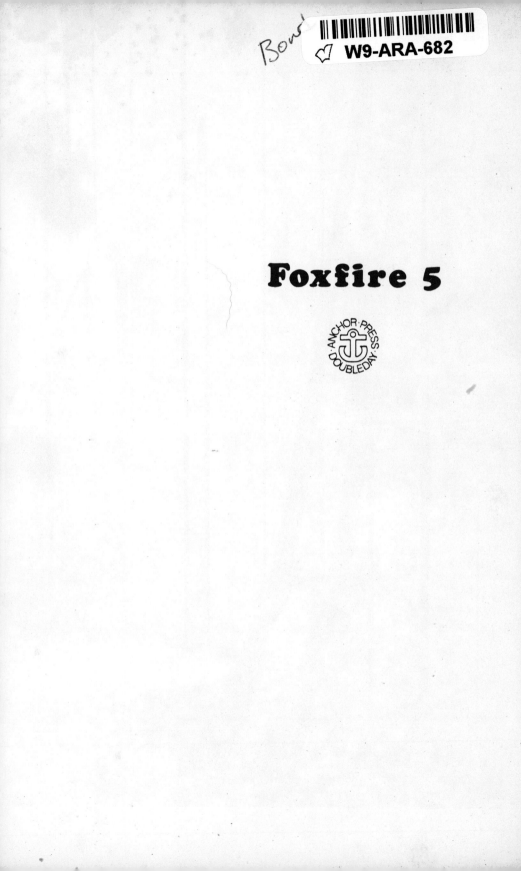

Foxfire 5

ANCHOR·PRESS·
DOUBLEDAY·

Foxfire 5

ironmaking, blacksmithing, flintlock rifles,
bear hunting, and
other affairs of plain living.

edited with an introduction by
ELIOT WIGGINTON

Anchor Books
Anchor Press/Doubleday
Garden City, New York
1979

Eliot Wigginton, who started *Foxfire* magazine with his ninth- and tenth-grade English classes in 1966, still teaches high school in the Appalachian Mountains of north Georgia and, with his students, guides the activities of The Foxfire Fund, Inc. His students have now expanded their efforts to include not only the production of the *Foxfire* magazine and books, but also the creation of television shows for their community cable-TV station, a series of record albums of traditional music, and a furniture-making business. Eliot Wigginton is also the editor of *I Wish I Could Give My Son a Wild Raccoon*.

Library of Congress Cataloging in Publication Data

ISBN: 0-385-14308-7
Library of Congress Catalog Card Number 78–055859

The Anchor Press edition is the first publication of *Foxfire 5* in book form. It is published simultaneously in hard and paper covers.

Anchor Books edition: 1979

Printed in the United States of America
First Edition

CONTENTS

This book is dedicated to those teachers who,
in hundreds of different ways,
have made their communities and their classrooms one.

INTRODUCTION

I t is late at night. Ronnie, one of my seventh-grade students, and I are in a Pullman sleeper on the Southern Crescent rolling toward Washington, D.C. He's never been on a train before, and he's never been to Washington. Through him, I find myself doing all this again for the first time.

Lost in the moment, we spent a lazy afternoon waiting for this train. We watched freights go by and counted the cars, waved at men on the platforms of cabooses, retrieved pennies we had put on the tracks, walked the rails, picked up loose spikes and pieces of railroad debris, and watched in awe as our train bore down upon us in the dusk, head lamp swinging, all noise and steam and metal and shouting men.

He's in the top bunk now, sound asleep. The last thing he said to me was, "Wake me up at every single station." Yes. That's just the way it was for me once. How could I have forgotten?

I have never been more conscious of the fact that teaching is best as a two-way proposition. We teach, and at the same time allow ourselves to be taught by those we teach. We talk, and at the same time, listen. We experience the world anew through another's eyes. And therein lies a part of the secret of renewal. It comes, in part, from allowing ourselves to accept from our students some of the same positive energy we try to put into their lives. We refuel each other.

Even more important is the fact that opening ourselves to our students has a vital by-product. The better we know our students and their environments and the pressures under which they operate outside the school walls, and the more completely we understand the ways they react to real situations in the real world, the better able we are to select appropriate vehicles and experiences for meeting their educational needs.

We get recharged, and simultaneously we plot new teaching strategies, and as we watch them react to those strategies that work, we get recharged again. Everything comes full circle.

Foxfire magazine, the contents of which make up these books, began as one of those strategies. Since my job in the local high school was to teach ninth and tenth graders how to write, a literary magazine seemed an appropriate activity. But it was only after one of my ninth graders took me to the head of Wolfork Valley one weekend and taught me how to find ginseng that the idea for making the contents of the magazine cultural instead of literary was established. Since then, I have watched students who had never written poetry and short stories with any enthusiasm work for months on articles that were rooted in their own environment and culture— articles that affirmed rather than condemned that background and provided a basis from which I and the students could analyze it in light of the national pop culture with which they were constantly bombarded. Had I not gone ginseng hunting with that student, the Foxfire story might well be a very different one.

Over the years, our organization expanded its staff and scope to include offerings within the local high school that incorporated, but went far beyond the hard skills of language arts: environmental studies, folklore, traditional music and record production, photography, and videotape and television. All are appropriate vehicles for passing on a myriad of basic skills, all are appropriate vehicles for helping students see themselves in relation to their own culture and to the outside world, and all are appropriate vehicles through which they can succeed and become self-confident and assured of their self-worth. An end result, of course, is that my staff and I have come to know the students even better as individuals for we have had to work closely with them in both of their worlds: the public school world through which they receive academic credit, and the outside world that provides the raw data for their projects. It is difficult for a student to produce a magazine article about some piece of culture, or a record album that features a local musician, or a cable television show about some aspect of the community, or an environmental-skills handbook for other students without knocking down the classroom walls and entering into a very different relationship with that outside world—and with the teacher who is assisting him.

It is impossible to be involved in education of this sort for any length of time and not be cognizant of the larger, overarching goal of education itself —a goal that goes far beyond the creation of a set of books and a series of record albums. Though our approaches may differ, here our mission as teachers is clear. It is, quite simply, to help our students master the information they must have to be able to take their destinies into their own hands. Said another way, it is to help our students come as close as is humanly possible to having control over their own futures. To start our students toward a life-style that matches their expectations. To move them toward the kind of independence that prevents their being eternally dependent on others. To give them tools for the long fight, and at the same time give them the human sensitivity they must have if they are to be part of the solution instead of part of the problem.

There's a good word for it: empowerment.

It's a tall order, but all of us who work with young people have a mandate to be about that business. It is why we teach. Football coaches do not work with students day after day only so that kids can master the specifics of the game of football. For the best of coaches, there is a larger goal: the personal rewards that accrue to their students from teamwork, self-discipline, and good health. History teachers do not work with students all year only to help them memorize dates and events. For the best of them, there is a larger goal: perspective. An understanding of the way human beings interact upon the globe, why they do the things they do and with what consequences, and how each of us—each in his own way—is part of the historical process. English teachers do not work with students all year only to help them memorize a poem or two, some rules of grammar, and some common themes in literature. For the best of them, there is a larger goal: a sensitivity to the voices within ourselves, and, by extension, a sensitivity to the whole of the human condition.

Empowerment.

Inevitably, we must evaluate. We ask the eternal questions that haunt all parents and all teachers and all adults who work closely with kids: "How are they doing?" "Has anything we did together made a difference in their lives?" "What do the answers we find tell us about our future thrusts and our future directions?"

I know that at our public school, through Foxfire, and in concert with the other teachers and administrators there, we have done part of our job well. A skeptical journalist visited our project recently and spent several hours talking with two of our former students, soon to be college graduates. I left her alone with them, and when she was finished, she and I had supper together, and she told me that it had taken her thirty-five years to acquire the self-confidence, sensitivity, and cultural and human awareness that those two students already had at the age of twenty-one.

But those two students, and hundreds like them, are also proof of the fact that we have not yet come full circle, and that our project and our school and our community have not yet begun to successfully address, together, one of our greatest problems. Those two students want to return to our county to live and work. The probability is that neither will.

For looming behind all this like the backdrop for a tragedy, and complicating our task immensely—perhaps impossibly—is the larger reality of Appalachia itself.

In the second quarter of the nineteenth century, the Cherokee Indians were removed from our part of the mountains under orders from Andrew Jackson. White settlers moved in, acquired land by lottery, and established tiny, essentially self-sufficient communities that were largely Scotch-Irish, English, and German. Gradually, a distinctive Appalachian culture evolved. Of special significance is the fact that, once established, these settlers achieved a measure of security from knowing that—though communally interdependent—as a group they had control over their futures. They had land, they had the ingenuity and the pride that comes from self-reliance, and they had each other. With the exception of natural catastrophe, they felt basically secure. A certain amount of effort provided a measurable amount of gain. Predictable results were the reward of measurable energy expended. Things made sense, life had a pattern, and the culture evolved accordingly.

This sense of control began to erode most noticeably with the various government programs that followed the Depression, and with the arrival of industries that were owned by large, non-local corporations. The natural resources and the non-union labor available in the mountains worked to the advantage of many of the industries but to the ultimate disadvantage of the Appalachian people, who lost control of those resources: who provided labor, but could not share in the ownership, leadership, control, or profits of those industries for their collective benefit. The steady conversion to a cash economy in the mountains made many families financially dependent on the jobs offered by those factories and assured them a continued welcome. Towns grew and became filled with stores that depended on cash from paychecks for their survival; schools and hospitals were built and roads were paved, and these services, which people came to depend on in turn, depended themselves on cash for their survival. Local business leaders came to wonder how they had ever survived at all without those industries, thus giving the corporations that owned them the final measure of control: "Unionize this plant, and we'll shut it down." And they weren't kidding. Suddenly, the executives of the industries, most of whom were from outside the region, became the new *de facto* powers in their respective towns. And with a notable few exceptions, the career alternatives available to most high school graduates centered around the family farm, some service occupations, and the closest available factory. Choose from those, or move on.

Granted, some went on to college and returned as professionals (teachers, doctors, etc.), but most communities could support only a few of these financially, and so most who left the region left for good.

For a time, all that was acceptable, if you will, for most people. Prices were generally low, taxes were low, expectations in terms of wealth and acquisition had usually been modest. The family land and the food it provided, and the family home on which there was no mortgage gave the illusion of—if not well-being—at least comfort and relative security. It would do.

During the years when most of the students I first taught were born, everything began to come unraveled. Prices began a long steady climb. Family farms and dairys went broke. Urban wages skyrocketed and further increased the attractions of urban life for the young. (Was it really true garbage men in New York City were making twice as much money as beginning teachers with Masters degrees in Georgia? Yes.) And rural factory wages stayed rooted at the minimum wage level. Relative urban affluence and increased leisure time fueled a dramatic increase in tourism into the mountains. With the tourists came the motel and fast-food chains and widened highways and junk craft shops filled with scented candles and toadstools painted on weathered wood—"crafts" advertised as "mountain made," but all executed by outsiders, and all making a travesty of traditional Appalachian craftwork.

And what had been a slow-paced, relatively invisible intrusion of summer people building vacation homes since the turn of the century in selected retreats around towns like Boone, Linville, Blowing Rock, and Highlands, North Carolina, turned overnight into the worst curse ever to befall the non-coal regions of Appalachia. In counties like ours, for example, where because of federal, state, and industrial ownership, less than 15 per cent of the land is available for private purchase, speculators cashed in on the demand for vacation and retirement homes and drove land prices and the resulting taxes to absurd heights. A land developer from Sarasota, Florida, recently told a friend of mine who was posing as a potential buyer that she should purchase a piece of land he was offering her at $3,000 an acre because in five years it would be worth three times that amount.

Throw fuel like that on the fire, and add to it the fact that some families *are* selling their land because they are being crushed economically, or because their children have moved away to find better jobs leaving the parents with no one to pass the family home on to, or because the children would sometimes rather see their inheritance in the form of cash rather than property; and combine that with a statewide push for increased tourism that creates the illusion of new wealth at the local level (most of the actual cash winds up in a very few pockets and rarely filters out to those who need it most) and brings in thousands more potential second-home buyers and the speculators who feed on them; and throw in on top of all that an average wage scale of $3.00 an hour ($5,760 a year before taxes with which you're supposed to raise a family in 1979) that perpetuates the fact of forced impoverishment for the bulk of local labor and condemns them to a future of a quarter-acre lot and a mobile home if they elect to stay here at all—add all that together and you have the makings of a home-grown, local disaster.

The fact is the county that is being passed on to our young people is filled with adults who feel powerless, and the young feel powerless in turn. It has all happened too fast. One of my best friends in this county, a young man with a wife and three children, lives in a small rented house and for two years has been looking for a piece of land on which to build a home. The family land was sold years ago when he was too young to have any influence over the decision, and one by one other tracts that he has wanted to buy have fallen into the hands of outsiders. "They've always got more money than us. We just can't compete. What's a fortune and a life-time mortgage for us is petty cash for them. They'll have two fine homes before we are able to earn enough to have one modest one—even with both my wife and I working. We can't compete with them. They've got us."

Perhaps it is part of the grand evolutionary scheme of things. The Creeks lost this land to the Cherokees, the Cherokees to the Appalachian whites, and now it's time for yet another shift—again at the hands of those who are more powerful or more shrewd or more wealthy. Perhaps it is all business as usual in the world, and our predetermined lot is to accept the shift gracefully and be glad for jobs as caretakers and custodians and cooks and make the best of it.

If this is true, however, then it imposes an ugly twist upon the educational goal of concerned and sensitive empowerment. Empowerment toward what? Toward a future as a mercenary who feeds on and accelerates the cultural destruction of the Southern Appalachians? Perhaps, but I hope not. Toward a future in Atlanta? Certainly, for those *who want that*. But if it is also empowerment so that those who choose to remain here will be able to take control of their own futures, and at the same time guide the futures of our counties in sensitive and caring ways, then we have a long way to go, for the plain and simple fact is that many of our graduates who *have* stayed here feel powerless—not empowered. And once a group of people has lost the feeling of some control over their futures, it has lost everything, for in order to have the energy to fight, there must be hope.

I don't suppose it would bother me so much if I did not take the job of teaching seriously. But I do, and so does my staff, and those students we work with are sharing with all of us a precious gift: their hopes and their aspirations and their fears. That's one of the hazards of getting to know students. Eventually they open up to you. And what they're telling us is that they're scared. Scared that there is no future here for them at all. And the same message is being echoed in communities all over the globe.

There are solutions.

In all the schools in this nation, we pay tremendous lip service to our mandate to "train responsible leaders for the future" and to "guide our students toward democratic and responsible self-determination." In most schools, the answer to this mandate takes the form of a toothless civics course and a powerless student government and an occasional speech at a student assembly where a business leader says things like, "You are the future of this country; one of these days we'll be passing the torch to you," and then leaves to have lunch with the Rotary Club.

The gap between the rhetoric and the reality is enormous.

Part of the answer, I believe, lies in programs of the type that Foxfire sponsors within—and with the vital support of—the public schools. Such programs build on and reinforce the basic academic skills that many teachers are struggling to help students master by putting those skills to work in the real world. But more than that, they also build students' self-confidence and conviction of self worth; they give students an intimate knowledge of the background and culture of their community, out of which the commitment to its future grows; and they give students a working knowledge of the mechanisms by which tasks get done in any community and in ways acceptable to the majority of those concerned.

Another part of the answer must involve the school faculty and administration as a whole taking its mandate seriously enough to build on and strengthen existing civics courses and leadership-training vehicles, such as student councils, and to offer solid experiential courses in such areas as county government and politics and future planning.

The next step is the hard one. As high schools become more and more concerned about the future options of their graduating students, as they begin to address more and more seriously the pressures in their communities that limit those options, and as they begin to become more and more skillful at the job of training students to function as responsible, thinking adults, the community leaders themselves must open their doors and enter into partnerships with those schools that are unlike any that have ever existed before. Regularly, decisions are made by county officials and business leaders that will affect dramatically the futures of those counties' students. But no students are involved—they remain outside that process.

Partnerships. What would happen, to take one example, if community leaders and businessmen, acting in concert with their high schools, began to create small demonstration industries and businesses at the local level that were culturally and environmentally appropriate, were owned and managed by their employees on a profit-sharing basis, and were tied tightly to high school courses in management, economics, business, and vocational and career education—courses that would lead to definite career opportunities and at the same time make tremendous contributions to the area's economy?

Partnerships. What would happen, to take another example, if community leaders and businessmen began to take serious steps toward highway beautification, strip development control, and the creation of city parks, and tied these moves tightly to high school courses in city planning, landscape architecture, and environmental design—courses, again, that would lead to definite career possibilities in that community and at the same time open to high school students another avenue by which they could make definite, specific contributions to the life of the community itself?

Partnerships. What would happen if community leaders and businessmen, recognizing the justifiable fears of the next generation, decided, in concert with high school principals and informed student organizations, to address the problems of tourism and second-home development? It might be decided, for example, to take advantage of the potential for tourism in creative ways, and to structure it so that businesses and organizations involved in serving tourists do so in such a way that tourists would have a culturally authentic experience that would be of maximum economic benefit to those who do not currently share in the profits. Craft shops, for example, might stock only traditional crafts purchased from area craftsmen (instrument makers, blacksmiths, basket makers, furniture makers) instead of Taiwanese imports. Restaurants might serve only traditional foods purchased from local farms rather than frozen cardboard hamburger patties purchased from regional distributors. Businesses that complied with the guidelines might be so identified, and tourists would be guided toward them specifically. Activities would be set up in such a way as to create the potential for saving the culture and celebrating it with pride and joy and making its future viable—not destroying it in a paroxysm of greed and self-interest and ignorant shortsightedness.

Partnerships. It is not enough to set up students for empowerment but at the same time give them no responsible, rewarding avenues for action. It is not enough to set up students for empowerment but at the same time allow them to believe that despite all the rhetoric about "bright futures," they are going to remain powerless. And it is criminal to set up students for empowerment but then limit their options for the future by selling their county out from under them.

Somehow the gap between what happens in high schools and decisions about their communities' futures must be closed in order to ease the transition between those two worlds and in order to make communities ever more responsive to the needs, fears, aspirations, and dreams of their children. That, or change the rhetoric.

We simply have to do a better job. There's a seventh grader asleep in the bunk above my head who deserves it.

BEW

PLATE 1   The Zoellner family portrait. Seated, left to right: Adolf ("Doc"), Will's mother, Margaret, Will's father, and Jenny. Standing, Carl, Irene, Will, Minnie, Col. Cobb (Louise's husband), and Louise.

WILL AND MAGALINE ZOELLNER

The story of Will Zoellner reveals a man of the mountains, a son of German immigrants, who is notorious among local folk for his epic hunting tales and respected in his profession as a blacksmith. This is the story of Will's life as a young man, a working man, and a family man. Included within the shell of the article are a number of hunting stories; some of them are so amazing that one wants to read them again and again.

From researching and writing this chapter, I have evolved a friendship with Will Zoellner that I will always cherish. In those first interviews when Will shared his life with me, I was a mere stranger. Later visits and interviews allowed me to see Will Zoellner as a man of deliberate character, who is strong-willed and honest, respected by many, and skilled in several lines of work.

Though Will leads a busy life, I always feel welcome in the Zoellner home. Now I go to see Will just to talk. He and Mrs. Zoellner are special friends I am privileged to know.

CAM BOND

Interviews by Cam Bond and Susan Van Petten. Photographs by Cam and Myra Queen Jones.

This here is a great big long story.

My parents came over from Germany on their wedding trip. Mother came from Bremen and Daddy came from Berlin. Mother was a cook and Daddy was a music teacher over there, but here he had eighty bee gums and he made more money with the bee gums than he did with the music, so he used both of them and he made a good living.

My parents left Germany because my father was a man [who] wanted to go where he wanted to and over there [in Germany] you had to check [it] out because everything was posted. You couldn't walk unless you had a permit. He was a man who wanted to see the mountains, and here he was free.

PLATE 2 Will with *Foxfire* editors Myra Queen Jones (left) and Sue Van Petten (right).

He could walk where he wanted to. Nobody said a word. That's where he wanted to go. His intention was to have a bunch of bees when he got settled, but he couldn't have them over there. So here he went ahead and bought eighty gums from the McCalls, and put'em up on Clear Creek.

They made honey to beat the band that day and time. There was white clover and the sourwood was in bloom. Everybody was raising buckwheat. (Now you never see a buckwheat patch.) So they had honey there by the tons, the prettiest white honey you ever saw.

Right after he got over here, he decided to buy some land, he liked it so well. His brother was a carpenter and he was figuring on coming over later on, and did. So they bought one hundred and twenty acres on the Walhalla highway and put up a pretty good camp while they was building a house.

Then he sent for Carl, his brother in Germany, 'cause he couldn't get a carpenter. (There wasn't no carpenters here.) So Carl came on over and landed in New York. He ran into a florist there who wanted to keep him there, but he says, "I'm going to my brother's and help him build a house, and I'll be back here when I get the house built."

Well, he let him go. So he come up here and put up that house with seven rooms, and all of the kids were born there. They's nine of us, five girls and four boys.

When Carl came over, he had a lot of property in Germany yet and he didn't have it fixed. So he says, "I'll have to go back and sell my property,

PLATE 3   Will, third from left, standing in board pile with others loading timber on train bound for Walhalla, S.C.

and I'm gonna settle here with you. If I get tired of working here, I can go to the florist in New York and pick up a big job there, 'cause it's already promised."

So Daddy said, "You help me build my house and the barn, and we'll get us a horse to plow and a milk cow, and we'll make it fine."

Carl went back to Germany and eventually ended up working with that florist in New York. He's traveled pretty much all over the world. [He] had a little house in Asheville he stayed in sometimes. He'd come by to see Daddy and Mother and make music and put on parties, then go back to his job in New York.

When I was around twelve years old, we gathered shrubbery for Carl to sell in New York. While we gathered that shrubbery, we'd have to spend a few days out there to get that country looked over and gather just what we wanted.

The galax and doghopper was up there. And princess pine [club moss]: we got a lot of them. Princess pine is just like a little pine tree that grows about four inches tall, but it's a bushy little thing. I don't think anything eats it; it must be poison. Not bad poison, though, because we handled it lots of times and then ate apples and things like that we never washed. Galax is not poison though. Deer lives on galax in the winter time; that's what they eat.

There's laurel and ivy [rhododendron and mountain laurel] that we took; small bushes with the roots on them so they could set them out. We couldn't make much off them because they were so bulky. The doghopper and galax was used through the window for Christmas decoration. They'd go to New York and decorate them bigshots' places with it, and church houses, too.

We took the shrubbery to Walhalla and put it on the train. There was no other way. Daddy had a team of horses we used. We'd load up five or six boxes of it and he'd take it to the station.

Daddy had a pretty nice home and they put up a building there for him to give music lessons in. He had sixteen scholars, and he taught violin and piano. His business did pretty well. His students were just people from around Highlands, especially summer people who wanted their children to learn violin and piano.

There was a man named Drewry Kelsey that came over from Germany, and he liked this country. He could go where he wanted; there wasn't no harm in going in any kind of place; didn't have to have a permit or nothin'. So he wrote back home how pretty everything was and there were more people who came over from Germany.

One was a man named Seizburger, kind of a preacher, school teacher, all-around man, and he and my daddy started a group of musicians who played at big old parties, weddings, and all that. There were about six or eight of them after they got started. They were all about the same age.

As Will said, "We was pretty bad about goin' to the dances." These parties that Will's father and his musician friends played for were in Highlands, North Carolina, and were popular among townsfolk as a form of weekend recreation. In the following story Will tells how he thought he had killed a bear one night as he walked home from the Saturday night dance.

Look what I done, by gosh, comin' from a dance to Highlands!

Rob and Henry Talley set up there this side of Highlands, and they said, "They's a great big bear in the road there every night, and once in a while you'll see a big painter [panther].

Well, I saw a wildcat walk up an' down the road there several times.

We was pretty bad about goin' to the dances there, and we all had half interest in Hall's Pavilion over there—we built that thing—cost us twenty-six thousand dollars, and they was five of us built it. We had a twelve-year lease on it. It was ol' man Hall's property. So we went over there, and as the big dance went on off, the boys said, "You going home tonight?"

"Why," I says, "ain't got no other way. Of course, I'm going home."

I lived out in the country, three and a half miles up this way on Buttermilk, what we called it. So it was 'bout two o'clock before I started home. I come on down to where Bob Reeves was a'livin' right around the mountain.

He didn't have no barn but fed his cow outside. She come over there on a little flat place right there on the side of the highway. She'd lay there at night. It was th'fall of th'year, an' I come on down that road there. The ol' cow seen me and she blowed at me, just like a horse that'd snort at somethin' like that.

I had an ol' ten-gauge shotgun layin' up there that I'd kept with me—killed birds with it. I'd hid it up there at the Masonic Hall, and I'd thought to myself, "I'll hide it here and when I go home tonight, I'll just pick it up."

Well, when I went on down the road, I heard the old cow blow at me, pretty high up there, 'bout twenty yards from where I was in the road. The moon was shinin' pretty well, but the leaves wasn't all off the timber. I could see that white face. She was a Guernsey cow, and the red on her didn't show up, just the white face. I thinks to myself, "There's somethin' there, 'cause it's so big."

I just throwed th'gun up and cut loose, by gosh, an' when I shot, it went down like th'*Titanic*. I went on down th'road an' got to studyin'—went about fifty yards. I heard it a'kickin' an' I thought, "By gosh, I want t'know what I killed. What could it be? It's too big for a bear or anythin' like that. I ain't going home till I see what that is."

I got my gun, loaded it again, an' eased on back up there, an' there laid Bob Reeves' cow. I knowed that cow well 'cause I saw it all the time. An' there laid his cow. I said to myself, "In the name of God, what in the world am I gonna do?"

Anyone could see it from th'road come daylight. I stuck that gun in the bushes an' went right 'round to Bob's house. They was all in bed, of course. I knocked on th' door an' heard somebody groanin'—nobody said nothin' much. I got to studyin' what I was gonna say when he got out of his bed. I said to myself, "It's got to be done. That's all they is to it," an' I kept on knockin'.

Finally, he says, "Who is it?"

"It's me."

"What're you doin' up here this time of night?" he says.

"Come out, I want to talk to you."

He said, "That's a darn poor time to come to a man's house t'talk."

"Mr. Reeves, I come down the road an' I killed your cow over there. Thought it was a bear."

"What? Kill a man's cow?" he said.

"I shore did."

"Well," he says, "are you crazy?"

"No. The boys had a bad tale out, an' th'cow was right there where they told me the bear crossed. An' I killed it."

"Well," he says, "you'll have to pay for it."

"I know that," I says.

He said, "I just don't believe it! What are you up to? Where are you from?"

I said, "I been to the dance."

"Well," he said, "where is the cow?"

"Over there at the barnyard."

Well, he got up and he and I walked on through there. He was mad as a wet hen. Got on out there and I said, "I've killed several cows and know pretty well [how to go about butchering the cow]."

He had all kinds of tools up there and I says, "We need a block and tackle."

He says, "Heck, ain't there some other way?"

I says, "I can skin her on the ground, for that's where she is. Spread out the skin and leave her a'layin' in there, and then when we get her dressed and her legs cut off, we'll just quarter her on the skin and hang her up."

"Well," he says, "let's make the best we can out of it. Dadburn the luck! A man killing a man's cow! It beats anything I ever saw!"

He never said no more.

It wasn't long till here come Fred Munger. Fred was the chief of police in town, and after the dance he come down there to go home. (He lived by there.) Fred come in there, and we just went ahead and took a hind quarter. We carried it over to Bob Reeves' house and hung it in the woodhouse.

I asked the ol' man how much I owed him. (I think he give twenty-seven dollars for the cow.) And he says, "You're just a loafering boy. You ain't got no darn money."

I says, "Now, Mr. Reeves, we're friends and I know you and all. I'm gonna do the right thing about it."

"Well," he says, "I wouldn't take a penny less than fifty dollars for her."

Now that was an awful price. You could buy a good cow for thirty dollars (well, my daddy did), and so I tried to pay him and he wouldn't take it. He says. "I tell you what you do. You hunt me a milkcow."

Well, I had lots of'em down on the farm, heifers and cows. I says, "That suits me all right. I got you fixed."

I went down and got him a snow-white Jersey heifer. Was gentle as she could be, but worth twice as much as the durned old cow he had. I'd been offered a hundred dollars for it a time or two. I wouldn't sell it. But I took it over to please the ol' man.

Well, you know how they done that day and time. There was no law. They just took the garbage and hauled it about a hundred and fifty yards from the hotel and poured it out.

Ol' man Munger had a board fence out behind the hotel. They said there was a bear cub [that was coming 'round there]. They was a hole in the fence, and the bear was a'working the garbage dump. Somebody or something had broke the board—big ol' wide board—and there was great big black wool a'hangin' there that looked like bear signs. It was just as plain as day. I had seen the place and all that, but I never did see nothing [like a bear].

Well, Jim Munger [Fred's brother] come down through there 'bout a month later. I had come on in and got about right where I had killed that cow, when a gun fired behind me. I thinks to myself, "Now they ain't nobody comin' this way except Jim Munger. They all been a'carryin' guns on account of the wild cats in the land."

And so I stood right still there awhile, and finally I thinks to myself, "If he sees me here in the road, he'll not come on." So I stepped in under a big spruce right there at the bridge an' peeped around, and here come Jim down the road. He was comin' ninety mile an hour.

I says, "Where you goin'?"

He says, "I kilt a bear up there."

I says, "You did?"

"Yeah, and I got'im."

"Well," I says, "you gonna leave'im?"

He says, "I don't know nothin' 'bout [how to dress] a bear. I killed'im and that's all."

"Well," I says, "let's go back an' git that bear. I like bear meat an' I want the skin anyway."

So he says, "Let's go."

We went on up there. Ol' man Perry had one of them coal-black, long woolly dogs, 'bout the first one I ever seen—great big ol' fat fella. And ol' man Perry had gotten a message to leave all of a sudden. Just him and his wife went to Massachusetts where they was from. I think some of his folks had died. And the dog wasn't at home when he left. So he went on and left the dog. And it was that dog going up to the hotel, getting in the garbage, not a bear!

The dog had been coming out of [that hole in] the fence. He'd been up there in the garbage pile. He'd come right out on the bank, fixin' to jump in the road, and Jim come by. The dog's head stuck right out, and the dog was tame as he could be. Jim just grabbed th'gun up an' shot his head off. The dog fell right into the road. Those things'll happen.

Munger had killed the dog near the side of the road. I went up there and pulled the ol' dog out. He was as fat as a butterball, by gosh. Great big ol' fat fella! I had to shake Jim's hand. I says, "Jim, you got ol' man Perry's dog!"

"Oh," he says, "it's a bear!"

I says, "Look at them feet. It's nothing but a damn dog!"

He says, "I know better." He went up there and looked at it. "Boy," he says, "what's that dog a'doing here?"

I says, "That's the only hole they is to get to the hotel that goes to the garbage pile up there. You got'im."

"Well," he says, "I can't understand. It looked like a bear. I just knowed it was a bear."

"It's a dog. And if you don't believe it, look a'here! It's got a collar!"

The hair was all over the collar and he couldn't see it. I took the collar off and there was ol' man Perry's name on it.

I says, "He give a hundred dollars for that dern dog over there in Boston."

He says, "The ol' man's gone off."

And I says, "Yeah. Well, don't say nothing about it. I don't want to pay for any of the thing."

He says, "I'm in for it hard enough."

I says, "I ain't gonna say nothin', but what you gonna do with the dog?"

He says, "What can we do?"

I says, "Leave'im a'laying."

"No," he says, "everybody'll see him."

I said, "We can't drag him across there with all that blood there."

And he says, "I'm gonna carry some dirt over on that blood."

Well, Jim went out there, and he carried mud out of the bank and put it all over the road. He started covering over that blood.

Next morning my daddy went to town with a load of milk and he said the whole road was bloody. Jim had throwed the dog below the road, and there he was. A hundred people seen ol' man Perry's dog.

Well, a few days later, ol' man Perry called up Fred Munger and told'im to go ahead and see if he could find his dog. He says, "I'll give you twenty dollars if you can find him for me."

Fred Munger, he found the dog down there, and he told Mr. Perry that the dog must of been killed.

When ol' man Perry come back, he raised cain. He says, "If I knowed who killed that dog, I'd throw me a dance from now on."

And Jim, he was scared to death, but he got out, got by with it. He didn't want to go to court. Nobody wanted to go to court.

"Well, I've got some awful fish stories . . ."

Well, I've got some awful fish stories. All my buddies was a'livin' then. Young, too. We went to Tugaloo Dam that you hear so much about. There's big rock bass and all that in there. There was six of us altogether— we went down to Turpin's boat landing and hired the biggest boat they had there. We were going to stay all day and all night. So we got everything rigged up and moved down into the boat landing.

We got out on the water and put out a two-hundred-foot steel set line, with two hundred hooks on it (a hook every foot). It took us about two hours to bait and drop it, then we went in the boat fishing. We caught lots of brim, mostly perch. We also got a lot of catfish.

Well, we went on back to the set line, and I seen the bushes shakin' on the other side where it was fastened. I said, "They's somethin' big on the set. Look at that alder bush it's fastened to. It's bending way over."

Teague said, "There might be two hundred pounds of fish on that line."

So we went on over there, and it was getting night and the moon was comin' up. We grabbed ahold of the bush and Teague pulled on the set line, and he said, "I'll tell you. This boat won't hold the fish that's on that line. Just pull on that line. You can't get a bit of slack."

So two of'em would raise the set line up, row the boat along. It was eddy [still] water, but it was getting cloudy. I told them we better get the fish off before the storm come.

Teague said, "You think there's a storm coming?"

I said, "Yeah, I sure believe it. It's black in the west, the wind is pickin' up."

We went down that set line. Throwed away lots of'em. Perch—I didn't like them. You have to scrape'em on the outside—not very good meat. We took the best of'em; we had some rock bass and crappy, and three deep-sea cat[fish]. One of'em weighed forty pounds—seventy-six inches long. We raised him on up and he soaked water all over us, flappin' around. I had to break his neck to keep him from jumping out. We had some pike, about sixteen of'em, two pounds apiece. Throwed most of'em away.

Got back to the campground just fixin' to get a big supper, and boy, you talk about a *storm!* It tore the tent down, tore down the stand I was cookin' on, tore the oil stove down, and we just squatted down in behind a rock till the storm ended about one o'clock. You talk about wet—hail, sleet, and everything! Brother, you talk about some pitiful fellas camping. Didn't have a thing dry. All the stuff we had was wet.

We come on out of there next morning, drove up to an old friend of mine's barn, and told him we wanted to lay down in the sun and rest awhile. We hung our stuff on the corral fence, and it got dry. We lay down under the trees and took a good nap, and cooked a big dinner when we got up, and he ate dinner with us. Just before we left, his wife and daughter came along and three more little fellas and they cleaned up what we had left. But we still had a lot of fish—had two ice boxes, and had to cut them fish to get'em in there.

The forty-pound catfish was the biggest fish I believe I ever saw. Couldn't get him in the ice box, so I cut him in half and doubled him back, put him in there so I could straighten him up and show him. I sold him to the man who used to run the hotel in town, for the boarders up there. It fed about fifteen or twenty people. They liked it, but I don't want no big fish. I like small fish.

"We took them big trips,... stay out three, four nights."

We took them big trips, went coon hunting, stay out three, four nights. Billy Neely and I went one time, before I was married. We went down into Blue Valley. There was an old fella there by the name of Mud Jones. He said the coons was eatin' his corn and stuff up. He said the woods were bound to be full of them.

I said, "What about us staying all night in the barn and hunting an hour or two?"

"Yeah," he says, "fine. Just make yourselves at home."

So Billy and I went out and the dogs treed something in a big poplar, and we looked and there was five coons in the top. One was *ungodly* big. So I started shootin' and shot the big one out first. We got'em all down, and Mud Jones, he loved coon. He wanted some, and we skinned'em there. The skins were worth twelve dollars apiece then. We got those five before twelve o'clock. Went on back and wasn't quite satisfied. We decided to go back and hunt another tree. So we went on up there and discovered a bear. (These dogs I had didn't know nothin' about a bear then.) But there was one old dog, he was runnin' but wouldn't separate himself from the other dogs. That old bear—he rared up. By God, he wouldn't run from those dogs! Great ol' whopper!

I had a double-barreled ten-gauge shotgun I got from ol' man Munger 'way back when I was a little boy. I'd fire a dram of powder and two ounces of buckshot, but you'd have to look out. It'd knock your head over easy.

I went on up the creek. I had a carbide light—took us about ten minutes to light it—and the bear stayed in the creek. The dogs were runnin' around and around. There was a whole lot of ivy bushes around there, couldn't see good in there, and it was dark anyhow at that hour at night.

Billy told me, "I've got a mirror down there that I can get. We can let the light shine in the mirror, and I'll spot him for you."

So he got the mirror and he let the lamp shine in it and it reflected on the bear. I could see the bear standin' up with his paws in the air, slappin' at the dogs. He was a buster!

I said, "I don't know if we can kill him or not, but I'm going to shoot him!"

He said, "Heck, yes, shoot'im!"

So I shot him in the breast, had a big old white square on his breast. He went ten feet up in the air. Them dogs all run off and we backed off, and I heard him a'moanin'.

I said, "I believe he died."

He said, "Don't get in there!"

I said, "I ain't *gonna* get in there." We knocked the carbide light out when we ran off, so we had to light it up again, then went back in there. He was gone, but I said, "He ain't fer."

The dogs wouldn't go after him. I said I believed we could find him, but I hated like dickens to walk in there [with] old rough woods, old dead timber, rocks and cliffs, and him not dead.

So I said, "I've got the axe."

He took the gun, and we went looking for him. We went around there and I saw where he went across a log, but he wasn't there. So I said, "Billy, let's call it off till daylight, and we'll come back in the mornin'. I bet he ain't a hundred yards from here."

The dogs wouldn't do a thing. They stayed behind us. Plumb scared to death. He wasn't dead. If he'd been dead, they'd go in there.

So we started back and got in the wrong direction, and I said, "I hear something, don't you?"

He said, "Yeah, what is that?"

I said, "It's that darn bear snorin'. He's layin' right over there in that dark place under that big hemlock. Yeah, that's him, he ain't strugglin'. We'll get him yet."

We eased on up, and there was his bed. A pile of alder bushes and other branches, about six foot high, a great big truck load of the stuff. And he was in that damn bed. I said, "I ain't going to bother him again tonight. I don't want to get him stirred up no more. Let him stay in there. The way he's a'breathin', he's nearly dead."

Sometimes he'd breathe pretty quick, then it would take nearly a minute before he'd get his breath again. So I said, "I'll tell you what let's do. Why not just stay here tonight?"

He said, "That'll be as good as anything. Would it hurt anything to build a fire?"

I said, "No, he ain't able to go on; he's stayin' in there."

So we built a pretty nice fire. There was a rock between us and him, about seventy-five yards away, but we could hear him if we listened right close. We'd both been up the night before, got pretty sleepy, and we laid on down, and he went to sleep. The dogs was all there with us. I knowed that old dog would raise cain if [that bear] come in on us. So I wasn't much uneasy. I had my gun in my hand; I went to sleep.

When I woke up, it was just breakin' day. I eased on up and listened. I never heard a thing nowhere. I said, "He's dead, that's what he is, Billy."

He jumped up and said, "Where're we at?"

"Why," I said, "don't you know where we're at?"

He said, "Oh, yes. What of the bear?"

I said, "Now that's what I don't know."

He said, "What do you think happened?"

I said, "He's either gone or else he's dead."

He said, "I believe he's dead. Let's see. The best thing is to put a load of shot in that nest and see if it moves."

I said, "No, I don't want to shoot him anymore. I'm going to throw a big rock in there."

I was about fifteen foot from him. I throwed a big rock in there, and the brush heap never moved. So I got the old hunting axe—mattock on one side, axe on the other. I just took the mattock side and poked it in there. That bear was spread out in there, darn cold. Brother, that was a big one—I'll tell you what's fact!

I told Billy, "We'll go and get Mud's horse, and we'll pull him out with a horse, and take him down to the barn and skin him."

We rolled him on out. I dressed him; took his innards out. He was still warm inside so the meat wasn't damaged, and we washed him out and laid him over a log so he'd drain.

Mud was down at the barn, wondering where we'd been. He said, "Yes, I'll take my steers. They'll go to him closer than the horse will. We'll drag him out to the barn and skin and fix him here."

So we went on up there, hooked the cattle to him, drug him through the brush, and brought him on down. It was about half a mile. He just run like a sled, his hair was so thick. We didn't have no way of weighing him, but we hung him up in front of the barn on a scaffold. We hoisted him up and skinned him. And by the time we got everything fixed up there, I guess twenty-five people was there. The whole settlement was there.

We laid him on out, gave each one a chunk—we were over thirty miles from home, and I wasn't going to carry no bear meat.

Mud said, "Will, why don't you leave a piece here and come and get it when you can drive over? It'll hang okay in my meat house till you can come and get it."

I said, "Well, that'll be fine." So I kept one hind quarter, couldn't handle the skin, no way in the world. It weighed over fifty pounds. We couldn't take it. We decided to tack it on the door and get it later, too.

About four o'clock in the evening, we moved on and crossed the line into northeast Georgia. Went on across the river. Billy said, "Let's shoot this dynamite in that big pothole out there." We had about twelve sticks of dynamite with us, so if we treed a coon in a cliff, we could just shoot it. He said, "I don't want to tote it anymore."

So I went over there, and it was just as clean as it could be, pretty full though. He said, "We'll get a tow sack full of the finest trout you ever looked at in that hole. My daddy and I used to fish it when I was a little fella. Let's just shoot it. You know how, and I've seen you try it out. Now don't tell me you can't hit no fish."

So I went ahead and made five shots, five sticks, and they all went pretty well close together. The water was tolerable low there, and I waded in there. I'll tell you what's a fact, there was two hundred pounds of fish there! Couldn't get but fifty pounds. The rest of them stayed there. We couldn't handle 'em. I've never seen the like of brook trouts, eighteen inches long, just as pretty as you ever laid your eyes on! The weather was so darn cold you couldn't stay in there long. They don't float [if you kill them] in the wintertime. They go to the bottom. Summertime they go to the top.

There was about six foot of water. I got me a little old sourwood twig with a little crook on the end of it, and I'd see one a'laying there, and I'd hook his gills one at a time. Billy was a'dressin' and I was a'pullin' them out.

He said, "Well, now let's go to the pin factory and lay out tonight, and cook and eat, where everybody doesn't know where we are and we got plenty of room, quiet, no trouble, nothin' botherin' us."

We started, but the fish got awful heavy, and we had a piece of bear liver (I really like bear liver), weighed five, six pounds, so we went on down there, stayed at the pin factory.

Somehow, somebody smelled them out, and he come down there just about dark.

He said, "I was just wondering why in the world this smoke was a'risin' down here. What are you all doin'?"

I said, "We've been a'coon huntin', bear huntin', fishin', one thing and another."

He said, "I heard some of the awfullest shots back across the mountain here about two to four hours ago. What do you reckon it was?"

"I just guess coon hunters."

He asked, "You didn't see nobody?"

I said, "No."

He said, "Must be somebody over there about that old still house." (We didn't know there was a still house there.)

So he set down there, and you talk about a man eating fish! Now he ate five fish over a foot long. I couldn't eat but one to save my life.

There was no law against dynamiting fish then. Wasn't no law there at the time anyway. It's illegal now. They'll put you away, by gosh, for ten years if you dynamite fish now. Wasn't no law much then. People'd make liquor wherever they wanted to and sell it to anybody they wanted to, and hunt and fish whenever they got ready.

Up there in Highlands, I worked with Gus Holt part of one summer. I think I was about eighteen years old. He run a gambling hall behind [his pool room]. After eleven o'clock, the police went to bed and the gambling hall opened up. (A. Henry and F. Munger, they was the two police there. One was the police and the other was the sheriff.) Outlaws come in there gambling. There they was until four o'clock in the morning!

[Gus] sold liquor and beer. I didn't sell nothing like that, but I watched the money part. [Men would come in there]: They'd shoot a game, get ripped, and out they'd go through the door, and you'd have to catch'em back and make'em pay. I done that: watched the game; when it'd get nearly over I'd get out there [and wait on'em].

Oh, they'd get in an argument, and then they'd have fist and skull there. I had to put a pistol on'em once in a while to keep'em going.

[There was one fella] this fella was an educated poker player. I could see that he was something. I didn't know what it was though. He was hanging around in there, wouldn't play much pool—shoot a few games. He just cleaned the tables and he wouldn't show off; didn't want people to know what he could do until he got well acquainted with everything, and then he cleaned up easy. So, he's hanging around there, and he asked me, "When is the poker time?"

I said, " 'Bout ten or eleven o'clock. When the police goes home, why they open up the gambling hall." Had a real place in there to gamble.

[This guy] carried a gun all the time. I saw his gun on him, but he didn't know it. I said, "You can't carry that gun in the gambling hall."

"Well," he says, "why in the hell, by gosh . . . what are you gonna do when they fire [at] ya?"

"Well," I says, "there'll be somebody there to stop that."

He says, "There's a man down here that's got a roll of money on him as big as my leg, and I got to have some of it."

I said, "You better get it honest. If you're a card player, get it that way. You got plenty of time. There's no killing or robbing going on."

He says, "I'll remember that."

He went on in. There was also a man from West Virginia, and one from Tennessee. The three of'em there; they'd buddied together (I found that out later), but they're no kin. They fixed it so that if one of'em made a big pile of money, why, they'd divide it up in the crowd. And they'd catch these other players there all with payrolls—[the] bigshots. There's two or three fellas, bigshots from Atlanta, and one from Wahalla. One of'em run a big outfit in Atlanta selling meat. Will Cleveland was there, too (the man I [later] worked for). And there was another fella from Franklin. He was an awful good poker player.

They took him on up there and started off playing poker. The man [mentioned by the "educated" player] laid out a roll of money of several hundred dollars. I knowed he was doing the wrong thing, but I didn't say nothing.

I told my boss man. He said, "I ain't got a thing to do with it, Will. You're running that." He says, "As long as they get along, by God, all right; if they don't get along, stop it."

One of the three men that buddied together had on a sweater, and he was the man to watch. He was taking the cards out and putting some more in. I fooled around there, so I could watch him.

One fella caught on [to what the man in the sweater was doing] and says, "Let's cull this deck of cards and get a new deck that's never been opened."

I says, "Now, that's orders."

And two of'em raised hell and said, "Hell no!"

One of those two says, "Ain't no use in changing cards. I'm just now getting used to these."

I says, "Vote on it. If there's more, by God, for it than there is against it, well, I guess we'll have it to do. If not, we'll go on."

They voted'em down; they went on. And one fella quit. He says, "I ain't gonna do it. I saw something I don't like." He quit and went to his home. [*Will never said which man left, but it was probably the man from Franklin: he was closest to his own home.*]

I stepped over in the pool room once more and fooled around. Turned my back and heard a gun a'firin'. I opened the door and looked on in there. I seen the fella go out the back. I says, "Who's that gone?"

They says, "It's some of them boys playing poker there."

I said, "What did he do?"

"Hell," he said, "he got a jackpot and left. Pulled his gun out, got the jackpot and left, and this fella [the Atlanta bigshot] out there reached in there to get a hold of the money and he shot his hand. Shot him through the hand."

"Well," I said, "okay." I looked out the door. He's out there under the street light. I don't know whether he's stacking the money or whether he was countin' it or what. He reached for his gun. When he reached for his gun, by God, I reached for mine. I shot him through the leg. He fell down on the sidewalk and throwed his gun in the road out there. Went out there and there's $750 on him. All the jackpot.

We took him to Doc Letman's hospital up there. Fixed him on up. He wasn't shot bad: shot right through the leg here. Laid up there about two weeks and went home. He was a Tennessee boy, and that's what he got.

I went ahead to take the money in there. Of course, you know how it was. Everybody said, "He got me! He got me! He got me!"

And I said, "Now, boys, half of it belongs to the room and the other part is gonna be equally divided between those that's lost."

Two of'em didn't have a penny to their name. They had to do something. They couldn't play on and they didn't want to quit. So, I divided the money up with'em even, and one of'em wouldn't have any. He said, "I've got enough to do me."

*By age twenty-seven, Will was caught up in World War I, had purchased
land, and was on his own.*

Daddy had some people clear three or four acres of nice land for a farm.
He raised a lot of stuff and finally got him four nice Jersey cows. (Us children was big enough to go to milking, you know.) [The farm] give us a
good living, and we made it fine there till we got to marryin' and scattering
out, and the farm kinda went down. But I stayed with my parents twenty-
seven years, except for the four years and twenty-eight days I spent in the
army.

Just before I went in the army, I bought a seven-hundred-acre piece of
land in Blue Valley. You wouldn't believe it, but I paid seven cents an acre
for it. I got it from Chester Young; he was a fireman. He wanted to leave,
and he owned that whole area in there plumb to Clear Creek. He said, "I'll
let you have seven hundred acres for seven cents an acre."

We run it out—seven hundred and fifty. I had the money. I paid him in
cold cash and moved down there. They was some neighbors lived there.
They didn't own nothing, but they was three or four nice places there. And
old man Burrell—he had a mans'on built down there on Mud Creek. Later
on, while I was in the army, Tri-State Lumber Company come in there. I
told Daddy to do the best he could [to watch my land], but he wasn't able
to run down there to see what was going on. There were some people down
there, Andy Brown and Lee Brown, so he got them to help him watch. I
had six hundred hogs in the woods down there, plus forty head of cattle,
when I went to the army in 1917. I had nine days to get ready, and I
couldn't do nothing about that land.

My brother Carl was exempt by some law through his work at the hospital. I told him, "While you're here, you go do the best you can with it.
There's five hundred bushels of corn in the crib and no road to it." It was
there for the hogs. When the mast didn't come, I'd feed them out of that,
and if the mast come, I'd have it layin' there.

Daddy and Carl sold a bunch of the stock, just left about fifty hogs in the
woods. When I come back, Daddy had sold all but about one hundred and
sixty-five acres of the land. But I couldn't operate that. I needed more territory. This wasn't enough territory to graze the stock.

My brother-in-law, Dick, had bought a mill of his own and had several
acres of land just out of Highlands. He said, "We'll saw that out." Well,
we worked there a couple of years.

He was a man who didn't want to hire much help, and we didn't saw but
about 20,000 board feet a day. I was looking after the timber logging and
hauling, and he was looking after the mill. We went fifty-fifty on it. And I
kept cattle right there at the mill. We got along fine, but timber got scarce

after about five years, and there was so much call for wood. See, the war was coming on, and they were buying up everything they could get ahold of.

I told Dick, "The best thing we can do is to go back of my daddy's place and buy about a hundred thousand feet up that creek there, and we'll make out better."

The government wanted mostly hardwood. We had been sawing mostly white pine and poplar. He said that would be all right.

So we went to the forest ranger, and he said, "I'll sell you the timber, the boundaries being the watershed of Georgia Creek. That'll be about 120,000 to 130,000 feet."

Well, we went to cutting the logs there, and I seen the war was getting red hot. They were calling them in from everywhere.

I said to myself, "I guess I better scat!"

Dick said, "I hate to see you go, but you're gonna have to go in the army."

I said, "No, not if I can get ahold of Ab Edwards in the West. I'll go to him and nobody will know where I am." (Ab Edwards was herding sheep in Wyoming.)

Lumber was so high, that's the reason we got into loggin'. Wasn't no building going on except the government was buying up airplane stuff. I went on over and checked up with my brother-in-law, Dick. I told him, "If I stay here, I'll just as sure in the world have to go, and if I go to the West, it'll take'em some little time to find out where I am, and I don't know if they ever will."

My brother-in-law said, "If you're at home, you're caught."

I said, "We'll make other arrangements then."

Well, Daddy told me, "Ain't you got some friends in the West?"

I said, "Yes, Ab Edwards is over there, and [some of his folks]. They've been herding sheep."

He said, "Well, do they want you over there?"

I said, "Yeah, I can get on herding sheep in a minute."

He said, "Well, if you go over there and don't write home and don't pass no letters through the mail, they don't know where you are. And if they ask me, I'll tell'em, I don't know; he disappeared and you'll just have to hunt him. And he says, 'They won't look all over the West about it.'

Well, I slipped away from home; I went to the West [to Wyoming], and Daddy didn't know exactly where I was. I thought I could get by that way. I went to Ab Edwards [who worked for ol' man Armstrong], and he said, "I'll get you a job. I'll tell you what to do; I'm delivering this milk for a boy here. You stay with the sheep when I deliver milk, and when I stay with the sheep, you can look after the cow."

Old man Armstrong was the supervisor there. He was a regular sheep man. Had . . . oh, millions of'em! And he hired these boys [including Ab] to take care of so many sheep there and yonder.

The boy there next to Ab Edwards had about ten thousand head and lost his health and got down and couldn't take care of the sheep. Needed a doctor to tend him. And that's how I got the job; taking the sick boy's place.

When Ab delivered milk the first time, I went over there to old man Armstrong, and he showed me all about it and gave me the guns and the shells and dogs. I soon made up with the dogs and run the sheep, and they seemed to like me pretty well. And I'd sleep there, but now, I thought I was safe. But I wanted to know from home. Of course, anybody would.

Armstrong came back to me and Ab one day, and he said, "Ab, I'm going to take Will to the dairy farm, and you get you another buddy. I need him bad, and I ain't got a thing in the world to pay him with. I'm going to let him milk them cows."

I told him I couldn't milk no hundred and fifty cows and get by. He said "We'll make arrangements."

His wife was older than he was, and he was an old buck. She couldn't get out of the bed. So they just had to go ahead and do the best they could about the rations. The rations was one problem when I was there, but I could drink all the milk I wanted—I could drink a gallon of milk whenever I got ready.

There were two more boys there, older than I was, pretty smart, and crooked as a dog's hind leg. They went ahead by gosh—the milk that wasn't sold, they'd set it up and make butter out of it, and they'd sell it to some other place. They wasn't getting much out of the butter business. And I told the old man, I said, "Them boys, by gosh, is just running that thing to suit themselves. You can't sell butter for twenty cents a pound and haul it fifty to sixty miles. You can't do it."

He said, "I'll see about that."

Well, the old man's wife got worse, went to the hospital, and he hung around the house right smart, couldn't cook much, just warm up stuff. I didn't care about that.

This was the first time Will had been far away from his home in Blue Valley. About this time, during his stay with Ab Edwards, Will attempted to write home in order to learn how his family was doing.

I got Ab to pass the message through his mother to my people. They wasn't too far apart—about two miles. That's the way I found out Mother got real bad sick. They wouldn't tell me exactly what was the matter with her. Dr. Hays was doctoring her. I tried to get word back and forth and couldn't get word of nothing. I wrote'em a letter. Took a chance on it.

That fixed it when the letter come to Highlands. The mailman looked at it, seen where it come from, and knew right then. [The army had] put out a reward. They'd give a hundred dollars if they could find out where I was.

The first thing I knew, here come a man out there. Jumped on the old man. I knew he was a government man because I saw him, but I didn't let him see me. I peeped through a crack in the dairy barn. He said, "Who are you workin' over there?"

Armstrong said, "I've got some boys here who were raised here in this section. Their daddy and mammy's dead, kicked out of the box."

Well, I hid in the stable when he come down lookin' around. The man said, "I saw a young fellow around the back here."

Mr. Armstrong said, "We have a fellow located here somewheres that is from North Carolina."

"Is he over at Ab Edwards' sheep herding, or is he here?"

Mr. Armstrong just popped off, "He's the best hand I ever had in my life. He milks forty cows in the mornin' and forty in the evening, and I don't want to let him go!"

The government man said, "That don't make any difference. *We* need him too."

So Mr. Armstrong come out and got me; introduced the man to me. We shook hands and he said, "You've got to join the army within nine days."

I told him "Okay." So I finished up there, and you know that old skunk never paid me a dime? I worked there for thirty days and nights and he never paid me a dime.

He said, "I'll send it home to your daddy and mother."

I said, "I need some to go home on."

He said, "You can get it."

I said, "Where *at?*"

"You can borrow it at the bank. I'll sign for it."

The bank was a hundred miles from there, by golly. I said, "We ain't got time to run around and go to the bank. Haven't you got the money?"

He said, "Yes, but I need my money. My wife's in the hospital."

I said, "You old tightwad. Take it and go to hell with it!"

I just grabbed my hat, hooked up the two horses to the dairy wagon, and I asked one of the other boys to drive me down to the cafe. It was forty miles. I never even asked for the team. I pulled on out, and the old man stood out there in the yard with his mouth open, and looked like a hollow tree. I had to laugh, I guess, at the old man. He never paid me a dime yet.

I caught the stagecoach to Red Rock, and from there I caught the train and come into Asheville. I got home, and the next morning, the man stood at the door. "Here's your card. You'll be examined tomorrow morning at nine o'clock."

I had to go to Franklin to be examined, and there was a whole bunch went with me. We stayed all night at Franklin, twenty-eight Highlands boys and forty Franklin boys. Out of the two crowds, thirty-two passed. Turned the others down. That day as the train came into Franklin, it picked us up at two o'clock and took us to Camp Gordon.

I was transferred from there to Camp Jackson. We had a few boys that was skilled, and they put us to work building the barracks down there.

I was a blacksmith then, and before I sailed across the Atlantic, I went to the Philippine Islands to shoeing school and showed them how to shoe horses and how to trim feet and everything. There was a fellow named Walker there. He was a German, too. Now he could shoe horses, but he didn't know exactly how to do it all. He didn't know where the dead line in the foot is, so I showed him all about where the dead line was and everything. I stayed down there about three months. We had a good time down there, but it didn't last.

Next thing I knew, I woke up in Hoboken, New Jersey. I stayed there till we got on the ship, then landed in Europe seven-and-a-half days later.

There wasn't nothin' I could do about fighting the Germans. If I would have just said I wasn't going, I would have gotten a bullet.

I went right straight over because they needed a horse shoer and I was one of the best horse shoers that had ever been in this settlement. There was lots of mean horses up there. I didn't pay any attention. I'd shoe them all—didn't make no difference *how* mean they were. I took a ahold of them and shoed them, and that's what the army wanted. I went straight over. They never gave me a chance to sell my stuff or prepare to go.

From New Jersey I went right straight to Berlin, Germany, on the battlefield. They gave us ninety wagons to haul ammunition in to the front-line trenches. I was the leader on ninety wagons. I'd ride my little saddle horse first, then the wagon train would follow me. We would hook up and leave at dark and come back at the crack of day. There was a big mountain there to cross over, and we could cross through that gap, but we had to make it at night so that the airplanes wouldn't see us and come and get us. Every once in a while we got hit anyhow, but they didn't get me. I did get gassed a time or two, and had a hole in my head from shrapnel. I stayed in the hospital a little while, about eight or nine days.

Carl, my brother, was gassed, too. He was a medical man in the army. I was there a year-and-a-half before he was called. He spent about six or eight months in the army.

The gas was the worst thing. A horse couldn't take a bit of gas. We lost most of our horses because they just couldn't take it. The Germans put it down and it settled on the ground and when the rain hit, it would dry us up. Lasted eight and ten days. By the time it would go away, they would shoot out some more. Finally we got the gas, too, and went to gassing them, but then the war ended.

When I went in the army, I weighed two hundred and twelve pounds, and when I came back, I weighed one hundred and twelve. I felt so damn bad I couldn't talk about it much. Didn't get nothing to eat! We had to steal everything we could find. It was pitiful. You had no friends, and what friends you had, they couldn't help you. I tell you, I seen boys cut up a dog and eat it just like they'uz eating steak. And you know what shape they was in. They'd fasted so long that they'd lost their minds. They'd eat anything—shoe tops was cut down, their shoes wouldn't stay on their feet anymore, they'd eat them.

Besides leading the wagon train, Will also tended to the army's horses, shoeing them or administering to their wounds.

I had one horse to get his ear shot off; it was hangin' on the one side. I said, "Well, the ear is still alive. It'd look awful if you cut it off, but you can go ahead and scrape it raw and sew it back down and it'll grow back."

"Fix it," he says. We laid the horse down and he sat on its head. I took the ear and scratched it all raw where it had torn, got it all to bleeding, put in nineteen stitches, by gosh, and a month later you couldn't tell it.

I took a piece of shrapnel out of a big water-cart horse—he weighed twenty-six hundred pounds. The cart carried over a thousand gallons of water. They used him on the battlefield, and a shrapnel busted and a piece of steel as big as my hand flew out and hit him over the hip bone and buried up in there. There he was standing in the barn by gosh for two weeks. They didn't know there was anything in there. A man come over to where I was and asked, "Are you busy today?"

I said, "I'm always busy."

"The captain told me you could go over to the barn and look at a horse for me. He looks like he's going to die. I don't know what to do with him," he says.

"You ought to have went in there. If he can't walk, open that cut and see if there's a piece [of shrapnel] in there," I said.

"How do you know?" he said.

"If there's anything in there, the seep, juice, or corruption, runs out of it, and you know whatever is in there don't belong in there."

"He sure has got somethin' seepin' down his ham plumb to the ground," he said.

I said, "There's a piece of shrapnel in there then."

"Can you get it out?" he said.

"Well, of course I can get it out," I said. "He'll die anyway if we don't." We went over there, laid that great big old horse down, looked like a mountain. Got a load of wheat straw from a a neighbor, spread it around in the yard, and had a harness you put on a horse to throw him. Just doubled his legs up and rolled him over on the straw. He never kicked, he was sick as he could be. I took my knife and cut in there, and brother, there come a quart of yellow corruption out. Had my big pot of water, four gallons, sterilized. I poured it all over and in that cut.

Then I reached down in there and there was a piece of old cast iron six or seven inches deep in the meat in his ham. I pulled it out and washed that hole out and sewed it up from the top down, and left a drain hole—put a little piece of rubber in the bottom of it, cut it off pretty short. Went back the next mornin', put some liniment all over it, and he was using the leg. There wasn't no bones broke, but this piece was in under his hipbone joint. He was lookin' around, and I seen he was coming out of it. I started on back and met the veterinary coming.

He said, "You're done here, are you? How's he doing?"

I said, "He's doing just wonderful."

I went back with him and he said, "Well, he's a'movin' that leg."

I said, "Sure! There's no bones broke, just inflammation struck him." In three weeks, by God, he was pulling the water cart again. Never limped, no scar, nothin'.

When *I* got that shrapnel, a big shell blew up and a piece stuck in my head. W. Arland was right there with me. It killed him—cut him slap in two. We were unloading ammunition, setting it up on the front line of the trenches, and the boys was in the trenches. The enemy was getting pretty weak by this time—they had been knocked around, and we captured twenty-eight prisoners. They just surrendered.

One night [when they] came in on us, there was a captain in there, and he knowed my daddy. I talked to him for a while. He says, "I am gonna tell you something. If you want to win this battle right quick, I'll tell you how to do it. There's a great big water pipe that comes down through this valley, and it's seven mile across. If that water pipe is hit, blowed up with a shell, this whole valley will be full of water fifty feet deep in less than two days. You fellows are up here on high ground, and they're down that in that basin. The battle is over if you bust that pipe."

He told me about where that pipe was and we shot several shells; took that big eighteen-inch gun and shot it in the air and let those shells fall down and blow up about two or three acres of land, and on the third shot they hit the pipe. I heard the tin rattling. I was down there in town unloading shells when they hit it. You talk about water a'going in the air fifty feet, and just like coming out of a big gun barrel! I told them, "We don't have but half an hour to get out of here."

We put the shells in the wagon and pulled out and by the time we got in the gap, it was about an hour later. I heard the shells hit the water, but I couldn't see nothing—all smoke around there. The next morning, I saw the Germans going in boats.

We was about three miles apart then and the water was still rising, but that captain had said that after it got fifty feet deep, it goes out, that there was a lake down here that would hold it. It was about eight miles across in three days. We went ahead and stacked arms, and they gave up.

I stayed in Germany until I got loose. You see, I was mustard-gassed and couldn't speak a word, and had that hole in my head. I'd take drunk spells, and they wasn't gonna let me go home. We had to have some guard duty there—a year or more before we could leave. So they took us fellows in the army of occupation. All those who'd work, put'em in there.

The mess hall was a half mile across the peak from the barracks, but there wasn't much use in going there; there wasn't nothing to eat. Hardtack was all you'd get. A cup of coffee once in a while, and it wasn't worth a darn. Couldn't drink it. And the water was no good.

Finally, I could get around pretty good and my voice come back. That had been the trouble—I couldn't talk. We had got gassed and [our doctors] sprayed our throats twice a day, every day for six weeks. That was the awfullest mess you ever saw. [When that] mustard gas got in our lungs, we lost our voices. We met all kinds of doctors. If we hadn't, we'd a'never been here now. And our hands, they was all sore, cracked up, lost my hair, teeth all out. It'd rot your teeth right out. I've got two plates now.

There were lots of lieutenants and captains there. Got the same thing. Some of'em was in bad shape. The army didn't want to discharge them because they knowed they'd have to give'em such a big pension.

There was an old fellow there from New York, Swanson—he was my right-hand man. He was a regimental supply sergeant. He'd check our stuff and tell us where to put it, how much, and where at. He and I worked together, pretty well all along. So he told me, "There isn't but *one* way to get out of this man's army. We'll die right here. We don't get nothing to eat. I want to go home to New York. I got a wife there and two daughters of mine that's married, and I ain't never seen any of my grandchildren, and I want to get out of here.

"I'll tell you what we can do. I talked to the major. He says he can get me out in ten days if I sign a slip saying I relieve the army of all responsibility for me from now on.

[*The men felt that the army didn't want to send them back home until they were either healthy or dead. That way, the army wouldn't have to pay medical bills and pensions once the men did get home.*]

"But the laws the army has now will all be changed in less than ten years. When all these laws are done away with, just as sure as twice two is four, if you're sixty-five years old, they'll pay you whether you're a cripple or whether you're sound. I've got a letter from home, and it said they know what's going on. We're not gonna stay in the shape we're in now. We're building up. We're going home. We won this war and we're going right up on out of here."

So we got to studying around about that. And Major Ward, he didn't tell you much of what he thought. (He was impolite anyhow.) He sat up there and he said, "I got gassed, too."

And he was there, sure enough. Got his horse killed. I saw his horse laying there and took the saddle off of it and brought it back to the company, back in the pouring rain and almost twenty-eight miles. Kept it down there, hid between my arms. Took it to region headquarters and showed him his saddle.

He'd talk to us same as anybody else, but he was in the army for from now on. He didn't want to go home. He didn't have anybody to go home to. So sure 'nough, that's what happened. Ol' Sergeant Swanson hit the nail on the head, by gosh. I come on in home and when the pension started, I got mine just the same as the rest of them did.

So the army said we could go home, but we had to find our own boat and fire it ourselves. We had a boatload, and a lot of them were wounded. There was a boat they said we could use, but they was three big boilers and there wasn't but one running. They told us, "If you all fire that boiler, we'll give you the coal and furnish food till you land in Charleston [South Carolina], and you're turned out to the mercy of the world."

I said, "Good enough." I had about three hundred dollars in my wallet, and a whole lot more in my gas mask and some in my shoes. I went ahead and brought my pistol back. There was nobody to take it off me because I was ranked the same as a sergeant. They wasn't hard on me. I didn't take it. It was a forty-four, and when I come home, I sold it.

So we came back and landed in Charleston. They was a big barracks there where they trained soldiers and kept'em till they'd get a boatload at a time and send'em over. We come back and stayed down there. They quarantined us for a certain time. It must have been ten or twelve days we had to stay and see if anything broke out among the boys. They was lots of smallpox and other disease over there. And that gas—it'd eat you up like cancer. You'd have to get that stopped. 'Bout half of us was turned loose. We got on the train, and the other half stayed on a while longer. There was four or five that died on the ship on the way home. Had to sink'em. The ride back was twenty-seven days. Eat 'taters and water. Got to Charleston the twenty-sixth of September.

Well, I finally got home. Dr. Hayes was the old family doctor, and he said, "I'll tell you. There ain't but one way for you to do it [recover]. You was raised in the mountains. You just go ahead and shack on out, just like you been a'doin'. Walk this fresh air out, and when you get able to do anything, I'd get you a logging job or start something outside. Don't work in-

side; don't fool with the shop no more. Your lungs is weak; you need air. Your throat's all blistered yet and your lungs is blistered. You got to stay out of that inside building."

Well, I piddled around there about thirty days and felt pretty good. Went ahead and bought me a big yoke of steers. Paid a hundred and twenty-five dollars for it. And my brother-in-law (he didn't go to the war, because something was wrong with him), a great big ol' thing, had a saw-mill, but couldn't get nobody to help him run it and he couldn't run it by himself. I said, "I'll furnish the logs, and you saw, and we'll go into lumber fifty-fifty." Lumber was a'sellin' to beat the band after the war was over. Everybody was busy on one thing or another—building airplanes and stuff like that. So I went ahead and bought a hundred acres of timber from the government in Blue Valley, mostly white pine—that's what they wanted for airplanes.

Well, I went to work there and hauled them logs. Skidded'em out with the cattle. I needed five yokes so I went ahead and got five yokes. Hooked'em to a tree—cut the limbs off and hauled'em. Then I'd take a power saw and saw'em into whatever they wanted. We shipped the lumber. We hauled it to Walhalla and put it on the train there. Put it on twelve by twelve sills thirty feet long, and just as straight as we had. We put in as high as twenty-four pieces. I built that wagon—big old logging wagon.

After we cut all the timber round about there, they were hollerin' for blacksmiths, here, there, and yonder, and Will Cleveland said, "Come right on here in the shop, and work with me. You're a good blacksmith."

I said, "Yeah, but you don't pay nothin'. You promise to pay, but you don't. You're working my brother, and you owe him five thousand dollars."

I worked there about three months. I think I drew about a hundred and sixty dollars, and he owed me, by God, nearly five hundred more. And I thinks to myself, "Well, goodbye." So I went ahead and went to raisin' hogs, cattle, sheep, and goats, and got acquainted with my wife.

I knew her way before I went to the army. I saw her sitting on a locust log over there on Piney Knob. She was maybe eighteen years old. My dad and I went fishing in that area. They lived down in Blue Valley. There was all kind of fishing and hunting going on there, and I got acquainted with her there.

We married in 1926, and we had two babies while we lived in North Carolina. (May was seven years old when we left, and Emily was the baby.)

I bought out the Brown boys, about two miles this side of where she lived, and I rented two other farms.

We fooled around in there. Then here come the stock law in there, and when it came I had so much cattle, so many hogs, I couldn't put them on my land and keep'em alive. I had to have that mast—the big mountains in there was covered in mast and white clover, and the hogs were doing fine. But then, ninety cents a head if you want to graze'em on the open range [government land, in this case]. I couldn't pay ninety cents for six hundred head of hogs with the rogues and rascals stealing half of'em. I was just getting enough out of them to do for meat. The cattle, they [the government] wouldn't let them go at all. They said that the cows would browse the timber down, wouldn't let it grow.

It had been burned every year. What was there was great big and the ground was clean. You could see five hundred yards in that forest. When you burn the mountains, that sterilizes the country, and every tree that was alive was loaded with acorns. That's what them old settlers wanted—acorns for the hogs.

They was hogs in the woods—you'd never miss'em. Everybody'd go and get him what he wanted. I marked mine, but it didn't do no good. If anybody else wanted one, he'd go get him. They'd pick the best ones, of course. I'd lose about twenty-five out of a hundred. We stayed there till the government closed us out. Why, there I was again.

After the government closed me out, I worked some for the Forest Service, helped build that highway into Highlands. Sharpened the steel and ran the hammer there. I stayed there till they run that road into Highlands, and I made a little money. Then I come on back home, and my oldest sister come give the orders all the time, and I didn't like it. She said, "I don't want you to leave. You stay *right here!*"

I said, "How can I make a living staying *right here?* I've got to have a decent job. I ain't workin' for no ten cents an hour."

I got tired of being bossed around, and I picked my wife and children up and we come to Rabun County.

I paid the house rent on a house for twelve months, and I worked with ol' man Tim Bell right in the middle of Clayton. He had a good set of tools.

Ol' man Bell, he give me two dollars an hour. (This was around '32, '33.) Two dollars to shoe a mule, and I have shod forty head a day.

Well, ol' man Bell got old, always growling around, bowed up, and I said, "Mr. Bell, I'll tell you. I've put up with this here arguing and growling around, you collecting up that old trash and bringing it in here, and it costs more to fix it than a man can get out of it. What'll you take for your tools?"

"Well," he said, "my wife has been sick and my son-in-law won't work and my daughter is telling me I have to feed the whole bunch and pay the doctor bills."

I said, "If that's the way you blow your money and then you come up and bellyache around me, more money, more money. We're all going to get throwed out of this thing if you don't pay the house rent."

"What?" he said.

I said, "John A. Wilson's been here five times this week, and he said he'll close the shop if he doesn't get his money."

"Well," ol' man Bell said, "dadburn it, let me have twenty-five dollars and I'll go down there and cool him off."

I pulled twenty-five dollars out of my pocket and give it to him. He went down there and cooled him down a little. It wasn't more than three or four days, he got on a drunk, came up to me, and wanted the rest, fifteen dollars more. He paid forty dollars a month.

There was a building and a big lot out front—wagons, truck bodies, and stuff in there, everything in the world a man could think of, we fixed it there. Sometime I'd get a friend to help me tear down a wagon or something. He'd take it apart so I could get to it and fix it, then he'd put it back.

Finally, one mornin' I said, "Mr. Bell, I'm gonna leave you."

"Why, dadburn, you can't leave!" he said.

I said, "I'm going to. I've got a set of tools at the house boxed up, everything that I need, and I'm going to move it right over here by Bob Hamby's place and go to work. And when I do, there ain't nobody in my way. I've got it all and I'm going to keep it."

He said, "You can't do that. All those tools here, I can't handle 'em no more."

I said, "I'll buy your tools. I don't need'em, but I know a man that wants'em, and I'll buy'em from you."

He said, "What would you give for'em?"

I said, "I'll give you five hundred for what tools you got, and the forge. I can shoe forty head a day, and it takes two ropes and another man and myself, and I can shoe any horse that's ever been born. I can make eighty dollars [a day]. And here—what am I getting? Making ten dollars a day, by gosh, and that's all! I can make eighty dollars a day just as easy."

"Well," he says, "if you're gonna leave me."

I said, "Certainly I'm gonna leave you."

He said, "You give me five hundred dollars, and I'll step off. Take the building, and you and John Wilson can fight it out."

I said, "We won't have no fight. I'll just write him a check and go to work." And I did.

So he took the five hundred dollars. He lived about eighteen more months. He fell and broke his hip and they took him to Greenville, South Carolina, and he never did get up no more. I went to see him at Long Creek just before he died. He was an awful wicked fellow. He was mean, he cussed, and he died.

Well, I worked there, and I made my big money there. I hired as high as five and six boys. My friends all helped me out. I stayed there about twenty years. I was right there with a great big building—fifty feet wide, one hundred feet long. That's where I built all the wagons and shod as high as a hundred head of horses a day.

Another thing—I had five camps that had about forty head of saddle horses apiece, and I'd go around and shoe them, drive around in a truck. We'd make no less than eighty dollars a day. I had the shop in Clayton fourteen years.

One man, C. W. Smith, a rich man, had forty head of horses and said, "Will, I don't want to be fooling with those horses. You go ahead and shoe them and watch their feet. I'm gonna turn it all over to you, and then when the camp closes, you write me a dun and I'll send you a check."

Well, he was a great big old fellow and worth about half a million dollars anyhow, and I said to myself, "That's all right, I'll do it."

Well, I went ahead and took the job. He had about forty head of horses over there, and some of them was durn mean. Sam Hill and I would go over there every two weeks and check the shoes, but they had small children and didn't ride too hard. When fall came, the camp closed and I sent him a bill. I figured two hundred and sixty-eight dollars. I saw it the other day in the book. It's still on the book. I wrote him a note and I heard the camp was closed, and how much he owed me. The check never came. I went over there. Lil, his oldest daughter, was there. She said, "Why, the old man's mighty feeble."

And she said, "Ain't that an awful price?"

I said, "Don't mention the price. Figure it for yourself, then you'll know what the price is."

"I'll tell him," she said.

Well, I never heared nothin' no more, and I went ahead and turned it over to Joe Davis for collection. He went over there and told them if they didn't pay the bill he was going to sell one of their cottages in front of the

PLATE 8 "I've hammered in the shop since I was six years old."

courthouse for cash. He told them he'd get for Will Zoellner what they owed him. So Smith wrote me a check, and the darn thing was bad. The bank wouldn't cash it. He drawed all his money out of the Clayton bank when the camp closed. So I showed Joe Davis the check. I said, "It's no good."

He said, "Let me have that check." Davis went in there, brought me my money, and he had to pay Joe Davis a hundred and fifty dollars, by God, for his trouble. The next year Lil Smith come to the shop. I saw her coming and I said to myself, "There she comes. The old man died out, now she's gonna take over. It's Lil Smith's camp now."

She come on in there. "Will, will you shoe some horses on Warwoman. They've been workin' as old farm horses, and they are down to the quick. They can't go. We need somebody to go over there and shoe 'em."

I says, "Miss Smith, I don't fool no more with you all. Your daddy done me so darn dirty and I don't want no more trouble. I ain't got time to be bothered that way. You get old Fred Turpin over there. He's a horse man. Get him to shoe them horses."

She said, "Oh, he don't know what we want. We want somebody that knows how to get a horse on the road and go."

"Get you somebody else," I said. "I'm through over there. I don't want to hear from none of your other folks. I went to your brother and told him

PLATE 9   Will's forge.

what his daddy done. He said that his daddy's and his businesses were two separate things, and that they didn't pay each other's debts. He told me that if I wanted the money, to go somewhere else. That's what Frank told me. A man talks that way to me, I don't want nothin' to do with the whole family."

Well, I'll tell you. I've hammered in the shop since I was six years old, and I worked with other blacksmiths, older people like Ransom Brown. He was a really good blacksmith. He'd been to a blacksmith school. And when he died, I bought his tools. And I went to blacksmithing. The rest of [my equipment] I got from other people. My brother hammered, by gosh, before I was able to hammer. Carl's older than I am. He hammered two years before I started. Then when I bought Ransom Brown's tools, I put Carl out of business. I bought two or three blacksmith books [that] tells how to weld.

Y'see, there's all kinds of steel. Swedish steel is the hardest steel to temper, and cuts anything. And there's nobody could temper that Swedish steel. It'll break or shatter. You can't use rainwater. You can't use stale water. It's got to be water that comes out of the mountain in a small stream. Then dip it on up and use it. If you don't, it just won't hold. I learned that just by experimenting. That's all.

Later I moved my shop over there at the house. I worked there about six years.

Then I went in with the Forest Service. They was building roads and they needed somebody to sharpen steel. D. C. Robbins was the supervisor. We finished that road from Clayton to Pine Mountain. Then we went over to Rock Creek and did that road up where them two fish pools are. That's a beautiful country out on Rock Creek there in Hiawassee. I worked over

PLATE 10 Will working at his forge. Some metals heating there require constant attention.

there two years. Stayed right there on the bank of the creek and eat fish. Boy, them was the most speckled trout I ever saw in my life. I'd go out and fish about a hour and have a hundred pounds. Then on Sunday, there'd be fifteen or twenty people come to see you, and we'd have a fish fry. We had a time there.

The government used to contract to have these roads built. When Ritter Lumber Company come, I put in twelve years with them. Worked out $47,000, and the government got half of it. They got forty dollars a month out of my pay. When I was with Ritter, I made more money there than anywhere. It's been twelve years ago when I quit. I ain't been workin' regular after I broke my hip. I went deer huntin' and rolled off a rock cliff, by gosh, broke my hip. I can still hammer, but not like I'd been a'doin'. I couldn't shoe a horse no more. That was the quickest money in the world.

With the Ritter Lumber Company, we had seventy-two men, started with ten head of horses, fine teams. We went to Coleman River first thing. They didn't have no spreads for the horses; the harness wasn't fixed. Ol' man Ritter had me to make a bunch of spreads and fix the harness. These horses that they brought in from West Virginia, they was old, couldn't stand up in these mountains here. I said, "You're gonna have to get something younger."

He said, "I can't find nothin' that's trained."

So I said, "Get the young horses."

So he come in here with seven teams of young horses. They was harness broke, and halter broke, but nobody had touched their feet. I got them stocks that had belonged to ol' man Bell, and took them over to Coleman River and put them up, and them horses tore them stocks *all to pieces,* and got on out alive, and I said, "Well, there'll never be another one put in them damn things."

I throwed the stocks away, and went and got me a big old robust fellow from West Virginia who had fooled with horses all his life, and two ropes, and we went to work. I'd just rope'em, by gosh, they'd fall, and I'd leave'em layin' right there till they got the shoes on.

You take a horse and lay him down and tie him where he can't get up, you can imagine about the second time you pick his foot up, he won't kick. I've had'em to bellow so you could hear'em two miles, layin' and bellowin' on the ground. Thought they's going to die. They'd never forget such as that. Then they'd come out there and pick their feet up just as *easy.* We tied a rope on each leg, and they couldn't do a thing, and get a man to sit on their head.

We logged that whole country plumb on into Hiawassee, to Wayah Bald, up on Jones Creek, Slick Shoulder, then we went in and logged up the [Chattooga] River to Highlands. Took those horses plumb up there; cut the trees down, the tops out, and gone from here. Them teams weighed three thousand pounds. Their feet were six to eight inches [in diameter].

We had an old drunkard with us. Ol' man Ritter thought there was nobody but him, and he was nothin' but a damned old drunk. I didn't like him, but there was a certain amount of stuff I had to do for him that was necessary. I knew he wouldn't make it long; he laid around drunk. When we got through with this one job, we went to Blue Valley. Ol' man Dennis was the supervisor of the horses, and come out to me and said, "Zoellner, we're gonna move. We're going to Blue Valley. You know that country. They told me you stayed up there and fished for years and years."

I said, "Yeah, I knowed the country before I come to Rabun. Who all is goin'?"

He said, "Well, about the same crowd."

I said, "Is G. R. [the drunk] going?"

He said, "Yeah!"

I said, "Well, I'm not goin'. I've seen the old drunk just as *long* as I want to. I'd go ahead and cook a nice mess of dinner when all the company was out on Saturdays and Sundays, and he'd come in there and drink the gravy off my soup, and there was the pot dry and scorched, and him a'layin' in bed drunk. I don't want to see him no more, and I don't want to hear from him no more."

He said, "Well, who is going to take care of the horses?"

I said, "You don't need no damn horses. You're crazy as the dickens using these horses when you can buy these cats [bulldozers]. One cat will log as much as four teams of horses will."

"Well," he said, "I'd never thought about that. Have you seen any loggin' done with these cats?"

I said, "Sure. All these boys around Clayton knows what a cat will do. Two cats will run that mill up there and pile the logs up so you can't see the mill."

He said, "I'm going to talk to the old man a little bit about that."

I said, "There's a man that knows what he's doin' when he hits the woods. He don't talk much, but when he talks, they's business behind it."

He said, "That's the man who come up here and told me to get you to shoe those horses. I know him. He said you'd shoe a horse or kill him. And not kill him by beatin' on him either. He'd kick till he died. If you go ahead and go over there, we'll need you to fix the riggin' on the cat. I got to have you anyway. If you'll go, I don't need G. R."

I said, "That's wonderful."

We went on over there and had a meeting at the bridge. Wilson Curtis was kind of a supervisor over the whole thing. And I couldn't stand him. He told me, "I'd fire you if you was a man of mine."

I said, "Yes, I'm durn glad I ain't. You ain't got sense enough to be a super over me." All the West Virginia boys bought stock in Ritter Lumber Company. They was all there, and we was all there with some good loggin' men from back in Shootin' Creek and Rabun's Fort. We all met there to see who goes and who don't, and what they need and what they're gonna have to do.

Wilson Curtis was a union man: "When you are on the job, I don't care if you strike one damn lick. If you were there at eight o'clock, and there at quitting time, you are paid by Ritter Lumber Company, whether you picked up a tool or not."

We got to talkin', who we needed and who we didn't need. Daniels asked Bill, "What do you think Will would do if I'uz to turn him loose in these woods?"

Bill said, "He'd log it, that's what he'd do. And he'd build you a damn road, big boy. It won't be Wilson Curtis going around there with a hoe, having sixteen boys diggin' the banks down with a hoe. You'll never find nobody to take Will's place!"

I never said a darn word. Sat right there. He said, "Now, what did you pay for this road here? Wilson Curtis worked *three months* on two miles of road, and there wasn't but one darn little rock to shoot there. You know it wasn't a big rock. Worked three months. Will would have had the whole twenty mile road built in three months."

Daniels said, "What about the shop work?"

Bill said, "Hell, he runs that shop, always got stuff ahead, and he keeps it that way. He don't never let it get down. All the trouble is, keep the rogues out of the shop, don't let them steal the stuff that he's got made." Old Wilson, he was walking the floor, back and forth.

Daniels said, "Tomorrow is Wednesday. In the morning, I want Will to get his boys he's been running with. The cat boys will have to get to where we're camped."

I said, "I don't know but one real cat man, and I don't know whether you'd like him or not—Wayne Smith. Best logger in the woods, but he won't take no bossing. Only way you can do with him is in the morning when you get out, before you go to work, tell him what you want him to do and leave him alone. If you meet him in the woods and change your mind, he's going to call off the cat and go home. He's independent."

Daniels said, "We won't have nothin' to'do with the cat. Charlie Curtis (Wilson's brother)—you and him gets along fine, but you and Wilson don't make it at all, so I'm going to let Charlie be with you, and you look after the road. Tell Charlie how to mark the cat roads. You was raised in here— use the old Three State Lumber Company skid roads. [They had logged that area when Will was very small.] You and Charlie see that we get the logs out, and the Smith boys is going to do the timber cutting. I'm going to contract the timber cutting."

[They were] good boys, too. They cut the trees down, trimmed it off, and cut the top out. That's all they done. The cats would go up there, hook to it, bring it right on in. Where the horses couldn't pull it at all, the cat could walk right on with it.

So I went on the road. We moved the shop in there, tore the one down at Coleman River, hauled it over there and put it up at night, so I'd have the tools covered up and locked up. I had my own tools.

G. R., he come over there and said, "How was it that I got kicked out?"

"Just because I said you didn't do a damn thing but drink liquor," I said. "You done it yourself. Going in the kitchen and spoiling my cooking, not feeding the horses you're supposed to feed. I got up at five o'clock and fed your horses, and what did I get out of it? Offered me an old drink of rotten liquor, that's all."

We went to work, and I'll tell you about the twenty mile road. Wilson worked three months on two miles of the road. There wasn't a foot of it ready to haul on. It was all tore to pieces, not smoothed off, no ditch above, a rock maybe in the middle of the road. Daniels said, "You go in there and get any amount of men you want."

I said, "I don't want but six."

"What? Loggin' a band mill with six men?" Daniels said.

I said, "We're not loggin' no mill yet. We're getting ready to log it. There are enough layin' by the side of the road to do you whenever you need logs. When you need logs, send your trucks over here. I'll see they'll be loaded."

I got Fred Henry there to load 'em. He was an old friend of mine. There was old Ted Bates, Fred Dryman, Roy Foster, and Charlie Bingham, one of the finest cat drivers there was. We all messed up together, and I told the boys, "Now, I've got to fix this road so they can haul the logs to the mill. It doesn't make no difference how many logs we've got on the road, if they can't get to 'em, the mill will go out. I'll see about the road, and you go ahead up there and cut up Persimmon Ridge. Cut all that timber up there."

Roy Foster and his buddy took a cat apiece and went up there. They snaked the logs down to a bend in the road, a nice place for loading.

That mill was in awful shape. Them old union men who'd been in there had logs scattered around everywhere. You couldn't walk in there, couldn't drive a truck in it. I told ol' man Hoyt, "You fix the mill yard and we'll give you some logs."

Ol' man Hoyt said, "He's talkin' business, boys. We got to do business with him. We can't turn a man down like that. There are five million feet to come out of them mountains, and we've got to saw it as it comes."

I worked one week on the road that Wilson had messed up, and creek-graveled it. I had four dump trunks and six good boys, and we had the prettiest creek gravel that you ever laid your eyes on, and a big gasoline-powered shovel to load the trucks with. By gosh, Saturday night come, ol' man Hoyt and Dedman went in there with a big fine automobile riding on that gravel road. It was just like a sheet. Hoyt said, "Boys, I would have never thought a man could get a road like that in this country in that little time." I had six boys. We worked though, I'll tell you that.

We broke several couplings skidding logs. They were overloaded a little bit, and I had to fix them in the shop at night. In rainy weather I could do a lot of work in the shop, and I was usually ahead. There were about seventy-five axes that had to be handled once in a while. But we got along fine.

Then ol' man Ritter died, and ol' man Dedman was old, and ol' man Hoyt was a big stockholder in the Ritter Lumber Company and he wanted his money. Georgia Pacific wanted to buy Ritter. I was ready to retire; I was seventy-eight years old. So we all got together, and Georgia Pacific went ahead and bought it, but there was a road to build back in Horse Cove—twenty-two-thousand-dollar road. And ol' man Hoyt and ol' man Dedman said that they couldn't leave until they built that road. "The government would sue us if we don't build the road, because it was in the contract."

There was a lot of [dynamite] shooting to be done over there. They had twenty days to get started on that road. I'd retired. I didn't want nothing to do with it. I said, "If you think I can't build it, you're just out of your head. If nobody wants it and can't build it, by God, I can show you how to do it."

So ol' man Hoyt said, "Ol' man Daniels told me that that road had to go through there, and in a hurry. We can't find a soul that wants to get in that country."

I said, "By God, I'll make you an offer. And that's all I will do."

Ol' man Hoyt said, "Pull it loose. I want to hear it."

I said, "You give me the cats. You've got the dynamite over there, five ton in that house over there. I want two cats—Wayne Smith is gonna drive one and Roy Foster is gonna drive the dynamite outfit. I need a man to pull my compressor where I need it."

It was the rockiest country, but the rock was soft. They didn't know it. Man could just drill it to beat the band. F.D. was my main buddy, big as a mountain, and brother, he wouldn't put out unless I was around there. He wouldn't run a jackhammer unless I was in seeing distance to save his life. He was a little bit off. I tell you I got some work out of him that ten other men wouldn't have done. One time there was a big rock in the road, and he says, "I believe I can turn him over without the dozer." It was about a half mile down the road. He went over there and he rolled that rock. That thing weighed over five tons. And it went plumb into Whiteside Cove when he turned it over. I never seen the like in my life.

He said, "We're building *roads* now, ain't we?"

Hoyt said, "Can you build it in three months?"

I said, "What are you talkin' about? I won't be over there more than fifty days."

He said, "A four-mile road through these mountains? It'll take you a year."

I said, "Bring that dozer over here." And we all got organized and somebody had put in a concrete bridge, had to have it there to get logs across, and it was *way* too high up in the air. So I had to shoot the darn thing out and put in another bridge. We done it. I hired a friend of mine with a concrete mixer and his crew, and I paid him out of my own pocket. We had to wait twenty days before we could get over it, but we wasn't near to it nohow. Had a lot of shootin' to do on the road before we got there. I told him I'd be sure I let it set up before we drove them big cats over it.

We had our camp right with us—two buildings, a big kitchen, and sleeping quarters. When we got off a mile away, we'd hook to'em, pull'em back to us. Had some of the best water over there I ever had. We got along just wonderful. We ate lots of wild meat. I'd go hunting at quitting time, and I come in with some of the finest pheasant you ever looked at.

We went on through there, at sixty days. Ol' Wilson came over there. He said, "I'm not working with Ritter's no more, Will, and I'm over there with my little union. We're a'cleanin' up—they've got property over there, and I'm takin' care of it. I wanted to see what you done while you was over here. They tell me it's sixty days you've been over here, and there's a lot of road built. Can I drive through?"

I says, "Why, sure! It's all ready except for the ditch on the upper side to channel the water coming down the mountain." By God, he drove to the other end, come on back.

He says, "I got to give it to you. You're the best man I ever seen in the woods all around. Goodbye, boys." Gone.

The job with Ritter gave Will numerous opportunities to hunt—on his own and with friends. The following are hunting tales Will entertained us with during our interviews.

[Once a bear got after me.] I got in a cave right here in Blue Valley. I went into the cave and the bear got around and got in front of the cave with me. Wouldn't let me out. It was called Billingsley Cave. It's right on the river over here, just above Pine Mountain up the river there. I had a little ol' cougar dog—I forget the name of it. We went in the cave because it got so cold and I thought it was sheltered a little bit there. I'd been huntin' and fishin' round about there, and it got late. I thought I'd warm up a little before I started across the mountains. It's about ten miles from there to where I had to go. And I had a knapsack full of grub, so I thought I'd eat a bit and start again.

That day and time we had flashlights, a carbide light. So, I knowed I'd make it, and I knowed the country anyhow. Well, I went on in there and that damned bear got in front of me. I couldn't get out. The hole in front wasn't but about ten feet square. In behind is thirty, forty feet. Room enough, by gosh, to put ten, fifteen head of cattle in there, after you get in there. And I wanted to get out of there, and he wouldn't let me. I just sorta rocked him with rocks and stuff, and kept on throwin' till finally I hit him in the nose with a big rock and knocked one of his eyes out, and he left. When he left, I went on out, and the funniest thing was, I didn't have my main gun—I just had a pistol. I didn't have but about seven or eight shells, and I didn't want to shoot until I absolutely had to.

After I got on out, he was right around the bend. The little ol' dog went after him. That little ol' dog was mean. He had a little bull in him or something. He was as mean as he could be, but he wouldn't bark. Went in there and he must've nipped him. When I got out in front of the cave, by gosh, he was standing right there next to the river, and I took my pistol on up. (I knew I hit him, but I didn't know where.) When I hit him, he jumped in the river and went on down the river and went back on out, and the little ol' dog went down by the side of the river. As the bear went up the hill, the little ol' dog cut him off. And by gosh, that bear ran off. I don't know where they went. He wouldn't bark, and I couldn't ramble around there. I waited some, and when I come on back out into the road, I said, "I hate to leave'em, but I can't afford to run around them mountains at night."

It was in the spring of the year, too. Rattlesnakes was out, and plenty of'em in there. So I thinks to myself, "My bear might'a killed him, can't tell."

So I followed the road and got nearly to the farm where I was staying. I got to the gate and it had a weight on it. [The dog would] take his paw and push it on over and run through, and I already had the gate closed. I thinks to myself, "It was either the [gate walker] or the dog. Wasn't nobody else over here."

[He'd come home by himself], but the bear'd hit him. It tore a great big piece out on the top of his shoulder. He was hopping on three legs. I took him in and doctored him.

Next morning, the Watson boys came in. They'd been over in at Hale Ridge with Tom Keith making liquor. I was afraid of'em. I had plenty to drink, but I just wouldn't fool with'em. They'd get on the drunk and get arrested. They'd tell everything they knowed. So I wouldn't fool with'em. They offered me a drink, but I didn't take it. I knowed who made it. And I didn't need it no-how. I had some better.

[I told them about the bear, and one of them said], "Let's just load up our stuff and go over there and see what's going on. I'd just love to have a cub bear."

I said, "It'd be nice if I had a cub."

He said, "Well, come over there."

We went on over around about [where the cave was], and if we'd had a dog, we'd had some real luck. But we didn't have no dogs. My little dog had got crippled by the bear just before that. I didn't take him.

We found where the bear had the cubs. The cubs was out somewheres in the woods. They was big enough to live, follow [their mother]. We found where they went across an old sandbar down there at the creek, and the little ol' cubs must have been about the size of a big house cat. We couldn't find'em.

I must have got that ol' sow bear. I think she was hurt, because she looked like she was hopping on three legs after I shot her that night.

Since we didn't have no dogs, we decided to get some bear dogs and come back the next night.

Well, the next night come and we went over there, and they had two bear dogs, sure enough. The ol' sow bear came right on into me. I couldn't run and rope the cubs then. I had to shoot her—just blowed her head off. Then the dogs left her and went right straight to the cubs. I heard the cubs a'squawlin' and by gosh, it was too late when we got there. Them dogs killed all three of them cubs.

So, we got the three cubs and the old bear. They was all dead. That ol' bear was poor, Lord, how poor she was! I thought she was starving to death.

I went on a big fox hunt one time with Bill McKurty and George Roland. Bill was from Mexico and George was from Texas. There was a pair now, let me tell you!

They were raised in the mountains and the woods, and didn't have no people or nothin'. So they went from coast to coast, from creek to creek, by God, and they had *forty* dogs. They had fox dogs, bear dogs, coon dogs, and hog dogs. They come down to the Brown place when I first moved in Blue Valley. They wanted to spend a week with me. I'd met'em before. That was before I was married.

I told'em, "There's lots of game in these mountains. It's rough, but I know all the country."

They said, "We want to have a *real* fox race tonight. Where can we have it?"

I said, "Right on top of Pig Pen [Gap]. They's a bunch of red foxes up there. Some of'em's old, some of'em's young, but they're just cleanin' up with the pigs. They've just eat every pig I've got."

They said, "We'll get'em then."

They had six of the prettiest dogs you ever looked at. (They didn't travel around with all of them forty dogs. They took the dogs of whatever they was hunting.) They had a big old rig for goin' in the mountains, and they even had a foldin' boat. So I took'em on top of Pig Pen.

They wouldn't get drunk, but they liked a little drink. I was makin' a little then. I had some in a gallon keg up by the Gibson Gap, and I got some.

Bill said, "Let me taste that stuff. I bet you made that."

I never spoke.

He said, "Did you?"

I said, "I did." Well, I had to make a living. Had five hundred bushels of corn, and couldn't sell it. I didn't have no road, couldn't get it out of there. And the hogs—there was big mast in the woods—they wouldn't eat corn, so I just went ahead and put in a sweet mash run.

He said, "It's green then. Let me have it."

He tried some and said, "Hey, George, I want you to taste this. I'll tell you, you can't quit!"

I said, "Now, boys, be careful. You're going to get drunk on that. It's powerful. We want to have a fox chase. Just take a light swig, and now and then take another. Don't overdo it, because I ain't able to carry you out of here, and it might come a little storm and I don't want you to get wet."

"Oh," they said, "we'll take care of all that."

So we took a swig of it. He said, "I'll tell you, Bill, I'm gonna have to take a little of that to my friends. He asked me, "How much of that you got, Will?"

I said, "We'll find something big enough to take along."

He said, "I'll tell you that beats everything I ever saw."

But I took a little swig, too, to show him that it wasn't poorly [made]. I was sipping a little along anyhow that day and time. I'd take three or four drinks a day, then go on about my business.

So we went on up there and there was the prettiest darn place to lay down. I got up there and they built up a little smoke [fire] in the middle there. The dogs wouldn't go! They wouldn't go out and hunt.

I says, "These dogs don't know the country."

Bill says, "When they find a fox, they're a'goin'."

I says, "We'll find a fox before ten more minutes, because there's a fox trail comes right straight out of Stony Mountain right up that ridge there, and it goes through Chastain's place. And right into this area here where the pigs is. That's what they're workin' on—them little pigs."

So, in five or six minutes, he said, "There's a fox!" And brother, that fox wasn't bothered [about dogs or people] way out in no-man's land where we were. People wasn't huntin' there much. So all six of them dogs, they brought that fox right in between us, ten feet from the fire. He was as big as a collie dog, a blood-red fox. Them dogs was about ten feet behind him. I tell you, it kept up for an hour. And never lost a dog! Tore brush, bushes everything down. Finally it hushed. Bill said, "What happens now?"

I said, "I believe they caught him."

Bill says, "You think so?"

"Yes, they run too hard and he run so fast he couldn't see he was a'going. The dogs was too close to him, and he just got hung off somewhere and the dogs was eyeing him. I heard a fight a little while ago, but I thought it was a dog fight."

"Where was it at?"

I says, "Well, right next to the road, where we come from, right on down the trail to the left, and that's where I heard'em fighting."

So I pulled out and they followed me up there and I got down there, listening. I heard'em down there in the cove. I says, "I believe [the dogs] did catch'im. I hear'em all brawling around down there, growling at each other."

We went down there and there was the fox. They tore him up. One of those ol' boys wanted the fox to mount.

I says, "Well, why not just skin him and let [the taxidermist] mount him that way?"

He asked me if I'd fix the fox. I knowed exactly what he wanted. He wanted the head left on him, just wanted him skinned and his feet left. I just cut his feet bone off under there and kept his original feet. The taxidermists can't make'em right. I skinned him in a few minutes and wadded him up and stuck him in my knapsack. He weighed about five, six pounds. Prettiest tail you ever looked at, and it was snow white. Just as white as cotton, it was!

The boys wasn't quite satisfied. So we went back the next night. We started there, but when we got to the Gibsons' yard, the dogs stopped in the road and separated; two, three went one way, four went one way, and two, three went another way. I says, "Without a chance, that's the kittens they're running out." ('Cause it looked like the fox they got the night before had been sucklin'.)

George said, "What do they do?"

I said, "They usually run in a hollow tree or some place like that, a sinkhole, maybe."

"Get up before the dogs catch'em!" he says.

I says, "No, one'll run till he gets caught."

So it wasn't but a few minutes. I said, "Wasn't that a tree dog down there?"

He said, "He's the best tree dog we got. He's got a fox down somewheres."

We went on down in the old field called the wet McCall field. There was a great big old chestnut log there, and that's where [the kittens] were—went up in that log, way up, and the dogs couldn't get to'em. It was too small.

I said, "There's nothin' to do but stick a stick in there and see about where he is and then cut a hole in it and get'em out alive."

"Oh," he says, "that'll be the day; that'll be the day!"

I cut [the log] open. It wasn't as much to it as I thought it'd be. It was hollow and pretty rotten. I cut it just exactly in the right place, right behind'em. I could see a tail. I went ahead and stuck some poles in behind him, so he couldn't back off and get out the back. Backed him up behind it and chipped down again. I reached on down there and got him right behind the ears, pulled him out and stuffed him in that tow sack. He was a pretty little fellow, 'bout eight inches long. Just as red as he could be. Prettiest tail you ever looked at!

He said, "I wouldn't take five dollars for it."

And I haven't. I had a crate down there that they hauled pigs in. It had a steel top on it, screen over it, and white oak sides. We put the little ol' fellow in there and that next evening, by God, he ate a big fish. I fried a big fish, and he ate it all up.

George says, "I'd love to stay another week."

I said, "It'd be nice. Farming time's coming and I'll have to be here regular."

He said, "I'll tell you what we'll do. We'll be back about the first of April, next year."

Well, they come every year while I was down there—every year for seven years they used to come down there. One time they stayed two months fishing and hunting.

Bill died right here. Bill McKurty run a drugstore right in this town, after he got old and couldn't get out in the woods any more. He was a druggist, a licensed druggist. Smart man. And he carried medicine along. You'd get sick in the woods, he'd fix you up. He was better than any doctor we got. You'd just have to be his friend. He was real good.

I killed a bear over here at Blue River, Tennessee. (That was the last work I did with Georgia-Pacific and Ritter Lumber Company. We built a big camp over there and were fixin' to log that area in there.) I got up in there and an old man come out and said, "I'll give some man a hundred dollars to kill that old bear. He's eaten fifteen of my sheep, and he's killing my cattle."

I said, "Where at?"

He said, "Right in that pasture, and I can't find a place in the world where he goes in that big wire fence—I spent thousands of dollars to keep that bear out of that. I put the fence up there, and an electric fence, and every morning I find a cow dead and half eat up."

"Why," I said, "I'll kill that booger in less than three days."

He said, "I'll give you a hundred dollrs in cash and a quarter of the bear if you get him."

PLATE 11 Will the storyteller. As Will tells a bear story, he shows us how the bear got into another man's pasture: "He'd get up on that rock and he'd jump on that poplar, and by God, slide into the pasture!"

I started lookin' for that bear with a man from Hiawassee who was operating a 'dozer. I went on up the next morning, and there was Charley Walls. He was a tax receiver in Hayesville, retired, and he come to Ritter Lumber Company as a kind of road supervisor. He was supervising that road up there in Tennessee. I didn't know the country. I wasn't raised in there, and he knowed how the roads was 'sposed to go in there.

I went on up there and [the man who wanted the bear killed] said, "See that nice cow laying over there? It's half gone. Bear got it *last night.* I've lost over three thousand dollars in the last two weeks—sheep and cattle up there."

I said, "The bear won't be there another week."

He said, "I hope that is true."

I looked around out there and Charley Wall said, "Will, why don't you get that bear trap that you made over there at the refuge and set it up here, and you can catch that bear the first night. All you have to do is just find out where he gets through."

And I said, "I never thought about that. That trap's over there snuggled up in the box, and the people can't get it."

So I went back to Hayesville. I had that trap hid over there. He and I drove around with the jeep one night, come back the next morning and brought that trap over there. And the next morning after that, we took it up on the river where we were building the road. I slipped out there and looked around about there. That bear was coming down the road we had built.

He'd go up a tree, and when he'd get up the tree, he'd crawl up on a high rock. There was a great big poplar standing right at the inside of the pasture. He'd get up on that rock and he'd jump on that poplar and by God, slide down into the pasture. The electric fence was *under* him! That's how slick that bear was.

"Well," I said to myself, "if I had time, I'd stay up there and shoot him, but I ain't got time to do it."

I had to work ten hours a day, and it was a long ways to go back and forth to the mill. The mill was about ten miles below us. (We was buildin' a road to get the timber out.)

So it got t'rainin' pretty heavy; couldn't work that evening and I went ahead and got the trap and come on up there and looked the situation over. And I says to myself, "If I set the trap outside [the fence], I might catch somebody, by God, having to walk around there. I'd better put it inside."

So I went to that old poplar where the bear jumped on that tree and slid on down into the pasture. I set that trap right under that poplar there and fastened it to the trunk of a [felled] birch that was about eighteen inches through and a hundred feet long.

I didn't have nothing but a little ol' scout twenty-two, about an eighteen-inch barrel on it and a few short cartridges left. I didn't have my shot-gun—it was still at Hayesville. I hadn't ever moved all of my stuff that was locked up in the tool shed. I couldn't get to it, and I hadn't nothing but that little ol' scout gun.

We went on up there and the bear had tore that fence all to pieces and pushed that birch tree to the roots through the fence, electric wire and all; tore everything up. He was in the river, and the river had caught the log and liked to have washed on down to a drift about a hundred and fifty yards down the river. He was a'sittin' up on the roots of the birch tree look-ing at us. He had both feet in that big trap [because he'd landed in the trap as he slid down that poplar tree into the pasture]. He was sitting up there, by gosh, looking at us. He showed his teeth when we come out there.

Charley said, "What you gonna do now?"

I said, "I'm gonna kill him with that twenty-two."

"Why, heck," he says, "you can't kill a bear like that that weighs six hun-dred pounds."

I said, "I'll show you."

I shot that bear right between the eye and the ear. There's a thin place there where the bone is soft. Went on up there about thirty feet from him—I tapped him right between the eye and ear and he went on down in the creek. I had to fetch the 'dozer to pull the tree out with the bear at-tached. I got him out in the road. I hung him on up. The 'dozer raised him on up, and we fastened him to the tree. Then I got him and took him on to the camp and skinned him. Told all them men we was having a feast that night. We had some fifty boys down there at that camp. An ol' man and his wife was cooking there—he was really a cook! Anyhow, they took a fit. Those were the prettiest hams you ever laid your eyes on!

I took one of'em and laid it on my jeep, went on up to the ol' landlord and got my hundred dollars. Boy, he took out a hundred dollar bill and gave it to me!

That ham weighed exactly forty-two pounds—the fattest dern thing I ever saw! Ate sheep! And hogs and cattle, too. That was about the fattest skin I've ever seen. I just cut down and it'd just come off, it was so loose and so fat. Then I took the skin on down to the camp and ol' man Demens, the Ritter Company supervisor give me twenty-five dollars for it.

I ain't scared of nothin'. A dog won't bite me. No, sirree! A bulldog will come like he's going to kill me, and it's all over. Cantwell Hamby had two down yonder, and he said, "I guarantee you'll be bit a dozen times if you get in my yard."

I said, "I'm not going in your yard as far as that goes, only if I have to."

Wasn't more than a year later, his boy and I (that was in my young days) was together. Cantwell's boy was makin' liquor up there at Hale Ridge—makin' big money sellin' it to Highlands. He couldn't get that still fixed up, and he got me to fix it for him. He had a condenser, but it wasn't workin'. The still was too big for the condenser.

I fixed it up and about one o'clock heavy rain come, and he was gonna take me home. We got just about within five hundred yards of his daddy's house (had a T-model Ford), and the rain was so hard he went in a ditch and buried the thing up, and it turned up and he broke his ankle. Couldn't walk a damn bit.

He says, "Go out there to my daddy's, and tell him about it, and he'll come out here and you and him carry me to the house. I'm too heavy for you to carry me."

I said, "What about them dogs?"

He said, "Oh, I don't know. You've been with me so much, I don't think they'll bother you. I don't think they're loose anyhow."

It was just a'pourin' down. I never saw such a rain in my whole life. I went out there and hollered a time or two and nobody answered. I opened the gate up. It was chained heavy, and directly I heard the dogs a'comin'. Oh, they was just a'raisin' hell! I was on the porch when the dogs come. They come in there and like to knocked me over.

The old man jumped up. Said, "Good God almighty! It's a wonder they didn't kill you!"

"Why," I said, "I'm petting them all over. They won't bother me."

He says, "You are the only man in the world that can get in here that way. Them dogs will kill any man that comes in here at night."

"I've never been dog-bit in my life. I've raised all kinds, bulldogs and everything else," I said. "Your son is out there with an ankle broke, wrecked that little ol' car and his ankle twisted, and I want you to come help me tote him in. He really needs to go to the doctor."

He said, "I'll take him in the mornin' first thing."

So we went over there and carried him in. He said, "Now you go on in the back room there and lay down and go to sleep."

I said, "No, I've got to walk on home. My wife is lookin' for me, and I'll have to go."

He said, "You're going to walk seven miles tonight in that rain?"

"I've got to be at home. It's gonna quit. It's just come a shower."

So I went on home. The next mornin', by gosh, he took him over to the doctor, and it took him nearly a year to walk. Mashed the bone in his foot. He's still a'livin', but he lives at Birmingham now. He could make some of the best liquor I believe I ever saw. Pure corn liquor, single and double it. Oh, he made a fortune with it. His daddy raised hell about it, but he married and moved out. Somebody said he's still a'sellin' it, and he's nearly my age.

When we revisited Will, we found him in the shop, repairing a plow. He invited us inside the shop to tell us about his big project and the other things that now keep him busy.

Now I do light mechanic and blacksmith work, but I'm not a mechanic. I don't work on the automobiles at all unless I have to. I work on mine a little but that's all. Right now I make light stuff in the shop, like cow bells. And there's a lot of grass cutting going on. I fix the grass cutters, swinging blades and stuff like that, and all kinds of light work. I'm fixing to make them tub chain hooks there to go on a team of horses to log with sometime tomorrow if I'm able. Got all this week to make'em, and I've got one more cow bell to make for the lady in Atlanta. She's got fifteen, but she wants a certain sound and it's hard to get out of any ol' kind of metal. She's with a musical group that is accompanied by the bells. I made the fifteen she's got. I've worked on'em so long that I hear'em during the night. It's misery sure enough. It gets a man's goat. All kinds of cow bells in it, too, and they ring them bells. But she says they lack one bell completely and two of 'em needs to be changed just a little bit. So I made two, and started on a third one, but I know one won't work, but the other two might. I made fifty bells, but only fifteen of'em would do. I sold'em to the farmers all along; I don't lose nothin'. I got a contract. I can't charge over three dollars apiece. Now she only has fourteen; I've got one more to make and I'll be through. There

PLATE 12   Will displaying cowbells he made in his shop.

was one of them bells had an awful time to get the bass out of it. But I got a lid off an old washing machine and it was the very thing. Just a coincidence. I thought to myself: That's just big enough to make it, and when I got the dern thing made, I'll be damn, we didn't have to touch it! Got it brazed, tempered, and she took it. She jumped over the moon. "That's it! That's it! That's it! That's it! Don't touch it no more. That's it!" So I fixed it up; she wouldn't even let me wash the dust off it. She took it home. Now she only lacks one bell, and I think I've got it here. The other'n—she could make out without it. Needs a little bit more brass. It's got kind of a dead tone. That's all that's a matter with it; I can fix it in two mintues. So, I'm getting along fine with it. I'm about ready for my money now.

It don't take a long time to make a bell if you got the materials. You can't get any old metal—it's got to be fourteen-gauge soft steel. Iron won't make no bell. It don't have a bit of sound. I made two or three and can't hear'em from here to the road top.

The best thing to make'em is that soft steel that they put in the bottom of pickups. You see, a big sheet there is six feet long and four feet wide. And it makes awful good bells. They all make the same sound. That's all the trouble. You have got to change the sound, so you put brass in it. And a little brass makes it a keen sound. I've been a'fooling with bells for fifty years, and I know exactly what to make if you can get the stuff to make it with. Use to be, you'd just pick up any kind of soft pot made out of metal. You could make a bell out of it easy. Now then, they don't do it. All this stuff we've got now is remelted stuff, and they put a little cast in it. And cast ain't got no sound at all. It kills the sound; that's what's the matter.

There's lots to it, I'll tell you. And you can take it on the anvil and as long as it's hot, it's got a different tone than it has when it's cooled off. You can't fix it till you make allowance. It either goes down or up. If it's high metal, it goes down. You have to get everything as near one kind of metal as you can. And that Swedish steel—it won't make nothin' at all. A woman brought me a silver pot the other day. It was s'pose to be solid silver. And she wanted a shovel made out of it. A shovel out of silver for the fireplace. I make shovels, knives, and all that, and I had a good little piece left over. And she says, "I'll give you that piece for making the shovel." So I went ahead and took that piece by gosh, and made a bell out of it. I sold the bell for twenty-five dollars. It was pretty as it could be! If you get it too hot, it'll just burn up to a puff of smoke. It's gone. You have to watch. Just a little bit red, you get it out of there or you won't have a thing left.

Will's pet project these days is caring for his pigs. He has four, but one pair is older than the other; the larger pigs are kept in another pen.

They come from a litter of sixteen. I sold the rest for ten dollars apiece, and the man give me fifty dollars for the old sow and two pigs. I bought'em in Toccoa, and everywhere I stopped on my way home, I sold one. I could've sold [my two] for ten dollars apiece, but I wanted something to fool with.

These larger pigs down here—I've never seen anything grow like these in my life! They were raised on Warwoman. I had these contracted before I got'em; I thought I wasn't gonna get them. They come here, and they was really poor, but they'd eat everything you'd put in there. They're gentle. Now they won't eat in the morning unless I rub their backs first. I feed'em pellets, and by God, they love it.

PLATE 14 Tinker McCoy and Mrs. Zoellner.

"I USED TO WEAR BLUE JEANS ALL THE TIME..."

When Tinker McCoy and I got into the *Foxfire* class, we learned that Will Zoellner had been interviewed by some *Foxfire* students, but Mrs. Zoellner never had. So we went to her house and talked it over, and she said, "Sure, I'd love to be interviewed because every time Will is being interviewed, I always leave the room because I feel it is his chance. But now it's my chance."

Mrs. Zoellner was born in the mountains of North Carolina outside Highlands in Blue Valley. Her maiden name was Magaline Webb. She has two brothers and two sisters living. Part of her family history is uncertain because, "The family Bible got lost and it's got all of their family and my family in it—all their ages. My uncle told me before he died, he says, 'You know how old you are.'

"I says, 'Yeah.'

"He said, 'I bet you don't.' So he said, 'You're fifteen year old.' Me and Will was married then."

The Zoellner house is rather large. It has a long hall, and all the rooms are big with high ceilings and open onto the hall. It has a fireplace and a wood stove, so the house stays very warm. They still drink water from a dipper and did not have plumbing until recently when Will got sick and they decided to remodel the house. Now it has a bathroom, and the ceiling has been lowered to make the house more suitable for winter.

We talked to Mrs. Zoellner and asked her some questions about her life and how she felt about the world today. She had plenty to talk about. I don't think she forgot anything that ever happened in her life, and she shared everything that she thought was important with us.

Article and photographs by Richard Henslee and Tinker McCoy.

We worked hard. I had to work from the time I was seven years old. My father made us. What he told us to do, we done it. And they never missed a Sunday taking us to church and Sunday school. They took us in the mule wagon. My daddy was a blacksmith. He also had a contract carrying the mail from Highlands to Cullasaga. My brother'd bring the mail from Highlands at nine o'clock, and he'd carry it from there to Cullasaga and back home, and my brother'd take the mail [he brought in] back to Highlands. He carried it for eleven years, and he had boxes on the road with peoples' names on them and he transferred the mail in the boxes. Sometimes I'd go with my daddy in the buggy and ride from home to Cullasaga and back. They wasn't but just two post offices between Cullasaga and Highlands. Highlands wasn't such a big place then. I think they was one market. Mr. Luther Rice run it. And Mr. Bascomb run the store. H. M. Bascomb.

And my daddy dug wells. He dug us a well one time. If you go too far down, you have to come out every once in a while 'cause the gas will stifle you. And he made the roller to roll him down in the well and roll the dirt out. And Loag Martin dug us a well over here on the old Mountain City Road. Me and him dug it together. I rolled him in and out. It was over thirty-five feet down in there, and we made a curb out of wood and dropped it down in there to keep it from caving. I remember he dug one for Mr. Dotson—150 feet before he struck water. I would be afraid to go down in it. I wouldn't go down in one for nothing. But I'd roll the dirt out for Loag. Use a great big old roller, and it's way wide. They make them out of straight dogwood poles, and they put a crank on them. You roll that roller and the rope would roll up in the middle of it till the bucket would come up to the top, and you reach and get the bucket and pour the dirt out of it and let it down again.

I wore blue jeans all the time when I was growing up till after I joined the church, but I wouldn't let the minister see me with my breeches on. Even though we had to work hard, we played lots of games, too. We played horseshoe. We called 'em "quates." And Daddy and Mother'd take us to Sunday school Sunday morning, and then they'd go up to see Granny, Daddy's mother, and they'd leave us there and we'd study up something to do to laugh at. We'd apron the roosters and make them fight. Just cut a hole in a paper sack and stick their heads through it and set them down and they'd go together and fight like everything. Daddy caught us one time about one of the rooster's heads a'being bloodied. He'd tell us we was gonna get a whipping, but he wouldn't whip us on Sunday. He wouldn't forget it. Monday morning he'd call us up and give'em to us.

Sometimes we'd carry the ducks up to the top of the hill, and we'd fly them ducks back to see them light in the lake. We'd carry them way up on the side of the mountain and throw them and watch them fly [back to the pond].

And we used to play:

> William Shinfull
> he's a good fisherman
> catches'em at hand
> put'em in a pan
> some lays eggs
> some lays none
> war brar limberlock
> three geese in the flock
> flock fell down
> the mouse run around
> o-u-t spells out
> on a rock dish cloud.

Whichever one it spelled out on, they'd go hide. And then we'd hunt them. We used to play all kinds of little old games. We'd get out of the night and play hide and seek till midnight.

And we'd jump rope. Jump it fifty times without stopping. We played you're out if you didn't jump fifty without the rope catching you. Then another'd take over.

And I'll tell you the saddest thing that ever happened in my life was when we was all together—they was eleven of us—and we'd have the biggest time in the world playing—get out and make swings; enjoy ourselves. But Leonard, the baby brother, he'd always have to be right where my brother Willy was. And we'd laugh at him. He'd do some little old tricks. He was the cutest thing in the world, if he was my brother. One time Willy was over in the garden, and the creek went across from the barn into the garden. My sister was over there, and she hollered and told'em, "Come over here." Says, "I want to show you something." And we all went over there but the baby. And they was a white swan, and its neck—you know how long their old neck is—over there, and it just stood there and wobbled its old head. Willy picked up a big old rock and throwed it, and Leonard was coming across the water gate and he hit him in the arm and just broke his little arm. And I happened to see him and I walked over there and I hollered out, "Willy, you killed Leonard." Willy just fell over. Fainted over as dead as I don't know. And mother come running down, and she was just hollering, "Lord, have mercy. It's killed him."

He'd raise up his little old arm and he'd say, "It's not broke, Mother," and it'd flop down here. I can just hear him telling her. And Willy wouldn't let him out of his sight till it got well. Daddy put his arm back together and splinted it and it healed up. You can't tell now it's ever been broke. Little bitty scar there.

Sometimes Uncle George Webb would scare us. He'd get a sheet and put over his head and cut holes in it. Hide behind something and scare us to death. One time we was trick-or-treating and we went over to Preacher Pick's and come back, and he'd hid at the gatepost and he come walkin' out. They's a big hollow stump right below the gate and it was full of glass, and my brother Ben run and jumped in that old stump and just cut his feet all to pieces. Mother and Daddy like to have never got the blood stopped. Uncle George never tried to scare us no more after that.

Daddy liked to scare old people. He scared Uncle Harvey one time, Uncle Harvey knocked him in the head with his walking stick. Mama and Daddy would go to see Grandma every Sunday and we'd do all kinds of tricks while they were gone; we'd sing, fish out of the creeks, ride the horses in the mountains, and we'd have just the biggest time. We wouldn't let Daddy know it when he came back. Mother caught up with us one time and said, "There's a wild Negro in the woods. Next time ya'll take them horses out in the woods he'll get everyone of you." That scared me. We never stole horses out anymore, to ride them in the woods. And I was going to my uncle's to come back with my sister one time. I was going up a trail way—there was a road that went around like that and back up and there was a trail way that cut across—that cut off about a mile of the road. I got up the trail way a pretty good ways and I seen an old man coming down the trail. They told me that there was an old man, a wild man that was going around pointing his gun in under every rock, so I thought it was him. I run back down the mountain. He had a pole of wood on his back and I thought it was a gun. I run back down the mountain and there was a big barn on the side of the trail—they called it the Miller barn. I went up in the barn and climbed up in the top of the barn as far as I could and I stayed there until dark. He never did come by, the old man didn't. I stayed up there until my mother and daddy came hunting me. I seen them coming, and they had the light. I was scared to holler at Daddy, afraid he'd thrash me all over the place. But finally I squalled out, "Here I am."

He come out and said, "What in the world are you doing?"

I said, "That old man got after me and I hid in the barn, run from him."

He says, "What in the world do you mean?"

I said, "Well, I was just going to stay here until morning, I wasn't gonna get down."

"Come on down," Daddy said. "That was Mr. McGee. They ain't no such thing as a wild man." So, I come on down, they took me home. Daddy laughed when he got home. He laughed until it made him cry. So from then on I wouldn't pass no one on the road. I'd hide. If I seen anybody coming before they seen me, I'd hide until they'd go on. And after that I'd slip off.

My brother got married, and he was coming home on Sunday morning and Mother wouldn't let me go to meet him. And I told her, I says, "I'm going out to Fred's to look and see if I can see him coming." We were all crazy about him. I didn't see him coming, I just kept going. I went on up the mountain and up by the cemetery (where Daddy and Mother's buried). Went on up and my granny was staying where I turned off the road to go through the Lost Gap. I went across the river, and the river is wide as from here down to Queens'. There were two big old pine logs that I walked across. I went on up into the Lost Gap and couldn't find him. There was a bunch of hogs on the side of the road lumped up. Stared at me and scared me to death. I ran back across the river. So as I came back across the river Granny seen me. Here she come. She said, "Where have you been? You slipped off."

I said, "No, I haven't slipped off, I was going to meet Willy."

She said, "I'm gonna tell your daddy." I went back by the cemetery and I found a little kitten, in the road. I stopped to play with the little kitten. I went on and the little kitten followed me. Got down on the mountain and met Mother and the baby coming. She was crying. She was sure I'd fell in the river and drowned. She said, "Where in the world have you been?"

I said, "I was just going to meet Willy."

She said, "All right. In the morning I'm gonna have Daddy to whip the skin off of you for slipping off." When Daddy came, Mama never told him. I was just tickled to death. I thought I'd get by. So the next morning she cooked breakfast, and he ate breakfast and all of us started out to work. Got up in the fields working and he called me. He wanted me for something. I went back and he had cut him a switch. He said, "I'm gonna learn you how to slip off, you don't never do that." Boy, did he give me a whipping. I learned better than to slip off.

We were all happy at home. Worked together. I raised calves. Trained steers. Daddy give me a calf—little calf—one time. I'd carry it in my arms [when it would rain] to keep it from getting wet. I'd carry it to the barn in my arms; and I raised it and I trained it to work. It'd plow. And it'd foller me. I could go in the mountains and it'd foller me just like a dog right in after me. And I rode it.

And my grandma, she raised her own meat. We raised our own. We generally had a big run of hogs. Will had the mountains full of hogs when me and him was married. And cattle and goats and everything else. We used to milk goats over at our first home at the WMU Camp, but we didn't use the milk. We'd give it to the pigs. We drank cows' milk. But now I can't drink cows' milk. I just can't drink it anymore. I've been used to this bought milk in my coffee. We sold our cows. Didn't have room for them over here. You remember when we had the last cow. We raised her in Mountain City.

The first job I had was when I worked for Miss Sloane at Highlands in the summers when I was seven years old in her boarding house. I cleaned rooms, made beds, done the dusting, and waited the tables. Forty dollars a month is all I made. Honey, I done work most grown women wouldn't of took. My sister worked there, too. My daddy told Miss Sloane I was too small, but she says, "I've just got to have her." Daddy let me go. He didn't want me to go, but he'd worked for her for years, too, and felt obligated. I stayed with her. They had a colored cook that'd been with them for twenty years, and she was just as sweet to me. I slept in the room with her.

Later I got married. I'll tell you how I met Will. He'd just come back from the First World War and he had hogs and cattle in the woods. And I'd been to Highlands and spent the weekend, with my sister, and I was coming back on Sunday morning riding my horse, and something happened to my saddle and I was off trying to saddle her. And Will and Mr. Cobb was coming up the road from his place and they stopped to help me fix the saddle. So he helped me back up on the horse, and he asked me if he could come see me. Now I never went out with no boys. I courted one boy before I met Will. And me and Will done our courting on the porch at the house. I was fifteen years old, and me and him married when I was fifteen.

Marriage is just what you make of it. It's nice if you get along with your husband, get along with the children. Sometimes it's rough.

We had six children: May, Emily, Earl, Charlie, Lucy, and Louise. I've been married fifty-two years. May, my oldest one, is fifty-one years old. She was born a year and two months after me and Will was married. And I never had no trouble with my babies. Never whipped none of them in my life but Charlie and Earl. They was in the [corn] crib a'shucking corn and they got to fighting—throwing corn at each other. Earl never would fight Charlie, but Charlie, he had a temper. I heard the corn a'going and I went over there. Earl was a way up in the crib. Charlie would say, "I'm gonna hit'cha." I listened at'em for a while, and then I eased the crib door open. Earl says, "There's Mama!" Charlie, he come down. I made them hug and kiss. Charlie, he didn't want to, but I made them hug and kiss. And they never did fuss no more. Wherever one was, the other was. They was some Speeds that had twins, Pete and Dood. And I got to calling my two boys Pete and Dood they was so close together. They was just sixteen months difference in them. They was right together, everything they done, till Earl was married. And Charlie missed him so bad. When Earl would come to see us and Charlie was here, they'd be right side by side. Charlie got killed down here in Mountain City. Truck run into Charlie and killed him. And one of my grandbabies got killed, too. Handyman from Ohio run into Robert. Robert would have been the same age as you, Tinker. He was the sweetest young'un. I miss him today. Sometimes I take a spell and break down.

Some of my children gave me nights of hard heartache, but I enjoyed them. I'd get out and play with them just like I was as little as them. Make sleds for them to play with. Come off of the mountain and play. Take care of them when they was sick. I used to use alum and honey to cure sore throat. And this here stuff you call boneset—it's the best thing for the flu. Make a tea of it, sweeten it and give it. It'll calm the fever down as quick as any doctor's. And catnip tea is good for little babies. Keeps hives broke out on them and lets them sleep good. And pennyroyal is good too. Pennyroyal

PLATE 17 Mrs. Zoellner and Tinker McCoy.

and ground ivy. I've got ground ivy out there on the bank. And Grandma Zoellner used honey and whiskey for a cough and wheezing. She had asthma and never did go to a doctor. And whiskey and wild cherry bark was the best remedy I ever took for rheumatism. I ain't took none of it in a long time. Since I was baptized. I'm afraid of it now.

But me and Will had a good life. Hard work. I used to love to help him in the blacksmith shop. I ain't able no more to help him. And he ain't able either, poor old feller. But I used to go from home and help him in the blacksmith shop over here at Clayton. [Will ran a shop there below Jowers. John A. Wilson owned it then, and Will started running it on May 16, 1933.]

I've done riding and breaking horses. And I used to shoe my jenny. You know what a little jenny is. They're a little like a mule—got great big old ears. My daddy showed me how to shoe them. I got to where I could fix the shoes and punch the nail holes in them as good as he could. And I'd take shoes off of horses when Will would be gone. I'd take pincers and pull them off. The last ones I took off a horse was Claude Smith's girl's horse. She'd come up here and Will was in the hospital in Atlanta. The old shoe was broke in front, and it would turn around crossways and the horse could hardly walk and she was cutting her foot on it. I told her, I says, "I'll take 'em off and you can ride her in the soft road and not get on the highway with her."

So she said, "Okay," and I just took'em off. She never moved while I took shoes off.

And I've hauled out acid wood and pulp wood and cross ties with the big old black horse I used to have since me and Will been married. Haul off

Pinnacle Mountain, and then I'd go to the house and cook dinner. Then go back to work and come and cook supper.

I've helped saw with a crosscut saw—helped the boys saw wood. Plow. We had a big fireplace and we burned wood. I'd snake wood up into the yard, and the boys—after they got big enough—they'd saw it up.

I even went and camped out with Will squirrel hunting with'im. We've had lots of good times going out camping. Listening to the dogs run, and Will killing squirrels. He came back one time with sixteen strung on a string. He likes them with dumplings and milk gravy on them. We've gone hunting and fishing and camping a week at a time. Will done the cooking and got the fire going. He's the best cook you ever seen. We'd eat what we killed and the fish that we caught.

I have shot squirrels for the boys before I'd let them carry guns. Dogs would tree a squirrel and they'd want me to go and get it. I've shot out squirrels out of a high tree. I beat my brother shooting one time. He shot four times at a squirrel and never hit it. I said, "Give me the gun and I can kill it."

He said, "Nah, you can't kill it," and handed me the gun, and put a shell in, and the squirrel started to jump from one limb to another and I shot it pretty in the head as you ever seen. I used to be a bad tomboy. I was risky. I'd risk anything. I've never had to shoot *nobody*, but I've shot at a man one time. He was drunk and aggravating me, and I told him not to come back again in my driveway no more drunk. So he went around and come back four times and stopped again, and I shot his back windshield out and his door glasses and he didn't come back and hadn't till yet.

I've never shot anybody myself, but I guess lots of it has gone on. One time two boys got in a fight near here over a gun, and one took the other one off and he never made it back home. They found him dead up there at what they call the Buttermilk Levels. He was sittin' on the side of an old road that went down there. He'd been shot in the back of the head, and then that boy had put his foot on his head to see if he was dead, and mud was on his head. Daddy found him [after they had] hunted all the next morning. And they couldn't find the boy that did it so they took out papers on him and found him and had him locked up. And [his father] got up and swore lies in the courthouse for him. Said his son was innocent. He didn't do that. And he got him out. Took everything he owned for him to pay him out to keep him from going for life. And that man was a preacher, and I told Daddy that we was gonna be baptized. And he says, "Who's gonna baptize you'uns?"

And I says, "Mr. —————."

He says, "He won't baptize my children," he says, "because I don't believe in a preacher that'll lie for his son after him killing an innocent boy."

The boy he killed was just sixteen year old.

But I always believed in the Lord ever since I was seven years old. I said, "Daddy, I'll never be baptized if you don't let me be baptized," but I still went on to church and on and on until I finally got baptized over here in the lake. All my people went to church and all my neighbors every Sunday; and the church was pretty big, but it wouldn't hold the people that went.

I love to be friends with everybody. I think I've got a lot of friends anyway. And I tell my children to love each other and live a good life and trust in the Lord.

If we don't do that, it's going to go to the bad and the world won't stand long. If everybody would get together and live right, serve the Lord more and have peace in all the states, I think that the world might stand longer.

IRONMAKING AND BLACKSMITHING

This chapter explores the roles ironmaking and blacksmithing played in the Southern Highlands during the nineteenth century and the early part of the twentieth. During this period there was relatively little industry in the area. The economy was basically an agricultural one, and the majority of people led a nearly self-sufficient, subsistence-level existence.

The chapter is divided into two main parts: The first covers ironmaking itself, and includes sections on blast furnaces, iron and steel, charcoal, and ironworks in general. There are also interviews with four people who are well informed about ironmaking, local history, or both. The second part is concerned with blacksmithing, specifically the work of rural blacksmiths, and includes sections on the basic procedures they employed, the tools they used, and lists different items they made. There are also interviews with five blacksmiths, and directions (with photographs and diagrams), for making the item each of them made for us. However, in a larger sense, this is not intended to be a how-to article; it seeks to enlighten the reader about an industry that is basic to the development of the Southern Highlands, and the country in general. Indeed, the metallurgical industry is basic to the development of civilization as a whole.

IRONMAKING

The first and simplest type of iron furnace was called a bloomery, in which wrought iron was produced directly from the ore. The ore was heated with charcoal in a small open furnace, usually made of stone and blown upon with bellows. Most of the impurities would burn out, leaving a spongy mass of iron mixed with siliceous slag (iron silicate). This spongy mass was then refined by hammering, reheating, and hammering some more, until it reached the desired fibrous consistency. During the hammering, the glasslike slag would be evenly distributed throughout the iron mass. This hammered slab of wrought iron, or "bloom," was then ready to forge into some usable object. There were many furnaces of this type in

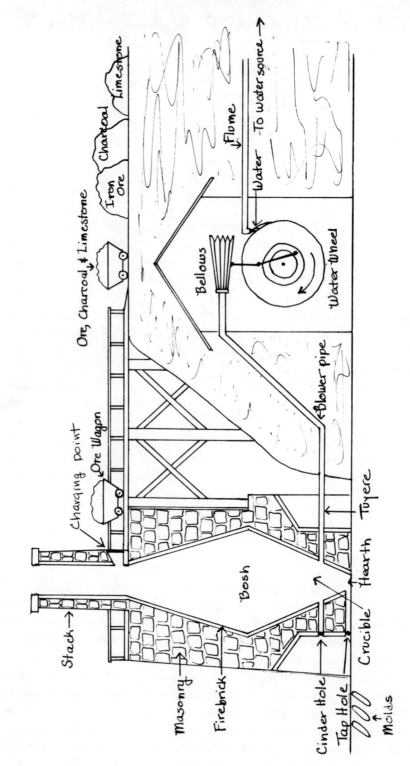

Ore, Charcoal & Limestone

Limestone

Charcoal

Iron Ore

Charging point

Ore Wagon

Bellows

Flume

Water

To water source →

Water Wheel

Stack →

Blower pipe

Masonry

Bosh

Firebrick

Cinder Hole

Tap Hole

Molds

Crucible

Hearth

Tuyere

PLATE 19

PLATE 19   Cutaway view of the old Tannehill Furnace ⚒ 1, which was put back in blast on September 19, 1976. It is located in the Tannehill State Park in Alabama. Diagram by Bryan Owings, courtesy of *Sparrow Hawk,* a project of the Bibb County, Alabama, Public Schools Bi-Centennial Commission.

The furnace is charged with iron ore, charcoal, and limestone, through a cupola in the stack. The charcoal acts as the fuel, and the limestone combines with the impurities in the ore to form slag, leaving relatively pure molten iron as the desired end product. The raw materials are kept at a point roughly level with the charging point and are run across a trestle in ore carts to the charging point. After the charge is ignited, the fire is supplied with a continuous blast of cold air provided by a large bellows, which is operated by water power. The air is piped from the bellows through the blower pipe, or bustle pipe, through the tuyère, and into the furnace itself. When the molten iron has collected to the point where it is about level with the cinder hole, or cinder notch, the clay plug is removed from the cinder hole, and the molten slag, which floats on top of the molten ore, runs off into the waste area. Then the clay plug is taken out of the tap hole, or iron notch, and the iron runs out into sand molds in the casting area. At this point the tap hole and cinder hole are replugged, and the operation continues.

The charging of a blast furnace is a continuous, twenty-four-hours-a-day, seven-days-a-week operation, while tapping of the furnace is an intermittent one. The furnace will stay in blast until the firebrick lining wears out, at which time the furnace will be shut down and repaired.

Colonial America, but they were later almost entirely replaced by cold-blast furnaces. The main drawback of this direct method of making wrought iron was its limited production. On the other hand, a bloomery required a much smaller investment of money and labor to set up and operate than did a blast furnace.

The first blast furnaces used a cold blast of air to feed the fire. They produced not wrought iron, but pig iron, which was cast into sand molds, called pigs, directly from the furnace. The pig iron was then reheated and cast into usable items, or treated in a finery and made into wrought iron or, less often, refined into steel. Blast furnaces of the nineteenth century were usually about twenty-five or thirty feet high. They consisted of an outer shell of rock with an inner lining of refractory brick and were capable of producing about two tons of pig iron daily. Four main ingredients are necessary to produce pig iron: iron ore, charcoal, limestone, and a continuous blast of air. The charcoal, an almost pure carbon fuel, aided by the air blast, burns, creating enough heat to reduce the ore to a molten state. Some of the impurities in the ore escape in the form of gasses, and most of the remainder combine with the limestone, which is the flux, to produce molten slag. The result is a relatively pure molten iron upon which the molten slag floats. The slag is tapped off into the waste area, and the iron is tapped into sand molds in the casting area.

PLATE 20 Professor Ray Farabee indicates the charging point of the old Tannehill furnace. Professor Farabee was the furnace master for the refiring of the old furnace.

Hot-blast furnaces work on the same principle as the cold-blast ones, except that the blast of air is heated before it enters the furnace. This method of treating the air blast was originally developed to enable furnaces to use anthracite (hard coal) instead of charcoal or coke. With anthracite it is possible to build a larger and more efficient furnace, but it requires the added boost of heated air in order to burn properly. Anthracite was not available in Georgia in sufficient amounts to be used in the blast furnaces, so the furnaces here were of the cold-blast type, using charcoal for fuel.

The first blast furnaces were located in areas where the right combination of natural resources occurred, i.e., iron ore, limestone, and wood for making charcoal. They were built by a stream with sufficient flow to turn a waterwheel to operate a bellows or blower. They were usually at the bottom or on the side of a hill so that the raw materials could be stored on a plane roughly level with the top of the stack to facilitate charging the furnace. The ironworks usually owned or controlled large tracts of forest to insure a constant supply of wood for making charcoal.

Charcoal Mound

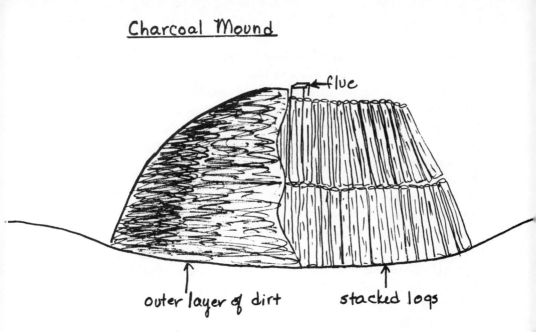

outer layer of dirt   stacked logs

According to the information we have gathered, charcoal was used almost exclusively as the fuel in blast furnaces, fineries, and forges in north Georgia. Charcoal, a wood product, is a relatively pure carbon fuel that gives off an intense heat when burned. It is produced by burning wood under carefully controlled conditions, in which only a limited amount of air is allowed to come in contact with the wood while it is burning. Actually, it is charred rather than completely burned. The production of charcoal is a time-consuming and exacting process, and the charcoal makers, called colliers, had to be very skilled in order to do it correctly.

The interview with O. H. Monroe gives a very good explanation of how charcoal was made, so here we will present only a brief description of the process. The collier in charge, whether he worked for an ironworks or was an independent operator, would procure the necessary amount of wood, cut in four- to six-foot-long lengths, to build a mound. In some cases the wood was stacked on level ground, and in other cases it was stacked in a pit. It was stacked "standing up" around a center pole (or a wooden box) the desired height of the mound, which acted as the main flue. When the first tier reached the desired diameter, a second tier, with a somewhat smaller diameter, was added. The irregular shape of the logs afforded air spaces throughout the inside of the mound. Then it was covered with dirt to seal off the air from the outside, but some small openings were left on the sides to ignite the wood and control the air intake. The collier carefully tended the mound, keeping it smoldering at a constant rate, until he decided that the wood was fully charred. At that point he closed the air intakes, and waited for the mound to stop burning and cool off.

A finery was often built in conjunction with a blast furnace. There the pig iron was converted into wrought iron by heating it in a furnace, using charcoal and a powerful air blast. Slag containing iron silicate was then added, and the heated, softened iron was agitated with iron tools, a process that distributed the iron silicate and caused much of the carbon, as well as impurities from the added slag, to come to the surface. The spongy iron mass was then hammered, reheated, and hammered some more, until the excess carbon and other impurities were removed. What remained was wrought iron, tough and fibrous, which was then hammered into bars that were available to local blacksmiths.

A forge, which is a small manufacturing plant, was usually built adjacent to the blast furnace. Here the pig iron and/or wrought iron was converted into usable items. Pig iron was cast in molds to make implements, such as pots, pans, heating and cooking stoves, and other things that wouldn't be subject to a lot of physical stress. Wrought iron was forged into things that would be subject to stress such as axe heads and horseshoes.

The term ironworks, or iron plantation, refers to the entire ironmaking complex. An ironworks generally included one or more blast furnaces, a finery, a forge, homes for many of the workers, and large tracts of forest land (sometimes thousands of acres) for the production of charcoal. Some ironworks also owned their own iron mines and/or limestone quarries. Many of them took on aspects of small villages, but whatever form they took, they all provided jobs for people living in the vicinity. In a number of cases in the South, slave labor was heavily depended upon to operate the ironworks up through the Civil War.

Ironworks that either didn't have their own iron mines, forest land, and/or limestone quarries, or could not produce all the necessary iron ore, charcoal, and limestone they needed, depended on people in the area to provide it. In some instances, independent operators would contract to provide all or a portion of the necessary materials. In other cases, local farmers would provide some of the ore, limestone, and charcoal on a piece-work basis, obtaining it during times when the farm work was least demanding. This was one way that people in a somewhat marginal agricultural area could earn money to buy things they could not produce themselves. No matter how an ironmaking operation was set up, it had a sizable economic impact on the community in which it was located. Bear in mind that during the nineteenth century and early part of the twentieth century, there were few wage-earning jobs available in the Southern Highlands, and the great majority of people lived on small farms and produced most of their own food and other necessities.

Wrought iron, the first type of iron made from iron ore, was the only product of the old bloomeries. It consists of iron and iron silicate, a glasslike slag in a physical, rather than chemical, association. The glasslike slag, largely responsible for the grainy, fibrous texture of wrought iron, makes it resistant to corrosion and fatigue, and gives it a toughness and ability to withstand stress which pig iron does not possess. The actual forging of wrought iron elongates the particles of iron silicate and distributes them evenly throughout the iron, thus creating the grainy texture. Wrought iron is perfectly suited for forge work because it is strong and malleable and takes a strong weld. It has all the right properties for tools and other implements that must withstand stress, such as hammers and horseshoes. Before the introduction of steel, wrought iron was the only ore iron product that blacksmiths used.

The first wrought iron was produced directly from the ore. After blast furnaces (which produce pig iron) were developed, it was made by an indirect process, in which pig iron was recombined with iron silicate, which was fluxed out during the production of the pig iron.

Pig iron is the product of blast furnaces. It comes out of the furnaces in a molten state, is immediately cast into molds called pigs, and is considered pig iron until or unless it is further refined. It does not contain the glasslike slag of wrought iron, and has different properties. Pig iron is hard and brittle, not malleable, has a grainy texture, and is not suitable for forge work. It was and is used primarily for casting into implements that may need to withstand heat, such as large pots and frying pans, but not for anything that must withstand stress. Pig iron can be further refined to make wrought iron or steel.

Steel is also a product of iron ore. It was first produced from wrought iron by a time-consuming and expensive process called cementation, during which strips of wrought iron were placed in clay containers that contained charcoal dust, and were fired in a furnace at a high temperature. The charcoal dust combined with the outer layer of the wrought iron, producing a steel outer surface on the wrought iron. Steel is now made from pig iron through a refining process in which certain alloys are added and some of the carbon is removed, leaving a specific amount in the steel. It has varying qualities of strength, hardness, toughness, and elasticity, depending on the amount of carbon and other alloys in it, and on how it is tempered. Steel is ranked by its carbon content—high, medium, or low; the higher the carbon content, the harder and less elastic it is.

Steel was not readily available to rural blacksmiths during the last century and the early part of this century, and they used wrought iron almost exclusively. It is now much more available than wrought iron. It has all the right properties for forge work and has pretty much replaced wrought iron in that field. However, steel does not resist corrosion the way wrought iron does, due to the absence of iron silicate, the glasslike slag that gives wrought iron this property.

John Bulgin, one of the blacksmiths we interviewed, explained, "A good steel is highly refined and made in a blast furnace. In its first casting they smelt the iron ore. And [then it's molded] in big pigs. Then they take that and resmelt it and add different alloys to make steel. Plain smelted iron ore [is called pig iron]. [Wrought iron, pig iron, and steel] *all* come from iron ore that comes out of the ground. A tooled steel is a high-carbon steel. It has gots lots of carbon in it to where it'll temper [hard], and it's strong. Hot rolled machinery steel [is] low in carbon and not supposed to harden. It's got its own strength."

The following interviews give insights into the development of the iron industry in the Southeast. Frank FitzSimons talks about the old Gillespie Forge in Hendersonville, North Carolina. Herbert Kimzey talks about the now defunct Habersham Iron Works and Manufacturing Company in Habersham County, Georgia. O. H. Monroe tells of the early years of the ironmaking industry in northwest Georgia in general, and the old Cooper blast furnace near Cartersville, Georgia, in particular. Ray Farabee covers the actual construction and operation of a blast furnace, the chemical processes involved, and the refiring of the old Tannehill furnace in the Tannehill State Park in Alabama.

Frank FitzSimons

Frank FitzSimons is a native of Henderson County, North Carolina, and during his long life there has acquired a great deal of knowledge of the area. For nearly twenty-five years he had a weekly radio show in which he covered various aspects of the history of the county. He has recently written a book, entitled From the Banks of the Oklawaha, *which includes the history, myth, and folklore of Henderson County, beginning with the first white settlers.*

While we were researching the ironmaking industry in this area, Mr. FitzSimons' name came up as a good source of information about the old Gillespie Forge in Henderson County. It was a small, family-type operation where they smelted small amounts of iron ore, and made longrifles. The

following information about the forge and the people who operated it is a slightly edited version of a couple of the radio broadcasts Mr. FitzSimons did as a part of his weekly series of broadcasts over WHKP, Hendersonville, North Carolina.

In the eighteenth and nineteenth centuries there were more than four hundred gunsmiths in North Carolina. Many of them were also blacksmiths, and some of them were also silversmiths or whitesmiths. [In Henderson County there were] two families that were famous in the early years of the nineteenth century, in later years, and down to the present time. One of these men was a forge master named Phillip Sitton, and the others were Matthew Gillespie, a gunsmith and the maker of the famous Gillespie longrifles, and his bachelor son, Phillip Gillespie, who was killed on an unknown battlefield and left a legend that persists to this day.

Forge Mountain is aptly named. It is that long mountain in Henderson County that lies between that south fork of Mills River and Boylston Creek. Drive by the road that leads by Mills River, or as some call it, the Hayward Road, [to the point] just before the bridge that crosses Mills River. There's a North Carolina historical marker [there]. It reads "Gunshop and forge set up four miles west of here, about 1804 by Phillip Sitton and Phillip Gillespie, and operated until about 1861." Phillip Sitton set up his forge on the side of the mountain and began to manufacture the tools needed by these early settlers here in our mountains; the axes and plowshares, hoes, and those things necessary to conquer the wilderness. He made them from the iron smelted from the ore that was dug from the mountainside and along Boylston, and he wrought them at his forge there alongside the same moun-

tain that took his name and had been known through the years as Forge
Mountain. The records show that Phillip Sitton was given a land grant
about the time he set up his forge, for three thousand acres of land. To
smelt and forge iron in those days here in our mountains required a
tremendous amount of wood [to make charcoal] to feed the fires that
melted the ore from which iron was extracted. It is presumed that the large
grant of woodland was given to Phillip for this reason. The forge was operated until the early years of the Civil War, when it was moved by the Confederate government and combined with another ironworks on the David-
son River. All that remains today to tell a body that here was once a forge,
is the name of the mountain and the pieces of slag and traces of ashes there
where Phillip Sitton once operated.

One of the earliest settlers in that same area, and at about the same time
that Phillip Sitton set up his forge and began to hammer out the tools of the
pioneers, was a man named Matthew Gillespie. The Gillespies were a
prolific family of gunsmiths who were famous in Rowan County, North
Carolina, for [their] longrifles [before they ever came to Henderson
County]. The early members of the Sitton family and the Gillespie family
worked together, and married together. It was naturally so because Phillip
Sitton worked with iron and the Gillespies made the longrifles from that
same iron, all there in the shadows of Forge Mountain along the waters of
Mills River. Matthew was the first of the Gillespie family in Henderson
County to make a rifle gun, and a'body who has one of those early mounted
guns with the initials MG engraved on it has a small fortune. Even so if
they have one with the initials PG, because Matthew's son, Phillip, became
as famous as his father. And the guns made by both men became widely
sought because of their balance and accuracy, as well as simple beauty.
Those same guns, rare today as they were plentiful in days now gone, are
still eagerly bought by modern-day collectors of guns.

Phillip Gillespie was born in Henderson County—was the son of
Matthew Gillespie. He was born in 1817, and while growing up worked
with Phillip Sitton at his forge. When he figured he had learned all he
could about smelting and working with iron, he followed in his father's
footsteps. Phillip set up his shop across the road from Phillip Sitton's forge.
These pioneer settlers in our mountains of western North Carolina came
from near and far to buy the rifle guns made by Phillip Gillespie. For those
days [he was] one of some wealth, because in addition to his gunmaking he
had a still. The brandy from his still was as eagerly sought as one of his
guns. In the days that followed a legend was born, and with it a mystery
that has not been solved to this day. Some say that the still with which Phillip Gillespie made his brandy was a government licensed one, while others

say it was a homemade one because mountaineers believed that it was one's inherent right to make and sell brandy, and such fruits of a man's labor should not be taxed. Some say also that it was apple brandy from the apples in his orchard down on the side of the mountain, while others say it was peach brandy from his peach orchard. Be that as it may, the gold coins poured in because that was the only coin that Phillip Gillespie would accept for the fruits of his labor, be those fruits of the Gillespie longrifle or those from the brandy of his still.

There is a secret locked away on some unknown battlefield in an unknown grave that holds the remains of Phillip Gillespie. One can say that secret is hidden in some unknown spot on Forge Mountain. When the Civil War started, North Carolina joined the Confederacy. Phillip Gillespie decided that it was his duty to defend his state from the invasion of the enemy. He cleaned, greased, and shined one of the longrifles made by his own hands, and got his gear ready to start on an early morning. There was one thing more to do before he left. Phillip Gillespie never married and he wanted to have something to come back to at war's end. That night when the moon came up, he slipped out, yoked his oxen to the farm sled, and in that sled he put an earthen crock [a crock that his mother kept in the springhouse], and in that crock he packed his leather poke filled with the gold coins he had hoarded through the years. Now, here again the story has been handed down differently; some say he put on that sled a jug filled with the brandy from the last run of his still. Others in the family say it was a fifty gallon oak keg that he filled with his brandy. Carrying his rifle and a pack and a shovel, by the light of the moon, he led his oxen sled somewhere up the mountainside of Forge Mountain. And in some cave, or maybe hole [he dug, he] buried his gold and his brandy and covered it so no man could ever find it. Before he marched off to war the next morning, he told what he had done, but he refused to tell where he had hidden it. Phillip Gillespie wanted to be sure his gold and brandy would be there when he came back from the war. But Phillip Gillespie never did come back, and here again the accounts in the family differ. Some say that the news trickled back to those in Mills River that Phillip Gillespie was killed in one of the battles around Chattanooga while firing his longrifle at the enemy. Others say that nothing was ever heard of him again—killed, it was presumed, at some unrecorded, unknown skirmish with the enemy. When the war ended and Phillip Gillespie failed to return, people began to remember his hidden crock of gold and the jug or keg of brandy. They began to search the mountainside, and folks have been searching till the present day. But Phillip Gillespie had done a good job of burying his treasure, and Forge Mountain has kept the secret very well.

PLATE 23   Judge Herbert Kimzey in his office.

Herbert Kimzey

Herbert Kimzey is a lifelong resident of Habersham County, Georgia. At one time he was the circuit judge in the mountain judical district, and is now a practicing attorney. Over the years he developed a strong interest in the history of his area, and as a result has gathered a great deal of information on the subject. Even though he was not specifically interested in the iron industry in northeast Georgia, he was able to give us information about the old Habersham Ironworks and Manufacturing Company, which operated in Habersham County from 1837 through the Civil War.

The Stroups were Germans. They came over to this country from Germany, and they played a large part in developing the iron ore in Habersham County and developing the tremendous iron manufacturing plants in northwest Georgia, and later in developing the iron ore in Alabama. Not long after the county opened for settlement during the 1820s, Jacob Stroup and a man I think was his son, Moses, moved into Habersham County looking for iron to develop locally. They were ironmasters; they would locate the iron ore and would manufacture it into merchantable iron. They moved into the area, and just east of where Demorest is now located, they found two deposits of highly usable iron ore. It was a very superior grade of iron ore.

PLATE 24 Plaque identifying the site of the now defunct Habersham Iron Works and Manufacturing Company.

Jacob Stroup was known as the ironmaster. Around 1835, as near as I can determine, Jacob Stroup got John C. Calhoun of South Carolina interested in developing the iron ore located in Habersham County. And John C. Calhoun was the man back of organizing a company to develop the iron ore and to manufacture it into the pots and pans and skillets. There was an ample supply of wood all through the county to make charcoal. At the fall of the Soque River where Habersham Mills is now located, there was ample water power to furnish air necessary to manufacture the iron. They appointed Jarvis Van Buren from New York to come to Habersham County to manage the company. The company was known as the Habersham County Ironworks and Manufacturing Company. It was incorporated in 1837, which was not long after the county was organized for settlement. They mined the ore at a location to the east of Demorest. They carried the ore in big ore carts along a road that is still called the Ore Road, although it hasn't been used for that purpose for one hundred and twenty-five years. There they built a furnace, to develop the iron ore into usable iron, and a manufacturing plant, to manufacture the instruments needed by the early settlers.

The iron plant in Habersham County was in operation by 1839, because in 1839 the legislature exempted all the hands working at the ironworks from compulsory jury duty, because iron was a great necessity to the early settlers, and especially to the state. This ironworks prospered. Jacob Stroup was the ironmaster, and Moses Stroup was later also an ironmaster. The plant continued in operation until the War Between the States. Some of the cannon and some of the armaments that were used by the Southern defenders of their state against the Northern invasion were made in Habersham County. I'm sure some of that iron went into the iron pipes [which were nothing more than what we would call a spear or a long pole with a sharp iron point on it] used by the Confederate troops to guard the Yankee prisoners in some of the Southern prisons because guns were real scarce. As far as I know, they never manufactured guns there, they just manufactured the heavier weapons.

This plant prospered until the War Between the States. Fortunately this area of our nation or state was free from invasion. The Northern troops could not or would not come across the mountains. After the South lost its bid for independence and the Northern troops moved into the area, the Habersham Ironworks and Manufacturing Company was destroyed by the Northern troops or went out of business. We don't know. The iron ore of this area was not used commercially after that date. The same Stroups went across Georgia after the Indians were expelled from [the northwest part of the state], where they developed the big iron plants over there where they had an ample supply of iron ore. Incidentally, the same parties, or their associates, all moved over to Alabama to mine ore farther over and started the big iron developments around Birmingham.

O. H. Monroe

O. H. Monroe was born and raised in the Cartersville, Georgia, area. For sixteen years before he retired, he was the Alatoona Reservoir Manager, and prior to that had worked with the Corps of Engineers doing surveys for the construction and operation of the dam, powerhouse, and reservoir. It was decided to put in a public visitors' facility in the Reservoir management offices where the visitors, as Mr. Monroe put it, "could become acquainted with the history of the Etowah River basin and the uses to which man has put the river and its immediate environs from prehistory to the present time." The focus of the research done to develop the visitors' center was the Cooper blast furnace, which was operated from 1845 up until the Civil War, on what is now Alatoona Reservoir property. The furnace itself is still standing, but there is little evidence of the rest of the ironworks. In the

PLATE 25 Mr. O. H. Monroe in front of the old Cooper furnace in Cartersville, Georgia.

process of gathering information about this particular furnace and its effect on the area for the visitors' facility, Mr. Monroe also collected a lot of information on the iron industry in the South in general. In the following interview with Mr. Monroe, he told us what he has learned about the Cooper blast furnace and the development of the iron industry in the South.

The iron manufacture in the southeast was sort of a late comer. Well, actually, white people didn't come into this area until about 1825, or 1828. The first ones who came were obviously traders, missionaries, gold miners, what have you, but the Indians were still here. As far as the whole country is concerned, this is not a pioneer story, but it is pioneer as far as this part of the country is concerned. People will try to tell you, "Oh, the first iron ever made in the United States was made right here." Well, that's not true, although some articles were. I have a section of the first railroad rail ever made in the U.S. It was rolled by Moses Stroup and used on the W&A Railroad when it was built from Atlanta to Chattanooga in the 1840s.

A lot of the people who settled here came when the ironworks were being established. Their names still persist in this area. The Stroups are all gone from around here, but there were some others who came here from England, Wales, Germany, and various other places on the European continent who were familiar with this type of work. They worked with and for Stroup, and later Cooper, in the operation of this facility and other facilities like it in the area. There were several; the Cooper furnace was not the only one.

It began in about 1837 as I recall. The Stroup family were the pioneers in iron manufacture in North Carolina, South Carolina, and Georgia. They didn't have the first furnaces in Alabama, but they were among the first. The first Stroup of whom anything is known—of whom I know anything—was a man named David Stroup, who was a soldier and a gunmaker in the Continental Army. Reared in Pennsylvania, he had emigrated to this country from the iron manufacturing part of Germany. He came to this country and settled in Pennsylvania, near the town of Alatoona, which is another story all its own. Among his children was a son named Jacob Stroup. He raised and commanded a company of soldiers in the War of 1812. After the War of 1812, he came into North Carolina and built the first iron manufacturing plant there. Later he came into South Carolina and built the first iron manufacturing operation in that state. Then he came into Georgia, in what's now Habersham County, up near the town of Demorest, and had a small operation there—operating on what people who used to mine ore here call "float." It's not a massive deposit of iron. It lies more or less every place in the ground. Some called it blanket ore, some call it float ore. It's usually pretty low grade. This venture was not too successful, but it did operate for a while.

Then he came into this county, which was then Cass County, now Bartow County. He sent his son Alexander here, and Alexander bought land lot 298 in the 21st district in the second section of Bartow County, from Jesse Lamberth on January 25, 1837. On May 11, 1837, Alexander sold this tract to his father, Jacob Stroup. Through that lot of land flows Stamp Creek, a pretty fair sized creek, and he had there a cold blast furnace. The principal product was hollow ware: household goods, pots and pans, skillets, and things of that sort. They made some pig iron too, of course, and other products, but as best I could determine the chief output was hollow ware. The Stroup family lived not too far from that furnace. Now just where, I do not know.

Before he left South Carolina, Jacob Stroup built a furnace and sold it to a man named Nesbit, and left his son Moses there with Nesbit to assist in the operation of this facility. Among other products that they made there were cannon cast for the Nullification Party. There was such a party in this country at that time—they were going to withdraw from the Union and get to heck on out.

Moses Stroup eventually came down into Georgia with his father, and at some point before his father died in 1846 or '47, bought his father out. Moses associated with the Coopers and a Welshman named Bobby Thomas, who had a furnace or a forge up on Alatoona Creek. Moses then went to Jones Valley, Alabama, now Birmingham, and acquired one or two furnaces. He built some other furnaces in Alabama, and was operating

them during the Civil War. But there were others in the iron manufacturing business here besides the Stroups and the Coopers.

Blast furnaces had to be built near a flowing stream. There had to be a
source of power to operate the blowing tubs, blowing engines, or the
bellows. There had to be something to force air into the furnace to get it hot
enough to melt the iron ore and melt the limestone (which was the flux
used) to achieve sufficient heat to melt the iron ore and convert it from the
raw material into pig iron, and the only way that could be done was by sup-
plying a source of air under pressure. The method was somewhat primitive,
but it worked. They used large bellows like a blacksmith uses. These were
much larger, and were operated by water power. Some of them used what
they called blowing tubs or blowing engines, which were nothing more nor
less than four large circular wooden vats, two of which fit inside the other
two. They worked up and down by means of a camming action from power
supplied by an overshot water wheel. One went up and one went down,
and then there was a larger wooden tank or reservoir, holding chamber,
whatever you want to call it, that held this air—collected it, in other words.
It was called a collector. Air went from that into the tuyère in the bottom of
the furnace, and gave a boost to the fire that melted the iron ore and the
slag. It caused the charcoal to ignite with sufficient heat to turn out the
finished product. All of these furnaces, without exception, had to have some
method of forcing air into the ignition chamber to cause the stuff to get hot
enough to melt. It was that simple. Now these were not the original primitive type where they built them up on a hill in merry old England and
depended on the wind to give them enough blast.

Mark Cooper's furnace near Cartersville was about a ten-ton furnace—that was the daily output. They usually kept the furnaces in blast
for a year. When a furnace was completed and put in blast, the first charge
was just dumped in a hole underneath the furnace to form a firm working
surface. It's called a salamander. They'd just dump that first charge, however large it was. They just dug a hole out in the ground there—that was a
one-shot operation, in a new furnace.

There was a piece of equipment in the Cooper furnace that's no longer
there—somebody probably sold it for scrap iron many years ago—called a
tuyère. It was a metal basketlike device, lined with firebrick, and it formed
a container to hold the fire and the slag and the molten iron. All these furnaces that I've ever seen have three adits, or three openings; an adit is a
miner's term for a hole to get into something. They had three adits. They
had one for the air, that was a pipe, a lightweight metal pipe that carried
the air from the blowing engines or the bellows or what ever source of air
pressure that they used, into the combustion chamber. They had another
adit where the iron came out into the casting shed. And then they had the

third that was called the slag adit. The hole where the slag came out was higher than the one where the iron came out. That was the dross; the waste. It was molten. You can believe it was molten. It was white hot and flowed like water. They plugged those holes, those two, with fire clay. And, of course, the air intake was not plugged, it just blew continuously, and gave the blast that caused the stuff to melt. In the case of the Cooper furnace, the air pipe would probably have been sixteen to eighteen inches in diameter, to let all the air they could get there to go into it. That entered the furnace higher up than the opening where the iron was tapped off.

When it reached the proper stage to tap (how they knew it was at the proper stage, I don't know), the first thing that came off was the slag. They used a long rod to push out the clay plug, and they still use something similar to that today in the Birmingham area. The rod they use out there now is an oxygen lance; it burns oxygen and just blows that plug out. By feeding raw oxygen against that hot firebrick, it just disintegrates. It is called a lance. Just a long metal tube. They tapped off the slag, and it flowed. It was just like hot water, and it flowed like hot water on out into the waste area, and after it got cool it was hauled away. Then the iron came off and went into the flasks if they were using flasks, but usually they just made pigs. I bet you don't know why it's called pig iron—the iron goes into a large trough called the sow, and then flows out of the sow into smaller troughs called pigs. The little pigs are nursing the sow. The troughs or trenches are made of molder's sand. When the pigs were cool, they'd hit them with sledge hammers, break them off, and go on and refine the iron into whatever they were going to make out of it. Sometimes it was reheated in what they called a sintering furnace, which they still use—remelted in other words—and cast in whatever form they wanted it. The sintering furnaces were upstream of Alatoona Dam. It was a reheating process. The pig iron, if it was going to be recast into a useful form without being forged, would simply be reheated and melted down again and probably have a little manganese added to it, and cast it into whatever form they were going to use it for. Now up here they had what they call a nailery. They made nails—you're familiar with the old cut nails—and they made a number of different articles for export and domestic use. They worked several hundred people at that enterprise. It was not a small potato; it was a rather sizable operation. That was after Moses Stroup sold out to Cooper, Stroup, and Wiley. Andrew Wiley, from New York, had a financial interest in it, and Mark Cooper had a financial as well as an operational interest in it. He was there in the remaining years as the operational head of the company, which functioned until 1864.

A man named Sherman came through; he was sort of careless with fire, and destroyed practically everything in this area. [The ironworks] never

PLATE 26 Head-on view of the old Cooper furnace. Terri Webb is standing in front of the furnace to give the reader an idea of its size.

PLATE 27 A three-quarter view of the old Cooper furnace.

operated after the Civil War, but during the war they did cast cannon and cannon balls, as well as other articles used by the military.

The iron industry started here about, as I recall, 1837, along in that period, and iron has continued to be mined sporadically in this area ever since that time. It isn't mined here now because it is low grade. Now we get iron ore from Venezuela that's a lot higher in Fe than our local iron. So it's imported and mixed with the native iron in Birmingham—the hematite. And it ups the grade on that. The local iron—there hasn't been a car of iron shipped from here in fifteen years or longer. I can remember when iron ore was mined here a lot, and it was shipped to Birmingham, to Gadsden, Rockwood, Tennessee, and to some places over in northern Alabama. But there hasn't been any shipped in a long while. It's just too low grade, not economically feasible or profitable to use it. Someday it may become so again, I don't know. Right now it is not and hasn't been for a long time.

Furnacemen judged the quality of iron ore by trial and error. A lot of these people had come from Scotland, from the north of England, and from Germany, where iron manufacturing had been going on for generation after generation. They were familiar with the ore, and they were familiar with the process for refining ore into pig iron and subsequently into wrought iron and so on. They found the ore just laying here all over the ground in some areas. A miner can look at a piece of ore and pretty well tell you what the iron content is without running it through a lab. They know—they can tell by the appearance and the feel of it.

Some of the ore occurred in many particle sizes. Hematite and limonite were the two main kinds of ore found here. Well, there was also specular hematite which is a gray iron, and it was used to some extent. The ore occurred in hunks anywhere from pieces as large as that sofa, down to a small particle size, maybe one-quarter inch or one-half inch in diameter. So they got it out in whatever size they could get it out in. It wasn't too material; they didn't run it through any kind of rollers to crush it—they didn't have any rollers to crush it with. They didn't have hammer mills, and they didn't have any of the type of equipment that's used now by miners to break ore down into workable size. It was nugget ore, just like it came out of the ground. Now for those great big hunks they'd have to take a gad and a sledge hammer—a gad is just a piece of steel like a wedge, round-pointed rather than flat like a wedge—and they'd drive gads in to make cracks and break it open where they could handle it; break it up into smaller particles. They obviously couldn't handle a piece as big as a sofa. Much of the iron used here came from what's now known as the Dobbins Mine. It was some distance away—I guess three miles from the furnace. A little old narrow-gauge railroad went over there. The better ore was, of course, mined.

They'd get it out in large boulders and break them up by main strength and awkwardness, and haul it to the furnace.

I know that some of the mining was done by independent operators. They were not working for Cooper or Stroup, and they were paid so much a ton, to get this iron out. The ore was mined at various points around this area in what were called wagon mines. A farmer would have a little outcrop of ore on his place. When the crops were in and he had nothing particularly better to do, why he'd take his boys out there and they'd start digging and hauling ore by wagon, and the ironworks would buy it and stockpile it. There was no large single source of iron.

As for the charcoal, I think there were sub-contractors who furnished it for so much a bushel. They went out and got the wood and burned it and sold it to the furnace operator. In that case, they were small businessmen. There were other instances where the land—large tracts of land—belonged to the ironmaster, or the furnace, and he would employ these people maybe on a contract basis, I don't know. I think most of it was done as piece work by independent operators, but I don't *know* that. I think that it was a joint effort on the part of a lot of people, and it gave employment to many people who normally had as their only source of income the little bit they could have made subsistence farming. That's what it was. There was no commercial farming as we know it today. It's the old saying, "they lived at home and ate at the same place," and they grew what they had to eat in large measure and had very little cash flow. So anything they could do that offered employment with compensation, why they would take up as a side line.

The making of charcoal was an interesting process. I have never seen it done, but I have talked to old timers who worked at what they called the "coaling grounds." It was interesting to know just how they did that. I had an old friend who lived over in Emerson, and he used to tell me how they made the charcoal. It was interesting, and I can see where it would work. He said that they would build what he called a hog pen. See, the wood was cut in four-foot lengths, like cordwood—pine preferably, because it split better. Easier to get out. They could use pine, or they could use oak. Those were the only two kinds of wood that they used. They would build a little hog pen, like a chimney—just get out in a saddle. You know what a saddle is—a spot between two high knobs on a ridge, a little flat area in between. They'd get in the saddle and scrape off a place. I've seen them that were, I'd say, fifty feet in diameter. Pretty good sized. Scrape it down to a mineral soil. In the center of that they would build a little hollow square out of the cordwood, and they'd bring it up to about five feet.

Around that they would stand cordwood on end leaning inward. It was supported by this little riser coming up through the center, the little hollow box, and they would set the cordwood out slightly at the bottom, and it'd go round and round till they reached the outer perimeter of the area that they were going to burn. That's the first course. Then, after they got out as far as they were going with it, they would extend this up another four or five feet. In the middle was the chimney, the hog pen, or flue is what it actually was. All wood. They'd come up with this second four or five feet just round and round like a clock spring, coiled you know; keep stacking it till it reached nearly as far out as the bottom course. Not quite. Then they'd come up another four feet, and stack another course around. When they got done they had a stack there, oh, Jim told me it must have been twenty, twenty-five feet high, and shaped like a stylized beehive.

They would cover this thing, soul and body, with pine straw, to a considerable thickness; six inches to a foot. Then they would put dirt on top of that, woods dirt, and it'd come all the way up, except right over the center there would be the chimney hole left. And they had it so fixed that they could cover that hole with flat rocks. That was the vent where the smoke went out. Then they went around the thing, and scratched little holes all around the perimeter of it, through the dirt and through the straw.

Now there was a shack called the charcoal burner's shack, right close by. He lived there, and his sole job was to take care of that fire. He had to be a person of some knowledge and judgment. After the thing was completed and ready to light, he would ignite it all around at these little holes. I don't know how many there were, but I would say there were probably six or eight, maybe more. Little tiny holes scratched through the dirt and through the straw, where it could draw. Handy there, he had a rock that he could lay there and stop that hole up. If it got to burning with too much enthusiasm, the whole thing would burn up. He left the center hole open until it started drawing. He had a ladder made out of a couple of poles with some cleats nailed on them, or maybe just one long pole with limb stubs and limbs left on it. He'd lean it against the stack and skin up there to get to the top. If it got to burning too freely, he would close that top vent, and go around and close the bottom vents and smother the fire down. This old black man said if you didn't do that that the thing would get away from you, and it'd just all go up like a Roman candle, and you wouldn't have anything but a pile of ashes left. It charred rather than burned. I don't remember if he told me how long it took to burn out; to "fire" one of these things, as he expressed it, but it was a matter of several days, and it had to be watched around the clock. Somebody had to be there and test it. By feel, I suppose, or by the sound it was making, and by know-how. He said that when the charcoal burner had judged that it was done, that he closed all the openings and just watched it till it got cold. But he didn't dare open it up. If you opened it up and let air get to it, you'd have the darndest fire you ever saw—shooo! it was gone. Away it'd go. He'd watch it for several days until it cooled off, and then it was ready to haul. to the furnace. If it was done correctly, and you got a perfect job, even that pine straw perfectly maintained its shape; it was charcoal, just like the wood was. The bark on the wood was still intact, and it looked like a piece of black wood and when picked up, it didn't seem to weigh anything. That's what they got the heat from.

I've seen a number of what they called coaling grounds all through here where I used to squirrel hunt. You can tell one as soon as you walk up on it. You'll see the charcoal on the ground. Charcoal never rots you know, it's just there, period, from now on. You'll find little particles of it, and sometimes fair-sized chunks. You look around closely, if there's a spring somewhere nearby, you'll see four big rocks and perhaps an old rotted sill laying there. Well, that was where the house was where the charcoal burner lived. Course there hasn't been any charcoal burned here in a long time—I'm seventy years of age and I have never seen it done, but I have talked to people who did it for a living.

The limestone was present here in abundance; you could find it most anyplace. People hauled it in by wagons. It was cheap, and labor was cheap. I would think [quarrying lime] was done on the same basis that the ore was mined. If a fellow owned a piece of land and had some limestone on it, and after the crops were laid by in the fall and he needed a little money, he'd just go out and get out a bunch of limestone and haul it down to the nearest furnace and sell it. I would think that's the way it was done, but I don't *know* that. Judging by scraps of it left lying around at the charging point, I'd say it was broken down a little smaller than man-size. Man-size rock is not rock as big as a man, but rock a man can handle in his two hands, pick up and carry, you know, fifty, seventy-five pounds at most. You could wander around there and find it on the ground—it was left there during the operation, and it's in chunks anywhere from two to four inches in diameter, irregularly shaped. They just broke it up with sledge hammers to where they could handle it with some facility.

One other interesting sidelight is that the first spiegeleisen ever manufactured in the United States was made here. That's a refined product of manganiferous iron ore, iron very high in manganese. If you just put raw manganese ore in a furnace, the blast is often sufficient to blow it away and you get no beneficial results from it. It takes manganese to make steel out of pig iron, so they took this highly manganiferous iron ore and ran it through a sintering furnace, and made it into little hard nodules of a mixture of iron and manganese. It was shipped from this region in wooden kegs to areas where the pig iron was refined into a more salable product. The first spiegeleisen made in this country was made up here on Stamp Creek. It was a rather primitive method, but it worked. Much of the iron around here had a lot of manganese in it.

Ray Farabee

Ray Farabee has been associated with the metallurgical industry for most of his seventy-eight years. At the age of sixteen he began working in steel mills, and at eighteen he entered the University of Alabama, later graduating as a chemical metallurgical engineer. He then worked in the field until he retired at the age of seventy. As he put it, "In all I've had twenty-five or thirty years' industrial experience, and twenty-five or thirty years' teaching experience."

Professor Farabee was chosen as the furnace master at the refiring of the old Tannehill furnace, a cold-blast furnace in Roupes Valley, Alabama, which had been out of blast for a least one hundred and ten years. The furnace was built around 1855 by Moses Stroup, on property he bought from Ninian Tannehill, who, up until that time, operated a forge there. In 1862 William Sanders bought Stroup's ironworks and formed the Roupes Valley Ironworks, which produced pig iron for the Confederacy during the Civil War. The ironworks was destroyed on March 31, 1865, by Union soldiers. Much of "Old Tannehill" (the furnace itself) remained, but never produced any more iron until 1976. The rest of the ironworks was destroyed.

David Thomas bought the property in 1868. The Republic Steel Company, which was formed by the Thomas family, deeded the property to the University of Alabama in 1952, for preservation and restoration. In 1969 the Tannehill Furnace and Foundry Commission was founded, and the property was turned into a state park. Almost immediately, clearing of the overgrown areas of the park got underway, and then the reconstruction of the ironworks itself was begun.

The Commission decided to refire "Old Tannehill" for the Bicentennial. At this point Professor Farabee was chosen as furnace master. On September 19, 1976 with the help of some fifty skilled volunteers, the furnace produced about two and one half tons of pig iron. There were between ten and fifteen thousand spectators there to watch the event.

Professor Farabee gave us this interview at Tannehill State Park in front of about twenty-five people at a small oral history workshop.

PLATE 28 Professor Ray Farabee, very pleased with the way things were working out during the refiring of the old Tannehill furnace.

You might say, "Why an iron blast furnace? What is the function of an iron blast furnace? Why did they ever have one?" It's to make pig iron, molten iron that can could be cast into shapes that our forefathers needed to cultivate the garden and fields with, like plows, and also pots, pans, syrup mills, things like that that they needed to live.

[The Tannehill operation] started back in the 1820s, and it was very small, naturally, to begin with. There were some small forges in this area prior to the time of the blast furnace. The property changed hands from the Tannehills to the Stroups, and the history I'll leave to someone else. Ethel Armes' *Story of Coal and Iron in Alabama* is a very good reference on it. They called it an iron plantation in those days. A plantation is generally where you have farms. They had people for labor, and they had to have grist mills and saw mills for cutting lumber—they had to have certain complementary industries to take care of the people and keep them going. So this was an iron plantation. Quite a village.

To come back to the [point], why did they locate here? Naturally, the raw materials were here. Water power—they didn't have electricity in those days, no kerosene oil either, they used pine knots and candles for lights. They didn't have any gasoline and very, very few steam engines at all, and they depended on water power. So here a beautiful creek ran swiftly down the line, and they built a dam, and then put a water wheel in to operate a bellows, just to blow, not continuously, but as you operate it mechanically. All of you have seen an old bellows—they were tied in so there would be a source of air for burning the fuel, which in those days was charcoal. They didn't have any coke—very little coal had been discovered in Alabama —[but they had] several thousand acres of forest, and they could burn that hardwood and make charcoal. Iron ore, which is iron oxide, in this case was located very close by up and down the creek, and they could haul it in [to the furnace] with ox carts. With the source of air from the old bellows and the water wheel, and the iron ore close by and the charcoal close by, it was natural to build a furnace here—it wasn't an accident, it was planned definitely, intentionally, and correctly. They also had plenty of limestone nearby.

They built the blast furnace. Another thing they had [close by] was a mountain of rock, sandstone, to build the outside of the furnace [with]. There are two parts to the furnace, an inside and an outside, we'll say, and the outside is a big framework of rock [made of rocks] maybe a foot and a half or two feet long and rectangular in shape, and they were stacked on top of each other to serve as the outside of this furnace—had to be refractory because it was going to be subjected to a lot of heat. [To shape the rock] they would drill holes with a star drill and a sledge hammer where they wanted to cut the rock. Then they'd drive wooden pegs down in the holes and pour water on those wooden pegs and they'd expand and burst the rocks in line with those holes. But they made a beautiful job of it. And the elevation of the rock [in its natural state] was important. There's a high hill which they slid the rock down to the furnace site, which was down by the creek where the air was. They took advantage of the topography —they built the furnace up so high, and then charged it by hand from the top by rolling wheelbarrow loads [of charcoal, limestone, and iron ore on a trestle to the charging point and dumping them in the top of the furnace]. It all tied in naturally to put a furnace in here.

Now, getting into the construction [of the furnace]—there's a hearth, or a crucible where the molten iron is collected, maybe a foot to two feet deep, three or four feet in diameter, and there's a flare-out portion just above the top of the hearth they call a bosh, about eight feet in diameter with a pull-in at the top. When the hearth is about four feet in diameter, the bosh is about eight feet high in the sloping out part, then converges back in toward the top for a total height of about thirty-one feet. So that was the outside furnace construction, built the hard way they tell me.

They had to set up a routine [to charge the furnace] with relative proportions of lime rock for flux, and ore, and charcoal. They had to put those three materials in there in definite proportions, and the furnace had to have air blown into it at the bottom at a certain definite rate. There had to be a systematic charging and handling of the furnace. It took an ironmaster, as he was called. He had to have experience, and he was skilled and highly respected. The raw materials were kept, say, thirty-five feet above the foundation of the furnaces down at the creek. The top was open, and had a trestle running across [from the area where the raw materials were kept to the top of the furnace]. It was made of heavy planks, and had a track on it. Men would roll wheelbarrows of raw materials over this trestle and dump them into the top of the furnace. As the iron ore came down, it was gradually reduced from iron oxide to metallic iron by the time it got down to the hearth. In the meantime, a lot of gasses were going up to the top. So, a man had to be kind of careful, or he might fall in that place himself. That didn't happen very often though!

[The iron notch] was plugged with clay. They would take a hunk of plastic clay, and make a slurry with part of it, smear that [slurry] in the hole, and then jam in the hunk of clay. They dried it very thoroughly. If they didn't, it'd crack open just like mud cracks in the sand. They had to treat it very carefully, make it air tight, so it would stay joined and not crack. A blast furnace this height would take four to six hours to produce molten iron. It would accumulate one foot of iron in the bottom, and it would weigh about two tons. They'd have about two tons of iron, and they'd open up the iron notch and let it run out. After it all ran out, they'd close it up with another plug of clay. Then they'd wait another six hours until another two tons had accumulated, and they'd open it up again. It was an intermittent operation as far as tapping was concerned, but a continuous operation as far as charging and blowing was concerned. [They'd] keep on charging, twenty-four hours a day, seven days a week. For a year if the lining would last, for three years if the lining would last—just as long as they could do it.

Pig iron [the type of iron that comes out of a blast furnace] has certain properties. It's not ductile—you can't draw it into a wire or shape it with a hammer, but you can modify it by burning out most of the carbon and most of the silicon, and practically all the phosphorus and do what you can with the sulfur, because it's a very detrimental impurity. The way they used to do this was to take the molten iron from the blast furnace and put it into a kind of an open mold, a puddling furnace, and surround it with iron ore, an oxidizing agent that would combine with the carbon and silicon and phosphorus and oxidize them out. Getting those bad-acting impurities out brought the [pig iron] down to a more pure iron they called wrought iron. The master (we'd call him a blacksmith, but he wasn't at that time) would roll that ball of semimolten iron into the slaglike stuff. The slag around it would oxidize those impurities, and he would come up with a ball of iron that he could take out and hammer—shape. They call that a forge [where the pig iron is made into the more ductile form of wrought iron]. That is a step beyond a blast furnace—they're changing cast iron into something that is forgeable, something they could hammer into shape and make into different things that have some elongation, some ductility, some toughness, versus the old pig iron. They didn't need toughness in a cast-iron pot, but they did need toughness in a hammer or an axe head. That's where the blacksmith came in. He was the skilled man for shaping these shingles. [A shingle is a piece of iron that has been treated in the puddling furnace and hammered into a bar, which is ready to be forged into a usable object.]

[The production of iron from iron ore] is not a melting operation, it is a reducing operation. You've got to burn the charcoal to carbon monoxide, not carbon dioxide. The carbon monoxide goes up through the charge and reduces the iron oxide to a metallic oxide—Fe_3O_4 to FeO to Fe to pig iron. In the meantime, the molten iron is coming down and some of the silica, the gang, is being reduced at those hot temperatures. You let it accumulate—this Number One furnace produced, I understand, six tons of pig iron every twenty-four hours. Compare that with a modern furnace today that makes six thousand tons of pig iron in twenty-four hours. Now, this was an old top-charging, cold-air operation with a crude balance. Today the modern furnaces are mechanized and computerized, and the operation can be controlled much better. You won't find pure iron ore (iron oxide)—there's always some sand connected with it or some clay stuff [mixed with it]. The function of limestone is to flux, lower the melting point of the gang material so it will come out as slag, separate from the molten iron which is on the bottom. The gang material in the iron ore—it's the undesirable portion. The desirable portion is the iron oxide which will furnish iron when reduced from iron oxide to metallic iron. It's *not* a *melting* operation, it's a *reducing* operation. Most of the gang material is siliceous, either clay or silica sand. Oyster shells are calcium carbonate, and they were used very early in the place of limestone. They had plenty of limestone and lime rock right around here close—pure almost, too.

When we started talking about getting some help, some folks experienced in the metallurgical industry here in this area were asked to volunteer to fire the old furnace, and many of them volunteered quickly. We went to work to repair the furnace, and it was quite a job, I can assure you, in the time allotted. During World War II, a lot of vandals came in and wanted to steal certain parts of [the furnace] and destroy things. Some folks put dynamite on the corner of this old furnace Number One ("Old Tannehill") and knocked the whole corner off, and that all had to be repaired. So when it came to reconstructing this furnace to get it going for refiring, there was an awful lot of work to be done. There had to be a trestle built from [the high elevation above the furnace] to the top of the furnace for charging it from the top. Then we had to go in from the foundation and rebuild all this part that had been destroyed. We had special engineers do that particular type of work ahead of time, knowing it had to be done.

In the hearth and bosh we put fine new refractory brick made by machinery—[put it in] brick to brick, they call it. We put steel bands around the lower portion to be sure we didn't have break-outs from molten iron and slag accumulating in there, because there's quite a heavy weight up above [when the furnace is fully charged and operating]. In the old bosh territory and in the upper part of the stack there was the old [refractory brick] lining—that was left because we decided it would be good enough. Somebody told me [the old brick lining] was imported from England. Our problem was to merge, join the modern refractory brick with the old existing material in the bosh area, and it was quite a job to do, and do in time, and dry thoroughly so we'd have no problems.

Another thing we had to do was to put a bustle pipe around the furnace to furnish air to the four different points, openings called tuyères. We had to get a welded steel pipe and a blower. The blower we used cost $15,000, but it didn't cost anything to Tannehill because a friendly foundry contributed it. In order to replace the old bellows with the electric blower, we had to have three-phase electricity at the site. Thanks to our power company, who co-operated and got us enough of the right kind of electricity, we felt at ease that we'd have plenty of air to carry out this operation. People began to donate things like that, and we got things together. It was hard, continuous work day and night to get it together, but we got molten iron from the ore. We produced about two and one-half tons of pig iron on refiring the old Number One furnace.

We have accidents with modern blast furnaces today. Maybe spend almost a million dollars for a lining—of course, the shell in this case is sheet steel, instead of the big old rock [structure] they had in those days. The lining might not last for six months. As a matter of fact, we've had that experience in just recent months about a big furnace losing the lining. It didn't last three or four months, played out, cracked, and sloughed away. Cost a million dollars or so. To get a good smooth performance out of a blast furnace the lining has to be taken care of.

In old furnaces, the reducing agent used was charcoal. In refiring the furnace, we used coke because we could not get charcoal. We had to take into consideration the impurities that are in coke today, like sulfur and ash content versus that in charcoal. But the charges in a modern furnace wouldn't vary much from the charges in a small old blast furnace, because you've got three things to do. One, you've got to reduce the iron oxide to metallic iron. Two, you've got to flux your gang material, which is silica clay—and it takes so much lime to flux so many pounds of silica clay. Third, you have to figure how much air you have to blow at what rate to burn a certain amount of charcoal to get carbon monoxide, which is the reducing agent for the gas going up through the ore as it comes down inside the furnace. So it's the same principle as it was years and years ago. Now we've got more sophisticated and accurate facilities like chemical analysis. We get chemical analyses of raw material very quickly today. We can get a chemical analysis of the iron in a matter of seconds after taking a sample. We have those wonderful modern facilities now.

BLACKSMITHING

Herbert Kimzey, previously introduced in the ironmaking section, here talks about the settling of north Georgia by the white man, and discusses the early settlers' iron needs.

"It is said that it took three generations to make an area civilized. The first generation brought in their goods on carts or wagons and built their very crude homes. Course, there would be no stores, no way to get anything. There would be no mills of any type. The second generation would build the grist mills and the other mills necessary to supply the needs of the community, and cut roads or pathways through the mountains. The third generation, of course, would find it well-settled and suitable for life; they would find the churches organized, and the schools organized. [They would also find] certain stores, blacksmith shops, grist mills, maybe a shingle mill, and other mills of that type.

"Iron was essential for the well-being of the early settlers. Most of them would bring with them a supply of iron, ten or twenty-five pounds, which had been manufactured from iron ore into iron that could be used for various purposes. Early estate inventories often list ten pounds of iron or five pounds of iron. They listed that as a separate asset of the early settlers' estates. The early settlers would make a forge like the blacksmith used, and with this iron and forge they would handmake the portions of their homes that were necessary to be built of iron. This would include perhaps the iron hook that hung in every chimney, on which the early settlers hung their pots to cook their food. They made their ovens out of iron in which to bake their bread and other food, and they made their iron skillets to fry their food.

PLATE 29   George Bulgin's blacksmith shop in downtown Franklin, North Carolina around 1909; from left to right, George Bulgin, Mr. Downs, Randolph Bulgin (George's brother), Jeff Betts, and Mr. Cabe. They are shoeing two of the horse's feet —the left fore and the right hind—at the same time. (Photograph courtesy of John Bulgin, George's son.)

They also used iron to make hinges, rims for wagon wheels, and to make necessary repairs around the home. These things were essential for every early settler. Also, in building a cabin or a church, iron was needed in a limited amount. One early settler, in describing the building of one of our rural churches, described how the settlers came with their crosscut saws to saw the planks from the timber for the floor, and the shutters on the windows and the doors of the church. Other settlers, of course, were busy cutting down the pine trees and notching them for the walls. At the same time there would be present one or more men with their forges, who would take the iron they had, heat it to a high heat with charcoal that was blown upon with bellows, and manufacture the few homemade nails that were used in the church.

"Most of the iron brought into Rabun County, I would imagine, would come through the Carolinas from the iron mines up in there, because you will notice that most of Rabun County was settled by North Carolinians or South Carolinians. Their main travel route actually went through Clayton over through Oconee County, South Carolina, and on into North Carolina. Most of their trade was east and west, that is, from the Carolinas into Rabun County. I imagine if a blacksmith in Habersham County needed, say, two hundred pounds of iron, he'd probably get one of these big old wagons and go down to Athens, Georgia, in all likelihood. Athens was a pretty good little old settlement, and some man there would probably wholesale it.

"But they would not bring in any huge hunks of iron; they would bring in the iron in sheets, probably two- or three-feet square, that could be cut into nails and things of that type. I can remember my father telling that when he was a boy, they would leave here in big wagons and go from here to Athens, down through Banks County. They would spend one night down in Banks County. The next night they would be in Athens and they would do their trading there. Then they would come home, and it would take them two days to come from Athens back to around Cornelia or Clarksville. One man wouldn't go alone; several would go together. At least four or five would go for the companionship, and the boys would go just for the fun of it. My dad said one thing he remembered was the fact that you could hear the dogs barking way ahead of you, and it would carry. With the wagon creaking and groaning every dog in a mile range would start barking behind and barking in front. Dad thought it was quite an experience for a ten-year-old boy to go on a fine trip to Athens and back. And they would buy a lot of supplies there that they couldn't get locally, like cloth, because there weren't many stores around here in the early days."

At that time the blacksmith played a vital role in his community and was generally accorded his due respect. There is hardly a facet of life his work did not touch upon; indeed without his skills, the prevailing life-style would have been extremely primitive. Most of the items a blacksmith made and repaired were either tools or other work-related items, such as harness fittings and ox yokes. In a culture where everyone, even children, had to work just to get by, it's not hard to understand how important the black-smith was. A typical farming family had to spend a tremendous amount of time at work, even with the basic tools available at the time. It would have been impossible for people to accomplish a given amount of work without the customary tools in the same amount of time it would take them with the tools.

The shop itself was often a place where people socialized on rainy days, and/or while they waited for something to be made or repaired. A trip to the blacksmith shop was a break from plowing or logging or hoeing corn, and people most likely looked forward to it.

Numerous things that everyone needed could be made or repaired only by the blacksmith, whereas today, many of these same things are easily available elsewhere, are replaced instead of repaired, or are no longer used. Most of the work done by "old time" blacksmiths was geared to the needs

PLATE 30 George Bulgin's first black-smith shop in Rabun Gap, Georgia, around 1906, set up for working at the now defunct Tallulah Falls Railroad; right, George Bulgin, left, an unidentified helper. (Photograph courtesy of John Bulgin.)

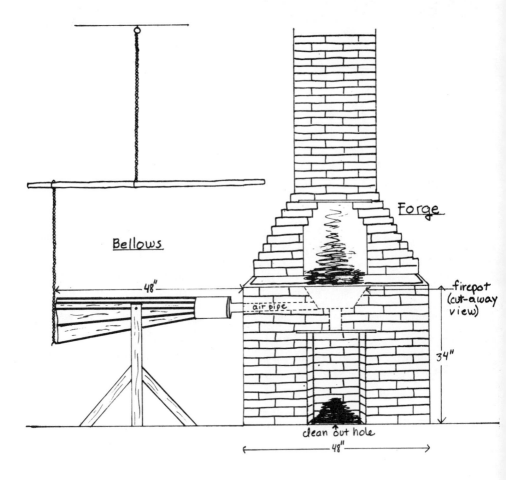

Bellows

48"

air pipe

Forge

firepot
(cut-away
view)

34"

clean out hole

48"

BELLOWS

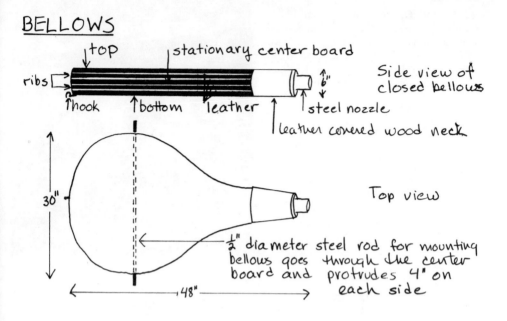

PLATE 32   This type of bellows delivers spurts of air, rather than one continuous stream, into the forge to fan the fire. It can be mounted at forge level and pump air directly into the forge, or it may be mounted close to the ceiling or in another more out-of-the-way place, in which case the air would be piped from it to the forge. The top, bottom, centerboard, ribs, neck, and valves are made of wood. All the hinges are made of leather, as are the sides, which allows the bellows to open and close and maintain a tight air seal at the same time. The valves are simple wooden flaps over the valve holes and are designed so they allow air to pass through them in one direction only. The bellows are mounted to a wooden frame by the steel rod that goes through the centerboard, and at the nozzle where it enters the forge or is fitted to a pipe that goes to the forge.

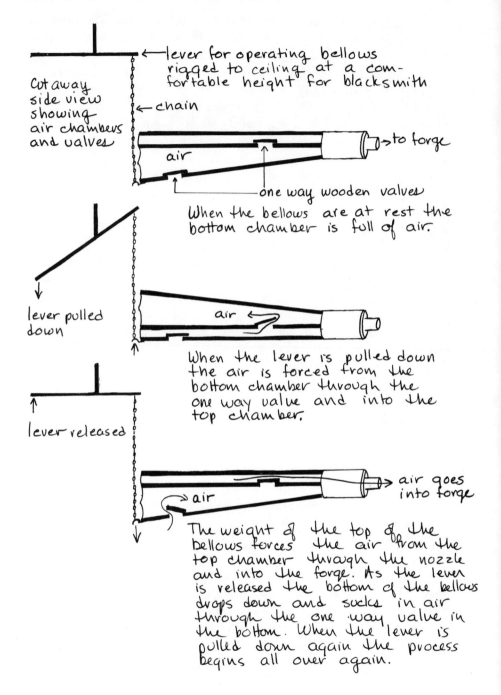

Cut away side view showing air chambers and valves

lever for operating bellows rigged to ceiling at a comfortable height for blacksmith

← chain

air

→ to forge

one way wooden valves

When the bellows are at rest the bottom chamber is full of air.

lever pulled down

air ←

When the lever is pulled down the air is forced from the bottom chamber through the one way valve and into the top chamber.

lever released

air

→ air goes into forge

The weight of the top of the bellows forces the air from the top chamber through the nozzle and into the forge. As the lever is released the bottom of the bellows drops down and sucks in air through the one way valve in the bottom. When the lever is pulled down again the process begins all over again.

of the individual in his/her endeavor to make a living. As society has changed, however, so has the work of the blacksmith. Much of the black-smith work done today is for industrial use, such as repairing heavy machin-ery or making a bed for a logging truck, or making personal luxuries, such as an ornate driveway gate, a candle holder, or a decorative mobile. Now, even making horseshoes and shoeing horses fits into the category of personal luxury. As a matter of fact, *many* of the items once made purely for neces-sity are now sought after as luxury items, such as handsome andirons, hinges, and cowbells.

A blacksmith forges objects of metal, typically wrought iron or steel. To forge metal is to shape it, by heating then hammering, or pressing it into the desired form. The metal is made stronger by forging, as it changes the grainy texture of it to a more fiberlike texture. The word "forge" also applies to the open furnace a blacksmith uses to heat metal—in a general sense, to his whole shop, and to a small manufacturing plant where iron is made into usable products.

There are certain basic requirements for a functional blacksmith shop. It must have adequate light, and enough space for working in, for tools, raw materials, and various completed items. It is desirable for it to have a fireproof floor, such as dirt or concrete. It must have worktables; all the shops we visited had large sturdy worktables, which in some cases ran all the way around the shop. Most important is the forge itself, a small open fur-nace that should be situated so that it does not create a fire hazard, and should be vented through the roof or wall. The forge also needs a bellows or blower system to fan the fire. One of the shops we visited had a forge made of wood and insulated with dirt, but the other four forges were made of non-flammable materials such as metal, brick, or concrete block. It is also necessary to have a coal bin or space to pile the coal, and a water tub (slack tub) for cooling and tempering items. The shop must also be equipped with an anvil and the proper variety of tools, which will be outlined in the fol-lowing paragraphs.

A well-equipped blacksmith shop can have a staggering variety of tools. Some are used for any number of different things, while others have very specific uses. While we cannot discuss all the tools, the following are the most common and basic to the time period we are talking about. On the subject of tools, Lee Tippett said, "My father took care of his tools. He *never* threw them down in the dirt, or on a rock. They's scarce. My daddy'd give me a going over if I throwed a tool down in the dirt or rock. And I'm glad he did. You have to respect tools. Good sharp tools are the name of the game."

Tools need to be easily accessible to the blacksmith while he is work-

PLATE 33 Handmade steel forge.

ing—especially with hot metal—and they need to be kept in good repair. The working surfaces of tools are tempered so that they will be harder than the metal being formed, but not too hard or they will crack, chip, or shatter when used. John Bulgin said, "Hammers are tempered. If you get'em too hard—some people do—a piece can fly off. I've got a scar on my leg; I was strikin' with a sledge hammer, workin' for the Forest Service. The tool we was strikin' on, the man had tempered it too hard, and a sliver flew off and went right in my leg. I thought somebody'd hit my funny bone. I went on strikin', and I felt somethin' warm runnin' down my leg and blood was just pourin' into my shoe. Had to bring me to the hospital and get it out."

PLATE 34 Side view of the tuyère iron (fire pot) for the old forge.

PLATE 35 Portable steel forge with hand-cranked blower.

PLATE 36 A modern, concrete block-and-steel forge with an electric blower and a cast-iron tuyère iron.

PLATE 37 A slack tub,

PLATE 38 An anvil—note the square hardie hole and the round pritchel hole.

Some tools are tempered to a higher degree than others, depending on the use. For example, cleavers, which are cutting tools, are made for either hot or cold work. A hot cleaver is not as highly tempered as a cold cleaver because it is used with heated metal, which is more plastic than cold metal. When working with hot metal, the tools coming in direct contact with it must not be allowed to get too hot, or the temper will go out of them. Years ago blacksmiths made many of their tools, which they were well equipped to do. Tools were probably difficult to obtain any other way, and very often they needed a special tool for a certain job which had to be tailor made for that job.

Of all the tools a blacksmith needs, the anvil is about the most important. The heated stock is placed on the anvil to be formed, whether it is to be drawn out, punched, bent, or cut. Some work can even be done cold if the metal is soft enough. The anvil is usually bolted onto a large, stable wooden block, which absorbs much of the concussion from the hammering. The wooden block may be placed directly on the floor, or it may be set into the ground a couple of feet deep. An anvil must never be hammered or punched directly. Its flat working surface is tempered, as are the tools, so they are harder than the object being formed, and a hard blow on the anvil with a tool could damage the tool or the anvil, or both. Anvils have a flat, tempered surface to work on, and a rounded horn (not tempered) that is used to curve objects. An anvil has a square hole in the flat surface, called a hardie hole, into which is fitted the shank of a hardie. A hardie is a tempered, wedge-shaped form that is forged somewhat like a chisel, and is used in conjunction with a hammer, or a cleaver and a hammer, to cut hot metal. The hardie hole can also be used to receive the bottom part of a swage, an iron block with grooves and holes of different sizes that is used to form hot metal into a specific shape. The hand-held top of the swage is used

PLATE 39   Hardie.

PLATE 40   Swage block.

PLATE 41   Swage block.

PLATE 42   Cross-peen hammers, above, and ball-peen hammers, below.

PLATE 43   Sledge hammers.

PLATE 44   Chisels.

PLATE 45   Cleavers.

PLATE 46   Tongs.

PLATE 47   Punches.

to complete the form. The anvil also has a small round hole, called a pritchel hole, that is used to receive the end of a punch when a hole is being punched through a piece of metal—so the punch won't hit the anvil.

Hammers are probably used more than any other hand tool. Blacksmiths use several different weights and sizes, depending on the task at hand. The heavier the work, the heavier the hammer needed for the job. Used directly on the metal being formed for welding, drawing out, bending, etc., they are also used with other hand tools, such as chisels and punches.

Chisels have a tempered wedgelike tip and are used for cutting metal. They come in a variety of sizes and are made for hot or for cold work.

Cleavers, also cutting tools, are very similar to chisels, have a tempered wedgelike tip, and are made for either hot or for cold work.

Tongs are used to hold items that are being heated or being worked on when they are hot. They can be made in many different sizes and shapes, and often a pair has to be made specifically to work on one particular thing.

Punches are used for punching or enlarging holes and for marking measurements. The tips are tempered and may be flat or pointed, round or square.

PLATE 48 Files—note the rasp at the left.

PLATE 49 Hand drill.

PLATE 50 Soldering iron.

Files used on metal are highly tempered and are used to smooth off rough spots or to reduce surfaces a small amount.

A hand drill is used for drilling holes. It can be fitted with steel drills or wood bits of different sizes. This particular breast drill is made so that the blacksmith can lean on it and put his weight into the drilling.

A soldering iron is used to melt solder, which is used to unite two pieces of metal without heating the metal to weld it. The old type of soldering irons are headed directly in the forge.

A hand-held hacksaw has a highly tempered blade and is used for sawing small pieces of metal. Years ago, blacksmiths made their own frames and bought the blades.

A traveler, or tire wheel, is used to measure the metal rim for a wagon wheel. The circumference of the wooden wheel (minus the rim) is measured by counting the revolutions of the traveler as it is run along the circumference, and that measurement is marked on the unformed rim. When the rim is completed its inside circumference must equal the circumference of the wooden wheel so the rim will fit very tightly on the wheel.

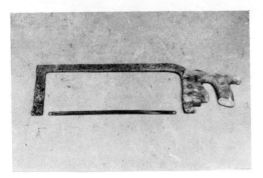

PLATE 51   Handmade hand-held hacksaw.

PLATE 52   Traveler, or tire wheel.

A grindstone is used for sharpening tools. The foot-powered ones were commonplace before the electric ones were developed.

Vises are used to secure objects while they are being worked on. The original ones were carved out of wood.

Mandrils are large cone-shaped forms used to form or stretch circular objects.

Most blacksmiths were skilled woodworkers as well as metalworkers. They were usually the wagon makers of their community, making all the wooden as well as metal parts for the wagons. They were also called upon to replace handles for tools, wooden parts for plows and other farm machinery, and to make ox yokes. They therefore usually had a sizable collection of woodworking as well as metalworking tools, but we shall concentrate only on the metalworking aspects of the trade.

PLATE 53   Grindstone. (Photograph courtesy of John Bulgin.)

The rural blacksmith primarily used wrought iron in his work. Some steel was available, but not in very large quantities. As mentioned in the iron-making section, wrought iron and steel are tough and malleable enough to be worked in the forge, but pig iron is not. Much of what they used to use came from the scrap pile, or was salvaged wherever they could find it. As Will Zoellner put it, "I'd use iron or steel, either one. It didn't make no difference, I just had to know what I had."

The fire is critical to the blacksmith's work because the iron or steel must be heated and softened in order to be forged or welded. Forge work requires a clean, hot fire, and in order to build a good one, the proper type of fuel must be used. It is important that the desired temperature for work-

PLATE 54   Mounted post vise.

PLATE 55   Mandrils.

ing the iron or steel be reached and maintained, both for the quality of the work and the energy expenditure of the blacksmith. For example, the forging temperature for wrought iron is between 2,100° F. and 2,400° F. If wrought iron is forged at a lower temperature, injury can be caused to the internal structure, which will weaken it. Also, it takes more energy to forge iron that is not sufficiently heated. If it's heated to too high a temperature, it can spark and splatter when hammered, possibly burning the blacksmith and/or other persons nearby, and each blow of the hammer can cause more than the desired change in the metal because it is too soft. Lee Tippet gave us his views on building a fire in the forge, "You can build any type of fire you want. Something the size of a froe blade takes a hot fire. If you was workin' on little bitty stuff, you'd have a small fire [not] a great big blaze. You judge by the color of the metal when to take it out. If it gets runny hot when you hit it, it'll come all to pieces. But if it's not hot enough, you can't do what you need with it."

Charcoal, the same fuel used in cold-blast furnaces, was used as a fuel by blacksmiths almost exclusively in north Georgia during the last century. Coal was not abundant enough to be profitably mined, and travel and shipping routes were not well enough developed to haul it in with any regularity. Some areas of Southern Appalachia had plenty of coal, however, and it is assumed that blacksmiths used it wherever it was available. As John Bulgin put it, "My dad used to get some blacksmith coal, but he used charcoal a lot of the time because coal was hard to get. Charcoal'll get as hot as coke, but it takes more of it. People would burn charcoal for my dad, and he'd buy it by the bushel."

And according to Lee Tippett, "You can make charcoal; my daddy used to make his. [He'd] dig a hole in the ground, set wood up in it—chestnut, chestnut oak, pine—cover it up with cane pumice and dirt, and set it on fire in there. It'd burn about two or three weeks, and leave these big chunks of charred wood, between a cinder and a piece of dry wood, and man it'll build a fire. They call it charcoal, but coke is what it is, wood coke. It's better than soft coal, but I don't like it as good as hard coal. Some people would rather have it." The great advantage of using charcoal was that it could be made anywhere there was an abundance of forest land.

Nevertheless, coal and/or coke was used by blacksmiths when they could get it. Anthracite, or hard coal, is an excellent fuel because it burns hot and practically smokeless, but it was not (and is not) mined in this area and had to be shipped in from quite a distance, probably as far as Pennsylvania. Bituminous coal, or soft coal, which must be coked before it is used, is much more plentiful than anthracite. It didn't have to be shipped in from as far away, and was used by blacksmiths when they could get it. It has many more impurities than hard coal, but they can be removed in the coking process. Coke is produced by the incomplete combustion of soft coal under carefully controlled conditions, in which most of the impurities are burned out and escape in the form of gasses. The result is a relatively pure, high-carbon fuel. Once soft coal is coked, it burns clean, giving off an intense heat.

According to John Bulgin, "They used to get blacksmith coal, hard coal freer from sulphur [and other impurities than soft coal], and it has to be good and clean to weld in. Whichever it is, you generally coke it, burn all the gasses out first. [Now] we just buy regular coke. Soft coal is not as good as hard coal in its regular state, but after you get it coked, get all the sulphur burned out of it, it's as good. What we get is coke from soft coal. See, coke is what they use in the furnaces to smelt iron with. To make coke they build up a fire in a pile of soft coal and burn all the gasses out of it. You can make coke in the forge, but you've got lots of smoke and heat while the gas is burning off. You don't get as much smoke about hard coal because there aren't as many impurities in hard, as soft coal. Blacksmiths do use soft coal, but as soon as it starts to burn, it cokes itself."

There are several basic procedures that all blacksmiths use to form wrought iron or steel in order to make it into a useful or decorative object.

Metal must first be cut in order to remove any unnecessary portion of it. For example, a blacksmith making a horseshoe would have to cut the stock off at the correct length for the size horseshoe he was making. Some soft, thin steel can be cut cold, but most cutting must be done hot. Cutting metal can be accomplished with a hacksaw (which is done cold), a chisel, a cleaver, or a hardie.

Very often a particular piece of metal must have a hole put in it. This can be done cold in some cases, but is usually done hot. In order to rivet two pieces of metal together, a hole must first be pierced in each piece. This can be done cold with a drill, which removes rather than displaces some of the metal, or it can be done with a punch—hot or cold, depending on the steel—in which case the metal is displaced rather than removed.

Metal is drawn out to make it longer and thinner without removing any of it. This procedure is carried out by placing the heated stock on the anvil and hammering it. For example, a blacksmith making a wedge for splitting wood would start with a rectangular piece of steel or wrought iron (shorter than the finished product would be), and draw it out longer and progressively thinner by hammering until it reached the desired length and acquired the right taper. In this process, the metal is displaced, not removed as it would be if a person carved a wedge out of wood.

Up-setting is the opposite of drawing. It makes the metal shorter and thicker. It is usually done hot, but can be done cold in some cases. For example, a rivet must be up-set in order for it to secure the pieces it is to hold together. In this procedure the unformed rivet (a short metal rod) is placed through the holes in the pieces of metal it is to hold together and placed on the anvil with the rod perpendicular to it. The top of the rod is then hammered, which causes its center to thicken, and the top and bottom to take on the shape of a nail head, thus holding the pieces of metal together.

Bending is a procedure that puts a curve or angle in a piece of metal. Unless the metal is soft and the bend slight, this must be done hot. Metal can be bent in several different ways, but only one will be mentioned here. For example, a blacksmith making a froe would have to bend the end of the blade into an eye to hold the handle. This is accomplished by heating the end to be formed, placing it on the end of the anvil horn, and hammering it around the horn until it makes a complete circle.

Today there are several different welding processes in use, such as oxyacetylene welding, electric metallic arc welding, electric carbon arc welding, and forge welding. Forge welding was the original technique and requires much more physical effort and time than, say, arc welding, but it was the only method of welding available to blacksmiths until the more sophisticated, modern welding equipment was developed. Forge welding is the permanent fusing of two (or more) pieces of metal by hammering them together after they have been heated until plastic. The heat partially melts the surface of each piece and allows them to combine into a single piece of metal, at which time, if properly done, the weld is as strong as the rest of the metal.

According to Arthur McCracken, in order to weld, "You put your iron in the forge, both pieces you're going to weld. When they get hot enough to weld, the sparks will be shootin' up out of the fire. Your welding compound is sort of a white powder. Put that on your iron while it's in the fire. When it gets ready get it out right quick [put both pieces on the anvil] and go to hammering on them. And they will stick right together. Take a really good blacksmith and he could weld so you couldn't tell even where he had welded it. Weld it and smooth it off with a file. You usually need someone else to hammer or hold the pieces together. Blacksmiths had to have a helper because when they were welding two pieces of steel together, the blacksmith got one piece and the helper got the other piece and they put them down to be hammered together. Then the blacksmith had one free hand with the hammer to hammer with."

Forge welding requires a high temperature. For example, wrought iron must be heated to 2,500° F. or 2,550° F. in order to take a good weld. Steel requires a lower welding temperature, and different types of steel require different tenperatures. Whatever type of metal is being used, if the temperature is too high, it can burn and damage it, but if it is too low, the result will be either no weld or a weak weld. Will Zoellner told us, "You can weld steel at a way lower heat than you can iron. You can see iron in the forge just blazin' up and full of fire, and you can take it out and weld it and it will hold. But if you do steel that way, it will come all to pieces. You hit that with a hammer, and it will bust into a thousand pieces. It will spray and burn your face and arms up. You just can't do steel that way. You have to weld it at a low heat. You put a piece of iron and a piece of steel in the forge—the steel will be ready [to weld] before the iron. Iron doesn't pick up the heat like steel does."

In order to complete a satisfactory weld, the scale on the surfaces to be welded must be removed. Scale is caused by oxygen from the air combining with the metal. This scale can be melted away by the fire under certain conditions, but most blacksmiths used a flux on the parts to be welded, which combines with the scale, reduces its melting temperature, and removes it from the surface of the metal. If the metal is not free of scale, the weld will either not take, or it will be brittle and weak. Lee Tippett used a homemade flux, which he mixed by combining borax, salt, soda, and blue sand, and he told us, "Flux cleans the metal when you weld, and it causes it to fuse together. You can't weld nothin' if it's dirty. You can't weld good without flux. You can't weld in a forge fire if there's even a trace of bronze or copper in the forge. Now why, I don't know."

Tempering, or heat treating, is a procedure that controls the hardness and strength as well as the toughness and plasticity of steel. Wrought iron has a hardness all its own, but cannot be tempered due to its low carbon content. Tempering will be discussed because rural blacksmiths were able to obtain and work with some steel, even though wrought iron was more readily available. Hardness and strength are sacrificed in varying degrees to toughness and plasticity, and vice versa.

The temper in a piece of steel depends on two things—the type of steel, and the use to which it will be put. Generally, the higher the carbon content of the steel, the harder it may be tempered, but the degree of temper possible also depends on the other alloys in the steel. The cutting edges of a drill bit for drilling rock, for example, would have to be tempered to a high degree of hardness to enable them to cut through rock. On the other hand, a sledge hammer would need to be tougher and less hard (therefore less brittle) in order to withstand the concussion of repeatedly striking steel on the anvil without chipping or shattering. Steel is tempered by first heating it to a high heat, then quenching it (cooling it rapidly in water or oil), then reheating it to a more moderate heat, and quenching it again when it is at the proper temperature for the degree of hardness desired. Conversely, the temper can be taken out of steel by heating it to a high temperature and cooling it very slowly, in sand or ashes instead of water.

Tempering different types of steel properly is an exacting process that takes a lot of "doing" to learn properly. Lee Tippett told us, "You have to have the right type of steel for whatever you're making. Say you were going to make a punch, you want a hard steel. If you're going to make a cutting edge for cutting wood, you want a hard edge, but you don't want it hard enough to break. That's what you have to learn. You've got to learn the right amount of temper that you need for your edge. You have to quench it—chill it sort of. You want a blue straw-color on a cutting edge. You have to brush off the scale so you can see your color. You watch your color as it crawls up the steel, and as it comes up, when it gets a certain length, you quench it."

John Bulgin offered this explanation, "In tempering, it depends on the alloy of the steel. I couldn't take a plain hot-rolled piece of iron, no matter how hot I got it, and quench it in water and temper it—if it's regular iron, it won't temper. [But] you can case harden iron. If it's tooled steel or spring steel, it will temper. You can heat a piece of spring steel (you don't have to heat it too hot) and put it in water, and it makes it just like glass, and it's dangerous because it'll fly out. M'dad never would even let us pick up a piece of spring steel after he cut if off a spring and put it in water because it was dangerous. A piece of drill steel like they use to drill rock with, they sharpen it, then it's tempered in water. And it's tempered hard, but not too far back. Just the cutting part—get it tempered too far back and it'll break off. A cutting tool you temper in oil. It makes a tougher temper, and you don't get it as hot. Say I was gonna temper a piece of tooled steel—sometimes I would get it—well, you have to find out what your steel is first 'cause some of it will temper at a very dull red. Some of it has to be brighter red. Then you quench that end as far as you want it tempered, and cool it off. Then I'd bring that out and polish the scale off to where I could see the color, and above where I wanted it to temper would still be hot enough to bring that heat on down, and bring it to the color I want. Either a straw or a blue. You drop it in the water to stop the temper as it goes on down. Or you might want it speckled like a guinea egg—that's how you do drill bits. Different steel tempers differently. A good piece of tooled steel you can temper just like glass, but then you couldn't hit on it. Dad used to make butcher knives, and he had a trough to temper it in. Generally he'd get a piece of flat steel in the forge, and then he'd lay the knife blade on top of that, and the trough had oil in it, and he'd get the blade on its edge and drop it in the oil, to keep it from warping. If he'd laid it down flat, it'd warp."

PLATE 56 Items once in common use, made by George Bulgin in the early twentieth century; from left to right, a pothook, fireplace tongs, a fireplace shovel, and a trivet.

The following is a list of the different things blacksmiths traditionally made and repaired in this area, compiled from the information we gathered. We doubt that it is complete, however, and welcome our readers to add to it.

Blacksmithing

forges
punches
chisels
cleavers
tongs
hammers, all sizes
hacksaw frames

files, rasps
forge and coal shovels
draw knives
horseshoeing tools,
    such as creasers, nippers,
   and clenchers

Farming

plow points
bits and other metal hardware
   for harness
horseshoes
ox shoes
ox yokes
tool handles
hoes
shovels
mattocks
go-devils
gate latches
grain cradles
scythes

sickles
digging irons
crowbars
cowbells
adzes
broad axes
wedges
barrel hoops
wagons, the wheels and all the
    wood and 100-plus metal parts,
    including brake rods,
    nuts, bolts, pins, washers,
    hound plates, tumbling rods,
    braces, etc.

Household

crocheting needles
knitting needles
large needles for sewing sacks
shoe buttons
button hooks
knives
ice tongs
trivets

hinges
door knockers
window hooks
shutter dogs
for the fireplace:
    pokers, tongs, shovels, andirons,
    cranes, pot hooks, jam hooks

Hunting

for guns:
   barrels, sights, locks,
   butt plates, trigger assemblies

and guards, grip rails
large and small animal traps

Logging

chains of various sizes
J grabs
turning links

peaveys
axes
bull hooks

Miscellaneous

froes	washers
nails	pins
screws	broom tiers
bolts	gouges
nuts	springs

The following account is from the shop book of blacksmith Jason Castleberry in Fort Valley, Crawford County, Georgia, for the years 1854 and 1855. It is intended to give the reader an idea of the large scope of, and the subsequent value to a community of, the work of a rural blacksmith. The staff of the State of Georgia Archives provided us access to the shop book.

Account for Dr. Thomas Lewis (1854)

February 10	1 backhand hook	.05
March 8	pointing 1 shovel	.30
March 8	1½ of iron	.08
March 9	resetting 1 shoe	.10
March 11	resetting 1 shoe	.10
March 16	putting 2 shoes on horse	.40
March 27	sharpening 1 scoter	.05
April 3	putting 2 shoes on horse	.40
April 3	1 new bolt for buggy	.15
April 13	sharpening 1 cotton shears	.05
April 13	shrinking irons on singletree	.06
April 21	sharpening 1 shovel	.05
April 26	pointing 1 turning plough	.35
April 26	1½ iron	.08
June 3	resetting 4 old shoes on horse	.40
June 3	pointing and making new wings for sweep	.40
June 12	sharpening 1 shovel	.05
July 6	putting 2 shoes on horse	.40
July 19	putting 2 shoes on horse	.40
July 26	1 new turning plough	.69
September 19	resetting 2 old shoes on John	.20
January 27, 1855	Received payment by note	

The listing below is a random selection also taken from Jason Castleberry's account book, for the years 1854, 1855, and 1856.

1 two-horse waggon	80.00
shrinking 2 cart tyres (.50)	1.00
mending staple for ox yoke	.10
1 crank for grind stone	.75
1 clevis	.25
making 1 key for ox yoke	.05
repairing 1 plowrod and 4 links in breast chain	.30
making one friziron for singletree	.12
making 2 window hooks	.20
making 1 latch for gate	.25
putting 2 shoes on mule	.40
putting rebit in gun lock	.10
making tongue pin for cart	.10
repairing 1 heelscrew	.10
1 new turning plough	1.12
making 6 nails	.06
3 hoops on tubs @ .15	.45
work done on trace chains	.10
putting rivit in pot hooks	.05
riviting 2 pair scissors	.10
making tap for coffee mill	.10
putting 1 bolt in lock	.10
making handle for frying pan	.25
work done on buggy step	.25
1 new grubbing hoe	.75
putting face on clawhammer	.25
making 1 spring for bridle	.10
sharpening axe and mattock	.05
putting clapper staple on cowbell	.15
making 1 drawing knife	.50
mending 1 chisel	.12
work done on pistol	.15
1 pegging awl	.10
mending 1 pair tongs	.15

Each of the five blacksmiths we interviewed chose the item he wanted to make for us, and we think we ended up with a good selection. John Bulgin made a fireplace poker, Will Zoellner a cowbell, Arthur McCracken a forge shovel, Lee Tippett a froe, and Duggan Ledford a pair of horseshoes. John Bulgin and Lee Tippett each have large shops with sophisticated machinery and still work full time; Duggan Ledford is a full-time farrier (horseshoer) who travels over a large area shoeing horses; Arthur McCracken is retired, but still does some blacksmith work in his small shop by his house; and Will Zoellner is retired, and has sold the bulk of his shop tools to Foxfire.

None of these men now fits the image of the village blacksmith under the spreading chestnut tree. However, except for Duggan Ledford, who is primarily a horseshoer, they all have done a tremendous amount of the handwork required of a blacksmith in this area some fifty and more years ago. Two of the blacksmiths we interviewed expressed pessimism about the future of the art. They felt that not enough younger people were taking it up. However, we would like to optimistically note that of the five men we interviewed, one is in his mid-twenties, one has a son working full time in the shop, and one has two sons working full time in the shop.

John Bulgin

John Alexander Bulgin was born into the blacksmith trade, and is still carrying on this family tradition. His grandfather was a very accomplished person, who, among other things, did blacksmith work. As a teen-ager, John's father, George Miller Bulgin, traveled to Chicago to apprentice with a blacksmith there, and later returned home and set up a shop of his own. John picked it up from his father, and John's son, Randolph, in turn, picked it up from him.

Mr. Bulgin and Randolph have a large shop behind Mr. Bulgin's house, a beautiful new semi-modern, spacious, cottage-type house. They recently finished a large addition to their work shop and put in a new showroom, where they display all their finished work that is for sale. They have a forge, which they do use, but most of their work is done with electric and gas welders and other large, sophisticated pieces of machinery that was unavailable during George Bulgin's time. The things Mr. Bulgin and Randolph make are mainly for fireplace use, and they will make and adjust items to the size and shape their customers desire. Some of the fireplace tools they make are shovels, pokers, brooms, tongs, holders for tools, screens, and cranes for hanging pots in the fireplace. They also make large and small candle holders, mend things for people, and do some special order work, such as large steel gates for driveways.

John Bulgin is most interested in and proud of his work and heritage. He

*keeps quite busy, but does find time to work in his greenhouse where he
grows many different kinds of orchids. While he is working you are most always certain to find Betsy, his dog, close at hand.*

TERRI WEBB AND MYRA QUEEN JONES

The reason I got started blacksmithing is I was born into it. My grandfather was a builder and worked with wood, brick, and iron, and could do almost anything else. He was also an architect and designed and built the old
courthouse at Hayesville, North Carolina. They made the brick for it at
Grandpa's brick mill, and he was the overseer of it all.

When my father, George Miller Bulgin, was seventeen, his older brother
took him to Chicago, and got him a job serving as an apprentice blacksmith. And he became a blacksmith. One of the first jobs he got when he
finished his apprenticeship was welding buggy axles in the forge at a buggy
factory. He did that for a few months to prove to himself that he was good
enough to go out on his own. So he came back to this area and set up a
shop in Rabun Gap, Georgia, and worked as a blacksmith for the Tallulah
Falls Railway. After they got the railroad finished, he set up a shop here in
Franklin, North Carolina, in 1908.

My father made froes, and remade axes when they got thick—they call it
up-setting the axe, which is just drawing it out thin again. He made single-
trees and doubletrees for plowing, and made plows for road work. Big,
heavy plows. He made wagons and remade wagons—not just parts, but
the whole wagon. He'd sharpen plow points and made new plow points.
Make chains, rock bits to drill rock, and go-devils. Make mattocks and
sharpen them, and wedges for splitting wood. And he made a lot of his tools
—hammers, chisels, and tongs. Sometimes he'd have to make a special pair
of tongs for one job, and maybe he'd never use them again. I've still got
those old tongs up there in the shop that he made special to do certain jobs
with. During his time, blacksmiths would pull teeth for people. I know even
after my dad died, some people kept coming to me to pull their teeth, and I
would pull them. Yeah, I did! I've got the forceps upstairs to prove it. People went to the blacksmith for just about everything. My father even made
knitting needles and corset stays.

Of course my father would shoe a lot of horses. It didn't take long to
make the shoes, and I've been told that my daddy and his brother could
shoe a horse about as fast as you get tire service today. They must have had
a fire going in the forge all day. Now, we may have a fire in the forge today,
and then maybe not for two or three days.

My father had to order stock from a wholesaler, like I do now. It's pretty
much basically the same . . . your round stock and your flat stock. The steel

PLATE 57   John Bulgin in front of his shop, holding the fireplace poker he made.

nowdays is called hot-rolled machinery steel. The hot rolled is just a mild steel, and that's what they call iron. Now wrought iron is hand wrought, which means it's handworked and formed. But that's the old method for making iron. What we make now is not out of wrought iron. Wrought iron was made around what they call blueberry forges. They were a hand operation, and they'd try to find a deposit of iron ore where there was a lot of wood. Where they could make their own charcoal. They used to have what they call a blacksmith coal, a dirt-free coal, that you could use to weld with. You have to have a real clean fire to make a good forge. You had to get it right close to the burning point. Now we use coke.

My father did invent things, but he didn't try to get anything patented. He made a lot of things that could have been patented. Blacksmithing wasn't the kind of trade where you would be out looking for work. There were always things to fix, but my father didn't get too much money for the work he did. You didn't get too much for anything you did back then. People would pay him in money, and he would take corn or meat, things like that. My father worked hard in the shop until he died at sixty-one years of age, in 1936.

My brother and myself took over the shop then. My brother's really more of a machinist though. Neither of us apprenticed like our father. We both just worked. We'd go to school in the winter and come by the shop in the evening to work. I worked in the shop full time until 1941. Then the war came along, and the power company hired me as their master machinist. During the war, a lot of metal was needed, and if I wanted some metal, I had to get my request approved. But working for the power company, if I needed something special, I could get it. I did a lot of work during the war. I had my welder and got all the work I could get welding. I did quite a bit of work for the government. They were in this area mining mica. Lots of times they needed things for the bulldozers, and I'd do what they needed done. I'd be up working till twelve o'clock some nights. In all, I worked for the power company twenty-eight years.

My son, John Randolph Bulgin, and I run the shop now. We have a lot of large machinery and don't even fire up the forge every day. We don't do forge welding. We do electric welding. The first oxy-acetylene process came into this area in 1918. We made all kinds of objects for a fireplace. We make screens, tools, and cranes [to hang pots on]. And we make candle-holders and froes. And I have made some of our hand tools, chisels, and hammers. We try to make what people want. All of the stuff is pretty as well as functional. Everything my father made was first of all functional, but he always managed to make them ornamental, too. I also restore old things people bring to me.

I'm as capable of doing different things as my father was. I've done most everything he did. If anyone comes in with a piece that's broken, we'll weld it for him. I enjoy being a blacksmith. I'm sixty-eight years old, and I've been in the shop since I was six. But it's hard work, and I don't do it full time now. However, my son Randolph does.

The Fireplace Poker

MATERIALS

1 30"-long rod of ½" (square) hot-rolled machinery steel for the main body of the poker

1 12"-long rod of ½" (square) hot-rolled machinery steel for the spur

flat black spray paint

DIRECTIONS

Mr. Bulgin used hot-rolled machinery steel for this poker, but he could have used wrought iron (as his father would have) if he had been able to get any. He assured us that a person could make this poker out of wrought iron the same way that he made it out of rolled steel, except that wrought iron would not need to be painted, because it wouldn't rust like the hot-rolled machinery steel would. In making this poker, Mr. Bulgin regularly used an electric trip hammer to do the heavy hammering, then did the finer hammering on the anvil with a hand-held hammer. In the following directions we will simply say, "Hammer the . . ."

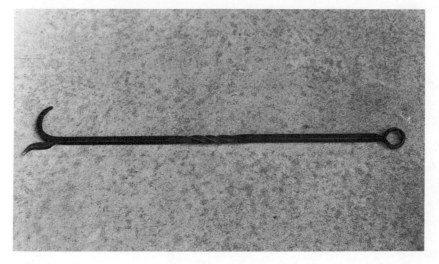

PLATE 58   The completed fireplace poker.

1. Use a hack saw to cut off a 30″-long length of the steel rod.

2. To make the ring to hang the poker from, heat about 3″ of one end of the rod until it's red hot.

3. Hammer the last 1″ of the heated tip of the rod and draw it out thin, about ¼″ in diameter, and about 5″ long. See Plate 59.

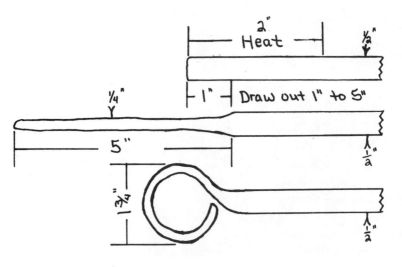

PLATE 59

4. Reheat the drawn-out end of the rod if necessary, and form it into a ring with an outside diameter of 1¾" by placing it on the horn of the anvil and hammering it over.

PLATE 60   Draw out the heated end of the rod before making it into a ring.

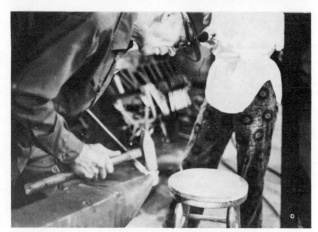

PLATE 61   Form the ring around the tip of the anvil horn.

PLATE 62   Draw out the other end of the poker with the trip hammer to form the point.

5. To make the point of the poker, heat about 3″ of the other end of the rod until it is red hot. Hammer the last 2″ of the rod and draw it out to about 5″, tapering it to a dull point. See Plate 64.

6. To curve the point of the poker, reheat it if necessary, place it on the thickest part of the anvil horn, and hammer it over into a gentle semicircle. Cool in water.

PLATE 63 Finish drawing out the point by hand.

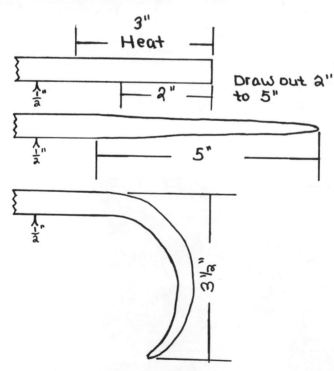

PLATE 64

PLATE 65 Form the curve in the poker point on the thick part of the anvil horn.

7. To put the decorative twist in the poker, measure a 6″ length in the center of the poker. Mark this 6″ length at both ends with a set punch. See Plate 66. Then, place this 6″ midsection in the forge and heat it to red hot.

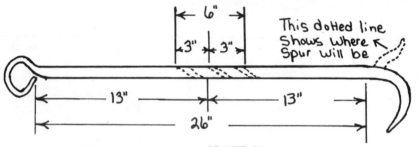

PLATE 66

PLATE 67 Marking the poker for the twist.

8. Put one end of the poker in a mounted vise just to one side of the heated 6″ midsection. Place a pair of vise-grip pliers on the other side of the heated section. Twist the rod one complete revolution with the pliers, thus creating the decorative twist. Then put the poker on the anvil and straighten it out if the poker was bent in the process of putting in the twist.

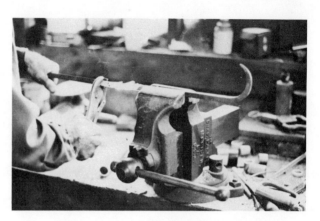

PLATE 68 Making the twist in the poker.

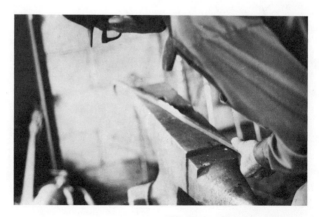

PLATE 69 Straightening the bend put in the poker when it was twisted.

9. The spur will first be formed, then welded to the poker. To form the
spur, heat the last 2″ of the 12″-long rod of rolled steel until red hot. Draw
the last 1″ out to 2½″ long, tapering it with a dull point on the end. See
Plate 70.

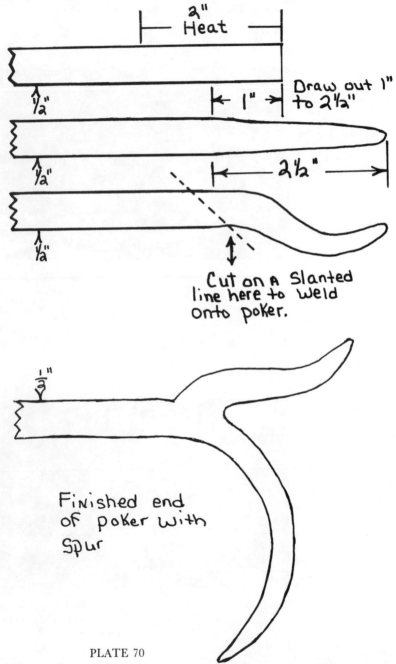

PLATE 70

10. If necessary, reheat the end of the 12″-long rod, and shape it into a spur on the anvil horn. Saw the formed spur off the rod with a hacksaw. See Plate 70.

11. Weld the spur to the poker in the position illustrated in Plate 70. (Mr. Bulgin welded the spur on with an arc welder. Before the advent of arc welders, the spur would have been forge-welded to the poker. A short piece of ½″ stock and the end of the poker would have been heated in the forge until white hot, then placed on the anvil and hammered together until they fused [welded] together. Then the spur would have been cut off to about 1″ long, drawn out, and curved, all after being welded to the body of the poker.)

PLATE 71 Drawing out the end of the twelve-inch-long rod, which will then be formed into the spur.

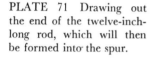

PLATES 72–73 Forming the spur of the poker, which will be welded on later.

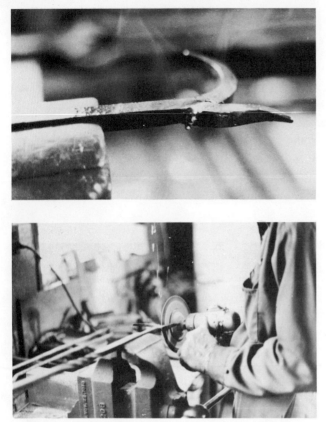

PLATE 74   The spur after being welded to the poker.

PLATE 75   Sanding off the rough edges of the weld.

12. To smooth off the rough edges of the weld, place the poker in the vise, and sand it with a hand-held electric grinder. (Before the advent of electric grinders, the rough edges of the weld would have been hammered or filed smooth.) This poker does not have to be tempered.

13. Now the poker must be sanded so it will take a good coat of paint to prevent rust. It will be easier if the poker is placed in the mounted vise for this. If you use wrought iron, it does not have to be sanded to be painted, because it does not have to be painted as wrought iron is very resistant to rust. (Mr. Bulgin used his sand-blasting machine for this but said it can be done by hand. Of course it will take a lot more elbow grease.)

14. Spray the poker with flat black paint and let it dry. Now it is ready to use.

PLATE 76   Nellie and Arthur McCracken on their front porch.

Arthur McCracken

While working on the blacksmithing article, we received an interesting letter from Bonita Mart, who now lives in New Jersey, about her father, Arthur McCracken, a blacksmith who lives near Cleveland, Tennessee. Mr. McCracken and his wife are really nice, hospitable people. After talking to them for a while, we found that he was a real handyman and skilled in many things besides blacksmithing. Mr. McCracken works with metal and wood, and makes furniture and toys for his children and grandchildren. He also keeps some ponies for his grandchildren. It was obvious to us that he cares very much for his whole family.

Mr. and Mrs. McCracken still do a lot of gardening and put up most of their food. Many things about Mr. McCracken impressed us, but the one I most admired was that he has never had a public (wage-earning) job. He has earned his living farming, blacksmithing, and sometimes cutting and hauling logs. These are some of the reasons why he has so much to be proud of, and why I enjoyed meeting him.

TERRI WEBB

I was born in 1897, on April 27. I married in 1920, and still got the same old girl. Nellie and I lived 'round about and rented for several years— Dennis Creek, Walker Valley, and Dry Valley. We bought this place in 1937, and we've been here since—about thirty years. We have eleven children. We've always lived on·a farm and had and killed two or three beef and two or three hogs a year. Put up fruit and beans and stuff. We raised cotton, and we'd take it and sell it and buy our kids a pair of shoes. I got to growing tobacco for four or five years. There's money in that. Also a lot of work. I've never had a public job, and the only outside jobs I've had were cutting or hauling logs.

PLATE 77   Arthur McCracken working at his forge.

I first got interested in blacksmithing when I was about fourteen or fifteen. The school teacher who was boarding there had a blacksmith shop and made his wife a shoe button out of a piece of wire. It was a pretty good one, too. I started to work with a fellow in his blacksmith shop, rainy days we'd work in the shop, and I learned what I learned from him, mostly. I was about twenty-five when I started out, up in Walker Valley. The shop belonged to him—we lived on the same place—and we worked there when we weren't doing anything else. It didn't take too long to learn [black-smithing]. I've always been kind of a handyman. I never was too much on welding, but I could do it, or used to. Used a compound to put on it as you hit it, make it stick better.

I'd say there were thirty or forty families in the area that I fixed and made stuff for. We just had a small outfit, kind of like what I've got here. I've made plows and horseshoes, knives, dog irons, pokers, and shovels. I've always farmed all my life, and just worked on the side in the shop. We sharpened plows and mattocks, fixed old wagons. I'd put spokes in wheels and then put the rim back on 'em. One time a fella brought in just a hub, wanted it rebuilt, and I never thought about it being wood inside, it was steel on the outside. I put it in the fire and burned the hub up! It took me half a day to make that piece of wood to fit inside there.

I worked with Frank Morgan for two years, then I put in m'own little shop. I didn't like shoeing the horses too much, but I didn't mind turning the shoes and fixing the shoes. [If a horse would] stand good, it was all right, but we'd get so many of 'em we'd have to rope and tie to get the shoes on. Never did get hurt though, too much. I made a lot of my tools, tongs, forge shovels, punches, chisels. I have a good punch I made from the spring that come out from under a freight train. The tools I use all the time are punches, chisels, draw knives, hammers, tongs, a hand saw, a brace and bit, and of course an anvil. The tongs are to handle hot iron with—I've picked up a few that were too hot—I can remember that! We never really had trouble finding materials. There was generally a lot of old stuff piled around. I have a lot of scrap metal out there I keep thinking I should make something out of.

There wasn't anybody else much around blacksmithing but Morgan and me. Some things I couldn't do that a regular blacksmith could do, such as weldin' tires and puttin' 'em on a wagon. Have to have them just the right length, weld'em, build a bigger fire, and get'em red hot nearly—they're loose when you put'em on—then pour water on'em, cool'em, and they get as tight as they can be. Well you can ruin the wheel if you get'em too tight, buckle the wheel.

I've never hurt myself badly in the shop. Burned my finger once. One time my little boy was fooling around in the shop and I was cutting holes in this piece of metal, and the pieces of metal was falling to the ground in little washerlike pieces. My little boy stepped on one of them and boy did he take off running! This blacksmith up yonder said he had a piece that got just hot enough. And boys would just bother him in the shop crowding around every day. He put that piece of iron in the fire and got it hot and took it out and hammered it. Those pieces of hot metal started flying, and they *all* cleared out!

The Forge Shovel

Mr. McCracken made a forge shovel for us out of scrap metal he had around the shop. A forge shovel is used to redistribute the coal and ashes in the forge to regulate the temperature of the fire. He said it was nothing of real beauty, but then his kind of blacksmith work has always leaned toward the utilitarian. It is a perfectly functioning shop tool.

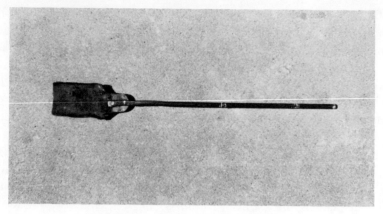

PLATE 78   The completed forge shovel.

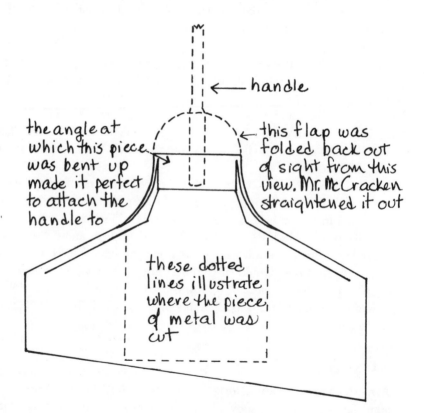

PLATE 79

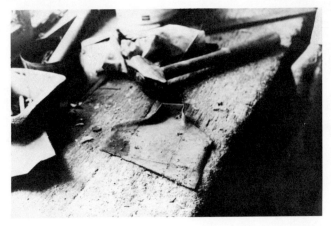

PLATE 80 The scrap metal used for the shovel blade marked to be cut.

MATERIALS

1 18″ length of ⁷⁄₁₆″-diameter steel rod for the handle
A 4″×7″ piece of ¹⁄₁₆″ thick fairly soft steel for the blade
A 1¼″ length of ¼″ soft steel rod for the rivets

DIRECTIONS

The steel rod for the handle, and the steel for the blade were both taken from the scrap pile. The rod was threaded on one end, but that posed no problem, and it just happened to be a good length. The piece of steel for the blade, however, was oddly shaped, and was bent in a distinctive manner at one end, which happened to be at just the right angle to attach the handle to (see Plate 79). He chose this piece of metal precisely because it was shaped as it was. The reader will most likely not find a similar piece, but a flat one, so the directions and the following diagrams will be for a flat piece of metal for the shovel blade.

1. Use a chisel or a set punch to mark off the shovel blade pattern (Plate 81) on the piece of ¹⁄₁₆″-thick sheet of steel. Be sure to include the dotted lines along which the blade will be bent, and mark for the two holes that must be punched in the blade to rivet it to the handle.

2. Put a protective apron of metal on the anvil. Using a hammer and a cold chisel, place the sheet of steel on the flat surface of the anvil and cut the blade out. Remove the apron, and place the point at which one of the ¼″-diameter holes must be punched in the blade over one of the holes in the anvil. Using a punch, punch out the hole in the blade. Punch the other hole the same way.

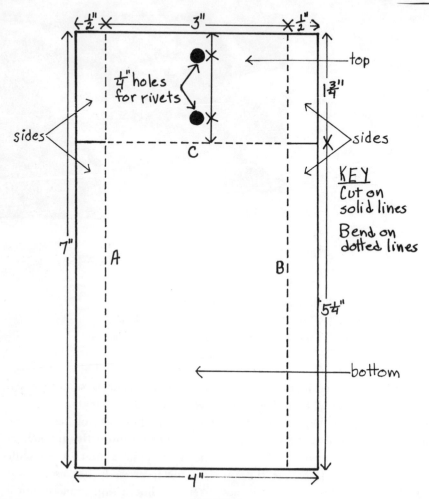

$\frac{1}{2}$"   ✕   3"   ✕ $\frac{1}{2}$"

$\frac{1}{4}$" holes
for rivets

top

$1\frac{3}{4}$"

sides

C

sides

KEY
Cut on
solid lines

Bend on
dotted lines

7"

A

B

$5\frac{1}{4}$"

bottom

4"

PLATE 81

PLATE 82 Cutting out
the shovel blade.

PLATE 83 Punching a hole in the top of the blade for one of the rivets.

PLATE 84 Bending one side of the shovel blade.

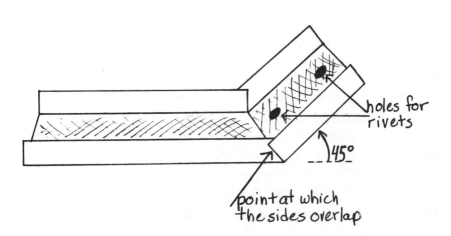

PLATE 85

3. To shape the sides of the shovel blade, place one side of the blade in the vise up to dotted line A. Hammer over the blade until it is bent at almost a right (90°) angle. Do the other side the same way.

4. To shape the top of the blade, place one side of the blade in the vise up to dotted line C, and hammer over the back of the blade until it is bent at about a 45° angle (see Plate 85).

5. Lay the blade on the anvil in such a way as to be able to hammer the sides where they overlap at the point at which the back of the blade is bent up at a 45° angle.

PLATE 86   The completed shovel blade.

6. Place the shaped blade in the vise and file smooth all the edges. The blade is now finished.

7. To make the handle, first saw off an 18″ length of the 7/16″-diameter steel rod.

8. The end of the handle must be flattened where it is riveted to the blade. Place about 3″ of one end of the handle in the forge and heat it until it is red hot. Place that end of it on the anvil and flatten the last 2″ of it with the hammer until it is about 3/16″ thick. See Plate 87.

9. Two 1/4″-diameter holes that correspond to the two holes in the top of the blade must be punched in the flattened end of the handle so the two pieces may be riveted together (see Plate 87). On the flattened end of the handle make a dot with a punch at 3/8″ from the end, and another dot 1 3/8″ from the end. Each dot marks the center of one hole.

10. Heat the flattened end of the handle until red hot. Place it on the anvil so that one dot is directly over one of the holes in the anvil. Punch out a 1/4″-diameter hole through the handle. Do the other hole the same way.

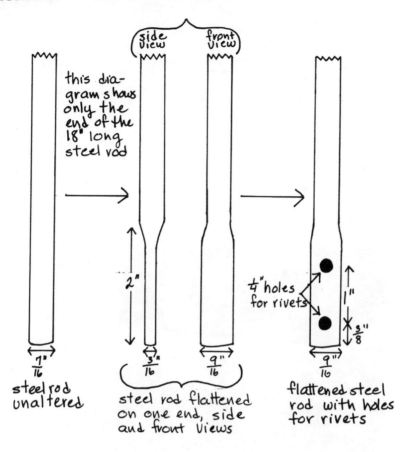

this diagram shows only the end of the 18" long steel rod

side view

front view

2"

$\frac{7}{16}$"

steel rod unaltered

$\frac{3}{16}$" $\frac{9}{16}$"

steel rod flattened on one end, side and front views

$\frac{1}{4}$" holes for rivets

1"

$\frac{3}{8}$"

$\frac{9}{16}$"

flattened steel rod with holes for rivets

PLATE 87

PLATE 88 Punching a rivet hole in the flattened, heated end of the shovel handle.

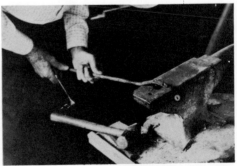

PLATE 89 Making the curve in the shovel handle.

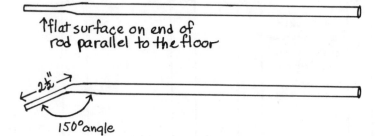

flat surface on end of
rod parallel to the floor

2½"

150° angle

PLATE 90

PLATE 91   A ⅝-inch length of a soft steel rod in the vise, to
be made into a rivet.

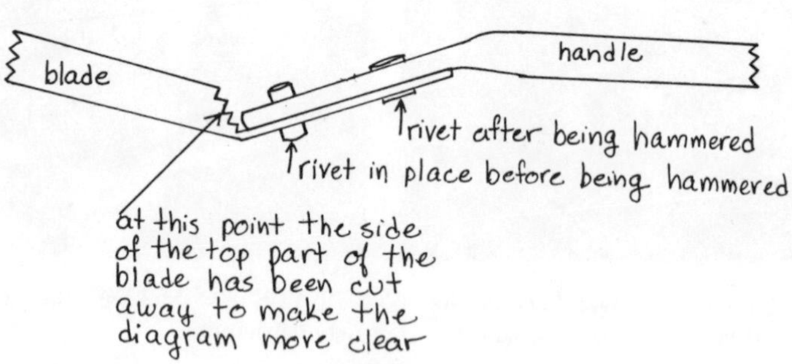

blade   handle

rivet after being hammered

rivet in place before being hammered

at this point the side
of the top part of the
blade has been cut
away to make the
diagram more clear

PLATE 92

PLATE 93   Making final adjustments in the curve of the shovel handle.

11. Now the proper curve must be put in the handle. Heat a section of the flattened end of the handle from 1″ from the end to 5″ from the end. Place it over the anvil (with the flattened surface parallel to the floor so the curve will not be out to one side once the handle is attached to the blade) at a point 2½″ from the end, and carefully hammer the end over until the handle is bent at roughly a 150° angle. See Plate 90.

12. The handle and blade must be riveted together. Saw off two sections of the soft ¼″-diameter rod, each ⅝″ long. Line up the two holes on the handle and top of blade, and tap one ⅝″ section of rod through one set of holes so it protrudes the same amount at each end.

13. Place the shovel lightly on the anvil so one end of the rivet rests on it. Carefully, so the rivet doesn't slip through, hammer the top of it until it is flattened on both ends, tightly riveting together the handle and blade. Do the other rivet the same way. See Plate 92.

The shovel is now finished, except for any necessary minor adjustments, like changing the angle of the curve in the handle, refiling any of the edges on the blade, or possibly tightening the rivets.

Lee Tippett

   Lee Tippett lives in Franklin, North Carolina, and has a large blacksmith shop next to his house, where he works with his two sons. He grew up working around the blacksmith shop on his family's farm, and around the age of eleven his father built him a shop. "My father taught me how to do it. He worked as a blacksmith only when he was a boy. And then on the farm he showed me how. He was a contractor, but he taught me how to blacksmith too. He taught me how to temper and all that stuff. He showed me how to sharpen plow points, build wagons, and all kinds of farm stuff, tools—we made tools. You learn a lot of it by yourself. You see something, you want it, and you make it." Mr. Tippett talked a lot about his father, and one story he told us was about all the hard work he had to do helping him. "I have an electric bellows. My dad had a leather one that you pumped. He'd say, 'Come on, Lee, pump a little harder, it ain't quite hot enough.'" So Mr. Tippett decided he would build an electric one that wouldn't be so hard to operate. "One day I told my father, 'If I ever get grown, I'll make an electric rig.' He got to work on this one. I got it made, and he came and worked on it."

   Every time we've been at Mr. Tippett's there have been several other people there, talking, watching Mr. Tippett or one of his sons fix something, or waiting to have something fixed. One time when we visited, his son, Joe, repaired a bent subsoiler, and another time Mr. Tippett had just finished a large rig designed to lift logs for a man who was building log cabins. He also has a couple of wagons around his shop that he intends to repair during the next year. In his shop we noticed a lot of heavy, metalworking machines and asked about them. He told us that most of those machines had been broken or thrown away because they didn't work. He took them apart, rebuilt them, welded them together, and made them look good as new. I think what fascinated me most about him was his ability to rebuild these complicated machines. Mr. Tippett was always busy working when we came to see him, but amidst all that modern machinery was a somewhat old-fashioned man who enjoyed his work and always had time to talk to us and show us what he was working on at the time.

TERRI WEBB

PLATE 94   Lee Tippett by his shop, holding the froe he made.

There were five generations of blacksmiths on one side of my family, and six on the other. Shop men is what I'm talking about. We've all been shop people down through the years. We've worked with our hands and made things. On my Tippett side, my great-grandfathers in England were ship builders. So we've always more or less had it handed down to us.

Blacksmithing is taking raw unformed iron [or steel] and making a finished product. Rough black iron and making a useful product out of it. What makes a blacksmith is—they had to have the iron and the tools and know how to use them, how to make things. Because there was no other way to get [certain things]. Necessity is the mother of all inventions. A blacksmith makes what other people want him to make. There've been many things I've made what people have drawn up, or whittled out of wood. The blacksmith was and is a much needed man in the community, and when [you can provide something people need] they think pretty well of you.

My father built a shop for me when I was eleven years old. At the old homeplace at Iolta. It was standing until two years ago when they tore it down. I worked there all the time I went to school, and after I married for a while. And my father taught me the trade. I mean he taught me how to work with these things and how to temper and how to weld. And some woodwork—I've done woodwork all my life, too, as well as steel. After a while I moved here and built this shop. Been here forty-one years. During the Depression I went to milling and logging, and really that's how come I have this shop here, so I could keep all my equipment in repair. And I've been a'working here ever since. Back when I logged, I logged with horses. We used header grabs and peaveys and axes and saws and chains, ropes and blocks to get logs out. It took a lot of work—course I believe we got as much out then as they do now. I've sawed hundreds of thousands of cross-ties. I cut crossties for years. I ran my own mill for fourteen years, and helped another man for three more years. I think what I was sawing was shipped to England. It was during World War II when we sawed the most of our ties. They'd take anything but poplar and basswood. I also cut a lot of timber for the coal mines—it was used in the mines overhead to keep the rocks and earth from caving in the tunnels. But I quit that in '46 and sold both teams [of horses] I had.

Back in the Depression I'd work for corn, meat, anything like that. But today I only take money. And most of the mountain people are honest. There are a few shysters, but our old mountain people are more honest than others. Of course, if they wasn't, they didn't get work out of me the third time. I'd do it twice, and the third time if they didn't pay me, I'd turn my back on them.

I logged and sawmilled and run the shop all of my life—that's all I've ever known. Oh I've built a lot of houses too. Most of the time I'd come back to the shop and work, 'cause that's where I like it best. Anybody wanted anything built, we tried to build it. Everything in the world from horseshoes to wagons. Pieces for reapers, plows, hoe handles, I've made it all, nearly. You'd be surprised what people want you to make. One time somebody asked me to make a gig to gig frogs with. Made two or three of those. I've made needles to sew sacks, knitting needles, quilting frames, repaired a lot of old spinning wheels. My father made broom tiers to tie brooms on, and I watched him and I did it one day when a man wanted one. By memory. I've made several wagons, and parts for hundreds of them. Baling-machine tongues and raking-machine tongues, and slats for claws on a reaper. Tractor parts—oh, I hated the day that tractors ever came to this country. I loved horses. We've made mine elevators and one time we made a railroad car for Gold City [a tourist attraction] over there, and we rebuilt saw mills and fabricated truck beds. My training back in my young years is what got me started. And I've enjoyed every minute of it.

PLATE 95   The finished froe.

The Froe

A froe is designed to split wooden boards (shingles) from logs for covering roofs. A wooden maul is used as the traditional striking tool, never a metal hammer or other metal instrument, which would damage the top of the blade. Everyone in the Southern Highlands used to have board roofs, usually of red oak or Spanish oak, before the introduction of tin roofing and asphalt shingles. A board roof that is put on properly will not leak, even though daylight may show through into the loft or attic. They age beautifully, and should be good for at least twenty-five years. (We have spoken to people who said they had board roofs which were in good condition after fifty years.) Following is an edited version of Mr. Tippett's comments while he was making our froe:

"The eye is the hardest part to get right. I always make my eye first. You make a cone in the eye, so when you put the handle in from the bottom, it'll wedge in and stay. You can't complete the eye until it's welded together, but I taper mine all along while I make it. It has to be big at the bottom and smaller at the top. After you get the eye made you've got it pretty well done. There's a whole lot of work in it.

"You have to get the blade all squared up with the eye. Now I draw out the blade and make a wedge out of it. This will be a quarter of an inch at the top, and as you use it, it gets thicker on the top all the time. Especially if you hit it with a hammer, so it's much better to use a wooden maul. You want the blade sharp. You hammer it down and make a wedge with a thin edge of it, so it'll burst the boards. You want it where it will start easy, but still split the boards. I sharpen mine where they're sharp. People say, 'Dull as a froe,' and they're all dull after you use 'em for a while."

MATERIALS

1 piece of tooled steel, 2¼" wide, ¼" thick, and at least 21" long
1 piece of white oak sapling, at least 2" in diameter and 14" long
1 steel or wooden wedge, about 1" wide
(The piece of steel Mr. Tippett used for the froe blade had been a spring for some sort of vehicle. It had a pronounced curve in it, and he had to flatten it by heating it, then hammering it flat.)

DIRECTIONS

1. First the eye, where the handle fits into the blade, must be formed. Measure and mark a 7" length on one end of the piece of steel, which will later be shaped into the eye. Heat about the last 8–9" of the measured end of the steel to red hot. See Plate 96.

2. Holding the unheated end of the piece of steel with tongs, form the last 7" of the heated end into a ring on the horn of the anvil. This ring, or eye, should be slightly cone shaped, with a 2" inside diameter on one end, and a 1⅞" inside diameter on the other end so the handle will wedge tightly into it (see Plate 96). The eye must be formed so that an imaginary line extending along the blade through the eye bisects the eye (see Plate 96).

3. Weld the seam where the end of the piece of steel forming the eye butts up against the side of the blade, to make the eye a closed circle. Mr. Tippett's son used an arc welder to do this, but before Mr. Tippett had modern

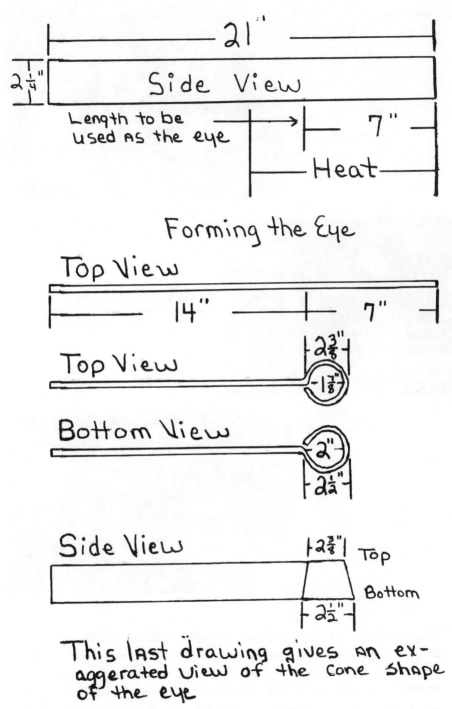

21"

2¼" | Side View

Length to be
used as the eye → | **7"**

— Heat —

Forming the Eye

Top View

— **14"** — | — **7"** —

Top View | **2⅜"**
-1⅞"-

Bottom View | **2"**
2½"

Side View | **2⅜"** Top

Bottom

2½"

This last drawing gives an exaggerated view of the cone shape
of the eye

PLATE 96

PLATES 97–99 Form the
eye around the anvil horn.

welding equipment, he would have welded it in the forge, which is a more
time-consuming process. First, he would heat a generous area around the
eye seam until white hot. Then he would apply a flux to the steel where it
was to be welded together and hammer the seam together on the anvil until
the metal fused together. Some reshaping of the eye would have to be done
after this.

PLATE 100 Side view of the eye before being welded together.

PLATE 101 Demonstrating how the eye seam would be hand-welded.

4. The next step in the process is forming the wedge shape of the blade. It is the bottom, not the top of the blade that is to be sharp (see Plate 102). Heat the whole blade until red hot. Lay it flat on the anvil and hammer it into a wedge shape, thick at the top and tapering to a point at the bottom. During this hammering, draw the blade out roughly ¼″, from 2¼″ high to 2½″ high. At the same time, hammer some of the metal up toward the top as shown in Plate 102.

5. Now the blade has to be cut off to the proper length. Measure and mark where the blade is to be cut, according to Plate 105. The blade will be cut at an angle. To cut off the blade you will need a hardie, a cleaver, and a person (striker) with a sledge hammer. Heat the part of the blade where it is to be cut off until red hot. Place the hardie in the hardie hole in the anvil, and place the heated blade where it is to be cut on the hardie. Hold the cleaver on top of the blade just to the side where the hardie is underneath the blade. (If the cleaver strikes the hardie when the blade is cut through, it will damage both of them.) Have the striker hit the head of the cleaver repeatedly until the blade is cut through. Reflatten the blade if this procedure bent it out of shape.

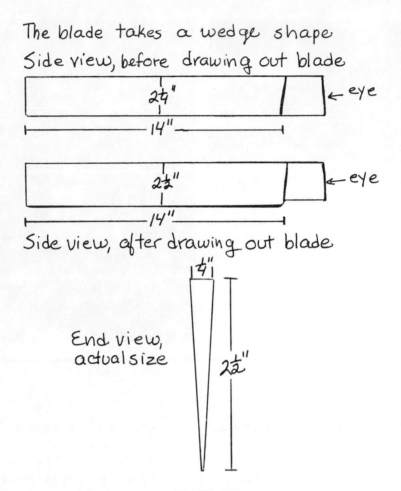

The blade takes a wedge shape

Side view, before drawing out blade

2¼"

14"

← eye

2½"

14"

← eye

Side view, after drawing out blade

End view, actual size

¼"

2½"

PLATE 102

PLATE 103 Draw the heated blade into a wedge shape.

PLATE 104 Straightening the curve put in the blade during the drawing-out process.

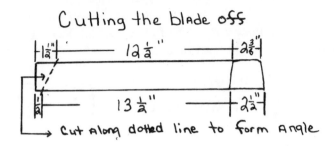

Cutting the blade off

Cut along dotted line to form angle

PLATE 105

PLATE 106   Cut off the end of the blade at the proper angle using a hardie and a cleaver.

PLATE 107   Hammer the end of the blade until it breaks off where it was cut with the hardie and cleaver.

6. The next step is making and putting in the handle. Cut the piece of white oak sapling off to 14″ long. Put it in a vise, and using a draw knife, shave it off until one end is 2″ in diameter, and the other end is 1½″ in diameter, tapering it gently all the way.

7. To put the handle in the froe, first clamp the froe in the vise with the sharp edge of the blade up. Then put the small end of the handle down into the large end of the eye and hammer it down until the large end of the handle is flush with the large end of the eye. It should fit tightly. Hammer the wedge into the large end of the handle (see Plate 108).

8. The last step is to sharpen the blade with a grinder. It should be quite sharp, but don't grind it too thin. Then smooth off the end where the blade was cut off (see Plate 109). The froe is now finished except for any minor adjustments that might need to be made.

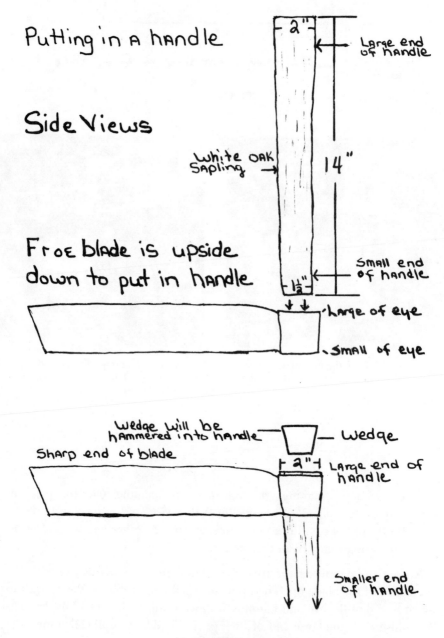

Putting in a handle

Side Views

White oak Sapling →

2"

14"

1½"

Large end of handle

Small end of handle

Large of eye

Small of eye

Froe blade is upside down to put in handle

Wedge will be hammered into handle

Wedge

Sharp end of blade

2"

Large end of handle

Smaller end of handle

PLATE 108

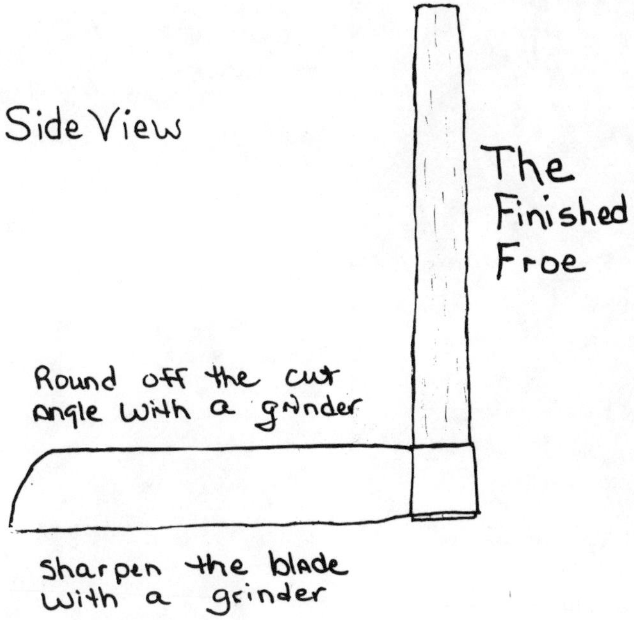

Side View

The
Finished
Froe

Round off the cut
angle with a grinder

Sharpen the blade
with a grinder

PLATE 109

PLATE 110 A wooden maul, which is customarily used with a froe to split shingles.

PLATES 111–113 Harley Rogers, demonstrating how to split, or rive, shingles—splitting the "bolt" which will then be split into shingles.

Will Zoellner

Will Zoellner is ninety years old. He started blacksmithing in Highlands, North Carolina, when he was ten years old, along with his brother, Carl, who at that time was twelve. The two boys set up a shop after being encouraged to do so by their father. They picked up bits of information here and there until they became very good at it. As a young man Will did other things for a living, such as farming and logging, but he always kept up with the blacksmith work. When he was in his late twenties he married, moved to Rabun County, Georgia, and worked full time with another blacksmith in Clayton, in a shop near the courthouse. He later bought the other man out and, in all, worked in Clayton fourteen years.

He then joined with a couple different logging companies, shoeing the logging horses and keeping the tools and machinery in good repair. After he retired from that, he kept a small shop next to his house in Mountain City for many years. Will has finally given up blacksmith work. He offered to sell his tools to Foxfire, and we gladly accepted. We plan to set them up in a shop and hope that Will will be available to spend some time teaching students to use the tools, even though he feels he no longer can.

MYRA QUEEN JONES

[Carl and I started blacksmithing because] everybody had tools all broke up there at Highlands. All of those carpenters up there, and nobody would file a saw. Axes and them mowing blades and everything was dull. Daddy said, "If you boys would go ahead and put up a shop, I'd help you all I can. There is an awful call for settin' horseshoes and fixin' the plows, sharpenin' them and one thing or another. It would be an awful good job for some young fella."

Carl said, "I believe I'll take it up." He was twelve years old.

I said, "I'll help him." And he got some second-hand tools, but not enough to amount to anything. We built a log cabin fourteen by eighteen feet—course the timber came off our place. It was a nice log house, and we sealed it with mud and rock. We made a pretty nice shop out of it.

Some old man over there had a pair of bellows, but didn't have no firebox. He said, "I'll let you have my bellows," and he brought them over.

Hans and John McCall were working for Daddy. They said, "We'll build you a little forge out of this gray granite rock, and get you a little coal,

PLATE 114   Will Zoellner in his shop.

and it will be just as good as any of these little fireboxes you can get. You
might get something better than this later on, but right now this will be
okay. You can do just as good as you can with any other high-priced rig."
Well, the next morning Daddy got the boys fixed up. We carried the rocks,
we got the cement, and we mixed some mortar up. We got the cement at
Basscomb's at Highlands at forty cents a sack. All we needed was one sack.
Daddy got a hundred pounds of coal from Walhalla, South Carolina. We
couldn't get it no closer. It was that big old lump coal.

Well we fixed up some shoes for Daddy's pair of little horses. We were interested in that kind of work. And I worked there. I wasn't but about ten or twelve years old. Mrs. Carr brought her horses over there. She had a fancy saddlehorse, and a buggy horse. We fixed all of them around there. Jim Bradley come up there with a bunch of plows wanting them sharpened. So Carl went to hammering. We didn't have anybody to tell us about the temper. That was the trouble. Tempering just hardens the metal.

Most of the stuff would break. You stick a piece of red-hot iron in a tub of water, and it's gone. You want to hammer it on medium heat. Just barely red, if you have to hammer it. If you burn the carbon out, you just might as well throw it away. If it burns white and it sparkles, you have burnt the carbon out and it won't hold. So that was the big trouble. We had nobody to tell us that the fire would ruin the metal. Old man Tweed Kellcey was an old kind of a rancher. He said, "Boys, I'll tell ya, you are getting your fire too hot. You're getting your metal too hot and you burn all of the carbon out of it, and by that time it's no good. You mustn't get it too hot—you should work on it in medium heat. And when you temper it, do it the same way. Just get it barely red. And put it in the tub just so deep. When it gets black pull it out and then watch till you see that blue coming on down there. Then after that blue comes gray and whenever that gray comes to the tip of metal, then stick it in the tub of water. Let it get cold."

Well Carl was slick to catch on. Some miner come in there and had a whole lot of chisels and stuff like that. He said, "I'll tell you right now I had a fella to fix them there in Virginia. Every one of them broke."

I says, "I can stop that. This man told me how to stop that."

Carl said, "Have you ever tried it?"

And I said, "Yeah, when you was gone one day I fixed a mattock. And there it sets. I done a real job on the mattock."

He said, "You never did that."

I said, "I did do it. I hammered it out and took a file and smoothed it off. And heated it till it was just barely red. And I held it in the water there about a quarter of a inch deep. And when it got cold I jerked on out and watched it. First, come a deep blue ring down, and finally it got lighter and lighter and directly the gray come and I stuck it in the tub and pulled it on out, and there it is."

Carl said, "It's perfect."

The miner said, "Do the same thing with the cold chisel."

I said, "I'll fix you one you can cut anything with."

He said, "A cold chisel won't cut no cold metal."

I said, "It will too."

Daddy said, "I've got a big cold chisel that my brother gave me that is dull as it can be."

The other man said, "Let him try it."

You can't temper nothing on the wrong heat. To temper you have to lay it aside and let it get cold. So you can just barely pick it up and cool it so you can handle it. Then you stick that in the fire, but don't stick it way down in there. Just to the cuttin' place about three inches, and you watch when it gets cherry red and take it out. If there is any black ends on it sometimes it don't heat all the way across. You just stick it in the forge and keep turning it around and around till you see a smooth dark red, then you stick it down in that tub. About a half an inch, and when it gets cold then check it out—it drys off quick. When the blue comes—if it comes too fast you didn't hold it long enough in the water. And you've got to come slow.

So the first one come and it run out on me, I didn't get it. I let it get away. He said, "What do you mean?"

I says, "I'll show ya what I mean. The temper outrun me before I could get it to the tub quick enough. I was too far off from the slack tub." So I heated it again and went on and did the same thing again, and he was standing there watching. I put it out there, and here come the blue down. The cooler it gets the slower it comes. And you can get it so cool it won't come at all. So it come on down there and here come the gray.

Daddy come out there and says, "Here's a piece of soft iron. Lay it down and lets see if it will cut it." I didn't know anything about cutting metal, but I know it was strong and wouldn't break. So he laid the piece of wrought iron up there, and he wanted [a section of it cut off]. I took a four pound hammer and set that cold chisel up there and tapped it. It cut it off just as smooth as it could be, and you couldn't tell it on the cold chisel.

Carl, he looked up at me and said, "Did he show you how to do that?"

I said, "Yeah. Kellcey did."

He said, "That's the man we need to get." But Kellcey was a man you couldn't keep inside. He wanted to be in the mountains.

So we pecked on there, and the first thing we knew he and I *both* couldn't do the work. Shoes come from all parts. We could nail the shoes but nobody could fit'em up and punch them. The shoe has to be punched so that the nail head [doesn't] wear off [causing the shoe to] come loose. You have to punch the [nail holes] from the inside first and the outside last. That nailhead goes down in that slot. It don't come off till the shoe gets as thin as a heavy knife. They stay right there. Sometimes they would wear the piece out in front and two pieces would still be on.

Carl got so far along that this man came up there and said, "You can come up and work for me for a dollar an hour." Back then it was *money*. And ten cents an hour is about what you would get when you work for the farmer. He went up there and made ten dollars a day. I took over at home then. I kept on messing around there sharpening tools. I got me a mowing machine sharpener. The old-time machine was pulled by horses. You just pull that sickle bar out and put it back in. You can grind them on that grinder and get them hotter than a 'tater. The temper runs out. You have to grind them right careful and not get them too hot. Take your time, and when it gets hot, quit awhile. Don't let them get blue—if you let them get blue the whole thing's gone. I run some on, but it wasn't no more than two or three weeks I knew how to do that. We had a wheel to grind a blade. You just hold the blades down there and grind two blades at a time. The farmers would pay five dollars for sharpening their sickles. I sharpened all of those sickles around there. I done all of that work first thing, I made more money than Carl did. I made twenty-five dollars a day.

I was working for Ransom Brown some. The school was up on the hill, and after school I would come down and work. Carl couldn't work a nail into a shoe, he was a little slow about nailing. He couldn't drive a nail just exactly like I could. I could shoe two while he was shoeing one. Bill Poss had forty head of saddle horses there and about ten of those were buggy horses. They hauled the mail from Dillard up there, and from Wahalla with horses. Those horses wore out a set of shoes every two weeks. So I went down there and they wanted to hire me. I says, "No, I'm just going to hang around here with Ransom Brown and Carl and just look around." I worked there way up into the night, business picked up so.

Finally, there was an old fella from Jackson County who come to Highlands there and put up a shop. Kellcey got him in there. Kellcey was a good friend of my daddy and all of us boys, but he really put us boys in a squeeze. He put us out of business with that other strange man. The strange man had a better set of tools than we did and more of them. But he didn't have it up here in the head. So he put his shop up on the other side of town, and we were down on this side of town. He put up a good nice shop, nothing that looked too well. A dry place to shoe, he had it level there. His shoes wouldn't stay. He had a pretty good business there but in less than a month we had it back. I saw him sniffin' around down there at our shop. Carl said to Ransom Brown, "That's the man that's trying to put us out of business. Coming down here to learn something. While he is standing around here let's not do a darn thing. Just let him set till he gets tired and will leave."

So he come on out there one day and he said, "I'll sell my tools and go back to the West. I like it the best here, but you can't make no money here. The payroll is weak. I'm not a blacksmith, I just can't get the shape like I want it."

Daddy said, "What will you take for what you got up there?"

"Well," he said, "I'll take a couple hundred dollars." I never said nothing.

Daddy said, "I'll run by some evening to see what you got." Our anvil was pretty light—it would bounce when you hit it pretty heavy when you turned those big old number four logging horses' shoes. It only weighed a hundred and twenty-eight pounds.

So we went on down there, and he said, "I'd love to swap you my big anvil for your little one." So we made an even trade. He took the little and I took the big one. It's sitting down there now. It's American Ross, they don't never wear out. Now don't never take a hammer and hit an anvil unless there is a piece of metal on it. [the hammer and anvil] are the same metal and one of them is going to break. They can't *stand* hitting each other. You've got to put something between them, like a piece of tin or a piece of light stuff. You don't get any money hammering on the anvil no how.

I fixed every thing that was metal. They would bring all kinds of stuff in there from the farms. I'd take the corn shellers that they run the shaft out of, and I'd put in a new shaft. I had a lathe, but it wasn't mine. Tom Roan down here was the first man to put the power in. I used his lathe. I'd put in new shafts, and put on a T-model Ford axle. They'd run into a bank and bend them, and they would bring them to me. I would straighten them up and send them back to them. Anything in metal I would work on. I would sharpen plows and make sweeps. Later on we got so many orders in for sweeps we couldn't handle them. Sweeps cut the weeds down where corn used to go. It works like a mowin' machine cuttin' hay, only this one goes under the ground and mowin' machine goes on top. I made knitting needles out of steel wire. Crochet hooks. And cow bells. But that day and time the metal was different. This metal now ain't got no sound. It's dead. It's got to be cold-rolled steel. Steel that I used to find in trash piles. I've almost stopped makin' bells. I can make one that looks good but not one that sounds good.

There are several hundred tools I use. Every once in a while you have to knock off and work on your own tools. You have to keep up with your own tools. The biggest thing is the hammer, you use your hammer for most anything there. I've got twelve hammers. I've got thirty-two tongs to pick up stuff with. I use them to get stuff out of the fire. I use a cleaver more than a cold chisel. A cleaver is just like a hammer only it has a blade on the back of it. Like a hatchet. I use them lots. You can handle them better. The metal lays on the anvil and you got all of your hands to work with. I got about eight or ten cleavers. And a hack saw but their soft blades don't cut no steel.

[Carl finally got out of the blacksmithing business.] So Doc Ledford told Carl that he would hire him over there at the base hospital. Said, "I need a man down in the boiler room to look at the steam, who knows something about steam and can build a fire in the furnace." Carl could fire these little sawmill boilers, so he was a pretty good hand. He stayed down there for years and years. And I finally moved into Highlands, but there wasn't any money up there. All credit. I finally moved down here to Rabun County, this side of the courthouse. I stayed there fourteen years.

The man that let me have the place wouldn't sell it to me, just leased it to me. The old building got rotten and the county wouldn't let me repair it. I would have had to put in a rock building or a block building. I says, "I'm not building on nobody's land but my own." So I pulled out there and went with the government. I worked these roads from Highlands to Walhalla sharpening their drill bits and sharpening their picks and mattocks. We also went on the road from here to Hiawassee. Spent my time there. And went to work for a lumber company. I worked twelve years with a lumber company [doing their blacksmith work].

PLATE 115   The cowbell, front view.   PLATE 116   The cowbell, side view.

The Cowbell

A soft steel [makes a good bell]. About a fourteen gauge for a big bell, and about a twelve gauge for a small bell. But you can't get the steel no more. Old shovels make a little bell; they won't make no big bell, but it's too high [tempered] a steel. It's hard to work. You have to heat it to cut it. I'll tell you what makes a mighty good bell. I've had a few of them. You know the lids off these metal barrels that some kind of compound comes in? The lids are a soft steel. I made my wife a nice bell out of it. There wasn't but enough there for just two.

You could make a dozen [bells] and *maybe* two would have about the same sound. It's impossible to make the sounds identical, [but you can change the sound of a bell] after it's all done. If you want a keener sound, you lay it on a certain dolly on the anvil, and flair it out. Stick it in the forge and get it good and warm—doesn't have to be red—and put it on the dolly and roll it around and tap it with a little-bitty hammer. If you've got one too coarse [sounding], lay it on the anvil on its [narrow] side and tap it on the side. Not too much though, just a little. That makes it [sound] cleaner.

People didn't put bells on every animal, just one in a bunch. Sort of the tamest in the bunch, who stays around where you can find it. Not these wild things—they will lead them way off. Take a good tame animal, put it where you could loosen the bell in case it gets too tight, and fasten it if it's too loose. So you pick your leader, and you can watch and see as you go around and check on them. Wherever that bell goes, they are close in hearing distance of it. They won't leave that bell at all. Sometimes you go out and find the one with the bell and the others ain't there, but two or three. And you wait about ten or twenty minutes and there they come sneaking out of the brush.

So many goes in a bunch. Let me say maybe fifteen head of hogs; sheep, they bed up as high as a hundred head, and cattle the same way. Horses is just as crazy in the woods with a mule as they are with another horse. Better. You put one mule in there with a bell, and the horses will follow him till he dies.

If you want to bring your animals in, just catch the one with the bell, and drive it in there and leave the gate open, and later on the others will come on in. The next morning sneak down and close up the gate. Some of the wildest few you ever let your eyes on takes up with that gang. [Say it's hog-killing time.] Tie the old sow with the bell in the lot. The others come that night, and in the morning when you ease down there and pop the gate shut, you got the whole bunch of them in there. Can't get out. We'd usually kill them right there. Just build us a big fire, get about fifteen or sixteen people, and just go ahead and stay there all night. Killed as high as seventy-five head.

When an old cow loses her bell, she's gone if you don't put another bell on her. She dries up, she comes to the gate before she dies. [If you] put another bell on her she'll go back. Get a bell as near as what you had on her. They go by the sound. If the sound ain't right, they won't take up with her, but if the sound's anywhere like the other one on the same cow, they'll soon take right back up with her.

Whenever a bell quits rattling [you can hear them all over the mountains], something's wrong. We'd go see about it. Sometimes a stem comes out, and we'd just put in a new one.

We could tell our bells by hearing them. And we'd know some of the neighbor's bells. Our dogs did too. They knowed our bells. They wouldn't bother at the sound of Billingsly's animals' bells at all. Them dogs, whenever they'd hear our hog bell they'd pull them ears together on top and look toward the sound, and look up at us, as if t'say, "There they are." Even the damn horse that I rode, whenever he'd hear a hog's bell we'd stop, go a little bit and stop, go a little bit and stop. I'd say, "That's not my bell, let's go." So we'd go on.

Will was unable to work in his shop while we were working on this article, but he was able to give us the directions from the comfort of his chair on the front porch. He let us copy one of his patterns, and gave us a bell he had made a year or so ago, so we could make accurate diagrams to go along with the directions.

MATERIALS

Sheet of soft $\frac{1}{16}$"-thick steel, at least $11'' \times 6''$ for body of bell
Soft $\frac{1}{4}$"-diameter steel rod, at least $13''$ long, for collar staple and clapper stem
1 eye bolt, $\frac{1}{4}$"-diameter stock, $\frac{1}{2}$" diameter inside the eye, to hang clapper stem on
1 nut for a $\frac{1}{2}$" bolt to form clapper
2 10 d nails for rivets
Brazing brass wire to seal seams, at least $12''$ long
Borax to use with brass wire

DIRECTIONS

For bell pattern and labeled parts of bell, see Plates 117 and 118.

1. Mark out pattern on steel sheet using a set punch, following the solid lines on the pattern.

2. Cut out the bell using a hammer and cold chisel, or a hammer and cleaver. (Lay a protective layer of metal on the anvil when doing this.)

3. Cut $\frac{1}{4}$" holes for the collar staple, for eye bolt for clapper stem, and for the rivets, using a drill or a flat punch which cuts out a hole.

4. Following the dotted lines on the pattern, mark the cut-out bell for the folds, using a hammer and set punch.

5. To bend in the four sides, hold the cut-out bell with tongs and heat one side in the forge. Place it on the anvil along the line down until it is bent in at a right angle. Do each other side in turn.

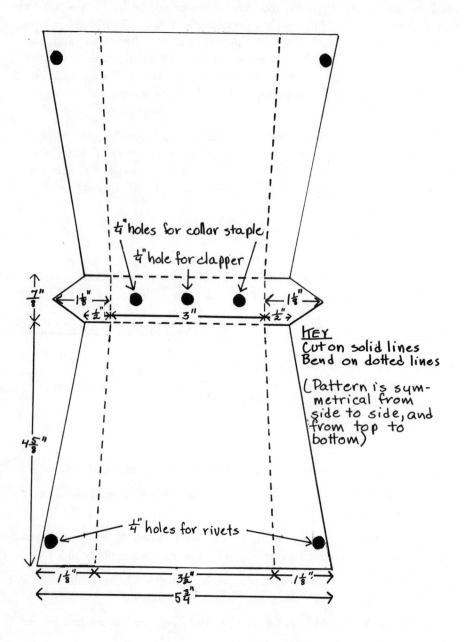

PLATE 117

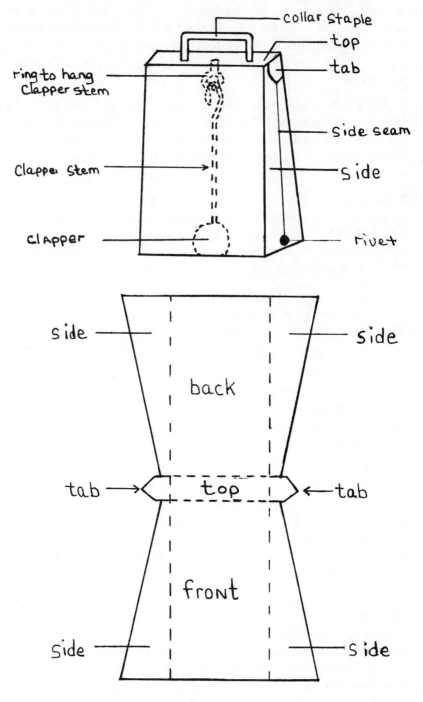

collar staple
top
tab
ring to hang
Clapper stem
Side seam
Side
Clapper Stem
clapper
rivet

side — — Side

back

tab → ← tab

top

front

Side — — Side

PLATE 118

6. Heat the top of the bell, holding it with tongs. Lay it flat on the anvil and place a flat ½" wide strip of metal across it, between the marks made from the dotted lines on the pattern. Hammer the front and back up into an inverted "U" shape, using the ½" wide strip of metal as a guide to bend the steel evenly.

7. Work with the bell until the rivet holes on the sides match up. The side seams should lap about ¼" at the bottom, and just meet at the top. Lay the bell on the anvil horn so that the horn fits inside it and one side seam is on the top surface of the horn, and hammer the seam together. Do the other seam.

8. For each rivet, use a 10 d nail. Put one nail through the two rivet holes on one side of the bell from the inside, so the head of the nail is on the inside. Snip or saw off the shank of the nail on the outside, leaving roughly ¼" protruding. Place bell on the anvil so the nailhead inside rests on the horn, and hammer down the protruding shank to form the rivet. Do the other rivet the same way.

9. Holding the bell with tongs, heat the tabs and hammer each down so it fits snugly against the side of the bell and seals the top of the side seams.

10. Cut two pieces of brass wire, each as long as the side seams inside the bell. Lay one piece along the inside of one seam, and sprinkle several pinches of borax along it. Holding the bell with tongs—carefully so the brass doesn't slip—heat the side of the bell in the forge until the brass and borax foam white, then turn clear. Take it out of the heat carefully and let it cool and harden. Seal the other seam the same way. The bell will not ring properly unless it is completely sealed.

11. Form the collar staple by flattening the 3" midsection of a 4½" length of the ¼"-diameter metal rod to about ⅛" thick (see Plate 119). Leave the ends of the rod round. At points 1" from each end, hammer the ends down at a right angle. Fit the ends of the collar staple into the two holes indicated for it in Plate 117. The ends should fit tightly, and not protrude inside the bell more than ⅛".

12. Cut two sections of the brass wire, each about 1" long, and shape each into a ring. Holding the bell upside down, put one ring over each of the protruding ends of the collar staple on the inside of the bell. Put a pinch of borax around each, and holding the bell upside down with the tongs, heat the top of the bell in the forge until the brass and borax foam white, then turn clear. Remove from heat and let cool and harden upside down. This seals the collar staple holes.

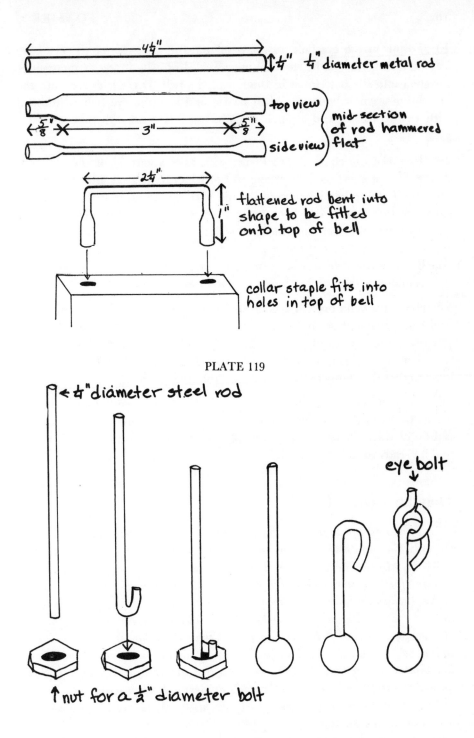

$4\frac{3}{4}''$ $\updownarrow\frac{1}{4}''$ $\frac{1}{4}''$ diameter metal rod

top view ⎫ mid-section
          ⎬ of rod hammered
side view ⎭ flat

$\frac{5}{8}''$ ✕ —— 3'' —— ✕ $\frac{5}{8}''$

$2\frac{1}{4}''$

$1''$ ↕ flattened rod bent into
        shape to be fitted
        onto top of bell

collar staple fits into
holes in top of bell

PLATE 119

← $\frac{1}{4}''$ diameter steel rod

eye bolt
↓

↑ nut for a $\frac{1}{2}''$ diameter bolt

PLATE 120

13. To put in the eye bolt, first saw off most of the stem of the eye bolt, leaving about ³⁄₁₆" of the stem. Using plyers, from the inside fit the stub of the stem into the hole for it in the top of the bell. Drive it tightly into the hole using a small hammer. Then secure and seal the eye bolt to the bell with a ring of brass and a pinch of borax, as was done with the collar staple.

14. To make the clapper (see Plate 120), take about 6" of the ¼" rod, double back a short section on one end of it, and wedge it into the hole in the nut. Holding the plain end of the rod with the tongs, heat the nut in the forge until its barely red. Then bring it to the anvil and hammer the nut gently with a small hammer until it is well rounded. You'll probably have to reheat it several times. (There is a simple grooved dolly made for anvils which makes this process easier, but it is not necessary.) This procedure not only rounds out the nut, but welds it to the rod.

15. Heat and bend over in a hook shape the plain end of the clapper stem at the proper length so that when it hangs from the eye bolt the clapper will just reach the bottom of the bell. Hook it over the eye bolt while it is still hot, then with plyers bend it closed around the eye bolt. Make sure it is done so that the clapper stem can swing from the eye bolt.

16. The bell now needs to be tempered. Holding it with tongs, heat it evenly in the forge by slowly turning it over and over until its hot enough so a drop of water "fries" on it. Then plunge it into the water until it's cool and it's ready to use.

Duggan Ledford

Duggan Ledford was born and raised in Franklin, North Carolina. He is the only blacksmith that we found who still works with horses. Duggan was not born into the blacksmith or farrier (horseshoeing) trade, but started by working for two years in Indiana breaking colts, then working for four years in Kentucky apprenticing to become a farrier. During this time he learned to shoe many different types of horses, including race horses, show horses, and pleasure horses. A farrier is a person who shoes horses, and is a blacksmith, but doesn't do all the other things blacksmiths do. Traditionally, a blacksmith in town did the horseshoeing for his area, but now it is done mostly by farriers who travel to people's homes to do their work.

Duggan travels over a large area to do his work, taking all needed tools with him in his pickup—a combination blacksmith and farrier shop. The back of his truck is filled with tools of the trade, and has a portable forge that can be set up in a short while. Duggan is the only man around this area who earns his living as a full-time farrier. He is considerably younger than the other men we talked to, but like those other men, he is very friendly and enjoys his work.

TERRI WEBB

I got interested in horseshoeing at a stable in Franklin, North Carolina, about 1967. That's where I started riding horses, and naturally, horse shoeing has to do with horses, and you can't get a farrier half the time. The farrier for the stable came out of Easley, South Carolina. And there was always a shoe off or something that needed to be done. Well the barn in

PLATE 121   Duggan Ledford by his pickup truck, which houses all of his horseshoeing tools.

Franklin burned down so that left me in the cold. So I got a job in Indiana breaking horses. Breaking colts. Horse people know each other, connections. So I went up there on a colt job, and it sort of got shaky and fell through. But I stayed in Indiana two years, and while I was there I started doing some shoeing for some old trainers. I shod horses with pads, and did corrective shoeing. The trainers gave me a lot of help and advice.

This guy that was coming out of Lebanon, Kentucky, Bobby Ishep, was shoeing horses, and he had been after me while I was in Indiana. He had been after me the whole two years to help him shoe horses, and I really didn't want to do it. And then I got to thinking; he was shoeing a lot of champion horses. American saddle horses. And so I went to Kentucky with him and started working for him. We shod saddle horses—some of'em world champion horses. We shod saddle horses professionally. On the side we had to shoe other horses. A few [Tennessee] walking horses, and a lot of Standardbred horses, which are trotters and pacers. Race horses. And we shod a few Thoroughbreds for secondary tracks. We didn't shoe any main track race horses, because the boys that shod them had licenses, and stayed on the track, and the horses were on the track and you have to have a license before you can shoe on the track. Bobby was in the process of getting his license, but he had more work than we could do, so no big deal.

[I finally left Kentucky in 1973] to come home. No farrier in the area. You can go about anywhere in the world and make a living shoeing horses. Or trimming horses. Their feet has got to be taken care of, no matter where you go. [Work] comes and goes. During the summer months you're covered up, and then about December and January you slack off, go way down. 'Course you've got to have a little time off. Horses in this country are really scattered out, and you have to go to make it. I try not to [go to too many shows]. You get a lot of mistakes. When you work a show you work for say fifty or one hundred dollars. And all you do is stand there. Okay, when a horse throws a shoe you got to go in there and you got seven minutes to put it on. And you don't know who the farrier was, and maybe he's just throwed it on and then you just can't get it back on. Man feels hard at you then because you couldn't get his shoe back on for him to show. Sometimes the shoe doesn't fit. Now if it was a top-notch show, it would be fine. But some of these little country shows, half the horses are crazy and you can get in trouble.

Accidents happen all the time, getting kicked, bit, or run over. I've been bit several times, but I've never been kicked real bad; oh, I've been kicked around, but not on the body, just on the arms and legs. [I like being a farrier] because you never stay more than a day with a customer, or more than an hour with a horse. You see, it's something new all the time. I've only got one or two places where I have to stay more than one day. It's your own business. It's a demanding business, but everybody's nice to you. All the horse people stick together—they know each other, like one big family. I know a lot of people. There are several people [around here who shoe horses], but not for their whole living. Just after work or part time. As far as I know, I'm the only full-time farrier in this area. Well, a lot of people can nail a shoe on. But here's not a lot of that going on because there's too many racing and walking horses that need pads, and a lot of corrective shoeing.

You go to a person's house and you don't know what kind of horse they've got or anything. And you look at the horse, the way he stands, his bone structure, the whole horse. Now, sometimes I shoe some horses where I just put the shoes on any way I can get them on because they're mean and crazy. They'd be better off if they was dog food. But you want to take pride in your work and fit the shoe just right, fix the angle, and you need a hard level place to shoe a horse really. I mean if you really mean to correct a horse, you have to see him standing, see his foot. I trim horses feet everyday. I could trim a horse's foot about as level as anybody. But I do make mistakes, and unless you really look at it, why he may be standing a little crooked. After you shoe a horse a few times you just know, and you do it automatically without really thinking about it.

A horse needs his feet taken care of starting when he's young. That's the time to trim one and get their legs straight when their bones are still sort of soft. But a lot of horses' feet are not taken care of when they're young, and so you see a lot of horses that wing out, are pigeon-toed, splay-footed, cow-hocked, and you really can't do anything with one after he's four or five years old. Almost all horses at least need trimming. If the horse has got a nice round foot, and you don't ride him much he may not need to be trimmed. He'll grow enough foot to where he walks, and it wears off and he doesn't get sore. He grows as much foot as he wears off when he walks. But if you rode him from here to Clayton and back, [about fourteen miles] on the pavement, he'd wear a lot of foot off. If you rode him on the side of the road, you wouldn't wear near as much off.

The reason they shoe horses in this country is because of the ground. Gravel. And there's no place to ride except on the roads, and the horse's feet just can't take it. The feet wear down more than the horse's feet grows. See, if you had two or three horses and you ride one till he gets sore, well then you put him up and get another one, and you can keep yourself a'going. In Florida, they don't shoe horses, they just trim them. Because of the sand in Florida they don't have to shoe them. But the horse's foot in this country just can't take it. Froze ground is just like pavement. Walking around on it barefooted beats their feet up. 'Course there's a lot of horses that aren't shod. But they're not used either. Some horses need to be shod every six weeks, and some do not. Some horses got good feet. About every two to two-and-a-half months is what I'd say is average. You have to play it by ear, really. Sometimes because of the weather I can't get to a person's house, and the first thing you know you are two to three weeks late and the

horse isn't hurting any more than he was two weeks earlier. I've shod horses
for ten years and every horse is different. You pick up one's foot and shoe it
this way and it won't work, and you'll have to shoe it another way.

A horse has got an angle to its foot [viewed from the side], and it's a
natural angle which is about fifty or fifty-five degrees. I got a foot gauge
that gives you the angle. When you shoe a horse you try to get him as close
to that angle as possible. It's according to his toe length—toe length controls
the angle. You cut his toe short and naturally his angle is going to be
steeper. If his toe's longer, his angle will be more sloping. Makes his foot
longer on the bottom. A club-footed horse will grow all heel and no toe, and
that puts pressure on his tendons. A flat-footed horse is the same way—you
need to trim the horse according to the way his foot grows, for his legs to
be comfortable. And not give out. You need to shoe the two front feet the
same and the two back feet. You see the two feet move together, travel together. There's nothing really different in the front and back feet except
that the front feet are round and the back feet are kind of pointed. They're
not the same shape, and they move different. I try to get the back feet either
the same length as the front ones or shorter. 'Cause they're the ones that
catches the front ones. The front feet have got to be out of the way of the back
feet. If they aren't, the horse will click and pop. [The angle is not the same
on the front and rear.] It's usually steeper on the rear. It's according to the
toe length. And according to the horse. But usually it's steeper. Some horses'
feet won't grow the same on both sides. One side will grow higher, and you
just naturally learn and know to trim it back down level with the other,
maybe just a little lower, so that in about two weeks it'll start catching up,
and by the time he needs shoein' it'll be just a little higher. Most horses do
best if they stand straight. Got to stand straight and their legs got to be
straight. Now you can trim their feet where they will stand straight and go
straight. In other words, you can leave one side higher than the other or put
something on the shoe such as a grab or outside caulk or inside caulk. To
turn the horse's leg so it goes straight. The short part of the horse's foot
comes off the ground first. And the long side last. That's the way you correct them. You just watch the horse go and you can tell which side they
come off of first.

There's different size shoes for different size feet, naturally. I buy shoes.
'Course every blacksmith buys'em. You can buy'em cheaper than you can
make'em. You try to fit the shoe to the foot. If the horse has a round foot,
you round the shoe to fit him. If he's got a pointed toe, you have to point
the shoe to fit the foot. If he's got one flat side or one round side, you just
have to fit it. A horse has got two posts on the back of his heel, where the
bars come in. That's where the shoe's supposed to come to, to fit directly
into his heel. Some people throw'em in too much, some people leave'em

stickin' out too much. But it's supposed to come right into the edge of his coronary band, just as straight as it can come. If he's crooked, it doesn't make any difference how it should fit, it should come right into the bar of his foot. Keg shoes will fit as well as handmade shoes.

The ones I make, I don't make for pleasure horses. I make them to put on with pads, for [Tennessee] walking horses and racking horses. And for shoes with pads you have to put your nail holes farther over on the inside. The store-bought shoes are made just right, the nail holes are perfect for a pleasure horse. Once you've fit the shoe, it goes on right. Some blacksmiths just take and nail the shoe on, then they rasp the foot off to fit the shoe. And that's not right. They'll quick a horse, get the nail hole over too far in the center of his foot. A horse is made to walk on the wall of his foot—not the sole. And that's why that's where the shoe is supposed to go, and there's supposed to be no pressure on the sole of his foot whatsoever. It's going against nature enough to put a shoe on one. A shoe doesn't help a horse at all. Other than protection. On a pleasure horse it's not too bad, because you've only got to shoe over the wall, and mud and water and stuff can still get in there, and keep the foot normal. And the frog is supposed to have pressure on it. It acts as a shock absorber and a blood pumper. In about six weeks when you get ready to shoe a horse again, the mud and the weight of the horse and him walkin' spreads the hoof wall over the shoe. That's one reason you have to reshoe a horse. It's not because the shoe won't stay on. A shoe can stay on maybe six months, but the horse's foot'll be a foot long and he'll be crippled.

A horseshoe nail is made in a wedge shape, wedged from the point to the head, long ways and sideways, and it tightens all the time as you drive it in. If you move that nail around, it works out a hole and it gets loose. I've tried this for an experiment. I just drove the nails all the way in the horse's foot straight and didn't let'em angle out. I let the horse out, and you'd be surprised how long the nails would stay in—and them not even clinched.

Some people don't even rasp the hooves off—they ride them on the pavement until they get their feet wore down so level, then just nail the shoe on. Just butcher it up. There's not too much in nailing one on if you fit your shoe pretty much to the horse's foot. If you go to fitting it in too close, you quick the horse. If you get your nails too far over in the horse's foot, why naturally you're going to get into the red stuff. And that creates trouble, it's just like mashing your fingernail. You can't let the blood or the pus out and that makes the horse have great pain. They will get to where they just won't walk at all. Another reason a horse needs to be shod is because of the gravel. Sometimes a little gravel will go in between the wall and the sole of a horse's foot and it goes upward. And some of the old timers have told me they have seen it come out up in their leg. Said they go all the way up in their leg. I don't know how, but all the ones I've ever seen come out in the coronary and right above the hoof. Then they bust. You see it in just about every horse in this country. Really I don't know how the gravel gets in there, it might work under the shoe on some of them. While you're shoeing one they might get an old shoe nail or something that goes between the sole and the wall and creates pus pockets as it goes. And I've cut several out—you just have to go in there and cut it out through the sole if it isn't too high and you can find it. A low one you can feel, press it and it's soft and the horse will give to it. You just get your knife good and sharp and cut through the sole and let the pressure off. And I have got to the point now where I don't cut it to the blood, just cut it real thin and let it kind of bust on it's own and it don't get infected. Stone bruises, stepping on something hard or sharp, is one way pus pockets come. Anything to irritate their foot can cause a pus pocket.

[If the hoof is not worn or rasped level], it'll cause quarter cracks. If you get a low place on the hoof, when you put the shoe on, and there's a space between the shoe and the hoof, if the shoe don't give, the foot's got to work down to it. And that can cause a crack, and it can pull on the nails. [Badly overgrown hooves] are caused by founder, usually. You see it in a lot of ponies and donkeys, not too much in horses. A horse's foot doesn't get out too long—it will get long, but it usually breaks off 'cause there's so much more weight. A thousand-pound horse puts more wear on his hooves than a five-hundred-pound pony. That's the reason you don't shoe many ponies. On a horse, I can shoe a horse on the front feet and get by, if he's not ridden in too rough a country, and not ridden too much. The weight is just about all up front on a horse. Next horse you see barefooted, you notice his front and back feet. The front feet are always short and raggedy lookin', and the back feet are pretty.

There's a difference in hot shoein' and cold shoein' a horse, [in the way you do it]. Some people want hot shod and some want cold shod. I don't know the difference. Only difference I can see is if you have a bad-footed horse, why that heat, have the shoe hot and put it on and it burns the foot level. They say anyway. The reason the old blacksmiths hot shod'em, because they were making the shoes, and if you cooled the shoe, you couldn't bend it with a big hammer, it'd break because of the temper. And they didn't have time to throw it down in the corner and let it cool, [without it tempering by accident], so they started fittin' it hot, and it was easier to hammer. That's one reason hot shoein' got started. And they'd burn the foot level and nail it on. They did not have time enough. They was gettin' fifty cents a horse, they had to shoe a lot of horses. And they'd furnish the shoes, usually. The burning of the hoof gives it better texture, toughens it, and blends it all in. It helps some horses, and some it don't. If I'm makin' a shoe for a horse, I fit it hot. I don't exactly burn it, but it'll sizzle a little.

The plow-horse days are over really. I still shoe a few work horses, but not many out-in-the-field horses. I trim up a few that they work through the summer months, but none that they *really* work. And now and then someone will have me shoe a horse they got to pull logs out with. Not many farmers shoe their own horses—the ones that know how are too old. They've always used a horse, worked a horse, that's why they got me now. They just use the horses to garden. And you see a lot of mules, and I trim a lot of them, but I don't shoe many mules in this country. They really don't need it. They're not used that much, used about two months out of the year. Don't shoe many, just wagon-train mules where they have been out on the pavement. They've got good feet, tough feet. Tougher than horses. They got a wall that's thick, you could drive nails backwards in their feet. [There are special shoes for mules.] It's a long shoe, you shoe a mule different than you do a horse. A mule is funny. You leave the shoe sticking out in back to hold him up. He don't forge, click and pop like a horse will, because his body's long. Short legs and got a long body. A horse is kinda short bodied and bunched up and their back feet will click with their front feet. Pull their shoes off. It's call forging.

[If a person asks me to shoe a horse in a way that's not good for it], I'll do if if I can't talk them out of it. Your walking horse people are hard on horses, hard on horses' legs. Because it changes the angle when they're shod with pads. And that's bad on their legs—that's the reason you don't see too many old walking horses. Or old Thoroughbreds. 'Course the Thoroughbred people shoe their horses and take the best of care of them, but they just burn them out. The horse just can't last. I think they should race horses at four years old. And let the horse mature. See they break them as yearlings. 'Course a yearling colt Thoroughbred is big, but his bones isn't mature, or his body. They just burn them out. When you start puttin' pads on a horse [as for a racking or a Tennessee walking horse] you take his frog off the ground and he gets no frog pressure, and his foot contracts. I've gone to putting silicone rubber in under the pads, which helps a little, but after a week or two, it doesn't help, because it gets all the flex out of it, and of course the hoof wall grows, which makes the space in there bigger. I used to use recapping rubber, cut little squares and put in there under the pad, and it gave'em frog pressure, but in two or three weeks it flattens out too, and the horses' heels contract. A lot of these walkin' horses you'll see weigh one thousand to fourteen hundred pounds. Big horses. And they'll have a little-bitty foot on'em—a foot 'bout the size of a nine-hundred pound horse. The heel contracts, it don't never open. They've got heel spreaders they put on'em, shaped like a frog, a V-shaped spring. You have to really be stout to put'em in, and it starts opening the foot gradually. But when you nail the pads back on it, why it can't open but so much, because the nails has got it fouled. The only way to do it is to just take the shoe off and put a keg shoe on them, which is a flat pleasure horse shoe with no pads, and turn them out into the pasture and let them stay out during the winter months of the day and get that mud in there and get their foot back to normal. Because those bones in the foot moves. And when they get them pinched up it can cause navicular disease.

If you're going to shoe all types of horses, you need an anvil and you need two rasps—one for the foot and one for the nails. A lot of people don't use two; I do, because they're high, and if you hit a nail with one, it dulls it. And I don't use dull tools, I wouldn't have a dull one. And you need a knife especially for trimmin' horses' feet, and you can buy a straight knife or a curved knife, a right hand or a left hand. And they're made especially for trimming horses' feet. They've got a special thing on the end for trimming the frog. And you need a pair of nippers to pull the shoe off with. You need a pair of ten inch nippers to cut nails with, and a pair especially to trim the feet with, real thin. And you need a rule to measure the toe length and a foot level, a clinch cutter, which cuts the ends of the nails that come through the hoof wall so you can clinch the ends of the nails. The old-timers used a clinching iron to clinch with, to [bend over the nail ends that come through the hoof wall]. Instead, I've got a clinching tool that pulls the nail over after you drive it through the horse's foot. They'd take and hold the clinching iron on the bottom of the nail and peck it down. Which is okay, it's a good way to clinch, but horses don't like you pecking on their foot much, especially up high. It's kind of tender. So I've got a tool that just reaches up and pulls the nail over, which is a new tool that old-timers didn't have. You also need a punch to punch the nail holes out in the shoe 'cause they may be closed up or you need to set'em over in the foot a little bit. Need a forge to heat the shoe with; tongs, couple different sizes of tongs for different thicknesses of steel; two or three punches for different size holes. I bought my forge. It's a regular farrier's blacksmith forge. Some blacksmiths make their forge out of car rims or anything. Now I'm wanting a new truck and a different camper. I'm gonna have a regular horseshoein' truck. I'm going to have a special camper made so the doors open on both sides, and I can have horseshoes on this side and nails and pads on the other side. And my forge will be in permanently. The way it is now, it's not in permanently because my camper is made out of wood.

I make my punches, and I have a handmade hammer I made, and that's about all. 'Course I made my foot stand. You can make hardies for your anvil to cut shoes off with. It goes in the big square hole in the anvil. I can't really make nothing t'speak of, but I *can* shoe horses. Now your racetrack horseshoers, when they're not shoeing they make all kind of tools. They're artists. They can make a pair of foot nippers, and that's really hard. When you put'em together, that's when you throw the curves in, and they'll just fly apart sometimes. And they'll cut a hair. Pull a hair out of your head an' just nip it. I don't know how they do it. You have to have a lot of tools. You can't take a claw hammer and a chisel and make nothing. You got to have tools. That's why I have a truck load of tools, and everyone asks, "What's all that?" And I need all of it sooner or later.

PLATE 122   The completed horseshoe.

The Horseshoe

MATERIALS

1 12″ × 1″ × 5⁄8″ bar of steel

DIRECTIONS

These directions will make a horseshoe in a size three—the type the average farm horse would have used. Two specific tools needed are a creaser to make the creases for the nail heads, and a punch for punching the nail holes.

1. Put one end of the steel bar in the forge and heat it until white hot.

2. Lay the heated end flat on the flat surface of the anvil and draw out the last 2½″ to about 3⅞″, being careful not to round out the bar as you draw it out (see Plate 123). Draw out the other end the same way.

3. To turn back the heel caulk, reheat one end of the bar, lay it on the anvil with 1″ of the heated end over the edge of the anvil, and bend it over at a right angle. Shape the caulk by hammering the top of it until it is 3⁄4″ long (see Plate 123). Do the other caulk the same way.

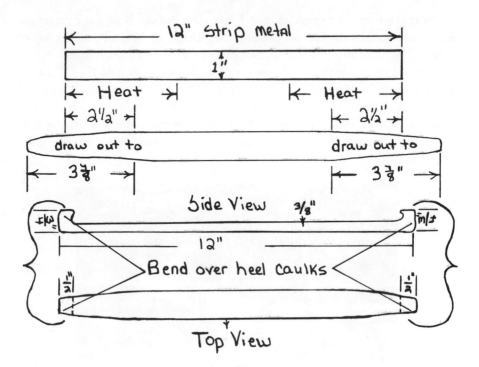

|← ——— 12" strip metal ——— →|

1"

|← Heat →| |← Heat →|
|← 2½" →| |← 2½" →|

draw out to draw out to

|← 3⅞" →| |← 3⅞" →|

Side View   3/8"

|← ——— 12" ——— →|

Bend over heel caulks

1½"   1½"

Top View

PLATE 123

PLATES 124–125 Drawing out the heated end of the steel bar, which will then be turned back to form the heel caulk.

PLATES 126–127 Forming the heel caulk.

4. The first bend the shoe will take is the toe bend. Heat the middle of the bar and stand it straight up on the anvil, holding it with a pair of tongs. Strike the top of the bar to put a slight bend in the middle (see Plate 128).

5. Bend one side of the shoe by heating that half and curving it on the large end of the anvil horn in a shape that corresponds to the one in Plate 128. Do the other side the exact same way. The shoe should be well rounded and symmetrical.

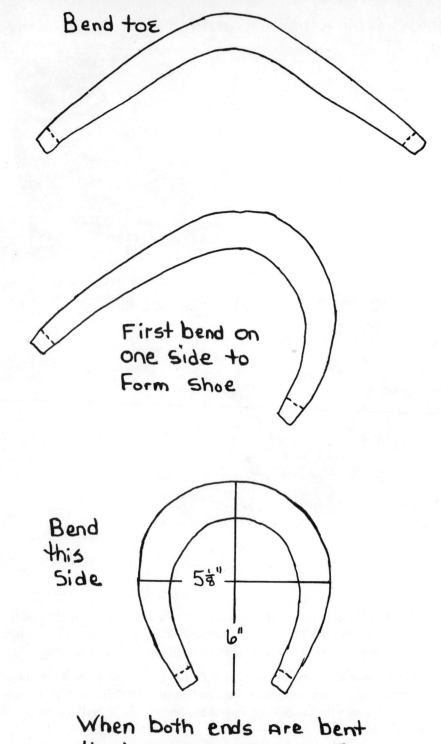

Bend toe

First bend on
one side to
Form shoe

Bend
this
Side

$5\frac{1}{8}''$

$6''$

When both ends are bent
the horseshoe shape is finished.

PLATE 128

PLATE 129 Putting the bend in the toe of the horseshoe.

PLATE 130 Putting the bend in the side of the horseshoe.

6. To put in the creases for the nail heads, first measure and mark where the nail holes are to go on the bottom of the shoe, where the heel caulks are turned down (see Plate 131). Mark the other side of the shoe. (The crease will obliterate these nail hole marks, which will have to be put in again in order to punch the nail holes.)

7. Heat one side of the shoe. Beginning 1″ from the heel caulk, make a ³⁄₁₆″-deep crease with the creaser, centered over the nail-hole marks, following the curve of the shoe. The crease should be about 3″ long, and end ½″ past the last nail-hole mark toward the toe bend (see Plate 131). Do the crease on the other side of the shoe.

Put creases in shoes

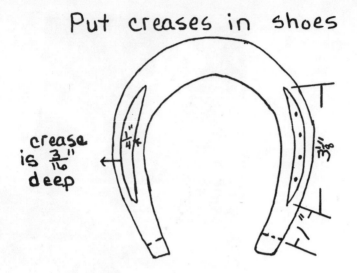

crease is $\frac{3}{16}$" deep

$\frac{1}{4}$"

$3\frac{1}{8}$"

$\frac{1}{8}$"

Punch holes

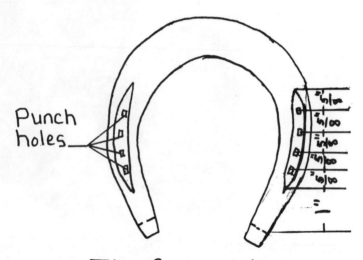

The finished horseshoe

note - When shoe is finished it will have to be shaped to fit.

PLATE 131

PLATE 132 Use a creaser to make the crease where the nail holes will go.

PLATE 133 Use a punch to put the nail holes, four in each side, right in the crease.

PLATE 134 Backpunch the nail holes to open them completely.

8. To put in the nail holes, mark their positions in the crease according to the drawing in Plate 131. Heat one side of the shoe and, centering the punch over each mark in turn, punch the holes all the way through from the creased side. Take care that the punch goes through to the hole in the anvil, and does not strike the anvil itself. Turn the shoe over and punch the holes back through from the other side. This is called backpunching. Do other side of shoe the same way.

9. The shoe is now finished except for minor adjustments in shape that may need to be made because of loss of shape while punching the nail holes. Any touch-up work on rough spots may be done now. The shoe is ready to be fitted to a horse's foot.

The following series of photographs illustrate step by step the shoeing of a pleasure horse. Duggan is using bought shoes, as the shoes he made for this article are not suitable for a pleasure horse. These photographs are not intended to teach anyone to shoe a horse. Never attempt to shoe a horse without the proper training.

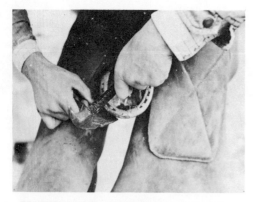

PLATE 135   Loosen the old nail clenches.

PLATE 136   Remove the old shoe.

PLATE 137   Trim the sole.

PLATE 138   Trim the frog.

PLATE 139   Trim the hoof wall.

PLATE 140 Rasp the bottom of the hoof wall smooth.

PLATE 141 Check to see that the hoof wall is level.

PLATE 142 Check the toe length.

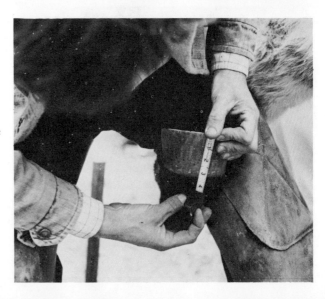

PLATE 143 Rasp away rough edges around old nail holes.

PLATE 144 Rasp smooth the edge of the hoof wall.

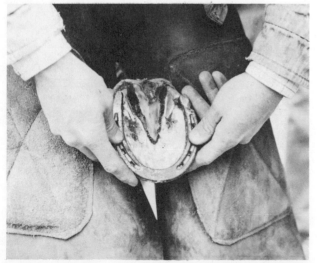

PLATE 145 Check the shape of the shoe against that of the hoof.

PLATE 146 Adjusting the shape of the shoe.

PLATE 147 Check the shape of the shoe once more before nailing it on.

PLATE 148 Backpunch the nail holes in the shoe, and nail the shoe on.

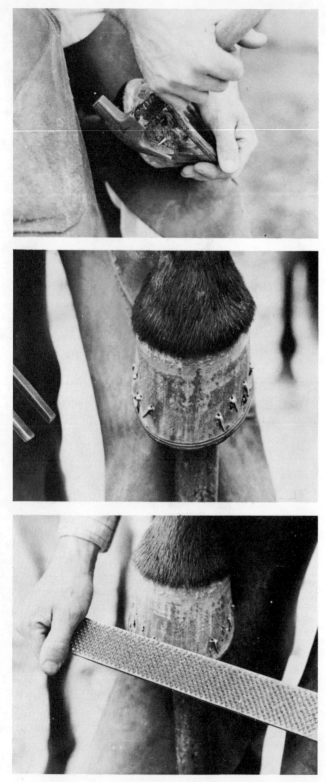

PLATE 149 Pull down excess length of nails.

PLATE 150 The shoe nailed on, with excess length of nails pulled down.

PLATE 151 Cut off excess length of nails.

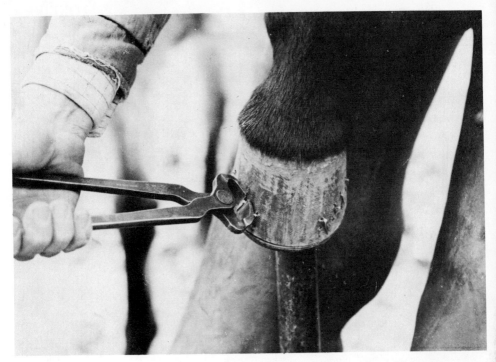

PLATE 152 Score the hoof wall directly under where nails will be clenched.

PLATE 153 Clench the nails.

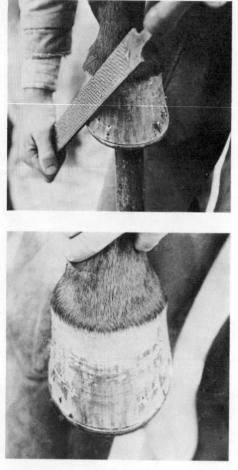

PLATE 154 Rasp off rough edges of the clenched nails.

PLATE 155 The completed job.

Today there are very few horses, mules, or oxen that are used for farming and/or logging. Because Duggan works primarily with show and pleasure horses, we asked Will Zoellner for some additional information on shoeing the different work animals that were traditionally used in this area. During Will's seventy-plus years of blacksmithing, he shoed every imaginable kind of farm horse, logging horse, riding horse, pony, mule, and steer. Here is what he had to tell us.

On the farm horse you have a straight plain shoe, no caulk in front at all, not necessary. Just a dull heel caulk all around for a big farm horse, not over three quarters of an inch long. He don't do nothin' but walk anyhow. If he overreaches and hits—lots of horses do in plowed ground, it's so soft and loose—it's because he steps way down when he steps, and before the

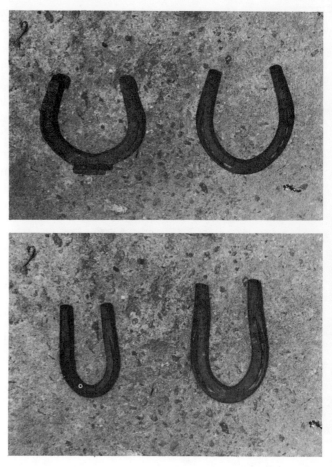

PLATE 156 Left, a machine-made logging horseshoe, with heel caulks turned and toe caulk welded on, and, right, a similar shoe without toe or heel caulk.

PLATE 157 Two different sizes of machine-made mule shoes, without heel or toe caulk.

front foot gets out, the back foot comes and catches that shoe and pulls it off. So you got to shoe him light behind and heavy in front to keep him going in that plowed ground.

A logging horse uses a big, sharp, square toe caulk, because if he gets on a slick place, by gosh, without a caulk, when he pulls, his feet will fly out from under him and he falls. The front-toe caulk goes in the ground and catches a rock or a root and he can pull. The toe caulk has to curve with the circle of the shoe—say the horse weighs a ton, he's got a toe caulk nearly an inch and three-quarters long. He also needs heel caulks, and they work the best coming down the hill. A toe caulk is added to the shoe, but a heel caulk is turned on the shoe.

For riding, you'd have a saddlehorse caulk, a small heel caulk turned over and not too sharp at the bottom. Nothin' on the toe, unless you've got a horse whose hind feet hits the front feet, then you've got to put a weight on in front to get that front foot out of the way.

You can shoe a mule, I guess, ten minutes quicker than you can a horse. He's got a little foot, a little leg, not so much trimming to do. Take a big sharp rasp, give it a lick or two, and it's level. Cut both sides down at the same time. If I had the shoes already shaped, all I'd have to do is turn a heel caulk and open or close the shoe. I liked to shoe mules. The thing is, mules is mean. Usually just put on a heel caulk, because they're usually used for plowing and farm work.

All the oxen I logged with I had to shoe. Oxen you have to put in stocks to shoe. I had one yoke I could shoe by myself, but I'd raised them from calves and played with them, and I could shoe them just like a horse, but

PLATE 158 Machine-made steer shoe, size three.

they were the only ones I ever found. The shoes I'd order from a place in Tennessee. You can make them, but I didn't. You can take a piece of four-inch-wide wagon tire and cut out the pieces and put the nail holes in there with a punch that's narrow at the point and wide at the top so you don't have to put that crease in there. The nail head would wear down, and still have plenty of shoulder to keep the shoe on. And they have a toe caulk. There are two pieces to each shoe because an ox has a split hoof, and you put in fourteen nails to the foot. You don't have to use them all. Steers don't wear'em out as fast as a horse does. You can leave them on a steer for three months. The foot gets so big he can't walk anywhere, you have to take them off, trim the feet, and put'em back, or put new shoes on. You can't bend cattle shoes—pot metal, they're hard. The cattle shoes come in different sizes, just like horseshoes.

A steer has a softer foot in the heel than the horse has. On steers you use little-bitty nails, smaller than you'd use with a horse. Shoeing cattle, you put'em in the stocks, and it's not near as big a job as a man thinks it is. They raise hell when you first do it, but after you shoe'em three times it don't bother'em. They get used to it. They know it takes so long, and they wait for you to get through so they can get out of there. The first time you do cattle in the stocks they usually lay down. And when they lay down they're too low, you can't work on'em. You have a strap you can put under him, and you have to roll him up and fasten him there. He can't back, he can't go forward, and they get so after a while they don't try to lay down. Don't do no *good* to lay down. The more you shoe'em, the easier they are. But don't quick'em. If you ever quick'em, you've got trouble. A steer takes a little longer to shoe than a horse. You can't cut none on his feet, you have to rasp him. His toes are limber. There's very little trimming to do on a steer's feet.

GUNMAKING

HISTORICAL OVERVIEW

There are those who argue that of all the types of craftsmen who were at work in the mountains during the days of self-sufficiency, those most challenged were the gunsmiths. And the best of the gunsmiths were, arguably, the best craftsmen, overall, in any community in which they worked. The production of few other items was more challenging, for the gunsmith was required to be a master in toolmaking, ironworking and blacksmithing, and the high arts of fine relief sculpture and inlay. The best pieces are priceless and so fearfully guarded that many collectors refuse to publicize the fact that they collect at all for fear of theft. These finest pieces work as intricately as Swiss watches, are as rugged and durable as Rolls-Royces, and are comparable artistically to fine paintings, music, or sculpture. Interestingly, they have the additional dimension that comes from their being, almost paradoxically, instruments of death—the tools by which enemies were slain, the frontier was conquered and tamed, and the table was filled with game. The fascination they hold for us is undeniable. Works of art that kill.

The subject is extraordinarily complex. So complex, in fact, that when I asked Wallace Gusler, former master gunsmith at Colonial Williamsburg, for the name of a history that I could trust, his reply was simple and to the point: "There is none." Every history written is accused of inaccuracy; every theory presented meets opponents and detractors. It seems almost impossible to pin down movements and schools and trends with real assurance, largely because of the frequent absence of signed, dated pieces that can be confirmed and accepted as prototypes. Gaping holes stud the logical, tidy continuum of design and development that some yearn for, and those holes get filled by hypotheses that are immediately contradicted. Others argue that there is no logical, tidy continuum anyway—that trends began independent of each other. And so the arguments continue.

Thus, you are going to have to forgive us if we tread carefully through this mine field as we try to put the gunmakers you are about to meet in some kind of historical context. For those of you who are interested in pursuing the subjects in greater depth, we have provided a Bibliography of the most often recommended books—and we wish you well.

The earliest and most widely used and available guns in our Appalachian settlements were the muzzle-loaded, flintlock longrifles. The term "rifle" itself is vital here, for it signifies a dramatic development in arms. It means a gun the barrel of which has a bore that has been "rifled." In other words, a series of shallow, spiral grooves have been cut into the inside walls of the barrel for its entire length to force the bullet to spin as it exits, thus giving it an extra stability and accuracy that the earlier "smooth bore" muskets and fowling pieces could not give. The best estimates, based on the existing evidence, are that the first rifle was a late-fifteenth-century German piece made for Maximilian and now owned by the Smithsonian. It is pictured in Blackmore's *Guns and Rifles of the World*.

The version of the rifle that came to America with the pre-Revolutionary War settlers was, basically, the result of the melding of two earlier design traditions. One was German. Several pieces from the second quarter of the sixteenth century survive. One is detailed in *Decorated Firearms* on page 108 (see Bibliography). It is a .50-caliber carbine with a wheel-lock ignition system (similar to the principle used by Zippo-type cigarette lighters) for providing the spark necessary to ignite the powder, a 25⅞-inch octagonal barrel, a full cherry stock, staghorn buttplate with a sliding horn panel covering a hole for the storage of several balls, a pronounced cheekpiece (as the gun was fired offhand with the stock against the cheek and not against the shoulder), and heavily inlaid and decorated as were most arms. The decoration of arms, in fact, is one of the earliest decorative traditions.

The second was French. Guns from this tradition were shoulder-stock (made to be fired while the gun rested against the shoulder) fowling pieces with a flintlock ignition system. Though historians disagree as to who designed the first flintlock (some attribute it to Marin le Bourgeois, who died in 1634, but this cannot be substantiated to the satisfaction of the most careful historians), all agree that it was a French innovation that appeared in the early 1600s and was definitely in use by the third decade of the seventeenth century (see *Decorated Firearms*, pages 3–6). Part of the credit must also go to Louis XIII who, through his extensive patronage of the Lorraine and Lisieux schools of French gunmaking, helped foster a climate in which such innovation could take place and focused it in the capital city. From Paris, the flintlock-ignition system spread rapidly through Europe and into England during the seventeenth century.

The wedding between the French and German traditions that is so vital to our early rifles took place when German gunsmiths adopted the French flintlock-ignition system and fowling-piece buttstock and produced a rifle made to be fired while the stock rested against the shoulder. An early example, dated about 1735 and described on pages 158–59 of *Decorated Firearms* has a bulky, rather inflated stock, a butt-trap with a sliding wooden cover, an octagonal .57-caliber barrel twenty-seven and a half inches in length that flares at the muzzle, is rifled with seven grooves, has an iron-bar rear sight and a simple brass blade for a front sight, double-set triggers, three ramrod pipes, a horn cap at the end of the forestock and relief carving on the stock itself. Significantly, the pronounced cheek stock has been modified into a smaller cheekpiece, and the flat sideplate for the lock (as opposed to the concave sideplate that disappeared in France about 1690) has been adopted. Also important is the relief-carved border around the patch box—a border in outline so similar to the brass plates that border early American rifle patch boxes that most historians regard it as the precursor of this American characteristic. This type of rifle is known as a Jäeger.

Jäegers arrived with the German and Palatine Swiss immigration to this country about 1709. These immigrants, along with a number of French Huguenots, settled in the Lancaster Valley section of Pennsylvania in a settlement named Hickory Town—later renamed Gibson's Pasture, and then, around 1729, renamed Lancaster. Others established settlements that later became the cities of Reading and Bethlehem. Lancaster, Pennsylvania, however, became the largest inland town in pre-revolutionary America. Since a high percentage of its population was German, and since a number of rifles were made there, that part of the country had a powerful influence on the development of the American longrifle. So powerful, in fact, that some historians make the facile assumption that the Lancaster County rifles were the most important influence of all. Men like Wallace Gusler quickly discount this, however, noting correctly that the movement of German gunsmiths throughout the colonies paralleled that of the Scotch Irish, and reminding us that there were Germans in the Shenandoah Valley by 1729; and that Winchester, Virginia, was laid off as a town in the 1740s, and there were Germans there. Gusler also notes that a man could argue that in those areas like Lancaster that were heavily German, the tendency might well be to hold onto a German design tradition more strongly, and resist design innovation longer, than in areas that harbored fringe gunsmiths who might well have been the real cutting edge of the evolution of the American longrifle.

In any case, the longrifle did evolve, combining the German Jäeger characteristics with those of the lighter, more slimly proportioned English fowling pieces, and adding the only purely American innovation: the two-piece, brass, hinged patch box. The result was known as the Kentucky

The Hunters of Kentucky

You gen-tle-men and la-dies fair, who grace this fa-mous cit - y, Just lis - ten if you've time to spare, whilst I re - hearse a dit - ty; And for an op - por - tu - ni - ty, con - ceive your - selves quite luck - y, For 'tis not of - ten here you see a hunt - er from Ken - tuck - y.

Chorus

O Ken - tuck - y, the hunt - ers of Ken - tuck - y; O Ken - tuck - y, the hunt - ers of Ken - tuck - y.

PLATE 159   2. We are a hardy freeborn race, each man to fear a stranger,
Whate'er the game we join the chase, despising toil and danger;
And if a daring foe annoys, whatever his strength and forces,
We'll show him that Kentucky boys are "alligator horses."
O Kentucky, etc.

3. I suppose you've read it in the prints, how Pakenham attempted
    To make old Hickory Jackson wince, but soon his schemes
    repented;
    For we with rifles ready cocked, thought such occasion lucky,
    And soon around the hero flocked the hunters of Kentucky.
    O Kentucky, etc.

4. You've heard I suppose how New Orleans is famed for wealth and
    beauty,
    There's girls of every hue it seems, from snowy white to sooty;
    So Pakenham he made his brag, if he in fight was lucky,
    He'd have their girls and cotton bags in spite of old Kentucky.
    O Kentucky, etc.

5. But Jackson he was wide awake, and wasn't scared at trifles,
    For well he knew what aim we'd take with our Kentucky rifles;
    So he had us down to Cypress swamp, the ground was low and
    mucky,
    There stood John Bull in martial pomp, and here was old
    Kentucky.
    O Kentucky, etc.

6. A bank was raised to hide our breast, not that we thought of
    dying,
    But that we always like to rest, unless the game is flying;
    Behind it stood our little force: none wished it to be greater,
    For every man was half a horse, and half an alligator.
    O Kentucky, etc.

7. They did not let our patience tire before they showed their faces—
    We did not choose to waste our fire, but snugly kept our places;
    And when so near to see them wink, we thought 'twas time to
    stop'em;
    And 'twould have done you good, I think, to see Kentuckians
    drop'em.
    O Kentucky, etc.

8. They found at last 'was vain to fight when lead was all their booty,
    And so they wisely took flight, and left us all our beauty;
    And not if danger e'er annoys, remember what our trade is,
    Just sent for us Kentucky boys, and we'll protect you, ladies.
    O Kentucky, etc.

---

rifle—not because it originated in Kentucky, but because it was called that
in the extremely popular ballad called "The Hunters of Kentucky" written
about the Battle of New Orleans. The name stuck, and now the term is generally accepted as meaning the American flintlock longrifle.

A commonly held notion is that the Kentucky rifle was of age before the
Revolutionary War. Joe Kindig, Jr., in *Thoughts on the Kentucky Rifle in
its Golden Age* (page 30; see Bibliography), says of the gun: " . . . it was
somewhat shorter and the butt was somewhat heavier than on rifles made
twenty or forty years later, but in general, the Kentucky had attained by

PLATE 160 Two rifles made recently by Homer Dangler of Addison, Michigan. At the top is a copy of a rifle made by J. P. Beck, and at the bottom is a copy of a rifle made by John Newcomer. John Philip Beck was a gunsmith of the Lebanon School in Lebanon County, Pennsylvania, from the late 1760s until his death in 1811. John Newcomer was a Lancaster County gunsmith who died in 1782.

this time that character that distinguished it from all other firearms. It had an octagonal barrel forty or more inches long [for greater accuracy], a full graceful stock of plain or slightly curly maple, a brass patch box, other brass mounts, and possibly one or two silver inlays. The patch box was plain with very little engraving and probably no piercings. The relief carving was simple and sparse." Though all this may have happened as early as 1750, Gusler says that there are no surviving dated pieces known that can support this. He states that the earliest known Kentucky-like rifle is one made by John Shrite in 1761 in Reading, Pennsylvania. And this rifle doesn't quite fit the description of the true Kentucky, for although it does have the longer barrel, it retains the German wooden patch box. The earliest known, dated, surviving piece carrying a hinged brass patch box is on a rifle dated 1771 that came out of the James River Basin School in Virginia and not out of Lancaster. And, Gusler continues, its patch box is naïve—obviously evolutionary and made at the beginning of the design's development. Guns with the fully developed brass patch boxes appeared in Pennsylvania by 1774,

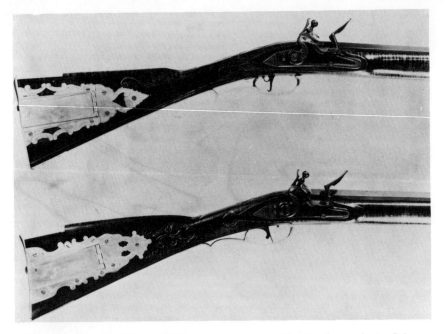

PLATE 161   The same rifles from the opposite side. At the top is the John
Newcomer copy, and at the bottom is the J. P. Beck copy.

and by 1776, they were everywhere. Their geographical distribution by
then, Gusler notes, was incredible. German gunsmiths were all over the
colonies and developing quite independently of any Lancaster domination
over the field.

In the twenty-five or thirty years following the Revolution, Kindig is convinced that the Kentucky was in its Golden Age with its extensive carving
and beautiful inlay and decoration. This period ended with the recession
following the War of 1812.

Another major design landmark appeared in America as early as 1776 in
a rifle owned by William Campbell: the substitution of iron trim (buttplates, sideplates, etc.) for brass and silver. In fact, says Gusler, the roots
of the tradition are probably French, since they continued the use of iron
mounts from the seventeenth to the eighteenth century. But iron mounting
is still regarded by many as an American mountain innovation. At any
rate, its use was in full swing in the late eighteenth and early nineteenth
centuries in southwest Virginia. Why iron? Some say it was a cheaper and
easier technique. But Gusler points to a letter dated 1810 that states
specifically that brass, in fact, is cheaper and more easily cast whereas iron
has to be forged and then filed. Gusler speculates that the reason for iron

mounting is probably tradition. There were three screws, for example, holding the French buttplate in place, and numerous Tennessee iron-mounted rifles have the same construction; two screws identically mounted on the back of the buttplate.

By the late eighteenth and early nineteenth centuries, there was an active gunmaking tradition in our part of the Southern Appalachians. Gunsmiths and their families had migrated down the Shenandoah Valley into Tennessee and North Carolina. Though the connections between the Pennsylvania gunmaking schools and our early settlers were numerous (it is rumored, for example, that one of Daniel Boone's [1735–1820] guns was a Dickert [or Dechard], made by Jacob Dickert [or Dechard], a contemporary of Boone's, in Lancaster County, Pennsylvania; and there were numerous Pennsylvania Dutch settlements in the area such as Burningtown, near present-day Kingsport, Tennessee), a type of longrifle evolved in our mountains that was almost without decoration or inlay. This was probably prompted by the conditions in the area—settlers could not afford to support and subsidize the gunsmith as artist. Some of the best examples of guns of this type are those made by the famous Bean family, which traces its ancestry to the McBain clan in Scotland. William Bean's family was one of the first to settle permanently in the territory that is now Tennessee, and their son, Russell Bean, was, in 1769, the first white child born to permanent settlers in that territory. (The family, by the way, later knew Andrew Jackson well during the time he sat as a judge in Jonesboro, Tennessee. It is said that Jackson once arrested and punished Russell Bean for slicing or biting off one of his baby's ears in a fit of anger caused by his suspicion that the child was illegitimate.)

The Bean rifles are almost devoid of ornamentation or frills, and Gusler hypothesizes that this would almost have to be caused by a lack of wealthy patrons on the frontier and not by ignorance. William Bean, who moved his family from Pittsylvania County, Virginia, would have had to have come in contact—if only through repair jobs—with the stunning workmanship the Simpson (in Staunton, Virginia) and Honaker (in Pulaski County, Virginia) schools were producing in the 1790s. Gusler admits that the Bean rifles, and those like them, have their own integrity, but he regards them as a degenerate style that cannot be revered as a high point in American gunmaking.

In an attempt to find out more about those gunsmiths that predated—and possibly influenced—the mountain gunsmiths working in our area today, we went to Kingsport, Tennessee, to talk to a gun buff and historian, Jim Moran. Here is what he told us:

"Jacob Gross, a German, came to Tennessee to the north fork of the Holston River. His first land deed was for 490 acres in 1790. No doubt his work influenced a lot of these mountain gunsmiths. He made a very good rifle. And the tendency—not only here but everywhere—was for the apprentices to marry into the gunsmith's family. Now that's a link between Douglases, Taylors, Wheelocks, Whitlocks, and Duncans.

"But the Bean clan was the biggest influence. They were English without a doubt, and the earlier ones were contemporaries of Daniel Boone. They were longhunters together. I have a rock in the back yard from Russell Bean's birthplace, which is only a few miles from here, and we know that Daniel Boone spent time there. Later, I'm sure Hacker Martin [see page 263] was influenced by their work. I know some of the farmers would bring old marked rifle barrels in and he would restock them, sometimes without buttplates and with a greasehole instead of a patchbox. I had one Bean rifle that was restocked by a Douglas who married into the clan, and he had a shop right close to Hacker's place. And I've seen four or five other rifles just like it.

"I used to have a Bean rifle that Charles and William Bean made for a J. Bean which could have been Russell's son, James, or his grandson, James or Jessie. And it was dated in the early 1800s, but somebody stole it.

"They evidently had connections with a Robinson and a Donaldson who were ironmongers who came out of Virginia. They had a bloomery over there in Virginia with a trip hammer and all. When they dedicated some bloomery named after Robinson's wife up here, Baxter Bean, who was sixteen at the time, won a foot race there. So there were connections there.

"I think to begin with that the mountain rifles were of smaller caliber than the average Pennsylvania [Kentucky] rifle, they had gotten farther away from the basic German Jäeger rifle influence, which was a big bore.

"It's hard to tell now, however, what the original calibers were because many of them have been freshened out so many times. Every time they were rebored and recut, that made them larger.

"The site of one old Bean shop is out this side of Jonesboro on the present Jonesboro road. There are two mill stones down there in a pasture where this place was, and when I first moved here in 1937, it still had the remnants of the water-powered sawmill there, and that was Robert Bean's shop.

"One of the famous gunsmiths I haven't told you about is Samuel Lafayette Click. Some of his descendants told me that he learned the trade in the penitentiary. He made the nicest half stocks—lock, stock, and barrel—that were ever made in the tri-city area. Even the latter-day Beans weren't making guns like Samuel Lafayette Click. He didn't put his hammers on with a screw. He had them on a spindle with a slotted nut on top. His better-grade later rifles had patent breechplugs. He made most of his barrels which he always marked. He moved up and down the north Holston River. Practically all big farms had a blacksmith shop. He would go and do all their blacksmithing and board with them—stay there maybe a month and usually make them a gun. The quality of the gun reflected the financial background of the people that had it made. He made some real fancy guns, and he did a lot of rework—restocking. I can spot his stocks. He was noted as a hard drinker, and an old timer told me, 'You know, he ruined nearly all the rail fences in Scott County.'

"I said, 'What do you mean?'

"He says, 'Well, he'd always go to Gate City, Virginia, and get drunk on Saturday and come back and get tired and lay down in the middle of the road and build him a fire and burn up the rail fences in the process. And what's more, he carried two converted Army Colts pistols, and if people came by in a wagon and kicked the fire out of the road because their stock was afraid to pass the fire, he'd come up shooting, and they were afraid of him. So they'd tear down a piece of rail fence to go around him.' They had rail fences on both sides of the road. Now that's true. I don't think that's a tall tale at all.

"Another tale on him happened down at Rotherwood below the big elm there. That was an Indian treaty ground. The first Indian treaties were under the big elm. DeSoto mentions the same tree. Well, they'd have shooting matches down there in the bottom below Rotherwood, and one Saturday down there, there was this fellow that owned some of these pegged boots, and he was laying over there passed out against a stump. Somebody bet old Samuel Lafayette, says, 'I'll bet you five dollars—(which would be the same as a hundred now)—that you can't shoot the toe out of old Joe's boot without bringing blood.'

"They had to discuss what shooting the toe out was. It had to be a bullet through both sides of the boot. Well, he hauls off and shoots Joe's boot, and Joe boils up and starts running, and they finally catch him and take his boot off and Joe hadn't lost any blood, so Samuel won his five dollars.

"He was operating, I'd say, about 1870. He tempered the steel for the Clinchfield Railroad. They ran into a geological streak over there that had a lot of silica or something in this limestone, and they weren't doing any good cutting that stone over there. So he tempered all their drill bits. That was before they had hydraulic drills. They just 'stood' around in a ring and whacked them with sledge hammers you know.

"But he was a good ironworker. Some of his pieces had solid wrought iron—not thin wrought iron like the Bean buttplates.

"Now I'm just giving you my opinion of the Smoky Mountain rifle. I do think that if the Beans did not bring the design in here from Pennsylvania, or a stop in Virginia, they did modify it to fit the frontier here. Here are the basic differences:

"One is the tang. The tang came down over the comb of the stock, and

PLATES 162–168 An original Bean rifle, part of a private collection in Tennessee. The hammer was made by Hacker Martin and added later. Note the distinctive trigger-guard, with its rear loop, as well as the distinctive sideplate. At some time the wrist portion of the gun snapped and was later reinforced with a metal sleeve.

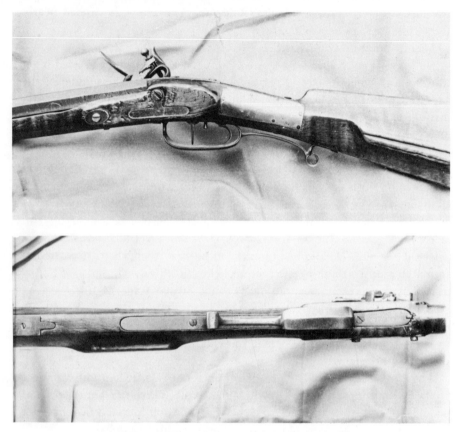

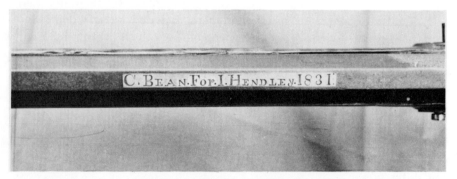

PLATE 163 The triggerguard from the underside.

PLATE 164 The original name plate mounted on the top flat of the barrel.

PLATE 165   The banana patch box and extended pointed bottom butt portion of the stock are typical Bean features.

PLATE 166   Additional Bean features include a long bottom portion of each buttplate.

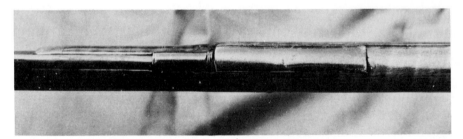

PLATE 167   an extended tab on the rear thimble . . .

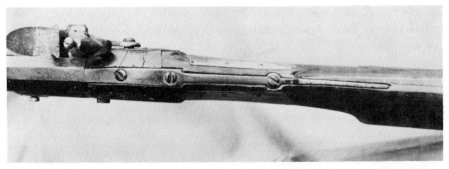

PLATE 168   . . . and a long tang extending up over the comb of the rifle stock.

in one or two cases came all the way to the buttplate. That took care of the reduction in the grip size of the stock. The Pennsylvania was husky in the small of the stock [the wrist], and when that was modified, that long tang braced that up.

"Another is the triggerguard. The two ends of the triggerguards in most cases were stronger. The design is very distinctive. Later smiths started duplicating it, but at one time, I think they all laid off of each other's triggerguards.

"And the patch boxes are different. Paul Fink had a Russell Bean rifle. Russell was a big man and it was the biggest rifle I've ever seen. Paul is one of the foremost historians in this area, and he said he had the history on it and thought it was a Russell Bean rifle. It was brass trimmed and its stock and all was original. And it had the double patch box—hinged in the middle. And the old Bean rifle that I had that was stolen had the double patch box.

"The rifles were not elaborately inlaid except every now and then in their late period they would make one for someone that was silver mining or some rich farmer. But the early ones were simple, and coated with a mixture of carbon black and varnish or linseed oil so that you would get no glint off the wood—no reflection from it. It was better for sighting, and you couldn't be spotted in the woods so easily. The finish was often applied to the entire rifle.

"Another modification that the Beans used a lot was the swedged barrel—the one with the flared end. It gave them better balance, possibly, but it also cut down on the weight in the middle of the barrel. Some of these had a marked flare to them, but most of the flare was eliminated through the years by the policy of cutting an inch off the end of the barrel to make the gun shoot accurately again after it had been worn out over the years by sand from the cleaning rod. They did that instead of reboring and freshening out the barrels, and it ruined a lot of them.

"The Bean rifles, as a general rule, didn't have the silver plate markings on the barrel. Because of the reputation of Bean rifles, many forgeries were made in later years. A rifle made by one of their peers would have the name of one of the numerous Beans engraved on it. Authentic Beans are now rare."

Later gunsmiths like Hacker Martin must have been influenced to some extent by the Bean clan as Martin learned gunmaking from his grandfather, who was a contemporary and neighbor of members of the Bean family.

In the nineteenth century, the Kentucky underwent several other modifications besides the trend toward iron mounting. Earl Lanning, a gunsmith in Waynesville, North Carolina, told us about one of these:

"Sam and Jay Hawkin went to St. Louis. They were Christian Hawkin's sons. This was about 1820. Now Christian Hawkin was a fine Maryland maker—beautiful art rifles—and he worked around Bladensburg, Maryland, where Carl Pippert lives now. His two sons went out to St. Louis, though, which was a jumping-off place for trappers and so forth. They set up their gun shop there, and found that these men needed a different rifle out West because everybody was on horseback, the terrain was much rougher, the game was bigger and harder to kill, and everything was going to see harder service and wear than it had back East. The guns needed to be shorter because of the horseback travel, so people were cutting a foot off the barrels and all. So the Hawkin brothers made a rifle that was shorter, heavier, had terrific strong breeches, and they beefed up the whole wrist portion so that if you had to knock a grizzly bear in the head, you might not break the stock; or if a guy got thrown off a horse some cold morning and the gun fell, it probably wouldn't break. Most of them were fifty-three or -four or -five caliber, and they had a gain twist barrel. It was just the ultimate in a big-game rifle at that time. It had good sights, good triggers, the locks were very good. It was the kind of gun that a guy could go out there in the wilderness and not have to worry about anything malfunctioning. If a grizzly bear got after you, you sure didn't want any problems.

"So the Hawkins were there when the big Rocky Mountain push started, in the 1840s and '50s, back when Bridger and all those boys were going out, and most of them had Hawkin rifles. They did a tremendous trade right there on that river. Now there's so much interest in that history out there with the primitives, and their rendezvous and all, that I'd say 50 per cent of the muzzle loaders made today are Hawkin types. Most of them are poor excuses for the real thing. But if I was going to hunt big game in the Rockies today with a muzzle loader, the Hawkin is the gun I'd want."

Other variations included the switch from flintlock to percussion-cap lock firing systems in the 1820s, and the shortening of the fullstock to halfstock in the 1830s. However, these modifications were overshadowed nationally by the advent of breechloading rifles and then repeaters, which made the muzzle loaders old-fashioned. Robert Watts, a gunsmith we interviewed in Atlanta, Georgia, said, "There was a transition period in the longrifle's history between the time when they were commonplace and the time when they went out of fashion. During that transition period, which continued into the early part of this century, a few die-hards kept using them, and people like Hacker Martin kept making them—barrels and all. These people were important because twenty-five years ago, you couldn't buy Douglas barrel blanks and brass buttplates and all. You could buy Bluegrass locks in

PLATE 169 George Lanning, a gunsmith from Fannin County, Georgia, holding one of his rifles. (Photo courtesy of Earl Lanning.)

most any country hardware store, but they weren't much good. They were cheaply made as replacement locks for shotguns and rifles."

In the 1920s, a tremendous revival of interest in the Kentucky longrifle took place, spurred on by enthusiasts like Red Farris, Walter Kline, Boss Johnson, Bull Ramsey, Bill Large, Joe Kindig, Jr., John G. W. Dillin, and many others whose names will be referred to frequently. Earl Lanning talked with us about the end of the muzzle-loading era, and the revival that is now in full swing—a revival that all the gunmakers we talked to are part of:

"The Sharp's rifle was the ultimate at the end of the black-powder days. It was a cartridge gun, but you didn't have to have any loading facilities for it. You just poured the powder in the case and stuck the bullet in it, and it was a great long-range gun. Then Winchester reared its ugly head with a repeater, and everybody didn't want no damn single shot. They wanted something that would shoot like all get out. And that was the end to all of it right there. The Sharp's rifle went right down the drain. If a guy didn't want a Sharp's, he sure didn't want one of those muzzle-loading things. He wanted a Winchester repeating rifle, and that killed it.

PLATE 170   Samuel Salyers, who built the second house in Norton, Virginia. He was the father of Col. Logan Salyers of Civil War fame. He is holding an early percussion rifle. (Photo courtesy of Alice Lloyd College Photographic Archives, Lyn Adams, and L. F. Addington.)

"So nobody wanted any of that junk up until about 1920 when this muzzle-loading rifle thing got started. Then it started to come back just a little bit, and most of it was centered around southern Ohio and southern Indiana. Of course, the rifles were used here all the time [in the Appalachians] because we were so isolated. They never went out of style here. I can remember when I was a little boy I had an uncle that had a muzzle-loading rifle—the first one I ever shot—and it was the only gun he had. He went squirrel hunting three or four times a year, and he could do the job with that. And then he killed hogs with it. And everybody's uncle had one back when I was a boy, and nobody thought much about it. Hacker [Martin] and a few more were still fooling around making them (but not as part of a revival necessarily). Hacker farmed a little, ran his mill, and piddled with these old guns right on. Bull Ramsey knew old Hacker in the early days, and got him to do some repair work for them back in the earliest days of Friendship, and Sunrise where the first match was held. Hacker would do repair work for them, and build a gun or two for them every once in a while. Bull got a few from this early period, as did several other men.

"Then the thing began to roll. Bill Large started in the late twenties

PLATE 171 Photo of a real estate exchange taken in Big Stone Gap, Virginia, in 1887. Note the percussion rifle one man holds. (Photo courtesy of Alice Lloyd College Photographic Archives, Lyn Adams, and the Filson Club.)

building some barrels (whereas men like Hacker had never stopped—they were among the few still carrying on the tradition, bridges between the two worlds). Hacker was a true gunsmith if there ever was one in the world.

"There are a very few people now still capable of [building one from scratch, including making the barrel]. There's just a tremendous amount of work in forging the barrel. I think Bud Siler [see page 283] and I together could probably do it. We've talked about it, but neither one of us has got enough energy to take it on. Wallace Gusler is a fine gunsmith and a wonderful craftsman, and he's made hand-forged barrels. But it's just not practical. A hand-forged barrel would cost a thousand dollars if made now. I guess people like Gusler would make you one right now if you wanted to get in on the tail end of the list, but I don't know what the bill would be.

"But you don't have to feel guilty anyway about using a factory-made barrel on a gun you might want to make. They were being turned out by manufacturers even back in the eighteenth century. They say that creeks around Lancaster County, Pennsylvania, were so polluted that they

PLATE 172   Uncle Sam Sloane and his homemade percussion half stock, muzzle-loading rifle. Photo taken in the early 1900s. (Courtesy Alice Lloyd Photographic Archives and Lyn Adams.)

PLATE 173   Two men, one with a homemade banjo and the other with a percussion, half-stock rifle. (Photo courtesy Alice Lloyd College and Lyn Adams.)

couldn't water livestock in them from the sediment and stuff from forges where they were making gun barrels. So those makers up there were all buying their barrels along with the imported locks—all that.

"Now that the revival is on, there are gunsmiths around that are making guns that are just as fine as anything being made back then—maybe better. Makers like Carl Pippert [Bladensburg, Maryland] and Wallace Gusler [Williamsburg, Virginia] and John Bivins [Winston-Salem, North Carolina] and Fred Riley [Tampa, Florida] are as good as they come. They're among the best, and what they make could fit right in with the best of the eighteenth-century work. It's revived now, and I don't think it will ever die out again."

THE HANDMADE ERA

Hand-forged Barrels and Locks: Wallace Gusler

Until parts for rifles were generally available to the gunsmiths through manufacturers, they were made by hand by the gunsmith himself. Few traditions illustrate more aptly the consequences of *not* recording traditions than the making of a gun barrel by hand. Wallace Gusler, the nationally-know gunsmith at Williamsburg, talked at length to us about the struggle he had trying to find a single living human who could show him how the barrels were once made. Finally he accumulated enough information to be able to do it himself, but the information did not come from that one elusive human fossil he sought (who apparently no longer existed), but from numerous individuals, each of whom gave him part of what he needed to know. Even today he admits that he is not completely convinced that the method he used at Williamsburg (and later trained gunsmiths there to carry on) is absolutely authentic historically. It was simply the closest he could come.

Making a barrel, of course, begins with a flat bar of wrought iron. The iron used in the Southern Appalachians often came from local bloomeries [see "Ironmaking and Blacksmithing"]. Robert Watts, one of the gunsmiths we interviewed for this book [page 366] said, "Mountain rifles were not all iron mounted, but a large percentage of them were. My theory as to why this is true is that local charcoal iron was much more readily available than brass. There were bloomery forges all over the mountains—even in north Georgia. One I know about was in the Lookout Mountain area. We used to go up there caving. Go up toward Rising Fawn, and you can still find slag left there. In fact, I still have some pieces I picked up there.

"I believe that a lot of the iron used on southern mountain rifles was refined there instead of being shipped in. I recollect reading somewhere that twenty-two pounds of wrought iron is needed to make a six-to-eight pound rifle because of all you lose in heating and reheating and grinding and filing. It would be a lot more economical—particularly if you were going to a remote area in a light wagon—to carry a finished rifle barrel than it would to carry twenty-two pounds of wrought iron."

And Jim Moran, a gun buff and historian we interviewed at length in his home in Kingsport, Tennessee, told us, "The McInturffs were in here in the early times over in Limestone Cove. Hacker Martin told me that the softest gun barrel he had ever freshed out was a McInturff barrel. They made a type of iron there that you could shave with just a drawknife. It was that

PLATE 174   A gunsmith and his apprentice hand-forging a gun barrel. (Drawing by Hershel House.)

soft. They cut the flats on the barrel with a drawknife—scraped them down. They strove to get real carbon-free charcoal iron because it would not shoot slick. It had a good velvety finish, and it held a patch. You didn't get a hop-skip with your ball inside the barrel like you would if you had slick spots in the barrel.

"And Jacob Gross' great-great-grandson told me that every winter he would go to Iron Mountain. That's Laurel Bloomery. He would go up there and stay two or three months working up a bunch of barrels. They made the iron up there. It was locally made. Of course, the guns that were brought in here with the settlers—that's a different proposition. But the ones that were made in here were made of locally produced iron by and large. Only a few gun barrels were brought in, and much of that was during a later period. There was one gunsmith, for example, either a Fairchild or a Douglas, who did a little flat boating. They'd go down the Clinch River on to Chattanooga carrying grain and hams and timber and stuff like that, that was going on down the Mississippi. That was a rough ride through there, and they sometimes took a big loss. But they'd usually leave the boat down there and walk the old Indian war path back bringing two rifle barrels. So some came in that way.

"Men would also take barges down to Knoxville and come back. I interviewed an old man named Jack Wolf about twenty years ago. He was an old man about ninety years old and was still shooting fish with a cedar heart bow. He told me a lot about boating and rafting. Once they had been to Knoxville and were getting ready to come back on the train and ran out of whiskey, and he went and asked the engineer to hold the train for him while he went and got the whiskey, but the engineer wouldn't do it. He was half-drunk then, but he had his tow rope. They carried those ropes back and forth with them since they were handmade and pretty valuable. So he took his tow rope and tied up the wheels of the train so it couldn't move. They put him in jail, and the others came home without him."

Wallace Gusler talked with us at length about how he makes a gun barrel in what he believes to be as close to the traditional method as one can come:

First he heats the flat bar of iron in his forge to the proper temperature for fusing the edges together, and then lays it on his suage block and welds the edges together, starting from the middle, around a long rod called a mandril. A flux made of borax, iron filings, and sand helps prevent the formation of scale and helps increase heat during the tedious operation, which requires hundreds of welding heats to complete. (Wallace told us that during the course of his research, he had found that the flux sometimes used in our mountain was made of mud wasps' nests.) The weld line can either go straight up the barrel, or around it in a spiral, depending on the smith's preference. During this time, the eight flat sides of the barrel (or "flats") are hammered in. They serve no functional purpose—just style.

Next the barrel is annealed— heated to a dull red and buried in the hot coals of the forge to cool slowly—and then bored. In boring, the barrel is set in a sliding carriage, lined up with a chuck, and held in place with wooden wedges. A bit turned by a heavy crank is attached to the chuck, and the barrel is pushed into it as an assistant turns the crank. In the early stages, the bit only hits the high spots inside the barrel, but after twelve or fifteen successively larger bits have been used, the last ones begin to cut the whole length of the barrel. The borings are saved for flux.

Then a square reamer is substituted for the bit, and any roughness left inside the barrel is polished off. Two square corners on the reamer do the cutting; the hickory backing piece simply presses the cutting edges against the inside wall of the barrel. Paper shims placed under the backing piece in-

PLATE 175 Wallace Gusler hammering the heated barrel stock around the mandril. (Photo courtesy of Colonial Williamsburg.)

PLATE 176 Wallace Gusler working at the Williamsburg forge. (Photo courtesy of Colonial Williamsburg.)

PLATE 177 Wallace Gusler hammering the flats into the heated barrel. (Photo courtesy of Colonial Williamsburg.)

crease the overall diameter of the reamer and keep it cutting and polishing effectively. Once this is finished, the outside flats of the barrel are filed and then smoothed and polished with emery. Since three of the flats will be hidden by the stock, only the top five are really polished.

Now the barrel is ready to be rifled. Spiral grooves running the length of the barrel are cut into the inside of the barrel. Their function is to force the lead ball to spin when it is fired, thus stabilizing its flight and giving it greater accuracy. The number of grooves cut into the barrel and the tightness of the twist vary depending on the gunsmith and on the style of the rifle. Since the grooves that are cut mirror the grooves that are cut into the rifling guide itself, a different guide must be used whenever a different groove pattern is desired. For example, if five grooves are to be cut into the barrel, the guide itself will have five parallel spiral grooves evenly spaced around its circumference. If each of the grooves is to make one complete revolution in each four feet of barrel length (a standard muzzle-loading rifle pattern), then each groove on the rifling guide will make one complete revolution of the guide itself in each four feet of length.

The grooves themselves are cut into the barrel with two steel teeth that are set into an iron rod mounted in the end of the rifling guide. Hickory shims behind the teeth—and under which paper shims are regularly added to raise the teeth—make the teeth cut more and more deeply as the job progresses. After the teeth are pulled and then pushed through the barrel once—thus making the cut for the first groove—the teeth are cleaned and the guide rotated to its next position [the neighboring groove] and pulled and pushed through again to begin cutting the second groove. This continues until each groove has been cut once. Then shims are added and the process repeated until the grooves are the desired depth.

Though there are almost no people alive who can demonstrate the traditional method of making barrels, there are a few left in our mountains who are direct, living links to the traditional rifling process. One is a man we found with the help of John Rice Irwin, who runs the Museum of Appalachia in Norris, Tennessee. His name is Charlie Blevins, and his father, who was a farmer and part-time gunsmith and blacksmith, was born near Rugby, Tennessee, in the same area where Charlie still lives. Charlie learned gunsmithing from his father, and though he no longer does it himself, he still owns some of the rifling guides he made while he was active. He ordered all his barrels unrifled and then rifled them himself using five grooves per barrel and one turn in four feet for his muzzle loaders. He claims that once the barrel was set up to be rifled, he could do the whole job in several hours, cutting them about $\frac{1}{32}''$ deep and using hog lard as the lubricant for the cutters.

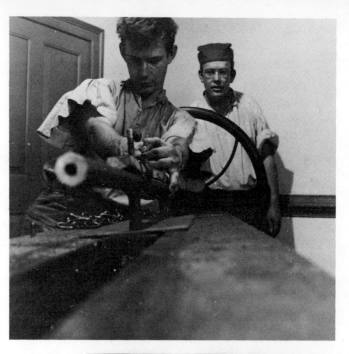

PLATE 178 Wallace Gusler and his assistant boring a barrel. (Photo courtesy of Colonial Williamsburg.)

PLATE 179 The end of the drill bit after one pass through the barrel. (Photo courtesy of Colonial Williamsburg.)

PLATE 180 The end of the square reamer that Charlie Blevins, a Tennessee gunsmith, once used to smooth and polish the insides of his gun barrels before rifling them.

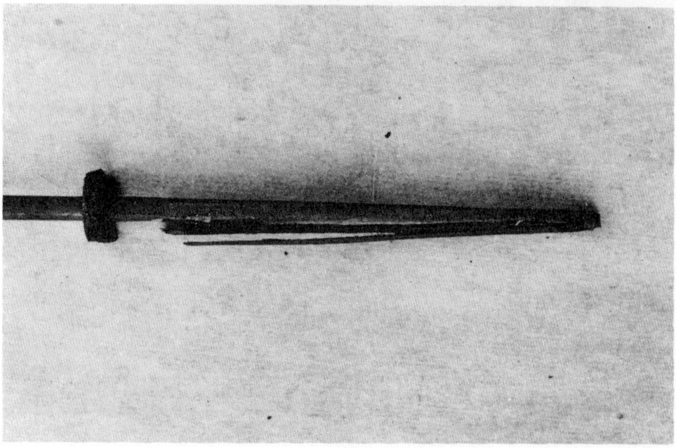

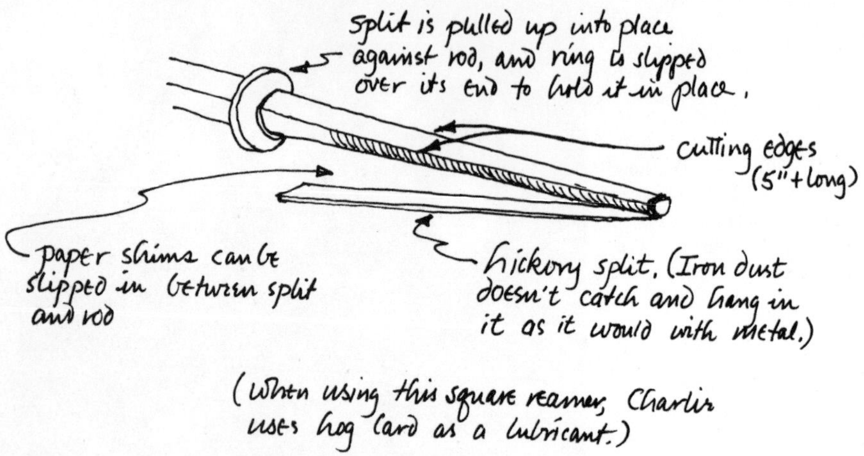

split is pulled up into place
against rod, and ring is slipped
over its end to hold it in place.

cutting edges
(5" + long)

paper shims can be
slipped in between split
and rod

hickory split. (Iron dust
doesn't catch and hang in
it as it would with metal.)

(When using this square reamer, Charlie
uses hog lard as a lubricant.)

PLATE 181   Diagram of a square reamer.

PLATE 182   The cutting teeth, though worn, are still visible in these rifling rods that
Charlie Blevins once used.

PLATE 183   The rod that
cuts the grooves in the
inside of the barrel is
mounted firmly in the end
of the rifling guide.

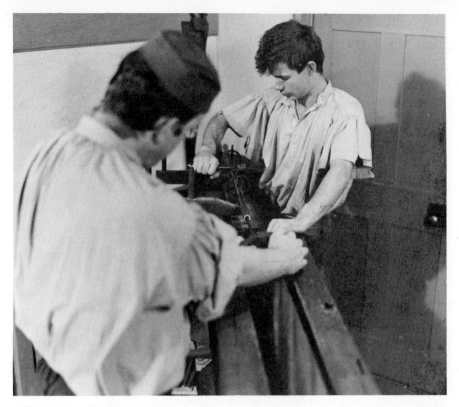

PLATE 184 Wallace Gusler and his assistant preparing to rifle a barrel. (Photo courtesy of Colonial Williamsburg.)

PLATE 185 A gunsmith and his apprentice rifling a barrel. Drawing by Hershel House.

PLATE 186 An old photograph of a mountain woman named Mary Owensby rifling a barrel. (By permission of the Doris Ullman Foundation and Berea College.)

The rifling guides he showed us were made by him out of yellow poplar poles, each spiraled differently depending on the gun being made. He says that a heavy charge of powder and a light ball required a barrel with more twists (the guide he is pictured with here has one turn in 14″), whereas a heavy ball being used with a light charge of powder needed less twist for accuracy.

In making his rifling guides, his first task was always to scribe the initial spiral line onto the pole itself so that he could begin the long whittling process. To do this, he used a trick his father taught him, which is illustrated in Plates 189–91.

To rifle a barrel, Charlie would slide the barrel into the two holes in the wooden blocks at the front of his rifling guide and then wedge the barrel into place from both sides to grip it firmly whether he was pushing or pulling the guide.

PLATE 187   Charlie Blevins with his rifling guide. The guide fits into the long
wooden box in the background. At one end the box has wooden teeth that fit into the
spiral grooves forcing the guide to twist as it is pushed into the barrel or drawn back-
ward through it.

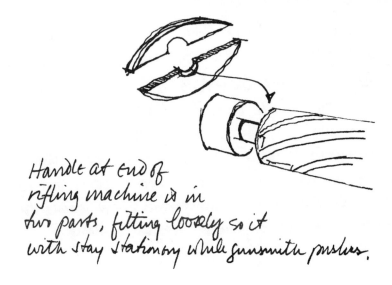

Handle at end of
rifling machine is in
two parts, fitting loosely so it
with stay stationary while gunsmith pushes.

PLATE 188

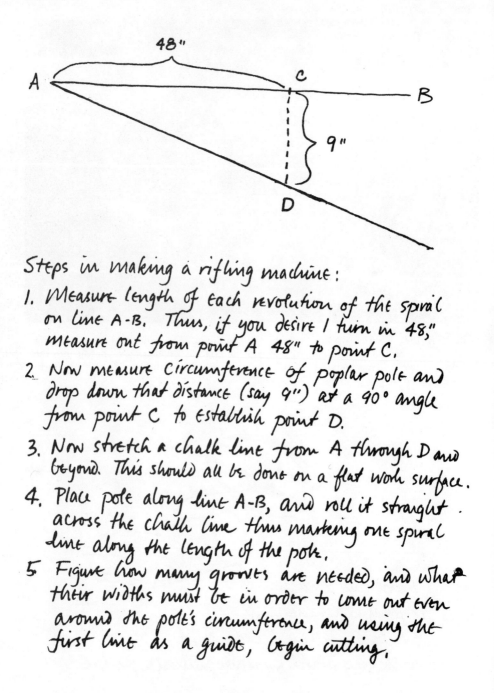

Steps in making a rifling machine:

1. Measure length of each revolution of the spiral on line A-B. Thus, if you desire 1 turn in 48," measure out from point A 48" to point C.

2. Now measure circumference of poplar pole and drop down that distance (say 9") at a 90° angle from point C to establish point D.

3. Now stretch a chalk line from A through D and beyond. This should all be done on a flat work surface.

4. Place pole along line A-B, and roll it straight across the chalk line thus marking one spiral line along the length of the pole.

5. Figure how many grooves are needed, and what their widths must be in order to come out even around the pole's circumference, and using the first line as a guide, begin cutting.

PLATE 189

PLATE 190 Charlie demonstrates Step Three in making the rifling guide.

PLATE 191 Using a paper tube, Charlie shows how he would roll a rifling guide across the chalk line to complete Step Four.

PLATE 192 To begin to rifle a barrel, Charlie pulls the guide back, inserts a barrel into the holes in the two blocks, wedges it into place, and begins to cut. The diameter of the metal rod closely matches the diameter of the barrel's bore. The rods are easily interchangeable depending on the rifle's bore.

PLATE 193 Wallace Gusler drawing out the tang. (Photo courtesy of Colonial Williamsburg.)

After the barrel is rifled, the gunsmith draws out the tang that holds the breechplug end of the barrel in the stock, and then threads both the barrel and its plug to seal up the end of the barrel. This end will contain the powder charge and bullet and is closest to the shooter's face, so it must be threaded tightly and well. After the touch hole is drilled, the barrel is proved by loading the breech end with four times the normal charge and firing it from a distance to make sure it will be able to stand the pressure of the explosions inside it as future shots are fired. If there are any cracks or swells, the barrel is rejected.

PLATE 194   In using his bow drill, Charlie often mounted the piece to be drilled (here held in his left hand) in a vise and then pressed the drill against it with his chest.

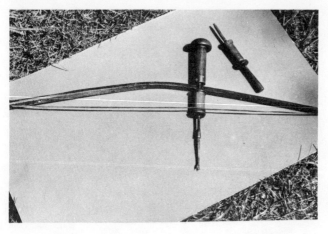

PLATE 195   A beautifully made bow drill used by an early gunsmith.

The touch hole, as well as holes that must be drilled in many of the other iron parts, was drilled by some early gunsmiths with a bow drill. Since more efficient techniques had been developed by the eighteenth century, Wallace Gusler regards the use of this rather primitive tool as an evolutionary throwback—a return to a less efficient past. Nevertheless, as Charlie Blevins demonstrated in Plate 194, he did use the tool frequently, making his bits from old files that he heated, shaped on his anvil, and then quenched in cold lead to temper (the hot bit would slide into the cold lead easily).

When the barrel was completed, the next part to be made was the lock [see pages 283–91]. Each of the pieces of the lock, starting with the cock and the lock plate, had to be forged out of iron and carefully filed and shaped—one piece at a time. The finished springs were tempered by immersing them in lead that had been heated to the boiling point, and then quenching them in linseed oil. Then, to remove some of the resulting brittleness, they would be heated slowly in the forge to soften them. The pieces of the finished lock would be case hardened by placing them in a crucible filled with powdered charcoal, ground charred bone, and charred leather. The crucible would be placed in the forge and the pieces inside heated red hot for five to six hours so they would absorb carbon and be converted into steel. Then the pieces would be quenched in water and the lock would be assembled.

Additional parts, such as the buttplate, sideplate, and triggerguard, were either sand cast from brass or forged from iron. On many rifles from our area, iron mounting was the rule, and so the blacksmiths would make these pieces also.

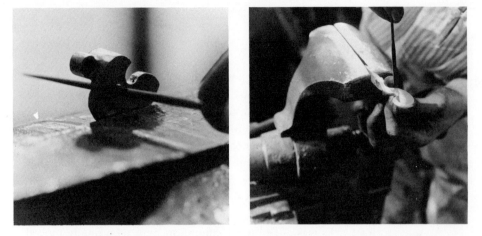

PLATES 196–197   Wallace Gusler filing a lock point. (Photo courtesy of Colonial Williamsburg.)

PLATE 198   Wallace Gusler tempering the lock in a crucible. (Photo courtesy of Colonial Williamsburg.)

Completion of the barrel, lock, and mountings brought the gunsmith to the point where he could begin the actual assembly. This process is described in the Hershel House section, and it remains in many ways much the same as it would have been in the days of hand-forged barrels and locks. The difference, of course, is that Hershel and his contemporaries buy their barrels and locks from mass manufacturers rather than duplicating the processes just described.

Powder, Flint, and Balls

As with barrels and locks, black powder, flints, and lead balls are now widely available to the gun enthusiast through manufacturers. Before this was true, however, all these items had to be made from scratch.

A few people still do it. Carl Darden, for example.

Carl lives on a mining claim in northern California with his wife and three young sons. One of several things that makes them special is that they actually live a self-sufficient existence rather than simply talking about it. Carl's steady stream of letters to us is filled with news of their activities and their dreams.

An ancestor of Carl's was a Tennessee mountain man who finally moved to California. As a teen-ager, Carl visited him often. In one of his letters, he said of this relative, "At night after supper, he'd sit by the big wood heater in the living room and tell me about the Tennessee mountains or about working on the Reading Railroad or on a steamboat on the Big Muddy.

"In those days, he kept an old Civil War musket which he let me hunt with. I thought it was the greatest thing a body could get hold of, and about the crankiest if you didn't keep it clean and well-oiled. . . . Like his boys, I took to the coastal mountains and the redwoods more and more. In my early twenties, I lived with my uncle some and split redwood fence posts for a living, and then I went to work on the county road near Annapolis, California, in sight of the blue Pacific. Lots of mountain men out there in those days. . . . We'd all go squirrel hunting on weekends and talk about muzzle loaders. . . . Finally, I got an old gun barrel for a couple of sawbucks from a gun shop, borrowed a set of files and carving tools, collected some selected scrap iron and a piece of seasoned maple from a nearby canyon, and began to make a muzzle loader bit by bit by hand and with no power tools. After two months of sweat, busted knuckles, dozens of mistakes, and asking gunsmiths so many questions that they started ducking out on me when they saw me coming, I finally put together a nice .25-caliber cap-and-ball rifle. That was right after I married Fran and we were expecting our first youngster. By that time I was a sign painter and was spending every spare minute target shooting and panning for gold on the Yuba River north of Grass Valley.

"After moving around some, I suddenly realized that I could actually do what I've always wanted to do: move into a wilderness place, take my muzzle loaders and my old-time home crafts and just plain live like my ancestors did. I'm sure they would have approved heartily. . . . Now we live full time in California's northern coastal mountains where I and the boys have walked many miles down old abandoned roads through frosty fallen alder leaves listening for the sounds in the crisp morning air that all hunters have listened for since the dawn of time. Even if I don't get a deer or bear, the day is made with an invigorating walk in the tangled closeness of nature. I show the boys edible plants, animal tracks, and what mushrooms are safe to eat. Both Mark and Antone know what greens to pick, what plants to stay away from, and how to find a clean spring to drink from. At home, they get schooling from Mama, and in the forest they learn the lessons of nature from Dad. They may well be the last of a fast-vanishing breed of mountain men.

"The big push today is to get out all the surplus people from the country and mountains into the cities where the government can keep track of everybody and their money. . . . People who are far back in the boondocks may avoid the big roundup. Right now, many wilderness areas in the United States are gated off and locked by the Bureau of Land Management and the U. S. Department of Agriculture. That much has been taken from today's Americans without even a whimper from freedom lovers. No longer can the venturesome soul pick up and head out for parts unknown and cut a living out from nature with ease. And most Americans have been led to believe that such a venture is unproductive and loutish. The few who have managed to do it in recent times have discovered that the job is rough, but the rewards of being self-sufficient are more than worth it in the long run. Caring for livestock and poultry happens to be a full-time, seven-day-a-week chore, and if a body wants to zip back and forth in an automobile and just goof off or work a town job, farming and homesteading should be studiously avoided. But if you want to be totally your own boss, this is a good way—maybe the only way—left to do it."

In his letters, Carl talks not only about the life-style he and his family have chosen, but also about making powder and flints for the muzzle-loading rifles he has made so much a part of that life. The following is a selection of material gleaned from several months' worth of letters to *Foxfire* beginning on April 29, 1977:

"We've begun to pick manzanita berries which Fran boils and makes jelly from the juice. It comes out tasting like crabapple jelly. The manzanita shrub is in the apple and rose family, and it's fruit is about the size and shape of a doby marble. The word manzanita means 'little apple' in Spanish.

"In about two more weeks, the spring gooseberry will be ready to pick, and wild strawberries are next. We've also been digging cattail roots, catching trout, digging clams at low tide, fishing for shoreline sea fish, catching crawdads, hunting quail, gathering about nine different kinds of wild greens, woodland spices, and many other goodies nature has to offer.

"Today I found a big hollow oak tree with bees in it and plan to drop it in a couple of days and recover both honey, and beeswax for candles. Should be enough honey to do us all summer. This summer the wild cherries and plums will come on, then the dewberries, native blackberries, and Himalaya blacks come on ripe, along with salmon berries, thimble berries, huckleberries, black raspberries, juniper berries, and red raspberries.

"I also hunt deer, bear, elk, brush rabbits, raccoon, and ring-necked pheasant, and chukar in season with my flintlock rifle and fowling piece. We've also given up 90 per cent of common grocery store food because it is overprocessed, has only half of its original food value, and is loaded with toxic poisons under the guise of food preservatives.

"Between gathering wild foods and purchasing decent old-time foods, we manage to spend about a half of what most families squander on food. When we prepare to bake bread, I dig out a container of hard wheat and grind our own flour with a hand-cranked grain grinder. If I kill a wild hog, I put up sausages with a stuffer, make salami, pickle and smoke hams and shoulders, and do all the other traditional things that should be done to any self-respecting hog.

"As time goes by, we spend more time purchasing, hunting, and producing good natural foods than ever before. Under close supervision, Mark, who is six, is learning to load and shoot a muzzle-loader rifle at moving and stationary targets so he can begin to hunt at maybe eight years old. The muzzle loader he owns is a .22 with a 40″ octagonal barrel made up as a Tennessee rifle. It's still eight inches longer than he is tall. He should grow that eight inches in the next two years easy. Mark loves to go hunting and fishing, and after his chores and home-schooling, he'll have plenty of time to pursue these two endeavors.

"Antone, his brother, is plain silly about trout fishing and huckleberry picking. Antone asks to go fishing about every three days.

"I know I was asked to talk about black powder and muzzle loaders, but when a fellow gets to talking about such things, to me it automatically includes everyday living and so many other thoughts; particularly such thoughts and feelings as our forefathers experienced back in the times when the muzzle loader was the only kind of gun mankind had.

"I won't ever forget the first powder I ever made and tried shooting in a cap-and-ball rifle. The mixture wasn't in the right proportions and the ball only went half way up the barrel. There I was with a hung bullet! Well, I had to take the barrel off the gun, put it in a vise and unscrew the breech plug and drive the thing on out with a ramrod. I was about as disgusted as a wet monkey.

"Another time I went buck hunting in California's Sierra Nevada Mountains and had left camp with an empty rifle. I hadn't gone more than a

PLATE 199 Drawing by Carl Darden.

quarter of a mile along an old logging road when I heard a sound from around the turn in the road. Easing forward slowly, I could see a nice forked horn buck feeding as I looked through the brush, and he was coming toward me slowly. At the same time it dawned on me that I hadn't loaded the rifle. As quietly and quickly as I could, I began loading the gun. First, I quickly poured a measure of powder down the barrel, then got out a greased patch and ball and proceeded to run the patched ball down on the powder. By this time my hands were shaking. Putting the ramrod back in place, I capped the tube and cocked the hammer. By now the buck was about fifteen feet from me, yet unaware I was a few feet away in a shaky cold sweat. As I slowly raised the rifle to fire, the deer sensed something was wrong and bounded away as my shot went wild. I tell you, I had to sit down and get ahold of myself before I went back to hunting—with a loaded gun this time. So you can get some idea what can happen when hunting with a smoke pole.

"Black powder is and isn't hard to make depending on which end you look at it from. It is a long and tiresome task if you make more than ten pounds at a time.

"Out on the West Coast, as in some southern states, the trend by the government is to prevent its sale with mountains of red tape. Making your own black powder, however, is not unlawful as yet, as far as I know.

"By weight measure, black powder is made of seventy-five parts saltpeter finely ground, fifteen parts charcoal, and ten parts sulfur. All ingredients must be fine ground separately. This can be accomplished with either a mortar and pestle, or with a hand-cranked flour mill. Never mix all three ingredients before grinding unless you want to turn your mill into a deadly grenade, or your mortar into a cannon that can blow off your fingers or even your hand.

"Then the ingredients can be mixed with a small amount of water so the mixture comes out with biscuit-dough consistency. Usually when I mix the ingredients, I add just enough stale urine to make the batch bunch about like biscuit dough. The urine, substituted for water, gives the powder more oxygen and higher performance.

"Flowers of sulfur is ideal for gun powder, and it can be bought in most drug stores in four-ounce bottles or pound cans.

"It can also be found in pure deposits around volcanoes, and in early times, because it was found where molten lava issued from the earth, the sulfur condensed around the rims of the volcanoes was called brimstone.

"Today, in certain places around the world, sulfur is recovered from underground deposits by pumping live steam underground through pipes. The sulfur melts and, being lighter than water, is easily pumped out at another point close by. Then it is pumped into big ships that haul it to industries all over the world. That's why you can buy a hundred-pound sack for about three dollars in most places.

"Saltpeter, the chemical that produces the oxygen for the other ingredients when lit off, can be made by putting urine and manure of any kind in a big cement tank mixed with water until you have about three hundred gallons mixed up. Then you put on a tight lid and let it sit for about ten months. You have to have a drain pipe and valve at the bottom, and a stainless steel filter screen installed beforehand or you'll have one big mess on your hands. At the end of that time, you run the liquid that drains off through ashes into shallow wooden trays lined with plastic sheeting and let them stand for evaporation in the sun. When the water evaporates, potassium nitrate crystals (saltpeter) will form in the bottom of the trays.

"In the old days in cities, most outhouses were fitted with trays or drawers under the seats that could be pulled out from behind the building. They had night-soil collectors who were paid so much every month by the outhouse owners to keep those drawers emptied, and they'd come around with a special wagon into which they dumped the contents. When the wagon was full, it was hauled out to where another fellow bought the contents and dumped it into concrete tanks where the bacteria works it just like yeast works wine or bread dough. Then the liquid was run through ashes into shallow tiled or plain concrete evaporating trays or basins to recover the saltpeter.

"Today, saltpeter can also be bought in most drug stores in bottles or cans.

"Charcoal provides the carbon needed when the powder is lit off. When burning, the carbon assists in making potassium carbonates and carbon sulfates during the one one hundredth of a second that it is burning. Most of this is released at the muzzle of a smoke pole in the form of powder smoke. Some remains in the barrel in the form of fouling and should be swabbed out about every third shot if the shooter wants the round ball to continue to shoot true.

"The charcoal should never be made from hardwood as hardwood has too much ash. Such woods as chinaberry, willow, cottonwood, soft pine with no knots, or redwood and Western cedar make the best grade charcoal. A fifty-five-gallon drum with a snap-on lid and a match-stem-sized hole in the lid set over a fire pit is a good charcoal maker. Take the wood and chip it or cut it into inch chunks and put a bucketful in the drum. Then build a hardwood fire under the drum and when smoke begins to spurt from the vent, light the wood with a match. When the flame goes out, your charcoal is made. Rake the fire out from under the drum, plug the vent with a bit of asbestos fiber or a nail that fits in tightly, and let the drum sit overnight to cook. You can then crush and powder the charcoal with a mortar and pestle, or run it through a hand-cranked grain grinder to a flourlike fineness.

"By the way, just yesterday I took time out and made a batch of powder, and this time, when I mixed the ingredients, I added homemade alder charcoal instead of redwood and improved the powder's performance 100 per cent. I recently bought a tight little sheet-metal heater stove for camp cooking and by accident discovered that getting a load of alder going good and then closing it up tight and dampering it until it went out and turned cold converted the alder into nice pure charcoal.

"When making black powder, never add any other ingredients or explosive powders unless you wish to turn your muzzle loader into a grenade that can kill you or cripple you for life. Keep your black powder stored in steel, airtight cans in a cool, dry place and out of the reach of children. My parents failed to do that, and I've carried powder marks on my face for the last thirty years. A ten-year-old may think he knows what he's doing, but ten years don't give him enough prudence to think many things out ahead of time before he lights that match.

"The nice thing about shooting black powder is that commercial black costs about two cents a round, and homemade about a half-cent a round. The flintlock is by far the cheapest to shoot. It needs no percussion cap primer—just a flint and primer powder. I'm freely giving the formula because any kid who can read can go into about any library and look it up if he wants it bad enough. And I'm not worried about mad bombers because most of them usually use other types of explosives.

"As far as flints go, sharp-eyed hunters using a flintlock will always keep their eyes open for flint, chert, agate, or hard jasper along river gravel bars and stream beds to pick up and bring home.

"Careful and artful chipping with a small hammer [see Plates 200–201] on a big block of wood with an old railroad spike driven into the center as a small anvil can net a hundred or more gun flints per day once the shooter gains experience in chipping stone. These same flints bought from a sporting goods store will cost from forty to seventy-five cents each. When I make them, I sell them to other shooters for ten cents each. Sometimes I trade flints for lead.

"Seems I've always been able to make good rifle flints for my rifle, and I've had a lot of shooters come and trade a lot of things for them. One fellow brought a goose and traded for fifty flints. I've traded for fresh salmon, crabs, coon hides, outdoor magazines, placer gold, fresh garden produce—one fellow even came and played his guitar for two hours in turn for a dozen flints. Best trade I ever made because he sang all my old fa-

PLATE 200   Drawing by Carl Darden.

vorite Appalachian mountain songs. You don't run into a trade like that very often.

"Picking the right stone to chip flints from requires about 50 per cent experience and 50 per cent intuition. Sometimes rejecting a chunk of chert, chalcedony, jasper, or agate turns out to be the right choice, and a flint-knapper may discard more material than he chooses when hunting gravel bars and creek beds for working material. Sometimes just looking can tell you that a stone will not break right to produce 'spalls' that can be worked

ONE WAY OF MAKING GUN FLINTS

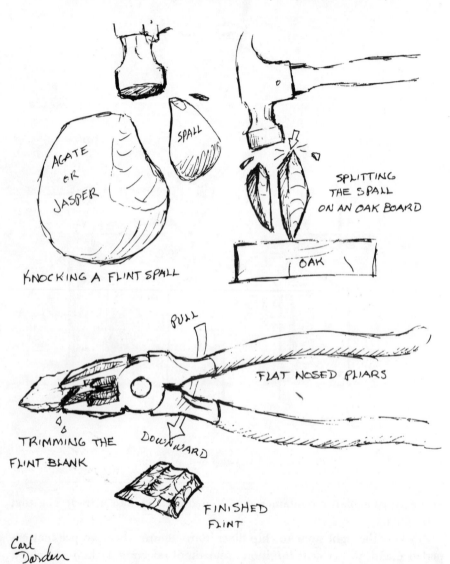

KNOCKING A FLINT SPALL

SPALL

AGATE or JASPER

SPLITTING THE SPALL ON AN OAK BOARD

OAK

PULL

FLAT NOSED PLIARS

TRIMMING THE FLINT BLANK

DOWNWARD

FINISHED FLINT

Carl Darden

PLATE 201   Drawing by Carl Darden.

into flints. I always carry a rock hammer and a gunny sack, and when I see a likely piece of jasper or agate, I chip a corner to see how it holds up. Like as not, the whole stone may shatter making it into leaverite (leave-'er-right there where you found it). When I find a good stone with no flaws or fractures with a hardness of more than six on the scale, I take it with me and keep on adding to what I have until I have about all I can easily carry. When I get this material home, I pile it in the back yard and work on it in my spare time. I remember once I brought home a real pretty translucent green rock. Weighed about twenty pounds. I worked it down into flints real easily, and a friend came by who owns a rock shop up north. He was looking at my flints when he came across the green ones and threw a cat fit. I asked him what was the matter, and he told me I had made flints out of a piece of jade. Didn't make any difference to me as long as they'd fire a flintlock rifle. I just couldn't help his hurt feelings a bit after the deed was done, so I gave him ten of them, and all the broken pieces I couldn't use.

"But it's a nearly dead art, and the man who takes it up, even for a hobby, is perpetuating a trade that once was one of the greatest industries in the civilized world—the last bit of man's stone age.

"It's a scary thought to know that so many people are alive today artificially because of modern inventions. The passing of such free cultures as the fruit tramps and the hobos and the gypsies are seldom thought of, let alone missed or wept over. But it's the same for the tinker, cooper, potter, woodcutter, blacksmith, miller, ferryman, old-time gunsmith, powder miller, horseback mailman, bowmaker, tanner, windmill salesman, general handyman, postmaker, miner, prospector, moonshiner, and a thousand other tradesmen that most parts of our society have forgotten or don't know anything about in this day and age of specializing. As a young man, I was a tinker (I still repair pots and pans rather than throw them away), coopered churns, buckets, and barrels; still make musical instruments, made whiskey and beer, mined placer gold, worked at blacksmithing, worked as a tanner and as a cowboy, explored unvisited places in the wilderness as a wanderer, made furniture, built cabins from materials at hand, made a few wooden water pumps, cooked meals for tunnel crews on a wood stove, made gun flints and arrowheads, smelted my own lead to make round balls from, and a dozen other self-sufficient and unique things few individuals even consider today. The arts and trades are being lost and forgotten at an ever-increasing rate, and if hard times fall upon us in some way or another, our survival rate will be low.

"In this day and age, there are few people who understand the rewards of starting from scratch to build something. When you want a thing badly enough, and you don't want to pay high prices for shoddy work, or you can't get it any other way, making it by hand always turns out to be the most satisfactory way if you're capable of making it and can get the materials. The American pioneer spirit isn't dead yet, but it's been pretty badly abused, misused, and avalanched with promises of the easy and luxurious machine-made life with hidden sacrifices to our self-respect and freedoms.

"And the way our lives are accelerating in these times, if we don't find a sensible way of slowing down, the sum total of mankind will eventually go collectively insane because of the rate we're going.

"I often wondered what was going through a man's mind when his power bill came to $35 a month—particularly when my power bill has never gone over $8 a month for our family of five people, and in the winter at that. Or what went through his mind when his food bill came to $400 in a month and his refrigerator was almost empty the week before payday. Or when he spent $60 for gas that month and $12 for oil and spare auto parts.

"Our move to the wilderness is to be a near-total break with society for as many reasons as both of us can think of. For one thing, our economy is getting ready for a big fall, and if a body has a way to make his own living instead of depending on what industry has to offer, the coming hard times can be weathered.

"The idea is to get by just as primitive and low-priced and with the lowest impact on Mother Nature as possible. Yet, one should be as innovative as possible without falling back on manufactured products that leave an impact on nature, or those requiring service maintenance that the owner can't do himself.

"Right now, we're living at the 1915 level, and regressing bit by bit. When we sell the car and buy a horse and ranch wagon, we will have taken the big step. Then we will be at the least point of impact on the balance of nature. That's one of the reasons we're glad we've decided to gravitate out into a wilderness area. Living close to product convenience tempts us to spend more and consume more.

"We have rejected 90 per cent of today's modern conveniences, including processed, packaged foods, TV, electric lights and appliances, electric tools, and other modern blessings. Our food is provided by our own hands or bought from natural-food stores and prepared from scratch in the kitchen. Brought down a raccoon yesterday that the dogs treed that went twenty pounds. The old muzzle loader roared, and the deed was done. Sure was good eating at supper last night. Gonna make a coonskin cap for Mark as soon as I cure the skin.

"Self-sufficiency and self-support breeds the kind of self-respect and confidence you can't buy off a supermarket shelf."

As the demand for powder grew in the Southern Appalachians, fairly large operations came into being for its manufacture. As Jim Moran told us, "Powder was made in this area. The big powder mill that was around here is gone now—the place burned up and all. But it was on Boozy Creek, and it was operated back in the early 1800s and possibly before by the Hughes family. They were also gunsmiths. They were somehow connected with the blockhouse which was on the Wilderness Road. That was where Boone wintered after his son was bushwhacked on the Wilderness Road. Now that was quite a settlement around there. One winter I went up on Timbertree Branch near the blockhouse site and there were about ten or fifteen cabins around there made out of poplar logs. They were only about twelve feet square—didn't have any windows or anything in them. I think they were the residue of that holdup of immigration when those people got that far and they were afraid to go on. I went back over there about five years ago, but there's none of that left there now.

"But these Hughes, they ground that powder on millstones. I found that out. I know one man who found the old order book for the powder mill. He had it photostated. That mill blew up twice. One time they found shoe tacks in the charcoal. The story was that it was sabotaged. One time it blew a fellow's hand off.

"Willow charcoal is what they used for the powder. And then saltpeter—you know you hear about saltpeter caves. Over around Saltville they've found a lot of the vats and stuff where they leached that out from bat guano. That was done during the Civil War. In fact, they've uncovered one of those caves in the last ten years or so and found the vats still intact in the cave. That's Saltville, which is about thirty-five or forty miles north of here. And the same thing in Big Stone Gap. Powder for the Battle of King's Mountain was made on Powder Branch near Erwin, Tennessee."

Another of these operations was located in Mammoth Cave. Recently, in a remarkable experiment there, potassium nitrate crystals from saltpeter were produced again in the traditional method. Carol A. Hill, one of the co-ordinators for the Saltpeter Research Group, describes the prodecure that was used that day:

"Before the 1870s, caves were the primary source of nitrate used in the manufacture of gunpowder. Saltpeter mining was one of the first major industries of the new frontier, and one of the principle objectives of exploring new territory was to find saltpeter caves. Caves were mined by individuals and also commercially for national defense purposes during the Revolutionary War, the War of 1812, and the Civil War. Many homesteaders in the Virginias, Kentucky, and Tennessee had their own individual saltpeter caves and from them would make their own gunpowder in home-constructed V-vats or 'hoppers.'

PLATES 202–204 The leaching vat or "hopper" was made without nails using a peg-and-hole construction. (Photos by Pete Lindsley.)

PLATE 203

PLATE 204

PLATE 205 Laying the drain trough. A foot adze and hatchet were used to hew the trough. (Photo by Pete Lindsley.)

"Making a V-vat entailed using a peg-and-hole construction. The holes were made with a hand auger (Plate 202); the pegs by whittling down the end of a log with a hatchet and then by trimming with a knife (Plate 203). The frame was then pounded together with a wooden mallet (Plate 204). A froe was used to make the side boards. Bolts of wood that were straight-grained and well-seasoned were the best for this purpose. The glut was used as a wedge to split the log base of the collecting trough. The trough was then hewn out with a foot adze and hatchet. After the hopper was constructed, twigs were laid in the bottom of the vat, and then wheat straw was laid on top of the twigs and along the side boards to help keep the vat from leaking (Plate 206).

"Cave dirt was tested for its nitrate potential by the following procedure: A footprint or mark was made in the dirt and left for twenty-four hours. If the print was scarcely visible by the next day, then the dirt was deemed high in niter. A mattock was used to break up the cave dirt, and a wooden salt-peter paddle was used for digging and scraping (Plate 207). The dirt was removed from the cave in gunny sacks and poured on top of the twigs and straw in the V-vat. Buckets of water were then poured over the saltpeter dirt to leach it of its nitrate or 'mother liquor.' The mother liquor (also sometimes called 'beer') would run down the sides of the V-vat and into the split-log base and out into the collecting trough (Plate 208). A dipper gourd was often used to transfer the mother liquor into a container (Plate 209). This same liquor was poured again and again over the saltpeter dirt because releaching caused more nitrates to be dissolved. According to the old reports, releaching went on until the solution was of sufficient density to float an egg.

"The next step was to combine the mother liquor rich in calcium nitrate with woodashes that contain high amounts of potassium hydroxide. The best woodashes for this purpose were made by burning hardwoods such as oak and hickory. The mother liquor was either poured directly over the woodashes or the woodashes were leached in barrels and the leachate directly combined with the mother liquor. Upon combination, a white haze could be seen (Plate 210), and this white precipitate (calcium hydroxide or 'curds' as it was called) would slowly sink to the bottom of the barrel. If the solution contained an excess of calcium nitrate, the product was termed 'in the grease.' An excess of woodashes produced a condition called 'in the ley.' The woodash leachate was poured into the mother liquor until the white curds could no longer be seen precipitating out of solution. The remaining solution thus contained the still soluble potassium nitrate. This solution was dipped out into an apple-butter kettle (or 'evaporator'), and a fire started under the kettle. Turnip halves were then thrown into the boiling solution to help keep it from foaming and to take up the dirty brown color. Oxblood (or alum) was also added to the boiling liquid and caused the organic mat-

PLATE 206 After the vat was completed, twigs and straw were used to line the bottom of the vat. (Photo by Pete Lindsley.)

PLATE 207 The mining operation consisted of scraping the rocks of loose dirt and carefully stacking them against the cave wall (rear of picture); breaking up the dirt with a mattock; loading the dirt into sacks using a saltpeter paddle (lower left of picture); and carrying the dirt out of the cave by wooden bucket or gunny sack. (Photo by Pete Lindsley.)

PLATES 208–209 The cave dirt was dumped on top of the straw in the V-vat, and water was poured over the dirt (Plate 208), picking up the soluble nitrates from the dirt and then flowing into the catchment trough. The "mother liquor" or "beer" was ladled into a container to be combined with the wood ashes (Plate 209). (Photos by Pete Lindsley.)

PLATE 210 When the leachate of wood ashes is combined with the mother liquor, white curds of calcium hydroxide form as a haze. (Photo by Pete Lindsley.)

PLATE 211 The final product: saltpeter crystals.

PLATE 212 Crystallized potassium nitrate crystals.

ter to rise to the top of the liquid and form a scum which, with continued boiling, was constantly ladled off. After a few hours of boiling, the hot liquor was poured through cheesecloth in order to filter out the remaining scum and organic material. Upon cooling, fine, bitter, needle-shaped crystals of niter (potassium nitrate) formed in the liquor (Plate 211). These crystals were then collected and dried (Plate 212). Potassium-nitrate crystals were far superior to calcium or sodium-nitrate crystals because they are non-deliquescent (do not take up moisture from the air) and, hence, would not make the gunpowder wet and unusable. The nitrate crystals thus obtained had to be further refined and purified. This purification procedure was done either by the individual and homemade into gunpowder, or it was done after the saltpeter crystals were sent to a refinery where the final gunpowder was made."

Lead was also mined in the mountains (one mine was located in Fort Chiswell, Virginia, according to Jim Moran), and the mountains are full of stories about settlers who accidentally stumbled across pure veins of lead back in the hills, carved out chunks with their pocket knife to take home, and then forgot where the veins were when they went back for more. Stories also abound concerning hunters short on lead who would exhaust all efforts to reclaim any lead balls they shot, whether it meant digging them out of a bear's hide or out of a tree trunk.

At any rate, the lead was melted in homemade ladles and then poured into bullet molds in much the same way as demonstrated by both Hershel House and Frank Cochran in later sections of this chapter.

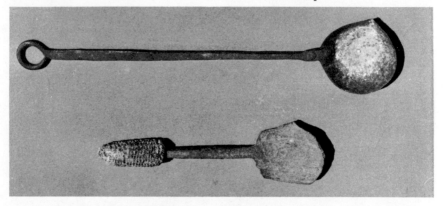

PLATE 213   Two handmade ladles used for making lead balls. The top one is hand forged. The bottom one, with its corn cob handle, was beaten out of pig iron on a buffalo head.

PLATE 214 Two crude handmade ladles for pouring lead bullets.

PLATE 215 A wooden bullet mold at John Rice Irwin's Museum of Appalachia.

WOODEN BULLET MOLD

THIS VERY RARE WOODEN MOLD WAS BOUGHT
FROM GUY BOWERS OF GREENEVILLE -- HE
BOUGHT IT FROM "OLD BLIND JIM CAGLE" OF
GREENE COUNTY, TENNESSEE; "OLD BLIND JIM"
MADE IT.

PLATE 216 A collection of cherries, the heads all hand cut, used for making bullet molds. The two halves of the soapstone or iron molds (the iron was annealed and relatively soft and easy to cut) would be squeezed together in a vise around one of the cherries as the cherry was turned by a brace and bit to create the mold. Often a gunsmith would supply a completed bullet mold and cherry with the finished rifle.

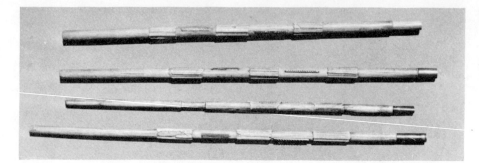

PLATES 217–218   Used "freshing" robs.

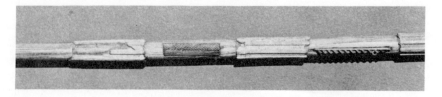

"Freshing Out" Barrels

Through use, the rifling inside a gun barrel got worn to the point where it no longer did its job. Though a barrel can now be freshed out by a number of more modern machine techniques, earlier gunsmiths were not so fortunate. They had two choices. One was to remove the barrel, take their square reamer and smooth out its inside, and rerifle it completely. This would change the caliber of the gun, but it is a method that was common.

Another was to turn out a wooden rod exactly the diameter of the rifle bore, and carve three bands into and around the rod and a groove down its length that connected the three bands together. The rod would then be inserted into the removed barrel, and hot lead was poured down the groove into the barrel itself. The lead filled the three bands, cooled, and then the rod was carefully removed, leaving a print of the inside of the barrel on the three bands.

Using these bands as a guide, two cutting blades made of files would be mounted in the wooden rod. One was wider and would not cut, but would polish the "lands" or raised portions between the rifling and remove the burrs left by the second blade, which recut the grooves one at a time as the rod was shoved through the barrel. When all the grooves had been gone over once or twice and the blade had stopped cutting, a paper shim would be placed under the cutting blade and the process repeated. Hog lard was the lubricant, as before. When the grooves were the desired depth, the barrel would be remounted in the rifle ready to use again.

It is said that Hacker Martin used the chaff of wheat as shims instead of paper. Since he was a miller as well as a gunsmith, this is likely. In early gunsmithing, as with most other mountain survival skills, one used whatever was handy as long as it did the job.

Hacker Martin

In this century, as interest in muzzle-loading rifles soared, collectors, would-be apprentices, and the curious found and celebrated the living fossils—those last links to the knowledge required to make a rifle—barrel and all—by hand. There weren't many of them left, and many of the ones they found then are dead now. One of the best known of these was Hacker Martin, who died in 1970.

The best account we were able to find of Hacker's ancestry and early history was put together by one of his apprentices, Robert Scott Carr, Jr., for the February 1968 issue of *Muzzle Blasts*. He gleaned the information from Hacker himself during the time they worked together. The basic facts are that Hacker's grandparents were of Pennsylvania Dutch stock and were part of that migration into the mountains of Tennessee that took place in the late eighteenth and early nineteenth centuries. Their names were Elbert and Sarah Martin and Abe and Deborah Keefauver, and they settled on Big Limestone Creek near Jonesboro, Tennessee. Davy Crockett was born on this same creek in 1786.

Hacker was born to Mary Ellen and John S. Martin on September 9, 1895, in the house built by Elbert Martin and Abe Keefauver in 1799. He was named after Newt Hacker, a judge in Jonesboro, and much of his early childhood was spent in the shop of his grandfather Martin, a professional blacksmith and gunsmith. Hacker went through the eighth grade, and his grandfather Keefauver wanted him to go on to college, but he decided to stay at home to help on the farm. He stocked his first gun in 1914 using a walnut post from the porch of his grandfather's house. And, like most mountain boys, following a tradition that still continues in full force, he became a fine shot. As Carr says, "Making the half-mile trip to Keebler Crossroad Store with a nickel in his pocket, young Hacker purchased a paper sack of black powder and, with a dime more, bought caps. With these ingredients and a muzzle-loading rifle, he brought home many a rabbit, squirrel, or bird to sweeten the pot. A man never went out to the store or to a neighbor's without taking his rifle. 'Most men would forget their hat before

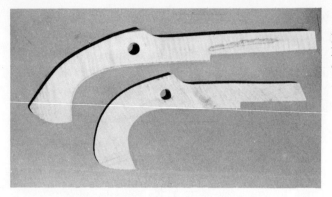

PLATE 219   Two patterns Hacker Martin used in the creation of his pistols.

they forgot their rifle, as one never knew when a fox, squirrel, or rabbit would run across his path,' related Hacker."

In 1917 he served with the Army Air Force in England as an aviation mechanic, and then he did a little shipbuilding in Columbia, Oregon, at the Columbia River Shipbuilding Corporation before returning home, at his father's urging, to east Tennessee, where, in 1922, he married Maude Bacon. Their three children, Raphael, Donis, and Betty Jean, are still living.

In 1940 Hacker and his wife bought the Cedar Creek Mill near Jonesboro, Tennessee. It had been built by Mrs. Martin's great-grandfather, Conrad Bashor, in 1840 near the site of the mill and shop that William Bean had built in 1775. There he began to build his reputation as a miller and gunsmith, moving later in his life to a larger mill in Appomattox, Virginia, where he died on May 22, 1970.

A large portion of the work Hacker did was repair work on fine rifles that were brought to him by some of the most famous collectors and museum directors in the country. But he also made numerous magnificent rifles and pistols himself. In an article for the October 1965 issue of *Muzzle Blasts,* Robert Scott Carr, Jr., tells a story that is revealing—one of hundreds of such stories that circulate about Hacker and make his guns so sought after and treasured: "Those who know Hacker and visit him in his shop admire him as the last of the only true artists America ever produced. The Kentucky riflesmith. Hacker believes to build a rifle like the old timers you must use the same methods and tools they used. Hacker tells of a collector friend of his who was showing his collection off to a famous gun expert. The expert, after looking over the collection, picked up a pistol Hacker had made for a friend only two weeks before. The expert told the owner that it was the finest pistol in his collection, and he proceeded to tell when the pistol was made and in what location. The collector had to take the lock off the

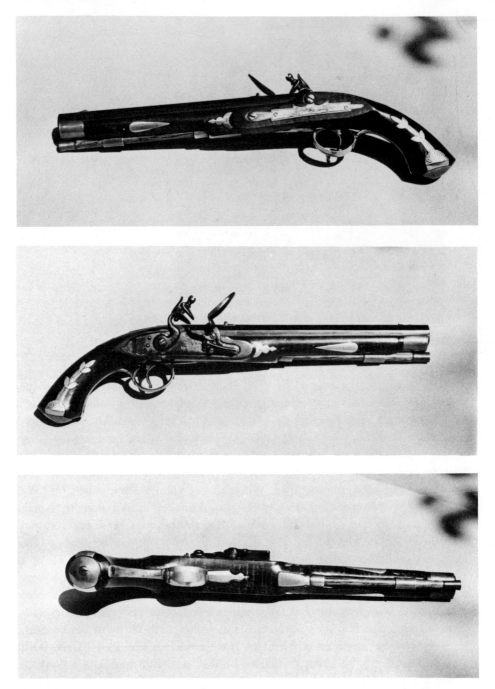

PLATES 220–222   A beautiful pistol, now in a private collection, made by Hacker
Martin about 1952 in his Appomattox shop.

PLATE 223   Gilbert Angel of east Tennessee with a Hacker Martin rifle. (Photo courtesy of Earl Lanning.)

pistol and show the expert the new wood before the expert would believe the pistol was a new one and not made in the late seventeen hundreds."

There are also stories that circulate about Hacker's legendary, quirky personality. The more we found out about him, the more fascinated we became. Since the Jonesboro area is not far from us, we decided to see if we could find some people who once knew Hacker, as well as track down the mill and get some photographs. We got more than we bargained for. We started the search with Earl Lanning, a gunmaker in Waynesville, North Carolina. He had visited Hacker on several occasions, and Hacker had made a rifle for him at one time. Earl produced a number of photographs for us that he had taken, which he invited us to use in this chapter. He also referred us to Garnett Powell in Johnson City, and Jim Moran in Kingsport—both gun buffs and historians. We found Garnett Powell easily, and he and his wife welcomed us into their home, fed us, and spent hours with us talking guns. Hacker's reputation was intact with Garnett. As he said, "Bull Ramsey was a good friend of Hacker and so was Red Farris. Both had told me what a great craftsman he was, and Bull had a fine flintlock rifle made by him.

"Bull and Hacker carried on a very active correspondence. Hacker was always writing Bull about carpetbaggers and damn Yankees who were always visiting him and eating him out of house and home. Letter writing

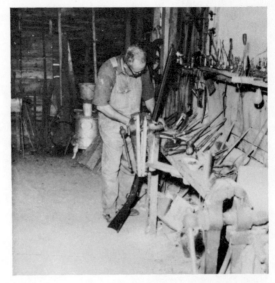

PLATE 224 Hacker Martin in his grist mill/gun shop in Appomattox. (Photo courtesy of Earl Lanning.)

PLATE 225 Hacker Martin holding a miniature flintlock rifle he made for one of his grandsons. (Photo courtesy of Earl Lanning.)

PLATE 226 Hacker Martin priming an Alfred Duncan rifle. Jim Holley stands in the background. (Photo courtesy of Earl Lanning.) Earl believes that the rifle is the same one written about on page 155 of *Lure of the Great Smokies* (see Bibliography).

PLATE 227 Hacker Martin firing the Duncan rifle. (Photo courtesy of Earl Lanning.)

was always a time-consuming bother that never allowed Hacker to get caught up with his ever-increasing gun work. He told Bull in one letter about a bulldog he had that would eat up every visitor or gunbug that dared to come around.

"I finally decided I had to meet this famous gunsmith, and during a spring break in school I went on a trip to visit Hacker. I finally located his mill and drove up in front of his house to be greeted by numerous posted signs—'No Trespassing,' 'Beware of Dog,' 'Trespassers Will Be Shot'— posted all around the yard and gate.

PLATE 228 Hacker Martin with his wife and granddaughter. (Photo courtesy of Garnett Powell.)

"Expecting anything, I cautiously advanced to the front porch and was met by the kindest, most gracious lady who informed me Hacker, her husband, was down in the mill.

"I threaded my way down the path and found a tall, fine-looking man who made me welcome. We became good friends and visited and corresponded until he passed away.

"I never encountered the legendary sour disposition that many said he possessed. It was always a friendly, gracious, and brotherly reception on my visits. Mrs. Martin was also a hospitable and generous hostess while I was in their home.

"Hacker taught me much about the old methods of gunmaking, as he did anyone who would take the time to ask and learn.

PLATE 229 Remains of
the mill and gun shop outside Jonesboro, Tennessee.

"He had little patience with the 'fast-buck boys,' as he called them, and
his time was too precious to waste on them. He always had time to visit
with his friends and people he liked.

"He was the epitome of the old-time gunsmith. The two-hundred-year-
old methods were still practiced by Hacker. He knew the secret arts of forging and tempering. I remember he would praise his young apprentice, Roy
Patterson, in all phases of his work, except Hacker said he never mastered
tempering springs.

"His favorite was a young man in Johnson City, Tennessee, named
Lester Smith. He was taught engraving by Hacker and did some stockmak-
ing for Hacker when he was at Gray Station making guns.

"Lester Smith could inlay metal to wood as perfect as any man alive. He
was a master engraver, and his work in his late years can be found in some
of the best collections in the country. Hacker felt that Lester's work was
exploited by some of the fast-buck boys. I agree with that. Lester never was
paid a decent price for his work. He was too much of a gentleman to pro-
test when things were misrepresented. He died a rather tragic death several
years ago. A few years ago another gunsmith that worked with Lester was
soliciting money to erect a proper headstone at Lester's grave.

"Several people who studied with Hacker are still around, but I've yet to
see any of their work that can compare with the old master. When Hacker
made a gun and put his finish on the metal and stock, you had to sometimes
remove the lock plate to tell it wasn't two hundred years old. Now that's
real art."

Garnett sensed our growing interest and offered that evening to take us
out to Hacker's old mill. We accepted immediately and found not only the
mill, but also his daughter, Betty, and her husband. They showed us

PLATE 230

PLATE 231 The head-
stone on Hacker and his
wife's grave.

through the mill and also gave each one of us one of the original paper sacks [see Plate 230] that Hacker had printed to sell his meal in. Betty also gave us directions to the churchyard in which he is buried, and in the last light of that day, we took photographs of his tombstone.

The next morning, Garnett took us to meet Jim Moran:

"I was introduced to Hacker Martin in 1944 by L. L. Hodges, who was gunsmithing then, and who was possibly related to Hacker through marriage. I went with L.L. to his shop because I had a gun that I brought up here from Dresden, Tennessee, that was discovered in an old cabin up on my grandfather's farm, and I wanted Hacker to repair it. I had been inquiring about gunsmiths in the area [trying to find someone who would fix it], and I had been out in the country and actually seen some of the natives still shooting with hog rifles—particularly down in Hancock County, the only county in Tennessee without a railroad.

"Hacker looked at the piece, kept it, and repaired it. I have a letter from him which he wrote me about the piece later. He had replaced a tube and a nipple for three and a half dollars, and had written saying that the piece was not worth the twenty dollars it would cost to rebore and rifle; it either had a welding flaw or a deep powder bed in it. Hacker had an old crank-operated boring machine, and it would have taken him two or three days to bore it out, so I never had the barrel fixed. I just used it as a wall piece. This gun was a J. and W. H. Mall, Allentown, Pennsylvania, Number 1657 rifle, restocked and remounted by Hilliary Jones of Dresden, Tennessee, 1800.

"I went to Hacker's mill to pick up the gun, and I remember that at the time, he had the top of it shored up with rough timber because it was about to fall in from an overload of at least 600 rifles and several thousand board feet of stocking materials, cherry and curly maple. He traded work for most of those guns with a Mr. Cooper who was one of the early 1900 dealers in Pennsylvania. He would bring his junk guns down to Hacker, and Hacker would repair some of the better ones for him. He sent me up in the loft and said, 'You pick around there and you can find a rifle that we can patch up to shoot a lot cheaper than the twenty dollars it would cost to fix up yours.' Well, I found an E. L. Pancost rifle from the Monongahela River, and it was a full-stock, back-action plains rifle with a nice curly stock. L.L. had bought this same rifle from Hacker and was squirrel hunting when the stock fell apart because of the glue getting warm and melting out. He told me when we were up in the attic that he had brought the gun back, but that the bore was good, and so forth. It was a .44 caliber. So I bought it for ten dollars, patched the stock and recently gave it to my son. That rifle killed the first deer killed legally in the State of Tennessee at Tellico Plains. And that same day I also bought two more for five dollars apiece, and Hacker restored those. In his attic, I remember two fowling pieces that were the silver-inlaid, early Spanish fowling pieces with very dark walnut stocks. I had a feeling for guns then, but I hadn't read enough about them to know what was what. I didn't take those.

"In a later visit, I found a Hudson Valley type, five-foot barrel, Indian musket up there without a buttplate and bought it from Hacker, and then Hacker found out what it was and never would repair it. He took it up to Virginia, and it burned up in his shop up there. But now that was one of the personal characteristics of Hacker. He was generous, and I was always fair with him, but I was a trader and he was a trader. If he thought I got the best of him (which is what he thought in this case) it would take me a year to repair the damage. I think I bought it for six dollars or so. He was selling most of them for five dollars.

"Hacker was notorious for his speed. He was one of the fastest workers I've ever seen. And he was from the land of make-do, of course. His carving tools were made out of old files, and he was a good steel-tempering man. He could make wonderful gun springs. He was always looking for old pitch-forks which he would use. And one thing he especially prized were the ele-vation springs from old horse-drawn road graders. They had some big springs in there to raise the blade, and they had cranks on them, and he was always looking for those things, and I found some for him. He wanted them because of the spring steel.

"And he always had a sense of humor. One of the first visits I made, Hacker was working on some pieces that he said were for the Smithsonian but might have been for Williamsburg. Both pieces were wheel-locks, and both Saxon-type or German-type rifles. One was ivory inlaid, and Hacker was doing some inlay replacing, and I asked him, 'What do you use? Ivory?'

"He said, 'No, just old bone. In fact, this inlay is out of the jaw bone of an ass.' And he would just laugh when he would make a crack like that.

"I remember another little trade I had with Hacker. One thing that ties this area in tightly with the Pennsylvania rifle industry is the lower Palatine German element that came into this section with the early settlers. Most of the gunsmiths in here were of German extraction. And there was a fellow here named Bernie Kiker; lived on the Nolichucky River down there, and he was a blacksmith, I think. He had collected some guns for a man in Washington that had migrated from this section. They were original flintlocks. I tried to run some guns down, but I was always too late because Bernie had been there first. This was about 1944, because Hacker had told me about Kiker first, and I went down to see him. He was an old man—about eighty. He had a little pistol lock that I bought from him—an English lock—and I was going to put it on a rifle. The hammer was missing or something, so I brought it to Hacker. Hacker recognized it at once. See, he had a good memory. He said,. 'I don't know whether I want to repair that or not. You got that from Bernie Kiker, didn't you?'

"And I said, 'Yeah.' Well, he finally repaired it for three dollars and a half. I guess he had probably offered Bernie a dollar for it, and Bernie wouldn't take it, and I bought it for maybe two dollars. One of those things. But it blew over. Hacker and I were basically good friends.

"Hacker was a mountain man in that he would stay away from the women for a long hunt every now and then. His wife and children would stay down at the home place and he'd bach out at the mill, and maybe he'd go home for Sunday dinner, and maybe he wouldn't. And his father was of the same stripe. He was a blacksmith—long beard—and he drove an ox and buggy. He had a brother that was a fiddler and made violins, and Hacker started maybe before his gunsmithing times fiddling and making fiddles and banjos. He made some fine fiddles.

"Later he bought the Isenberg Mill over around Appomattox. A fellow from here went over there and apprenticed and worked with him for a while. His name was Robert Carr, and I have a letter here from Hacker saying, 'My new apprentice is doing fine.' The first time they came back, we had them to dinner a night or two before Christmas, and then they invited us out there and we talked until about twelve o'clock about this and that. I remember we had some cinnamon bread or something exotic in keeping with the mill. We had a nice visit. Then, about two weeks after that, I got this letter from Hacker. Maybe somebody had been kidding him. Mutual friends would. kid Hacker about things and get him upset. But it's a hot letter. It said, 'I don't want any east Tennessee Jew city slicker coming over here with a bunch of brats (I had six children) and staying around my place and eating me out of house and home.' That was the essence of it. Now that shows you that when Hacker got stirred up, he was really stirred up.

"He was working on a piece down there one Saturday, and people kept coming in to get five pounds of meal or something, and they were bothering him, and he made a mis-lick with a hammer and ruined the piece. He was working in front of the window at his bench, and he took that hammer and let out an oath and threw it through the window and took about four panes of glass with it. Well, for the next four or five years, he had a pillow stuck in it. Of course, he could have fixed it. I guess I have some of his habits. I don't get around to fixing things.

"There were several earlier periods in Hacker's life. Once they tried to lock him up for being a deserter in World War I—or draft evader. All the time he was in the Canadian Air Force. Now he didn't want to be drafted, and maybe at that time he had long hair. I've seen one picture of Hacker in his younger days and he had long hair. That was not too different at the time, and yet it *was* depending on where you were. Anyway, he ran away and went to Canada. I heard him say that, and I saw a picture of him standing by an old Jennie. Now maybe he was a mechanic, and maybe that's where he picked up some of his skill. If he wanted to, he could be a pretty good machinist depending on the demand.

"And then during the Depression he was in Florida with an apprentice named DeVault. He was on the Tamiami Trail and had a one-cylinder gas-oline engine, and DeVault told me that it broke a piston ring one time and Hacker made one out of wrought iron, and he brought the old engine back up here with him. He was making tourist-type trade things down there, and DeVault said that for two months, all they lived on was oranges. Hacker couldn't sell anything. Couldn't buy any groceries.

"When he got into making guns, I think that his later decorated rifles were mostly the result of customers who wanted show pieces, and he changed his trend from the simple work to pieces like that because that's where his bread and butter came from.

"Hacker could stripe his ramrods by hand. He'd just get a piece of steel wool with some of that nitric acid—his hands were always eaten up—and he would start down there at one end and just s-h-r-o-o-o-m. And that was it. Grab up a piece of toe sack with linseed oil and go over it real light to kill it.

"Hacker is important for a number of reasons. For one thing, he preserved a lot of the individuality and the spirit of freedom—'if you're right or wrong, by God, do it.' He was full of it.

"But even more important, his greatest influence was gathering the remnants of a past and sort of reintroducing and modernizing the methods enough to make them economical. At a time when these other shops were falling down, he did get around and get up some of the tools, and he must have picked up some of his know-how about making pieces from descendants or old-timers that were still surviving in the neighborhood and told him how they did it. For a while, he did weld his barrels, for example. He lap-welded them, of course—he didn't spool-weld them. But I've seen him make barrels. He used the same sized scelps they made on these forges for wagon tires. It was just about what he wanted. Maybe work it down a little smaller or something like that. Later he went to manufactured barrels a good bit.

"But he never went to machine screws on his serious pieces. He had some screw dies, and I've seen him make screws. He'd take a piece of ⅜″ rod and grind it down to make the screw and the tip. Then he'd saw it off and work out the screw heads.

"But Hacker was here, and Ferris and Cline, they knew it and they came

PLATE 232 Hacker Martin and his apprentice, Lester Smith. (Photo courtesy of Garnett Powell.)

to Hacker. They had the interest and they had the guns, but they had to get back to [people like] Hacker to find some of the background. He was a living fossil, if you want to put it that way. He wouldn't chew Bulldog tobacco, for example. He made his own twist.

"And I've seen Hacker grinding barrels. He had an old grindstone about three feet in diameter and a foot thick rigged up down there on that waterwheel, and he'd grind them on that."

Both men talked at length about an apprentice Hacker had named Lester Smith who stocked and inlaid many guns for Hacker. With Garnett's help, a number of letters Hacker wrote to Lester were made available to us, and portions are excerpted here as being especially revealing of a master gunsmith always under enormous pressure from the outside. The first, dated November 9, 1944, was written during the time one of Hacker's sons was serving in World War II, and Hacker was first approaching Lester about working with him. Portions read:

". . . How is the gun work getting along? I am swamped with it, as usual. Butchered a beef this morning and have a mess on the stove about tender enough to eat right now (eight o'clock P.M.). I wish you were here to help me polish it off! Or, better yet, bring your belongings and come for a six-month stay. There is a plenty of all sorts of old gun work, and in between jobs we could play the fiddle and tell big tales, etc. There is a reasonable amount of cash return, too, although a fellow is not likely to get to be a millionaire at it (not with present income tax). You might be surprised if you knew how much I have saved up in the last two or three years, and I have been sick, more or less, and just dragging along more than half that time. If the gun trade slacks up (it has not slacked for more than seven years), the mill will keep two or three hands over busy if the trade is pushed a little, which is not much trouble to do. Maybe we can make some ar-

PLATES 233–236 A flintlock rifle, now in a private collection, beautifully stocked and inlaid by Lester Smith.

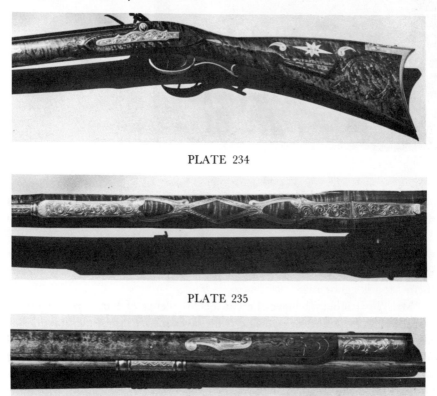

PLATE 234

PLATE 235

PLATE 236 The forestock of the rifle. Note that even the thimble is beautifully carved.

rangement so we can be of some help to each other. I can furnish you with plenty of stocking jobs right now, and any other sort of old-time gun work you might like to try. I see that you are not afraid to tackle any work about a gun, and that is exactly what it takes. I had a good man helping me once, but I could never get him to try any barrel or stock work—he was afraid he would spoil the work and would never tackle these jobs, though I asked him to many times.

PLATE 237 Hacker Martin and Jim Holley with some of Hacker's rifles. (Photo courtesy of Earl Lanning.)

"I would be glad if you can arrange to do a few jobs of stocking on old-time full-stock Kentucky rifles for me sometime about the beginning of this coming year—sooner, of course, if you are able to. If you lack some tools, I will gladly make you some—the right gouges, chisels, saws, etc. speed up the work very much. I need some more myself—just keep putting off making them—too doggone busy.

"Mr. [Jim] Holley believes he can get us plenty of barrel iron (tubing) just the right bore and size outside. This saves most of the time making barrels as I have had to make .45-caliber barrels from .25-caliber blanks which is quite a reaming job and takes as long, often, as rifling six or eight barrels would take. I grind one octagon in an hour or two. I will furnish the buttplate, guards, triggers, locks, and barrels, and the brass for the patch boxes, thimbles, muzzle caps, etc. Also the coin silver for the inlays, and I would be glad to know your price on making a stock (I would furnish curly maple) with, say, twenty-four silver moons, fish, fancy hearts, etc. on the stock, and finished with nitric acid and red shoe dye, like that dandy job on the old rifle you got from me. Boy, how I wish this blasted war was over and I could build a good big brick shop with lights in the roof on the north side and some machines handy to speed up the work.

"You and me, with two or three other men I know of could really amount to something making guns, pistols, etc. If my boy gets back from the war safe, he aims to help make guns, and I know of two other fellows who want to, but are tied to other jobs on account of the war.

"Hoping to hear from you soon, I am Sir, Sincerely Yours, Hacker Martin."

Lester began working with Hacker, even though sick with a disease that would take his life at an early age. Hacker was constantly worried about Lester's health, though he was pushed simultaneously to produce more work. It must have been a difficult time for him. In a letter to Lester dated February 9, 1945, he wrote:

"I've been making some more set triggers, and hope to have a dozen sets done by tomorrow quitting time. Mill work is light—bad weather—but the gun business is rushing, as usual. Heard from Jim Serven out in California. He only wants us to make him up five Kentucky hog rifles—all flintlock. He would furnish old barrels (to be newed inside), part of the buttplates, guards, and stuff, and all we do is do the rest. New stocks, new inlays, new patch boxes, new triggers, new thimbles, new ramrods. Why not make new rifles and be done with it, I ask you? Be worth $400 to $500 to make up the five as he wants them.

"I know where we can sell, for cash, between 200–300 hog rifles. So if you know of anybody you can get to help you make stocks, etc., it would be a good idea to get them started. There will be plenty of guns to fix up, but prices may not continue high after the war ends, or slacks off. Meanwhile, go right ahead on the three rifles you have—but be careful of yourself, and don't go at it too hard or hurt yourself in any way, for a fellow can do only a certain amount of work without harm.

"Say, I forgot to give you a sack of cracked wheat before you left the mill. It might be good for you as it is full of vitamins, minerals, flour, bran, hearts of wheat and so forth—besides, it eats mighty fine mixed with cream and sugar and a small chunk of butter the size of your fist—if you like butter.

"It makes the sick, well, and the well, weller.

"Have you got your shop covered yet? I hope you have it fixed up snug and warm so you can be comfortable while you make guns. I often let my fire get too low, or go out, when I get busy on a gun, which is not good for what ails you, or me.

"Drop me a few lines once in a while and let me know how you are getting along. You won't have to wait for your money when you get the rifles fixed. I may have a little work to do on the locks, etc. after you get through with the stock. That fancy one has to be changed back to flintlock and some work done on the lock of the new one you are fitting up. Keep track of all your work so you can charge enough, for that is the most important part, or so it seems to me!

". . . Ole man Bull Ramsey and Red Farris are wanting a big bunch of

Kentucky flint guns and pistols made. Boy, what a life. Once I wanted all the gun work I could do. Now I want all the help I can get, and can't get it! If it was not for you, I would sure be out of luck.

"Well, I'd better close. It's about bedtime and I am getting cold. Let me know when you get the guns ready. Best of luck. Your friend, Hacker Martin."

In a third letter to Lester, dated March 23, 1945, more of the pressure that Hacker was under is revealed, and it is easy to see why he might have been worried by and suspicious of some of the people who crowded around his shop:

". . . What we need most is a bunch of good stockers like yourself. I doubt if there is a dozen real top-notch gun stockers in the U.S. right now.

"Heard from B.R. a few days ago. He got home safe and sound, but had to detour about two hundred miles to get home. Boy, I don't think so much of him as I did before. He didn't pay enough for the rifles he got from R.C. and you in my opinion. He bought a couple of real fine rifles off an old lady on Beaver Creek for twenty-five dollars, one about brand new. Worth fifty dollars each. Well, maybe it's none of my business, but he looks more and more like a cheap sh—t to me. That rifle he got from you really should be worth sixty-five dollars at least the way guns sell now where he is.

"I believe he is wanting to get you away from me so he can have you to make stocks for him all the time. Well, it's a free country, and all I can say is I hope you don't quit me. In fact, I believe you can do better with me than you could with him—or anybody else, for that matter. I have worked on his guns almost entirely for the last six months. Guess how much cash he paid on this work? You'll have a fit! Thirty dollars cash! Of course, I got a mess of old second-hand railroad tools and junk—a lot I never needed nor wanted for that matter. Mostly stuff picked up for nothing, or next to it.

"Boy, wait till you see a letter I got from Red Farris about us and our gun work, especially stocks! Red is, as you know, Secretary of the NMLRA. He broke down complete. Even says we ought to charge *more* for our grand, sweet, fine, artistic gun work, by Gorsh! Wants us to come up to the big show at Cleveland and show the Dudes how we rowell out barrels and chop out stocks, etc. Can you imagine you and me surrounded by a couple of thousand gun bugs, each asking forty-nine questions a minute, [and us] trying to work at anything, much less a gun, under such conditions? Me, well I can't do any noticeable amount of work with two or three people talking to me at once. How about you? Red even offered to pay fifty dollars on our expenses there and back. Well, Ol' Red is a pretty good feller, at that, and is willing to pay a fairly decent price for fine work. He wants some of the old plain iron-trimmed walnut-stocked Kentucky rifles like used to be made around here so much back about the time of the Civil War.

"Red is even wanting Bull, him, and us to get into the gun business all together. He and Bull would do the advertising, we would get to be famous, do all the work, and they would get the money. What do you think? *I* think we need no advertising. No help selling guns. Nobody to spend the money we make but us. . . .

"Trusting you are enjoying good health and hoping to hear from you soon, I remain, yours Sincerely, H. Martin."

Hacker remained his own man to the end, and when he died at the age of seventy-five an article about him appeared in the July and August 1970 issues of *Muzzle Blasts*. Its author, Ogilvie H. Davis, said in part, "Most every collection of note in the country today has a rifle by either Hacker Martin or Lester Smith. All are dearly cherished possessions, for there is just no finer work available."

Fine work is being done today by a new generation of gunsmiths, but in the minds of those who knew Hacker, there will never be another quite like him.

MAKING THE NEW ERA POSSIBLE

Today, muzzle-loading rifles are being made by thousands of men and women. Some are high school students working in industrial arts classes making rifles as their term projects; some are adults who are making one rifle for their own use, or who turn out several a year as a hobby; some are adults who make their entire living serving the demand for guns in a field that has exploded in popularity.

No matter who they are, however, almost all have in common the fact that they have been vastly aided by the availability of generally reliable gun parts from an impressive array of manufacturers. Arguments about which company supplies parts of higher quality go on endlessly.

One thing that is sure is that the suppliers are out there, and most of them mean to be around for years to come. Some of them—The Golden Age Arms Company in Delaware, Ohio; Log Cabin Sports Shop in Lodi, Ohio; Dixie Gun Works, Inc. in Union City, Tennessee—offer almost every part imaginable. Others supply only barrels and have become successful at that specialty: G. R. Douglas Company in Charleston, West Virginia, for example, or Bill Large in Ironton, Ohio. It is interesting to imagine the reaction of an early barrelmaker if he were to see the recent article about Bill Large by Dr. M. P. Graffam in *Muzzle Blasts* and read, "I asked him how long it takes to make a barrel, and he said that he starts on a batch of twelve

PLATE 238 Wig looking at a lock with Dottie and Bud Siler at a picnic table in their back yard.

at a time. Automatic drills are used, one drilling at a rate of seven inches a minute, and the others at a slower rate, ⅝ to ⅞ inch per minute. Reaming takes from three to five minutes. Rifling from fifteen to fifty minutes depending on hardness of the steel used and the caliber. A breech pin can be made in from five to seven minutes. The plain, average barrel takes a total of about two to three hours, breech pin included."

Some companies offer knives and accessories, others produce powder, and some survive by marketing books about muzzle loaders. Some are family operations that are relatively small and personal but highly successful. Bud and Dottie Siler are typical. At one point in his life, Bud wanted a muzzle loader but couldn't afford to buy one. A man in a hardware store told him about Earl Lanning in Waynesville, North Carolina, so he looked Earl up and the two became good friends. Occasionally he and Earl traveled together to visit other gunmakers, and as Bud's interest grew, he designed and made a few locks for friends who were assembling their own rifles. Now he and his wife run a thriving business from their small home's basement, producing the nationally known Siler lock full time.

The Siler family began in the mountains with the arrival in this country of Plakard Dedrick Siler, one of whose sons, Weimar, was a fifteen-year-old drummer boy at the start of the Revolutionary War. Bud's father, Clifton K. Siler, was part of the Macon County, North Carolina, branch of the family—the same branch that produced Rufus Morgan (see pages 391–441 in *Foxfire 4*).

Bud and Dottie now live in Asheville, North Carolina, in a pleasant oasis of a home/garden/orchard surrounded on all four sides by crowded highways—the newest symbol of Asheville's tremendous growth—and have built an unassailable reputation producing one of the finest locks in the muzzle-loading business.

Article and photographs by Mark Palpal-lotic with help from Mitch Walker.

Bud and Dottie Siler: Lockmakers

BUD: The history behind these guns is the reason I got interested in them to start with. One of my ancestors, Jacob Siler, was supposed to have made a gun for Daniel Boone. The rifle is in a private home near Washington, D.C., now. That ancestor is supposed to have moved south from Pennsylvania with the Boone family. When you read the history of Daniel Boone and the frontiersmen, there's the fact that muzzle loaders are something you can have and use today that they also had and used then. Earl and I got started in it like you all are doing: going out and meeting people and developing a real interest.

Earl started in this thing before I did. He started in about the early fifties, and I started in the early sixties. He would travel around a lot. He wore a car out trying to meet people he'd heard about like Hacker Martin and Carl Pippert. He'd find out where they lived and just go visit and talk with them and learn all he could.

I guess Hacker Martin was the character of all characters. I didn't meet him, but Earl met him and can relate some really classic stories about him. Hacker made a rifle for him. Hacker had signs all around his place that said, "Beware of Mad Dogs," "Keep Out." You could feel very unwelcome, I heard, at Hacker's unless he knew you. He was just a mountain character, but they said he really had a knowledge of music. He could tell you anything about classical music, or anything. Stradivarius violins and how they were made. Anything. I'm sorry I didn't get to meet him. He could forge the barrels, and nobody else could do that I ever heard of in modern times. Wallace Gusler and one present gunsmith at Williamsburg can do it now, but I don't know anybody else that can *forge* the barrels. But yet Hacker forged his, I am told. That was handed down in his family, you know; it's just an art that was never forgotten in his family. He didn't have to go out and get taught or read about old methods. He just learned it from his forebears. But he sort of turned into a recluse and moved up into Virginia and bought a farm up there. He just didn't like to have too many people coming around.

Now there are a lot of people around who can hand *rifle* a barrel today. That's an art that just never did die out. It's the *forging* the barrel from a flat piece of iron that did die out. Even some of the early gunsmiths bought their barrels already forged but unrifled. They'd keep their tools sharper and possibly do a better job of rifling than the factories. But the middle-eighteenth-century gunmaker would start with a flat piece of iron, heat it, form it around a mandril, lap-weld it together, and then rifle it. Then, from about 1800 on, most of the gunmakers bought their barrels already welded by a factory and saved money by rifling themselves.

When they welded their barrels, one method was to have a seam all the way down the length of the barrel, and the other method was to spiral it just like a barber pole. And to make locks, they would heat the metal red and shape it on an anvil. They then had to file it because the old gunmaker didn't have surface grinders and band saws. Hacker Martin could forge a lock. I've got one of his frizzens that he did that way.

Another way today is to take a hacksaw and saw the parts out. I've done that, too. You start with a block of metal. It's tough going, but it can be done. There's several good blacksmiths around. Hershel House could probably do it. I know Hacker Martin could. Wallace Gusler at Williamsburg has done it. But it's always a slow, hard job for me. I'm not a really good blacksmith.

Before you could get these investment cast locks, if you wanted to build a rifle you had to locate an old lock from an old gun wreck and incorporate it into the new gun, or sit down and whittle it out somehow—saw it out or blacksmith it out to make up your lock. Even those weren't widely available. Then we found out we could apply this lock need to the casting process. That way you could get parts much cheaper than trying to machine them. For us, it was then just a matter of designing our particular lock.

DOTTIE: One of the reasons Bud started in the lock business was many of his friends around here were building guns. Bud specialized in the locks, and he got encouragement from his friends, and he put their locks together [for them]. He might not appreciate me saying this, but he is a craftsman, and he's known as one of the better lock men in the U.S.

BUD: I got a lot of encouragement from Earl and George Shumway and John Bivins and Bill Large.

DOTTIE: He just made a close fit, and all these parts are precision. He gets more satisfaction working in metal than wood. Maybe someone else did the stock better, or the engraving, but Bud's talent seemed to be locks.

BUD: Some people are better in metals, and some in wood. There's an art to all of it, but I do better in metals.

DOTTIE: For each lock part, he made the pattern and the mold himself. And he built my wax machines that I work on. Most all of it he has done by hand.

BUD: The lock we designed is actually more or less a copy of a rifle in the Pennsylvania Historical Society. It's an eighteenth-century style—middle to late eighteenth century.

We designed it because eighteenth-century guns were popular, and we felt like it would continue and get more popular with the Bicentennial approaching. Then people decided they wanted them, and now we can't make enough [to supply the demand]. It started for us in 1967, full time, that is. Had to hand make them before that.

PLATE 239 Dottie holds the mold for one of the lock parts in her left hand. The vertical tube injects hot wax into the mold, and when the wax cools a moment later, Dottie separates the two halves of the mold, inspects the wax piece for any flaws, and if it passes inspection, drops it into a box ready to go to the caster.

DOTTIE: We were still working [at other jobs] before that. As orders increased and we got calls, we were able to quit our jobs and go into it full time. Before that, I was a legal secretary, and Bud worked for the U. S. Geological Survey.

BUD: I was in the water resources division checking water supplies in western North Carolina and north Georgia. I didn't have any training in machinery. I wasn't the first to get into the lock business. Bob Ditchburn was one of the first I knew of, and I think there was one right before him that started in investment casting, and processing locks: Bob Chadwick in Pennsylvania. Russ Hamm came in there also. Now those were the three I know of that were first, and I really got the idea from Bob Ditchburn. I have to credit him with helping me a lot. He's at Gettysburg, Pennsylvania. He doesn't advertise his work, though, and it's hard to get locks [from him]. He's a fine craftsman, but his interest is in archaeology and fine gun restoration and rifle making.

But investment casting has really caught on. The reason so many gun products are investment cast today is that it makes a faithful reproduction of whatever you're trying to produce: either a lock, buttplate, triggerguard, or any hardware for the gun. Each part is identical to the last one, and any type alloy can be cast.

It starts out as a wax pattern that's injected into a mold, and for each steel part that you want later on, you have to have one wax pattern like it [Plate 239]. The caster sprues the wax pieces on a tall form called a "tree." Then he dips the tree in ceramic slurry. They're dipped about eight times in this ceramic. It takes about a week to do this. Then they turn the tree upside down and burn the wax out of it in an autoclave. They turn it back up and heat it to about two thousand degrees. Then they pour the steel in the ceramic shell at three thousand degrees, and it fills all of the cavities. When the steel cools, they chip the ceramic off—it's only about an eighth of an inch thick—then sand blast the steel parts and saw them off. They can't use the same mold again, obviously. This is called the "lost wax" process, precision casting, or investment casting.

Any of the hardware on the gun can be cast: the buttplate, the trigger-guard, the thimbles that the ramrods fit in, and, of course, all lock parts, and breechplug. It would even be possible to do the barrel. One of the modern pistol makers uses investment castings for the barrels. The advantage is that it's fast and you don't waste materials. There's little machine work to be done, so you're not wasting chips and borings and this sort of thing.

It is a really old process. Benvenuto Cellini did it during Da Vinci's time. They did it in gold and bronze. They couldn't do it in steel. That was the only difference in them and us today. They didn't have the alloys we use today. But they could do it in brass and bronze, silver, gold, and *possibly* iron, but we are not sure iron was used in pre-twentieth-century times. I have read the Egyptians used lost-wax casting in gold three thousand years ago.

There are eleven cast pieces to each lock. There's a little spring called a sear spring and the screws that aren't cast. I don't make the screws. They're done on an automatic screw-making machine. They're my design, but a company makes them according to my specifications, several thousand at a time. There are eight screws per lock. I don't assemble locks anymore, but made hundreds of locks until three years ago.

I used to do that but had to get rid of some of my equipment because my shop is small and it got too crowded. I hated to give up lockmaking. But now I sell them as kits, just like you see right here [Plate 240]. I also include a red plastic plug that helps in the assembly and then is discarded. It screws in a threaded hole, and it helps line up the bridle before you drill it. It's not part of the finished lock. When you get the kit, you've got to do some drilling and some work yourself. Just drill and tap it, and there are three parts you have to harden. The frizzen has to be hardened and tempered, the fly, and the tumbler. The springs are already hardened. Using an electric furnace is one way to harden parts. An acetylene torch is another.

PLATE 240   A finished Siler flintlock, at left, beside its component pieces.

PLATE 241   A finished Siler flintlock.

Most people use acetylene or a propane torch and heat the part red. That's about fifteen hundred degrees. And then you quench it in oil. When you quench it, that causes it to get glass hard—too hard to use it for anything because it's so brittle it'll break. So then you temper it. You reheat it back up to a lesser temperature—something like six hundred degrees, four hundred, or whatever the part calls for—and that softens it to the point that it's usable. It's still hard enough to give good service, but it's not so hard that it will break in use.

The springs are already hardened because that's pretty critical. You can miss a little bit on some of the other parts and still not affect the use or life of the lock.

DOTTIE: With each kit we sell, we send a sheet of instructions, and have them simplified as much as we can so that one can understand exactly what to do [see Plate 240].

They aren't very hard to put together. This one [Plate 241] has had a lot of finish work done on it to make it look pretty. But it doesn't take all that to make it operate. You can leave it with a sandblast finish and still have it operate perfectly. But the spindles on each end of the tumblers need to be turned and smoothed so that they will operate freely. The gates have to be ground off or filed, and then you drill and tap the parts where necessary.

BUD: One fellow claimed he could do one in forty-five minutes, but I don't really see how. I've heard a lot of people doing it in three hours. To finish one up like *I* like it takes about eight hours.

DOTTIE: But he's a perfectionist.

BUD: Someone who had never done one before, he'll fumble around some, and so he ought to spend two or three days on his first one.

The most basic thing you need to do a really good job is a drill press, because if you try to drill it with a hand drill, you're liable to get slanted holes and wobbly holes. It would probably still work, but you wouldn't be real happy with it.

We've got two sizes of locks in this eighteenth-century style, and we have two percussion locks that are the same style, but percussion is a later system. A lot of people like to do like Hershel does. They want to have a gun that they can take one lock out [and replace it with another]. Shoot flint one day and percussion the next day. Use the same gun for different matches.

Our lock would look out of place on a large match rifle, but it *would* work. It'd fire a cannon if you wanted it to. That's why I have two different sizes. One for a small slender mountain-style rifle, and the other one for a larger, early-period rifle.

The small one wouldn't be suitable for a large rifle as far as looks go. In fact, the musket locks are bigger than what I have. The original musket lock is about six and a quarter inches long, and this is five and a quarter. The musket lock was made out of really heavy stuff, too, so it won't break in rough field use because there wouldn't be any way of fixing it on the march. If you broke a sear in a musket then, you were just out of action. Or a spring or anything. That spring, you know, is kind of a sounding board for that little click you hear. It has a kind of ring to it that's real pleasing [laughing].

And now we are developing a left-handed lock that will be the same style as this lock. That's a need that's been neglected in this style lock. That's what we're working on right now—trying to get it done.

We wholesale at least 90 per cent of our locks. We do our own packaging and shipping. The flintlock kits run $32, and percussion kits sell for $19.50. And the left-handed lock that I'm going to have will be $32 also. We mail'em all over the U.S. I don't guess there's any state we don't send them to. Mostly California, Michigan, Illinois, Indiana, Pennsylvania, and we

LOCK INSIDE:

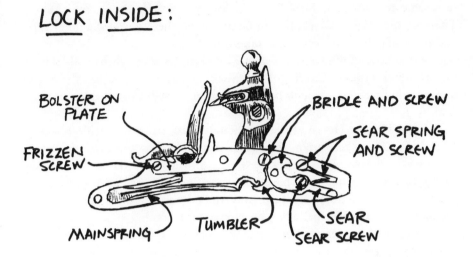

BOLSTER ON PLATE

BRIDLE AND SCREW

SEAR SPRING AND SCREW

FRIZZEN SCREW

MAINSPRING

TUMBLER

SEAR

SEAR SCREW

LOCK OUTSIDE:

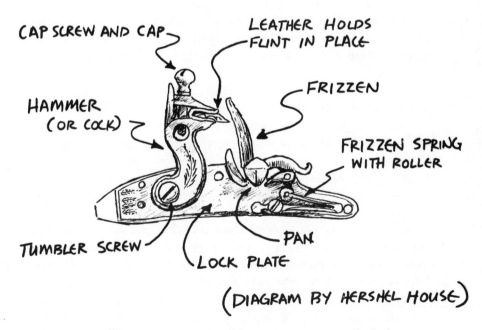

CAP SCREW AND CAP

LEATHER HOLDS FLINT IN PLACE

FRIZZEN

HAMMER (OR COCK)

FRIZZEN SPRING WITH ROLLER

TUMBLER SCREW

PAN

LOCK PLATE

(DIAGRAM BY HERSHEL HOUSE)

PLATE 242   This diagram by Hershel House shows the parts of a lock.

sent some to Australia, New Guinea, Africa, Canada, Spain, and Japan. There's a big interest developing in Germany on these muzzle-loading rifles, and there may be a market there someday.

The first advertising we did was in Friendship, Indiana, where they have the National Muzzle Loading Rifle Shoots; and we went up there and showed what we had. Enough people saw it and liked it to get us in production.

We met Hershel House at that National Muzzle Loading Rifle Shoot at Friendship. Thousands upon thousands of people show up at these shoots, and they have two big matches each year and about three smaller turkey shoots in between that. And that's where you meet all the gun people.

DOTTIE: We had a booth set up, and we had our lock at the booth, and I remember meeting Hershel when he came by the booth.

BUD: He had written us, but we hadn't met him before.

Once you get into this gunmaking, it's like a disease. I don't call it a hobby. It's more like a disease. You can't get out of it. I've seen people come here, and you know they're so excited they are hooked for good. And they stay that way. I've seen people in their seventies that have been at it for some years now, and they're just as interested as they were when they started years ago.

One reason it's growing, I believe, is the fact that it's something you can do at any age. It's not something you are likely to outgrow. And you meet so many darned nice people. Seems like everybody that's into muzzle loading is nice folks. And they can get together for shoots, etc. Also you never learn all there is to know. That's another reason why people keep their interest going.

DOTTIE: I'm glad the interest is there, because I really enjoy being able to work at home. I can put my blue jeans on and run downstairs to work.

BUD: You get a lot of nice comments, too. Letters. And you feel like you're doing something to help people. I got a phone call today from Joe Scorsone who built a gun for a man who was from Bob Brownell gun supplies in Iowa, and he called him from Iowa and told him he just couldn't praise it enough. Well, that makes you feel good. Joe just had to call me and tell me.

DOTTIE: You know the feeling you get when you finish a piece of furniture, and when it's all shiny and pretty. It's kind of like that with this. When you know you've done the best you can, send it out, and get a letter back of praise and thank you, it's a good feeling. A feeling of satisfaction.

BUD: I really think this demand will keep on going, too, because of the big interest people have in it right now. It's so big that I can't imagine it dying out. It's growing. Look at Earl's classes [in gunmaking at Haywood Tech in Sylva, North Carolina]. If the locks ever *did* go out, the backup for me, I think, would be in the investment-casting business itself. I'd kind of like to get into that *if* this ever runs out. At least that's an interest I have. But I don't foresee this business slowing down unless the gun-control laws reached the point that they actually put the squeeze on the muzzle loaders, too. But we don't foresee that right now. I do foresee the fact that it's really going to hurt the sale of the more modern-type rifles and pistols—particularly pistols.

DOTTIE: All of which could make this kind of gun more popular.

BUD: A lot of people claim that's one reason this type of gun is getting so popular. They feel the handgun is going to be restricted, and now at least they'll have something they can practice a sport with. I just hope guns like this are never used for crime. It's hard to imagine. Shoot at somebody and miss and have to stop and reload! I heard of one man that reportedly committed suicide with one back about 1940. He shot himself, but that's the only time I've ever heard of anyone getting killed. They're used for shooting matches, sport, and hunting.

I really encourage people to try making a muzzle loader, rather than buying the ready-mades. If you want to try it, you should get with someone that's good at it, like Earl Lanning [instead of learning from a book]. Attend the class he teaches. If you don't, you'll fumble along with several rifles over a period of several years before you turn up with something really good. But you can take that class at Haywood Tech in eight weeks—or however long it lasts—and you can come up with a rifle that you'll be happy with because you've got somebody to show you every step, the right way, from the start to finish.

And use good parts. There are a lot of locks and barrels being made in Italy, Spain, and Japan, but they're not top quality, and usually the user is disappointed after he finds out better a little later on. In a way, it's a shame to think people are wasting that much money that they are going to regret later. Get off to a good start with top materials and proper instruction if possible, and then enjoy it as long as you live.

Garnett Powell

Garnett Powell has watched the field grow over the years, and he feels strongly that access to parts has been one of the greatest benefits of the current revival. When we asked him to elaborate, he did.

One thing that has come out of all this is the ready availability of things like hardware for a reproduction, Kentucky or mountain style, Bean rifle. Few people have access to original parts. And I think the reproduction parts are justifiable. Not everybody has the technical skills of the blacksmith necessary to sit down and forge all this out. And if he had the skill, chances are he might not have the forge and the tools and the anvil and things needed to make the parts. Most people today use the investment-casting process, and this lets you produce hardware at much less cost than hand forging. The availability now of swamped barrels is one of the best aspects of the current revival. Making one of those by hand would be an almost impossible task for most people, but at the same time, they still have to use some of their ability as craftsmen to inlet the barrel, which is not an easy task because of the curvature. So it isn't all done for them. Some craftsmanship is still required.

One thing people buying reproduction parts need to watch out for is the quality of what they buy. A person buying a kit is, with a few exceptions, buying a lot of junk. Many of the parts are made in Spain with questionable metal. In fact, a lot of the cheap rifles that are being sold today by some who advertise in magazines are Spanish or Japanese junk. You'll notice in recent *Buckskin Reviews* that John Baird has criticized the NMLRA for carrying advertisements for this crap in *Muzzle Blasts*. A guy takes his life in his hands with it. He would be a fool to ever shoot one of them. On a correctly made barrel, breechplugs are threaded and seated on good solid binding threads, where on some of these imported pieces they are just stuck in with a weld to hold them. Of course, this is where the maximum chamber pressure is generated, and it can blow the whole business right back in the shooter's face. And there go your eyes. But John Baird has led the fight against this inferior stuff, and we owe him a real vote of thanks for taking issue and in trying to protect the newcomers who might buy this type of gun unwittingly.

It's silly to settle for inferior parts when there are parts around that you can count on. You can count on a Bill Large barrel, for example. Unlike many on the market, the Large barrels are still cut. With a cut bore, the edges of the lands are sharp so that when you put the patch in there, they actually cut into the patch and hold onto the ball to get a good seat. I'd say the largest maker of barrels being made today are Douglas barrels—they are made with a swedged bore. This is actually a bore that's thrust into the metal under pressure instead of being cut, and the rifling is very shallow by nature because the swedging process can only go so deep. This works fine for a cartridge rifle, but with a patched ball I personally prefer a deep-cut bore. I think there is a difference. I have a rifle with a Douglas barrel that is a good shooter, but in my experience it can in no way duplicate a cut rifle barrel for accuracy. You take a gun that has been freshly recut or "freshed out" as the old-timers said, and it will shoot rings around a gun that has been shot several hundred times to where the edge is worn off those lands. Bill Large's barrels are extremely accurate and precise because of his cutting

PLATE 243 T. J. Cormack shooting a Hawken rifle at an early NMLRA shoot. (Photo courtesy of C. Frederick Beck and Garnett Powell.)

process, and he's one of the few men, to my knowledge, in the world today that's making a barrel of that precision. When Bill's gone, that will be the end of a great era. The type of barrel that he makes costs you about twice as much as an average muzzle-loading barrel. That's why some of the great barrelmakers of the past are just topics to talk about now. Someday I predict a Bill Large barrel will be revered like a Harry Pope barrel is today.

Now in patch boxes and this type of thing, I would go to Log Cabin Sports Shop in Lodi, Ohio. I know Dan Kindig. I knew his father, Wes, who founded the organization, very well. They have been selling muzzle-gun parts for years, and everything that Log Cabin sells, to my knowledge, is quality that you can depend on. They probably have one of the largest selections of patch boxes, hardware, barrels, nipples, drums—the whole bit—a builder would ever need.

On the subject of locks, there have been some real good locks made and offered to the trade over the last twenty years. When I first got into this business, there were probably one or two people like Hacker Martin capable of making a good flintlock. But in the last twenty years, there have been some real good locks offered, some of which—if you had an old rifle minus the lock, and it was a particularly good style—you could just take and almost fit them into place. In flintlocks, I seem to encounter more people praising the Siler lock than about any other. The fitting of it is very precise. Again, this is due, I think, to the casting process that he's using. He's able to produce a quality piece at a reasonable price.

Now with all these quality parts around, there's no excuse for settling for cheap, inferior stuff. And there are enough new parts around now that you can almost duplicate any style of old rifle, and all for a reasonable price. Take the Hawken rifle, for example. There have been several firms that have made and offered bastardizations of the Hawken features and used the name, but most of them were just trying to capitalize on the name and their offerings in no way resembled a real Hawken. But now Ithaca is putting out the Cherry Corners Hawken kit [Cherry Corners in Ohio had been putting out an authentic Hawken but couldn't produce them fast enough and so sold out to Ithaca under the condition that they would continue the quality], and from general appearances it's a reasonable-looking replica. This arrangement gives a person like me, who might want a Hawken to shoot, a chance to have a fairly authentic replica—a safe one and a well-made one —with the actual features of the Hawken as far as physical design and basic features are concerned. And it's a step in the right direction because the only other way you can get a Hawken replica is to hire a custom gunsmith to make one, and the cost would be rather expensive. But here's a chance for under three hundred dollars to get ahold of the parts and assemble your own with the drawings they provide. These are some of the things that I think have been good about the revival.

THE MODERN GUNSMITHS

Of gunsmithing today, Garnett Powell said, "In my opinion, today there are probably more people practicing the art of muzzle-loading rifle making than you would find at any time since probably 1850. And many of them are highly competent. Many of them are as good as some of the golden-age makers. There is still that element that just throws something together, but by and large, each rifle that these people make is an improvement over the one they've made before. It's a learning continuum and they're developing, and you watch people in the process of the fourth, fifth, sixth rifle, they begin to acquire the skill of inletting and the skill of working with wood, and the rifles improve.

"The tendency in the first rifles is to make them too heavy in the forestock and wrist so that they are more like a club than a firearm. I've seen old rifles where the forestock was almost paper thin the whole length of the barrel. People say, 'Well, that was bad in a way because it made the gun fragile,' but that was done for the purpose of balance and holding. Rifles that were

typical of the frontier period were the longrifles, and the longrifle name itself denotes the purpose. The purpose was accuracy, plain and simple, and
that's why the barrel length [was long]. By the time the pioneer settler got
to this part of the frontier, the buffalo were gone. About the largest game
they'd encounter would probably be a bear, and of course, we didn't have
grizzlies. Just black bear. And a deer or a black bear can very easily be
brought down with a .38–.40 caliber. So most of these guns were really for
rabbits, squirrels, and so forth, for the table—thus you hear the term 'squirrel rifle.' And the barrel was made real long and of small caliber for extreme accuracy. And one turn in forty-eight inches was a pretty standard
bore twist. In muzzle loading, if you increase the twist, you begin to lose accuracy. They hit a happy medium of where they had the ball spinning just
enough to stabilize it, but at the same time not have so much spin on it that
it would cut down on the velocity and reduce the killing impact. One turn
in forty-eight inches became fairly standard, and this again accounts for the
long barrel. And on a full-stock rifle, if you had an extremely heavy stock,
you would have something so heavy that it would be real difficult for a person to hold up and shoot. It takes a fine gunsmith to take that wood down
to where he can produce a full stock and yet come up with a piece that's
light enough that you can take a bead and hold it steady enough to bark a
squirrel in the top of the highest tree. Some awful fine copies of the walnut-
stocked and iron-trimmed mountain-style rifles are being crafted just over
the mountain from here in nearby North Carolina. I've seen some that were
true copies of the fine Bean rifles made around here."

Whether making true reproductions, modified reproductions, rifles of
their own personal design, or simply hammering together inexpensive kits,
the tradition of making rifles in one form or another is alive and well. Each
maker is different. Some, like Wallace Gusler, can take justifiable pride in
the fact that they can make every single piece that a rifle requires—and they
are paid in the thousands of dollars for their mastery of the art. Most are
satisfied with less, but they take pride in the finished piece nevertheless.

In the following sections, we present six men we interviewed, each of
whom is unique in his own way. The first, Hershel House, built a rifle for us
using a combination of purchased parts (the barrel and lock) and parts he
made himself as we watched. Through Hershel, we can see all the steps involved in putting a rifle together.

Because of space limitations, we could only ask the others to show us
some of their rifles and talk about their work. Despite this limitation placed
upon them, we think you will get a good idea of the range of styles being
produced from Jim Chambers' eighteenth-century Lancaster, Pennsylvania,
reproductions through Joe Farmer's Bean-style creations.

If you yourself become interested, check around in your own town. Chances are there are several gunsmiths within a few miles of your home who would be willing to give some help.

Hershel House

"Anybody that tries to write a treatise on riflemaking from start to finish . . . is a candidate for an insane asylum. Several famous authors have tried it, and who is fool enough to try to make a rifle from their written instructions?"

Hacker Martin, as quoted in the August 1970
issue of *Muzzle Blasts,* page 9.

Subscribers to our magazine have been urging us for years to do a series of articles on gunsmiths. It is such a complicated subject, however, that we shied away from it. Two of us finally decided to take it on, however, during the time we were each making a flintlock rifle with the help of our high school industrial arts teacher, Des Oliver.

While this was going on, we got a letter from one of our subscribers, a Marine helicopter pilot named Jim Wright, about a friend of his, named

PLATE 244

Hershel House, who specialized in building Kentucky flintlock rifles. He urged us to visit and interview Hershel, and so we got in touch, and Hershel offered to let us stay with him at his small farm for a week and document the making of one of his rifles.

Hershel put us up, fed us, and worked with us that whole week to build a rifle so we could photograph the whole process. On the last day, we all went down into a field beside Hershel's house, set up some targets, and fired the rifle Hershel made. The very first shot hit the target.

Hershel has always lived in the area around Morgantown. His great-grandparents settled in Woodbury, Kentucky, only a few miles away from Hershel's present home, in the 1890s. Woodbury is located on the Green River, and it was founded in the 1840s when the river was dammed and a lock put in to open the river to trade. Steamboats brought mail and supplies up from Evansville, Indiana, and lumber was shipped out. Residents of the area used to take weekend river excursions to Mammoth Cave, still one of the most popular tourist attractions in the country.

Hershel's great-grandmother ran the hotel in Woodbury. Grandma Finney, as she was known, died in 1947 when Hershel was six. His grandfather, known in the area as a fine squirrel hunter, is eighty-seven and has been partly responsible for Hershel's interest in flintlocks.

Though the dam and the locks at Woodbury have fallen into disuse now, Hershel still goes to the river, passing his old home and the old hotel, and he remembers waking up to the sound of boats blowing at the lock at dawn when he was a boy.

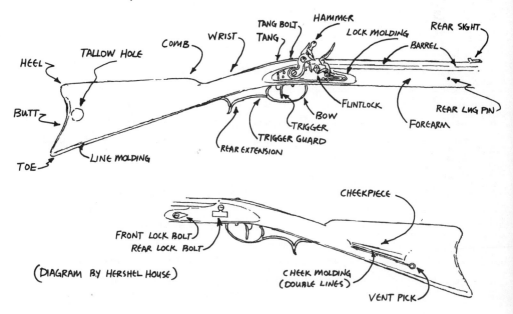

PLATE 245

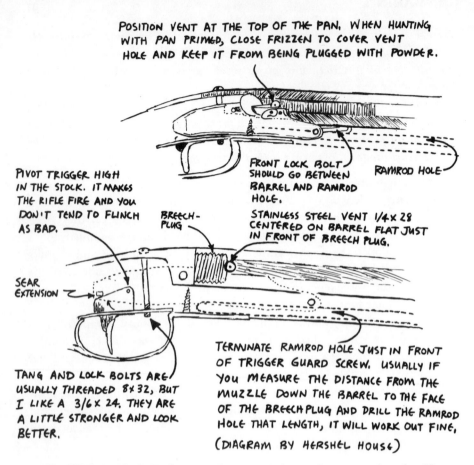

POSITION VENT AT THE TOP OF THE PAN. WHEN HUNTING WITH PAN PRIMED, CLOSE FRIZZEN TO COVER VENT HOLE AND KEEP IT FROM BEING PLUGGED WITH POWDER.

PIVOT TRIGGER HIGH IN THE STOCK. IT MAKES THE RIFLE FIRE AND YOU DON'T TEND TO FLINCH AS BAD.

FRONT LOCK BOLT SHOULD GO BETWEEN BARREL AND RAMROD HOLE.

RAMROD HOLE

BREECH-PLUG

STAINLESS STEEL VENT 1/4 x 28 CENTERED ON BARREL FLAT JUST IN FRONT OF BREECH PLUG.

SEAR EXTENSION

TERMINATE RAMROD HOLE JUST IN FRONT OF TRIGGER GUARD SCREW. USUALLY IF YOU MEASURE THE DISTANCE FROM THE MUZZLE DOWN THE BARREL TO THE FACE OF THE BREECH PLUG AND DRILL THE RAMROD HOLE THAT LENGTH, IT WILL WORK OUT FINE.

TANG AND LOCK BOLTS ARE USUALLY THREADED 8 x 32, BUT I LIKE A 3/6 x 24. THEY ARE A LITTLE STRONGER AND LOOK BETTER.

(DIAGRAM BY HERSHEL HOUSE)

PLATE 246   Hershel's diagram offers several tips on the construction of a rifle.

Hershel has always been interested in old things. His grandmother on his father's side ran the last grist mill in Morgantown. He found a mill of his own in Gilstrap, Kentucky. It had only been used for one year before the engine broke, so the owners used the engine for junk iron and the almost new mill sat covered in hay for nearly fifty years. Hershel bought it, and later bought a blacksmith shop where he found an engine that he plans to hook to the mill.

He first began working with guns around 1956 when he found an old half-stock percussion rifle in a barn. It had belonged to the father of the woman who owned it, and she let Hershel have it. He fixed it, got it firing, and got a tremendous amount of pleasure out of it. Then, in 1959, he saved enough money to buy the materials he needed to build a longrifle to use for squirrel hunting on the river, and to shoot at area shooting matches.

In 1961, he joined the Marines for four years, and when he came out of the service he found out about the National Muzzle Loading Rifle Association and joined it. It was through association with that group, and through attending their annual shooting matches in Friendship, Indiana, that he met such men as Earl Lanning, Jim Chambers, George Shumway, and Bud Siler—all men who were interviewed about gunsmithing for this book.

Hershel takes great pains to make sure the rifles he builds are as authentic as he can make them. The one he made for us is the very simple, basically plain, but very reliable mountain rifle known in his part of the country as a "poor boy's rifle." He has researched all its features carefully, and feels sure that its design is accurate. Unlike the products of some of the other gunsmiths that were interviewed for this book, this rifle has a tallow hole instead of a patch box, no buttplate, and no decoration except a few shallow parallel grooves carved into the stock to emphasize the lines of the rifle.

Hershel has also done some personal research into the differences between the performance of flintlocks and caplocks:

"Beginning about 1830, there was almost a universal changeover to the cap system. It was partly because one of the aspects of the flintlock was that it was awful vulnerable during rainy weather. You couldn't hardly keep the priming dry. When damp, the guns sometimes misfired or fired slow. There were two ways around this. Some hunters had a hood made out of the leather from a cow's knee that slipped over the entire lock. The gun was loaded and primed and kept on half-lock, or safety position; when game was spotted, they removed the hood, cocked, and fired. The other method was, when it began to rain, to pour out the priming powder, peg the vent with a small feather, and thus close off the main charge. Then, when you wanted to shoot, you just removed the feather, reprimed the gun, and shot.

"But when the cap system came in, the lock was either taken out and completely replaced, or the flint hammer was taken off and replaced with a percussion hammer, and the vent hole bored out and a drum or nipple put in. Then you just used a copper cap. When it was hit by the hammer, the cap would pop like a modern cap, and a jet of fire went down through a hole and into the main barrel, and this was more reliable.

"But if a man takes the time to learn, a flintlock can be just as good. A good flintlock is pretty darn fast, and they're a lot more colorful and more closely linked to early history [which makes them additionally attractive]. Plus, there are certain advantages. If a flintlock fails to fire, all you have to do is take a little vent pick and go in and clean out the vent hole and fill the pan with fresh powder and fire away. If a caplock fails to fire, you've got to take the drum or nipple out with a screwdriver or wrench. So if you're in

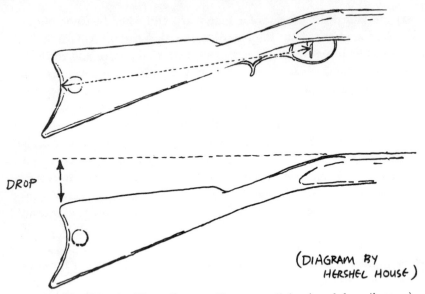

DROP

(DIAGRAM BY
HERSHEL HOUSE)

PLATE 247   These diagrams illustrate pull (top) and drop (bottom).

the woods and your caplock misfires, you're in big trouble. With a flintlock, you can correct it pretty fast, even if you have to pull the charge.

"Also, if you lose your little box of caps, you're in bad trouble. But you can always find a flint somewhere. In the haste of battle or the hunt, it was also hard to reach in there and find one of those tiny caps. So I prefer a flintlock myself, and that's mostly what I make."

Hershel charges $500 for the type of rifle he made for us, and he guarantees it for life. If it has to be repaired, he'll do it free of charge. Partly for that reason, he always has more work than he can get to. Another reason is that his work is authentic. "I try to get my guns as close as possible to the old styles. I think that's one reason that my work is fairly popular."

On top of that, he's one of the nicest people we've ever met.

Article and photographs by Doug James and Jeff Lane.

Choosing the Stock and Pattern

Select a piece of wood at least 5′ long, 10″ in width, and 2″ thick. This would be suitable for two stocks. If the stock is not kiln dried, it should be air dried for at least four years or longer, to allow for a minimum of warping and shrinkage. Most rifle stocks were made of curly maple, and sometimes walnut and occasionally fruit wood such as cherry and apple.

Since this rifle is for an average-sized man, the pull will be 13½″. The pull is the distance between the trigger and the center of the butt (see Plate 247). Your drop will be 2¾″ for the average man. The old rule of thumb

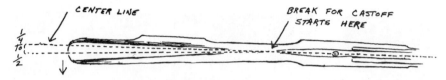

CENTER LINE

BREAK FOR CASTOFF
STARTS HERE

¼ to ½

PLATE 248

for measuring pull was to stick the butt of the rifle at the elbow and reach for the trigger as if you were going to fire it (see Plate 244).

The castoff is the slight curve of the stock between the wrist and the butt away from the face at the cheekpiece (see Plate 248). It enables you to get the rifle into your shoulder without having to lean into it, and also keeps the gun from kicking you in the face.

To get castoff in your rifle, first draw a straight line from the center of the muzzle to the center of the butt. Then make a dot at the extreme butt ½″ to the right of the line for a right-handed man, or ½″ to the left of the line for a left-handed man. Then draw another line from the center of the breechplug to that dot. That will give you your castoff.

Barrels

This rifle barrel was bought from G. R. Douglas, a barrel company in West Virginia. It's a rifled .45 caliber with ⅜″ across the flat. Barrels come in 44″ lengths, but Hershel shortened it from the muzzle end to 42″ to give it better balance (a procedure, incidentally, that is recommended by the company). Later on he will cut his stock to fit the barrel. The breech is already threaded to ⁵⁄₁₆″ with 18 threads per inch.

The mountain gunsmith went to an iron furnace to buy iron straps (flat bars of iron) and welded his own barrels in his forge. He also reamed and rifled their barrels (see earlier section on Wallace Gusler).

When using a Douglas barrel, note that there is always some runoff. The term runoff refers to the fact that in the boring process, the hole does not stay true but varies to one side or the other down the length of the barrel. G. R. Douglas stamps their name on the side of the barrel to which the runoff goes (the point where the distance between the end of the hole and the outside edge of the barrel is the least). This brand name should be placed *down* in the stock so that the gun will shoot high instead of to one side or the other. To compensate for the fact that the rifle will shoot high, the front sights should also be left high. This is actually an advantage, as a high front sight compensates for the fact that after a few shots with black-powder rifles the heat waves coming from the barrel will cause a lower sight to "dance" or float.

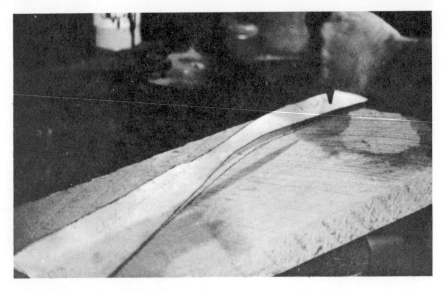

PLATE 249   Hershel takes one stock pattern he has selected, lays it down on a slab of curly maple, and traces around it.

PLATE 250   Hershel cuts out the butt of the rifle on the bandsaw.

Cutting Out the Stock

After drawing the pattern on the stock blank, cut around the outline with a bandsaw leaving the lines.

PLATE 251   The stock blank after it has been cut out, and before channeling for the barrel has been done.

Inletting the Barrel

To establish the position for the barrel groove, measure $\frac{3}{8}''$ from the outside edge of the stock on the side that the lock will be on, and draw a perpendicular line down the front of the stock. This assures that a maximum amount of wood will be left on the other side for the cheekpiece. Then place the barrel's end against the stock and trace around it as shown (Plate 252).

Hershel uses a spindle shaper and a special octagonal bit to shape the channel for the barrel. When cutting the groove, he is careful to leave all the lines so that he will get a tight fit. Before he had the shaper, he used a

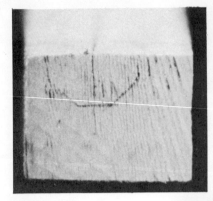

PLATE 252 To draw the shape of the barrel on the end of the stock, first center the barrel on the original line drawn down the length of the top of the stock. Then drop the barrel half its width and trace around it.

PLATE 253 Hershel cuts the back of the breech flat so that the breech of the barrel butts up flush.

skill saw. He would first set the blade to cut half the depth of the barrel, and would then mark around the barrel at the end of the muzzle (Plate 253), and saw the two deepest lines as shown in the illustration. Then he would reset the blade, saw the two shallow lines, and chisel out the wood from the channel.

The mountain gunsmith would scribe a line on each side of the barrel down the length of the top of the stock and channel the groove out with a series of box planes.

Breechplug and Tang

Hershel uses a standard machine-made breechplug measuring $\frac{5}{16}''$ by 18 threads per inch. These are available from any gun dealer.

He first takes the breechplug to his forge and draws out the tang to a spear point. This spear-point tang was characteristic of the mountain rifle in Virginia.

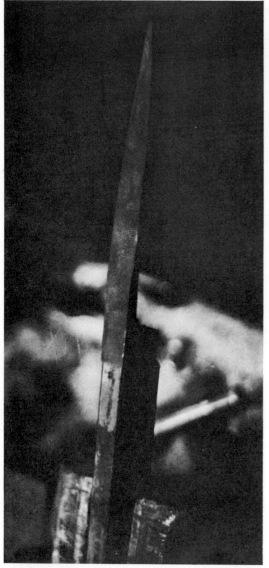

PLATE 254 This is the tang after being drawn out and shaped in the forge. This must be done before the tang and its attached breechplug are mounted to the barrel to avoid damage to the barrel in the drawing-out process. Most of the old mountain rifles had long tangs.

After drawing out the tang, he attaches the breechplug/tang assembly to the barrel and punches a line with a cold chisel on the underside of the breechplug, as shown in Plate 255. Then he inlets the breechplug itself into the wrist so that the tang will lie flat on top of the wrist, draws around the tang, and chisels out the appropriate amount of wood to inlet the tang and allow it to lie flush with the top of the wrist. He then removes the barrel/breechplug/tang assembly from the stock to prepare for the next step.

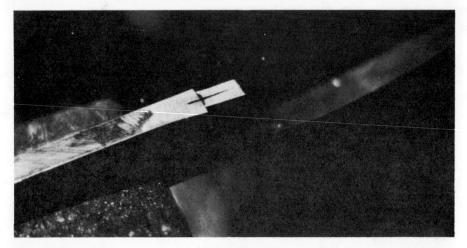

PLATE 255   Note particularly in this picture the line made across the underside of the breechplug and the barrel. Hershel does this as a precaution so that if the breechplug was accidentally moved or taken out (or taken out on purpose for a thorough cleaning or to check the bore), he could remount it in precisely the right spot.

PLATE 256   The tang inletted into the wood.

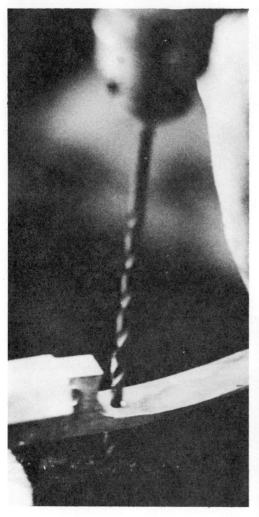

PLATE 257 Hershel drills a hole into the tang for the bolt that anchors the rear of the barrel. This bolt goes through and screws into the trigger plate and anchors the tang.

PLATE 258 This hole is for the screw that taps into the trigger plate and anchors the tang.

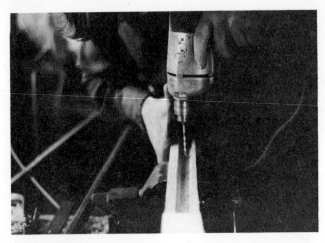

PLATE 259   Hershel drills feeler holes to make sure that the long drill bit drilling the ramrod hole is on course.

PLATE   260   The   first feeler   hole   centered   between   the   lines   for   the ramrod guide groove. The distance between these two lines is three eighths of an inch.

PLATE 261   Here Hershel has cut out the barrel groove and is ready to cut out the ramrod guide groove. To draw the half circle for the groove, he puts a three-eighths-inch ramrod against the front of the stock, leaving one-eighth inch between the barrel groove and the ramrod guide groove, then traces his half circle. He cuts this out with a   special   rounded   bit   on   the   spindle shaper.

Drilling and Shaping Ramrod Hole

To position the ramrod hole, Hershel sets it up right under the barrel groove. Then he goes to the point shown in Plate 259 and drills a hole directly in the center of the barrel groove. He draws two lines ⅜″ apart with that hole directly in the center, as shown in Plate 260, then matches those lines with the lines at the muzzle, as shown in Plate 261. Next, he takes a special round-bottomed shaper bit and shapes the groove. The depth of the groove should be set to where there is approximately ⅛″ between the barrel and the bottom of the ramrod groove. If you don't have a router or shaper, you have to chisel out the groove, which Hershel has done previously.

Then he drills his ramrod hole. He uses a long drill bit he made himself. These bits are available, however, from Log Cabin Sports Shop in Lodi,

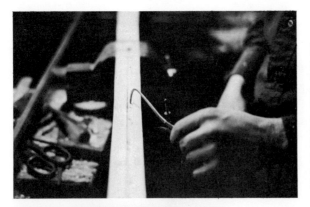

PLATE 262 Using a caliper, he checks to make sure the distance between the ramrod guide groove and the bottom of the barrel is only about one eighth of an inch along the entire length. This will insure that the ramrod hole will run straight on through the forearm.

PLATE 263 The special bit Hershel made to drill the ramrod hole. To make the bit, he heated it, beat it flat, and ground and filed the edges and tip down. This bit is $2\frac{5}{64}$ of an inch in diameter.

PLATE 264 Ready to drill the ramrod hole through the forearm.

Ohio. He drills the ramrod hole into the forearm about 1½". Then he drills a hole directly in the center of the barrel groove at the end in the path of the ramrod groove. These holes are "feeler" holes to make sure the drill bit is on course. The feeler holes are about 1½" apart. To know when the ramrod hole is deep enough, he puts the drill bit inside the barrel and wraps tape around the shaft of the bit. As soon as the tape meets the end of the stock, he stops drilling.

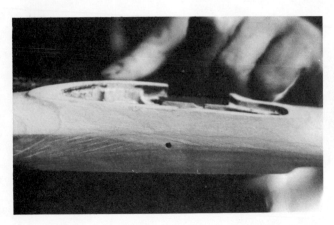

PLATE 265 This is the last feeler hole to determine if the ramrod hole is still on course. The trigger-guard will cover it when the rifle is finished.

Lugs

Lugs are the pieces of steel that are inset into the underside of the barrel and secure the barrel to the stock. Hershel uses three lugs, which he makes from a ½" square piece of steel stock, as shown in Plate 266. He cuts it lengthwise twice into four equal pieces.

Next, he makes all the necessary cuts to inset the lugs into the underside of the barrel. He uses a dovetail notch (see Plate 267).

PLATE 266 To make his lugs, he takes a square piece of steel stock and cuts it twice lengthwise to make four pieces.

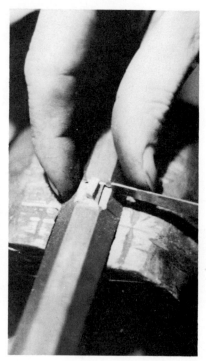

PLATE 267 Hershel cuts the dovetail groove in the barrel for one of the lugs. He also uses this dovetail notch to mount the front and rear sights.

PLATE 268 Hershel files down the rough edges of the barrel after he has inset the lugs.

PLATE 269 One of the lugs completed and inset into the barrel.

PLATE 270   After taking all the parts off the lock (the "guts" as they are called), Hershel places the lock plate on the stock in the proper place and traces around it. (Note the lines on the stock for the ramrod hole and barrel groove.) The top of the pan should be about lined up with the center of the end of the barrel.

The Lock

Every basic mountain rifle that Hershel has seen has a good late-period (1800–1940) English lock. In his opinion they were the best locks of that period. These locks were imported from Birmingham, England, a lockmaking center, in large quantities and sold through hardware dealers in the eastern states. They were either made by hand or drop-forged. "It has always been a mystery to me how the mountain gunsmith living in inaccessible areas was able to obtain these fine locks. I'm sure the gunsmiths made locks from time to time and were capable of doing it." Since most of the mountain rifles had these English locks, Hershel uses replicas of them (obtainable from Log Cabin Sports Shop or Golden Age Arms Company in Worthington, Ohio, or Dixie Gun Works in Union City, Tennessee) on all his mountain-style rifles.

To position the lock, it must first fit tight against the barrel and even with the breechplug so that when the spark hits the powder, the powder inside the barrel is not too far back to be ignited. The lock is then positioned so that the two lock bolts go into the right spot (see Plate 270). One goes between the barrel and ramrod hole, and the other goes into the breechplug for support. Finally, the bottom of the pan (the part of the lock that holds the powder) has to be aligned with the vent in the barrel (see Plate 270).

PLATE 271 Hershel holds the lock over a candle so soot will collect on it. When he places it into its proper spot on the stock, the soot will rub off and reveal the high places so he'll know what wood still needs to be shaved off to make a tight fit.

PLATE 272 The lock is held in the right position so that Hershel can mark the right location for the trigger.

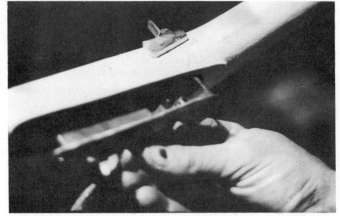

To find out where the vent must be drilled into the barrel, he puts the ramrod into the barrel as far as it will go—until it hits the breechplug—marks the ramrod, and uses it as a ruler to mark the right spot for the vent on the barrel.

After it has been determined where the lock must go, the hammer and the guts are removed. The rib or the bolster around the pan is inlet first. When the rib is fitted into the stock, he traces around the rest of the lock and chisels out the excess wood so that the lock fits snugly into the stock. Putting soot on the lock (see Plate 271) is an old trick that helps here.

After he has chiseled out the spot for the lock, he puts all the parts back into the lock and chisels out more for these. He then drills a hole for the part of the lock that the trigger trips.

When setting the lock, he sets it deep so it butts up against the barrel. There should not be a space between the side of the barrel, where the vent is, and the pan, or carbon will build up and corrode the barrel and lock.

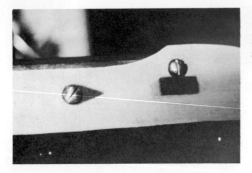

PLATE 273 The completed sideplates after they have been inletted into the stock.

Sideplates and Lock Bolts

Hershel made the sideplates from an old piece of iron that was once a cultivator guard. Using a pattern, he traced them on the iron, drilled the necessary holes *first,* then cut them out with a hacksaw and filed down the rough edges.

Most of the true old-time mountain rifles didn't have lock plates. The lock bolts were simply tightened snug against the wood.

Making the Trigger

Hershel first cuts out a piece of blank steel for his trigger, as shown in Plate 274. Then he files it, as shown in Plate 275. Next he takes it to the anvil and beats it to flare out the pad (the part you pull with your finger when shooting). He then cuts down the thickness of the trigger, as shown in Plate 276, and smooths it and shapes it so that it looks as shown in Plate 277.

PLATE 274 The trigger blank before any filing or shaping has been done. At this time, the blank is about one and a quarter inches square.

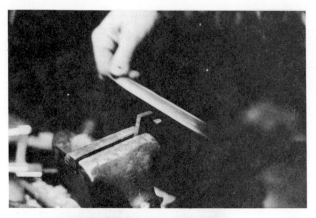

PLATE 275 Hershel shapes the trigger blank with a file while taking off the rough spots left from cutting it out.

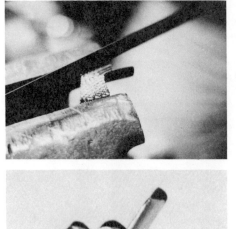

PLATE 276 The trigger blank was one quarter inch thick. As this is much too thick for the final product, except for the trigger pad itself, he rasps about one eighth of an inch off each side, scoring it with a hacksaw to make the rasping easier.

PLATE 277 The finished trigger, ready to be inserted into the gun.

He makes his triggers because he likes to make as many parts of the gun as possible. They can be bought, however, from gun shops, but they would have to be smoothed. He says, "It's just about as easy to go ahead and make your trigger yourself. If you buy one, they run about two or three dollars."

To set up the trigger, he positions the trigger to fit against the sear. This insures that it will fire instantly. He also has to get his pull right. To do so, the trigger should be positioned so that it is about fourteen inches (or a little under) from the butt, depending on the size of the man. The old-time way of measuring was to stick the butt of the rifle in the crook of your arm and reach for the trigger as if you were going to fire. If you can reach the trigger comfortably, then the pull is right. (When a man had a gun made for him, he'd check the pull on the patterns that the gunsmith had and choose the one that was the most appropriate for his arm length.)

Then he chisels out the wood where the trigger goes into the underside of the stock. The trigger has to work free.

To drill the pivot hole (the hole that holds the pin that holds the trigger in place), stick the trigger into its place and drill through the stock and trigger at the same time. The hole should be high for leverage so you won't have to pull hard to make the gun fire. To make the pin for the trigger, Hershel takes a small finish nail and cuts the head off. Then he buffs the nail so the trigger will move freely without catching.

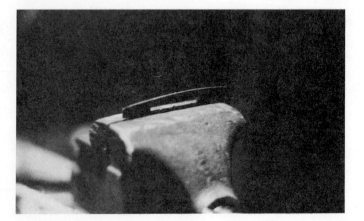

PLATE 278 The trigger plate, which is about three inches long. It fits under the triggerguard and helps stabilize the trigger and provide an anchoring point for the tang bolt.

Trigger Plate

The trigger plate is a piece of metal 3″ long that anchors the tang bolt. Hershel cuts the trigger plate out of a piece of steel $\frac{1}{16}$″ thick. After cutting out the trigger plate and shaping it, he drills a row of holes in its center, then files out the extra metal (see Plate 278) and smooths it. The slot is where the trigger goes.

PLATE 279 Hershel drills the hole in the tang that the tang bolt goes through in order to mark the place on the trigger plate where a hole has to be drilled for the tang bolt.

He then inlets it into the stock at the wrist. After inletting it, he drills a hole into the front of it small enough so that he can thread it with a $\frac{3}{16}''$ tap. He then threads it, and drills from the trigger plate up to and through the tang. He then countersinks the tang so that the head of the bolt will sink into it. After countersinking, he bolts the tang to the trigger plate.

Triggerguard

The grip rail is the rear extension of the triggerguard that your hand fits around to help hold the gun into your shoulder. To make the grip rail, Hershel takes a $\frac{3}{8}''$ piece of steel rod and rips it down the center for a distance of $2\frac{1}{2}''$ (Plate 280) and cuts it off $\frac{1}{2}''$ below the slot. He takes the rod to his forge and flattens the end, then puts the end into a vise and spreads the two wings so they are opposite each other. One end should be about $\frac{1}{2}''$ higher than the other. Then he flattens the two wings a little as shown in Plate 281.

Then he curves the short piece of metal sticking up between the two ends of the grip rail to match the curve of his finger. After curving it, he smooths it with a rat-tail file.

PLATE 280 The metal rod Hershel used to make the grip rail. First he cuts about three inches into the rod with a hacksaw (see slot in rod above), folds the two halves back, and cuts the rod off at the point just above his thumb.

PLATE 281 Hershel has flattened the end of the grip rail and formed a curve for the owner's fingers.

PLATE 282 The half-completed triggerguard.

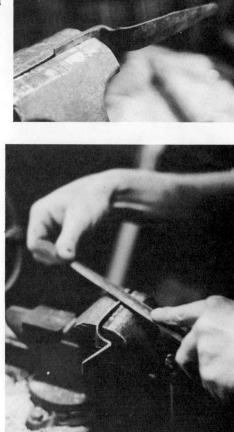

PLATE 283 Hershel uses a vise to do most of the bending of the trigger-guard. Here he smoothes the sides of the lower part of the triggerguard.

The triggerguard is the round bow that goes around the trigger. To make the triggerguard, Hershel takes a steel rod $5\frac{1}{2}''$ long and flattens it out. Then he bends it into the shape he wants, as shown in Plate 282. The distance between the square end and the first bend is $1\frac{1}{2}''$. The widest part of the triggerguard, which is the bow, is $\frac{7}{8}''$ wide.

Before he makes his next bend, he files down the rough sides of the trig-gerguard. After he has filed it smooth, he makes the final bend at the spot he is pointing to at the back part of the triggerguard in Plate 284. The back part of the triggerguard should touch the trigger plate when bent down. After Hershel has made the triggerguard and grip rail, he rivets and solders the two pieces together. He sets the grip rail against the trigger-guard, then drills a hole $\frac{1}{8}''$ in diameter through both pieces, and counter-

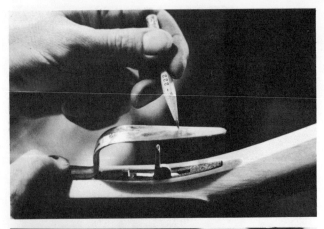

PLATE 284 Hershel points out where to bend the back of the triggerguard. The part of the guard that is bent down will touch the trigger plate.

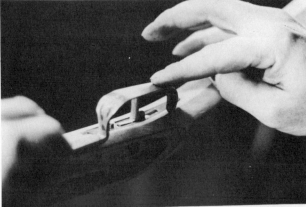

PLATE 285 Hershel lays the front part of the triggerguard on the trigger plate and stock to position it.

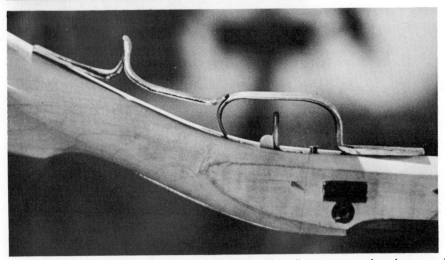

PLATE 286 Hershel gets ready to bend the grip rail up to meet the triggerguard to which it must connect. Here the triggerguard is laid out to determine the right place to attach the grip rail.

PLATE 287 To rivet the grip rail and bow (triggerguard) together, Hershel drills a hole through both pieces the size of the nail he is going to use as a rivet. Then he runs a nail through both pieces, cuts it off a little long, and pounds both ends flat.

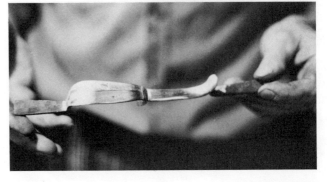

PLATE 288 Hershel solders around the rivet for reinforcement. Here is the completed triggerguard and grip rail after being soldered, filed, and smoothed.

sinks the hole so that the rivet will sink slightly into the metal. After that, he puts the nail in and flattens it out on an anvil. Then he solders the joint to make it tighter and improve the appearance. Then he files and smooths the rough edges. Instead of soldering the guard and grip rail, the old-timers would have bronzed them or braised them in a forge.

The guard he has made here is one of the typical guards. Other trigger-guards and grip rails had low grip rails or came with a reverse grip rail that locked your hand into place. Some triggerguards have thumb latches.

To inlet the triggerguard and grip rail, Hershel first lays the two ends that will be inletted into the rifle into place on the stock and traces around the ends. Then he removes the triggerguard and grip rail and chisels out the wood for the front, inlets it, and then does the same for the rear. He then drills two holes, one into each end, and screws the assembly to the stock.

Filing and Rasping the Stock

When Hershel starts rasping, he takes the big rasp and cuts the stock down to almost what it will be when finished. Then he takes smaller files and files rough scratches out of the stock. One of the common mistakes made by most builders is leaving the wood on the forearm and the front extension of the stock too heavy and bulky.

PLATE 289 Hershel inlets the triggerguard. He is careful to inlet the front of
the triggerguard first and screw it down to
stabilize it before pushing the back into
place and inletting it.

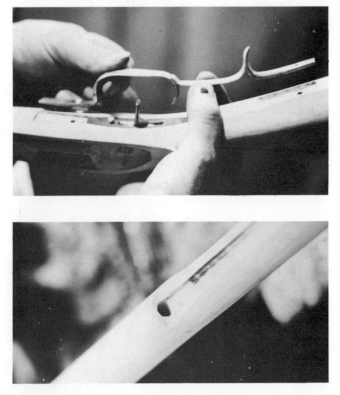

PLATE 290 Hershel puts
the completed triggerguard
into place, and is ready to
screw it down. After securing the triggerguard, Hershel rounds the front part
of the triggerguard to
match the roundness of the
stock.

PLATE 291 The ramrod entry hole before it has been rasped down.

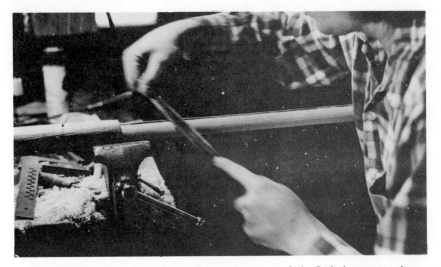

PLATE 292 Hershel rasps the forestock to smooth it. It is important that he does not leave too much wood on the forestock or it will be bulky and heavy.

PLATE 293 The butt of the stock after it has been rasped down.

He cuts the front extension down to a feather edge. The forearm should be rounded out—not left square. Another mistake often made is that the builder may want to round or roll over the wood around the trigger. It should be left flat so that the trigger plate and lock have a flat surface to rest on.

The barrel should not be in place at this point or it may be hit by the file and scratched.

Cheekpiece

First Hershel draws the cheekpiece onto the stock, then he cuts out around it roughly with a hand saw. He says, "You make it proportional to the size of the gun. I judge the shape of the cheekpiece by eye. Don't make the cheekpiece too long, and keep it shallow. If you don't keep it shallow, it will tend to kick you in the face when you shoot the gun."

When he has shaped it out roughly, he finishes it with chisels, files, and sandpaper.

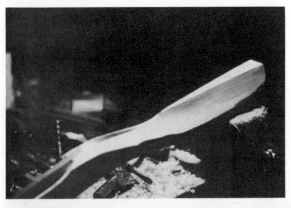

PLATE 294   Knocking off the majority of the excess stock with a rough wood rasp, Hershel files down the stock for the cheekpiece. Note the sweeping motion from the wrist to the butt.

PLATE 295   This is the cheekpiece after being cut out. Now only sanding is needed.

PLATE 296   Here is the cheekpiece showing the eyelets that will hold the vent pick.

Ramrod Pipes

Hershel makes the pipes to hold his ramrod out of any piece of thin metal —he made the ones for this gun from a water heater jacket. First he takes a ⅜″ drill and a piece of paper and wraps the paper around the drill, leaving ¼″ of paper extra on each side. Then he takes the paper, which is now the pattern, and traces it onto the metal. Next he cuts out the pieces, and makes the pipes. He starts by putting one in a vise and bends it, as shown in Plate 297.

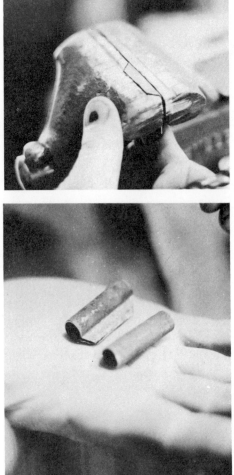

PLATE 297   The first step in bending the ramrod pipes is to bend the metal ends up about one fourth inch parallel to each other.

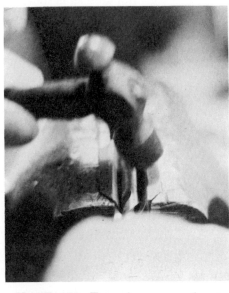

PLATE 298   To make a ramrod entry pipe round, Hershel bends the piece of metal around a three-eighths-inch drill bit.

PLATE 299   The finished ramrod pipes are one and a half inches long.

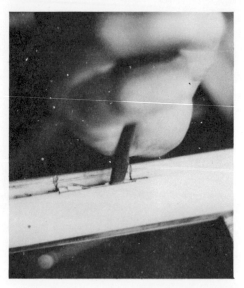

PLATE 300   Here Hershel is chiseling to inlet the ramrod pipes.

After the edges have been bent, he puts the drill bit onto the center of the piece of metal and bends it around it. The edges, which are ¼″ wide, are left over to form flaps that nails can be driven through to hold the pipes in place.

He then takes a rat-tail file and files the roughness out of the entries of the pipes. He flares the front of the entry pipe to allow the ramrod to enter more easily.

To position the ramrod pipes, Hershel measures 3½″ from the muzzle to place the first one. The second goes halfway between the first pipe and the ramrod hole in the forearm. To inlet the two ramrod pipes, he lays the pipes on the ramrod guide groove with the lips (edges) up. Then he traces their outline onto the stock and chisels them out. Then he cuts the slots for the edges or lips, and sets the pipes into place.

After inletting the pipes into the stock, he drills one hole for each pipe through the stock and the pipe edges. Then he puts pins made from small finishing nails with their heads cut off into each hole, securing the pipes in place.

Sights

Before Hershel makes the front sight, he cuts the barrel off to the dimensions he wants it to be on the final product. He lets his barrel hang over the stock about ⅟₁₆″. After cutting the barrel, he files the end of the barrel where the rifled grooves are. He files the grooves at the crown of the muzzle to make it load easier.

PLATE 301 Hershel drives the copper base plate into place. The front sight will be mounted on top of this copper base.

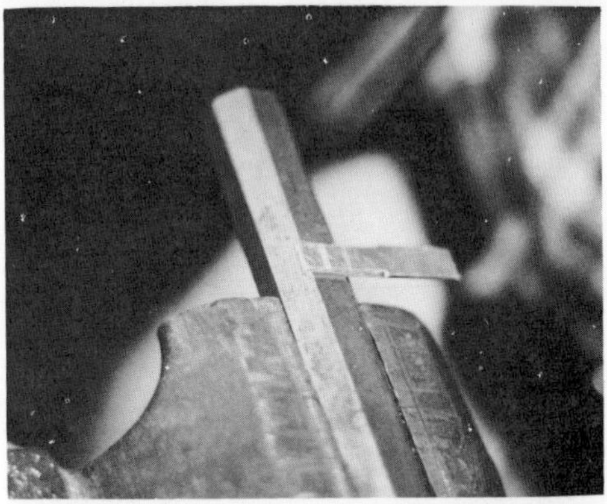

PLATE 302 The plate is now in place and ready to be cut off. Note the groove cut into the center of the sight where the silver blade will go.

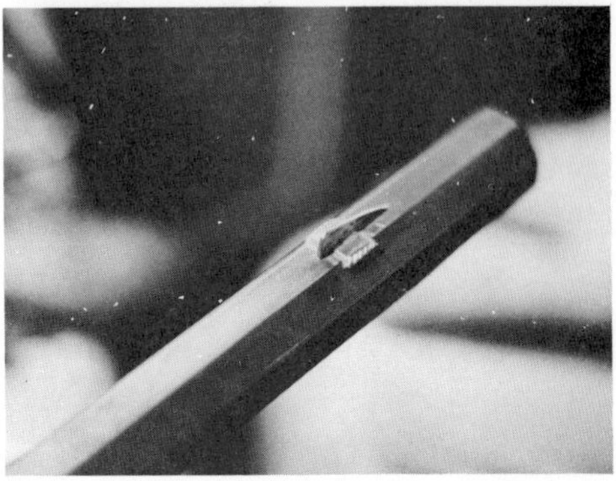

PLATE 303 The completed front sight with the silver blade soldered on top. Hershel made the silver blade out of a silver quarter.

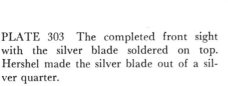

The base of the front sight is made from a piece of flat copper. Hershel then takes a silver quarter and cuts out the shape of the blade with a hacksaw and smoothes it. After that, he takes the copper plate and mounts it on the dovetail groove cut for that purpose. Then he puts the blade into place and solders it on. He uses hard-core silver solder.

The hunters in old times knew what they were doing when they set the front sight down on the barrel. They used a low silver blade. When polished, it was easily visible even in bad light. In the woods in dim light, it was a common mistake to take in too much front sight and overshoot game. Hershel's grandfather, who was a notorious squirrel hunter in this region (Herschel Finney), told him that the best sight was one made of bone. This type of sight picked up the largest amount of light and was easily seen. The only problem was that it was easily broken.

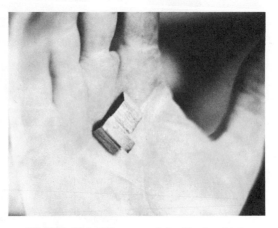

PLATE 304   The rear sight blank which is cut out of a piece of half-inch-square steel stock.

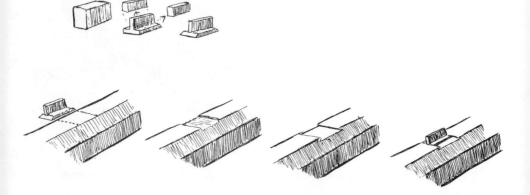

PLATE 305   Diagram by Hershel House.

PLATE 306 After completing the rear sight, Hershel rounds one end of the groove of the sight with a drill.

Because the shooter of today uses his rifle a good deal in match shooting, he prefers to have a sight a great deal higher, for reasons described earlier.

For the rear sight, Hershel cuts out one half inch of square steel stock. He uses the same metal that he used to cut the trigger. Next he beats down two sides on the anvil. Then he takes his drill and starts to shape it out as shown in Plate 305. After shaping the rear sight, he levels up the bottom. Next he determines where it is going to be placed on the barrel. He does this by holding up the rifle as though he were going to shoot it, placing the rear sight about ten inches from the breechplug. Then he has someone move the rear sight up and down along the barrel, focusing on the front sight, until he gets the least amount of blur around the notch on the rear sight. He marks that spot and mounts the rear sight in place, cutting out the place for it with a hacksaw and a three-cornered file (the three-cornered file is used to get into the undercut edges). Then he drives the sight into place and does the final shaping and cleaning. One advantage of the muzzle loader is that the sights are out away from your eye.

Stainless-steel Vent

Hershel sets the hole for the vent right at the junction of the breech and the barrel. He lines the hole up so that it is at the bottom of the powder pan. After this is done, he bores a pilot hole into the barrel, using a number three drill bit. Then he takes a $\frac{1}{4}''$ by 28 threads per inch tap and taps the hole. Then he takes a $\frac{1}{4}''$ stainless-steel rod and taps it. After tapping it, he drills a $\frac{5}{32}''$ hole into the end of the tapped rod almost $\frac{1}{8}''$ deep. Then he screws the rod into the barrel with the hole facing the inside of the barrel.

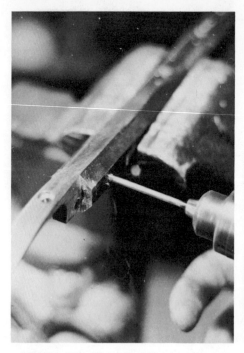

PLATE 307   Hershel drills the pilot hole   PLATE 308   Here is the stainless-steel
for the stainless-steel vent.   vent after being threaded.

Next he cuts the rod off flush with the barrel, and drills a $\frac{1}{16}''$ hole into the
rod until it breaks through into the hole drilled from the other end. This
opens the vent and completes it.

The better guns have vents made of stainless steel. By putting a stainless-
steel vent in the gun, it fires more quickly and prevents the snapping and
hissing that sometimes happens on guns without the vent. A man who has
worked with both kinds of guns will know the differences between them
well.

Stainless-steel vents may be purchased at any of the muzzle-loading supply houses. They come ready to screw in and finish.

Tallow Hole, Vent Pick, Decorative Molding, and Feather Hole

It is rare to see an old mountain rifle that doesn't have a tallow hole—
especially if it is a southern-made rifle. The tallow hole goes on the side of
the rifle that the lock is on. The tallow hole is centered up and down, and is
about $\frac{1}{2}''$ from the butt of the stock.

PLATE 309 The   com-
pleted tallow hole.

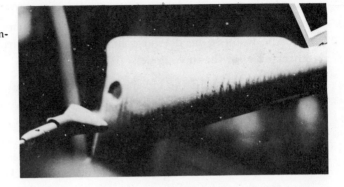

To make the tallow hole, Hershel drills it with a brace and bit about
½″–¾″ deep. Old-timers made a mixture of beeswax and beef tallow
to go into the hole. They heated the mixture in a ladle and poured it into
the hole. They would put this mixture on the patch to make the ball go
down the barrel easier and also to help keep carbon from building up in the
barrel.

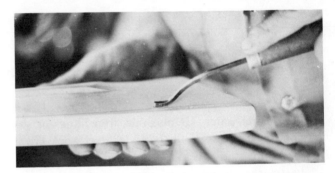

PLATE 310   Here Hershel is using the checking tool to
cut the small groove up the butt of the stock. This decorative groove is one fourth of an inch above the bottom edge
of the butt tapering to the bottom edge of the stock just
below the center of the trigger plate. He puts one of these
grooves on each side of the stock.

MOLDING: Hershel cuts his decorative molding with a checking tool. The
groove is just a simple line cut along the edge of the stock for style. Some
rifle makers add a good bit of decoration, but a simple mountain rifle like
this one would not be that fancy.

VENT PICK: The vent pick is used to make sure the vent is open and not
clogged. This should always be checked before the rifle is taken out and
shot. The vent will sometimes get clogged when the rifle is left sitting between hunts or shooting matches. Hershel makes the three eyelets to hold

the pick out of nails, the heads of which are cut off. The shafts of the nails are bent into the shape of a U. He drills holes where the two points will go into the wood so he doesn't split the stock. He drills six holes under the cheekpiece for the three eyelets.

FEATHER HOLE: In the old days when rifles were used a great deal, vent holes burned out rather fast. Stainless steel was unknown. Some fine English guns had platinum vents, but they were expensive and unattainable in the backwoods. When vents burned out, a rifle would leak the powder charges during the loading process. Thus, hunters, when loading their rifles, would first plug the vent hole with a small turkey or chicken feather shaft, which kept the charge from leaking. The feather was removed after the rifle was loaded and before the lock was primed. A special hole was drilled underneath the rear of the stock just behind the triggerguard and usually centered with the cheekpiece. The feather was kept there.

Raising the Grain, Staining, and Browning the Barrel

Before Hershel can put a finish on the stock, he must first raise the grain. He does this by wetting the stock with a wet cloth, then resanding when it dries. He does this about three times—or until the grain doesn't raise anymore. He does this so that if he ever gets the gun wet, the water won't raise the grain and ruin the finish.

Hershel uses nitric acid to stain the stock. It is cut one part nitric acid to three parts water. He also puts iron filings or steel wool into the solution, and the acid eats up the filings or steel wool. He adds this material until the solution is static (won't take any more). When heat is later applied to the barrel, the dissolved steel rusts and gives the stain its color. Mix this in the open air, for it is important not to breathe the fumes of this solution as it may sear your lungs. Mix the stain in a crock so the heat generated in the process doesn't burst the container. If the solution starts to react with the container, soda water will neutralize it.

After adding the iron filings, he applies the stain to the stock, then heats the stock with a propane torch. This is the same method used two hundred years ago: They used aqua fortis (old name for nitric acid) and held the rifle over the forge to heat the stock. He goes over the stock with the torch until he gets a glaze on it, and then rubs it down with some thinned, boiled linseed oil and a piece of steel wool. Next he heats the linseed oil into the stock using the propane torch, paying special attention to the nooks and crannies that he couldn't get to before without burning the stock (linseed oil won't burn and acts as protection in these areas). The color of the stock will deepen into a mahogany color by the following day. The next day he

PLATE 311 The stock before applying
the heat to the stain. The stain has already
been applied.

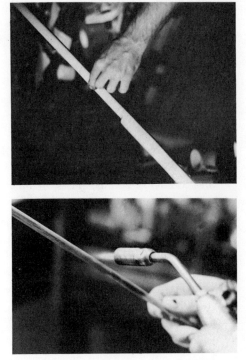

PLATE 312 Here Hershel is heating and
setting the stain into the ramrod.

applies boiled linseed oil, full strength, three or four times. The linseed oil
that has been put on helps keep the stock flexible so it won't dry out and become brittle. It also builds up a fine, old-time-looking finish. Continue to
apply a coat of linseed oil once a day until a good finish has been achieved.
Never hang the gun high on a wall or above a fireplace as the stock will dry
out.

Hacker Martin explained the stock finish he used to Ogilvie H. Davis in
the August 1970 issue of *Muzzle Blasts:*

We usually use nitric acid and water, half and half, with some steel
wool eaten up in it to make the color black. This we smear on the well-
sanded stock with a small cotton rag which is held in the split end of a
small stick. This protects the fingers from being burned by the acid.
The new stock is then sanded down and smeared with Esquire brown
shoe dye. Then the stock is lightly sanded down again and rubbed with
wool waste. Next, we go over the stock with a swab dipped in linseed
oil, in which there is about one ounce of turpentine to the pint of oil.
The stock is then wooled and oiled several times.

When the stock looks nice enough, it is let dry good, and then waxed with the best floor wax available, or varnished a few times with Spar Varnish. For a top job, use red violin oil varnish. It imparts a finish slick as glass.

To brown the metal parts, Hershel first cleans and shines them. To get the barrel clean, he drawfiles it with a metal file until all the scale and oil is removed down to fresh metal. When he drawfiles the barrel, he also knocks the sharp corners off the octagonal barrel. He does this to break up the glare of the sharp corners; the glare impairs the shooter's vision and tips off game. After filing, he sands it down with sandpaper. Do not put your hands on the filed or sanded parts or fingerprints will show in the browning process.

After filing, the barrel is plugged with a dowel rod and the vent with a toothpick. For our gun, he applied paste bluing to the barrel, and then brown bluing. This gave it a nice old-time dark-brown look. To apply the brown, he heated the parts and the barrel with a torch and applied the browning solution, which turned them to a rusty brown. Then he applied the bluing compound by just rubbing it on straight from the bottle.

The reason he did our gun this way was that we were in a rush and had to have it finished. The better and older way of applying browning solution takes about a week to do, whereas the above only took one day. With the older method, the barrel was stripped, and then a cotton swab was used to paint the barrel and the other metal parts with a browning solution. This can be obtained from Log Cabin Sports Shop now, but was made from home recipes years ago. A recipe from *The Science of Gunnery,* published in 1841, follows:

1 oz. Muriate Tincture of Steel
1 oz. Spirits of Wine
1/4 oz. Muriate of Mercury
1/4 oz. Strong Nitric Acid
1/8 oz. Blue Stone
1 qt. Water

These are well mixed and allowed to stand to amalgamate. After the oil or grease has been removed from the barrels by lime, the mixture is laid on lightly with a sponge every two hours and scratched off with a wire brush every morning until the barrels are dark enough, and then the acid is destroyed by pouring boiling water on the barrels and continuing to rub them until they are nearly cool. Presumably "muriate tincture of steel" is ferrous chloride ($FeCl_2$), "spirits of wine" is ethyl alcohol, "muriate of mercury" is mercuric chloride also known as corrosive sublimate ($HgCl_2$), and "blue stone" is copper sulphate. Another recipe for "Birmingham Imitations" calls for the following:

1 oz. Sweet Nitre
½ oz. Tincture of Steel
¼ oz. Blue Vitriol
6 drops Nitric Acid
14 grains Corrosive Sublimate
1 pt. Water

When the barrels are dark enough, drop a few drops of muriatic acid in a basin of water and wash the barrels slightly to brighten the twists." [This obviously refers to finishing a "twist" in shotgun barrels, the final acid wash to remove some of the brown finish.]

It is important that all grease or oil be removed using lime as mentioned. Dust hydrated lime on a cloth pad and rub vigorously, renewing the lime as necessary. Otherwise, boil the barrel in a weak solution of lye. Do not handle the cleaned barrel in the bare hands as oil from the skin will leave finger marks. When boiling, if you do it that way, put wood plugs in the ends of the bore and hold by the projecting ends.

We found these recipes in *For Beginners Only,* by B. M. Baxter, published by the National Muzzle Loading Rifle Association.

After sitting overnight, a fine coat of rust would cover the barrel. Give it another coat of solution, being careful not to touch the barrel. In humid weather, the barrel will rust rapidly. Repeat the process for four or five days or until it has a good coat of rust. When it has a good, even rich covering, scald the barrel by holding it under a hot faucet until the barrel is hot. This will neutralize the acid in the browning solution. Then give it a good coat of linseed oil or motor oil while the barrel is still warm.

Hacker Martin explained his bluing and browning process to Ogilvie H. Davis in the August 1970 issue of *Muzzle Blasts:*

Gun browner is made by taking a pint of water, a pint of rubbing or radiator alcohol, mix and throw in a handful of Bluestone along with a teaspoon of nitric acid. Shake the mixture well and set away for a few days. If you want it extra fast, add a quarter of an ounce of Corrosive Sublimate of Mercury. Wet the iron with the solution, then let it set until dry and rub off with steel wool, wet again and repeat until the brown suits you. This may take three days or three weeks.

You can blue the above by boiling the rust off in plain water, then wooling down, continuing until the color is dark enough to suit. No trouble getting this solution to take hold. I wipe the surplus grease off a barrel, and smear it on hard. I scrub the iron, in fact—no trouble in getting it to stick. Do not get the mixture on your skin, as too much will cause a burn.

For applying the mix, a piece of rag set in the cleft end of a wooden stick is fine. This can then be thrown away when the job is done, as the acid eats up the stick pretty fast.

Hardening the Frizzen

To harden the frizzen, Hershel heats the frizzen to a light orange color and dips it in light motor oil. If the metal is too soft and won't harden, then it has to be half-soled. (This means attaching a second piece of harder metal to the face of the frizzen.) The latter was the case with our rifle. The frizzen was too soft and wouldn't harden, so Hershel had to harden the frizzen by adding a piece of hardened steel he cut from an old file. It was cut to

PLATE 313 Hershel uses a piece of an old file to make the frizzen piece. He rivets it to the face of the frizzen and then grinds the rough edges down.

PLATE 314 Here Hershel is ready to cut off the excess metal from the old file and then remove the excess edges with a grinder.

fit the face of the frizzen. Then he ground down the surface and the edges with an emery wheel. He then drilled three holes through both pieces of metal for the rivets. Before he pulled the rivets down tight against the frizzen, he heated the file piece and quenched it in oil to anneal it and keep it from breaking.

After he had it riveted on and filed down to fit exactly, he put the lock back together, adding a piece of flint, and checked it to make sure it would spark properly. If it had not sparked properly, he would have had to put it back in the forge and heat it hotter and repeat the process.

One of the better sparks is a yellowish-orange spark. The hottest spark is a white one that just sits and sizzles. That spark is too hot, and it means the frizzen is too hard. To take some of the hardness out, he would have to heat it a little. A beginner should probably buy an already-assembled lock. These locks will spark properly when brought.

Ramrods

The size of the ramrod should be about ⅜″ in diameter at the tip for a .45-caliber rifle. To make the one for our gun, Hershel started with a straight hickory rod ½″ in diameter and worked it down to ⅜″ on one end tapered down to about ¼″ on the other so it won't stick in the pipes in wet weather.

Hershel has made his ramrods before, but now he buys them from Log Cabin Sports Shop at ten dollars a dozen.

To make a ramrod, Hershel just cuts a piece of straight hickory one inch square and uses a drawknife until it is round. "Don't ever buy one of those dowel rods from a hardware store. If you get a ball that's hard to drive down the barrel, the dowel rod might break and might go through your hand."

The rod must be made out of a good piece of hickory that has the grain going straight from one end to the other to prevent splintering with use. It should always be cut a good deal smaller than the ramrod hole in the forearm. The reason for this is that while hunting in humid or wet weather, the rod might swell in the forearm and get stuck.

Molding Lead Balls

Hershel first cut some small pieces of lead from the big chunk of lead he has. Then he placed them in his ladle in the forge and melted them down. After they had melted, he poured enough molten lead into the mold to fill it; then he opened the mold allowing the hot ball out and cool. He

PLATE 315   This photo shows Hershel's
.445 mold and .315 mold. These molds are
for .45-caliber and .32-caliber rifles.

PLATE 316   Hershel pours
hot lead into a mold and
makes a ball. The gunsmiths
call it "running bullets" or
"running balls."

poured about two or three balls first and then put them back into the ladle
to be melted again. He did this to warm the mold for easy use.

Whenever he found a ball with an air hole or bubble in it, it was a sign
that the mold or the lead wasn't hot enough. These were remelted because
they would not shoot properly.

The ball should be five thousandths of an inch smaller than the caliber
of the gun so that there will be room for the patch around it. The size of the
mold for a .45-caliber rifle should be .445. After the bullets are poured, the
spur left on each (where the lead entered the hole in the mold) should be
clipped off (called "spurring" the ball), using the pinchers built into the
mold. Cut the spurs off as close to the ball as possible.

When loading the ball into the gun, Hershel tries to load with the spur
up. If what is left of the spur went down the side of the rifle, it might affect
the ball's course. To prevent this, sometimes Hershel will take the butt of
his knife and pound down anything left of the spur.

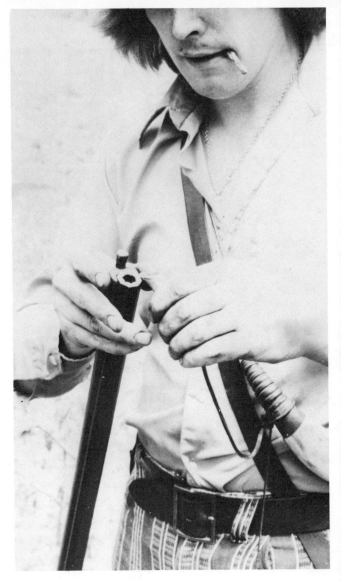

Loading and Firing

Before you fire a new gun, you should first dry the barrel with a clean patch and blow down the barrel to make sure the vent is clear. (After firing, blowing down the barrel creates moisture inside that helps break down the carbon that tends to accumulate inside—and keep the vent clean.) Also clean the vent with the vent pick.

Next Hershel takes his powder—a 45-gram charge—and pours one charge down the muzzle of the gun. He uses a piece of denim cloth for his

PLATE 318

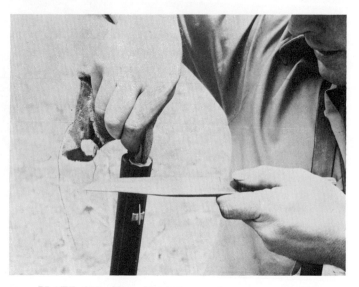

PLATE 319   Here Hershel cuts the excess material
of the patch off.

patch. For target shooting, he uses a spit patch—he spits on the patch before putting the ball on it to help the ball slide down into the barrel and
also to break up the carbon from the previous shot as the ball is shoved
down. Spit patches would not be used in hunting as the charge is often left

in the gun for a long period of time before shooting, and the spit patch would tend to rust the inside of the barrel. For hunting, he uses a patch lubricated with tallow and beeswax, or sperm whale oil (which is the best lubricant of all, but almost unobtainable nowadays). After doing this, he takes his patch, places it over the opening of the barrel, places a ball on top of the patch, taps it down into the barrel the depth of the ball, and cuts the cloth patch off as shown in Plate 319.

Then, using the ramrod, he shoves the ball and patch down the barrel to the breech, and seats it well by tamping it.

He then pulls the hammer back to half-cock and primes the pan. He uses a finer powder for his primer than for the charge. To prime the pan, he just fills the pan full of fine powder. Then he closes the frizzen over the pan. Now the gun is ready to fire.

PLATE 320 After cutting off the excess patch, Hershel prepares to ram the ball down the barrel.

Loading The Flintlock Muzzle Loader

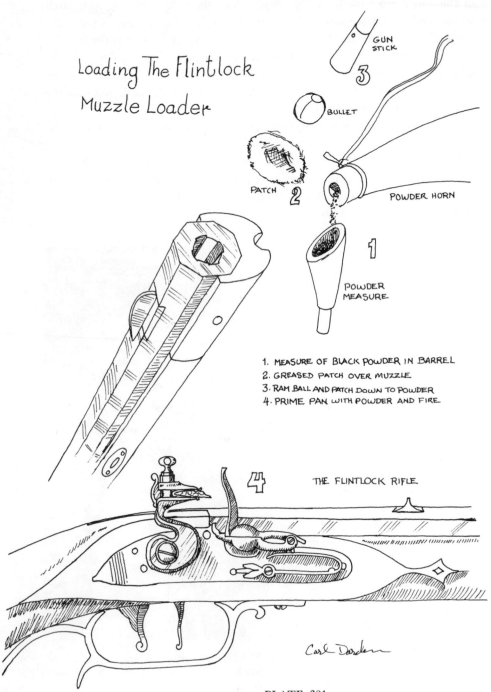

GUN STICK

3

BULLET

PATCH

2

POWDER HORN

1

POWDER MEASURE

1. MEASURE OF BLACK POWDER IN BARREL
2. GREASED PATCH OVER MUZZLE
3. RAM BALL AND PATCH DOWN TO POWDER
4. PRIME PAN WITH POWDER AND FIRE

4

THE FLINTLOCK RIFLE

Carl Darden

PLATE 321

PLATE 322   Wig fires the completed rifle.

After a few shots Hershel pulls the lock out to check whether or not powder or carbon is leaking out between the pan and the barrel down into the lock mortise. If it is, it can be stopped by either filing the bolster flat on the lock or setting the lock in a little deeper. Powder escaping into the lock mortise will eventually cause the lock to rust on the inside and cut the life span of the rifle.

To clean the gun, he runs a patch soaked in hot soapy water down the barrel. He does this a couple of times and then runs a dry patch down the barrel to dry it out and prevent rusting. He also swabs a little hot soapy water over the lock to help break up carbon. He said, "If you clean the barrel and lock and keep it clean, it will fire well. After cleaning the barrel, pay particular attention to the lock and oil both it and the barrel with a light coat of oil. For extra protection, you should also oil both the inside and the outside of the barrel with a light coat of light machine oil the day after cleaning."

PLATE 323 Joe's home where he lives with his mother is also home for numerous chickens and dogs.

PLATE 324 The front of Joe's shop.

Joe Farmer

Joe Farmer is one of several gunmakers in the Waynesville, North Carolina, area. When we first drove to his home, high on the side of one of the hills overlooking the Allen's Creek section and surrounded by apple orchards, we noticed right away the number of animals he had around the place. He laughed and said, "I like dogs, and I raise fighting chickens. I have seven dogs. Most of them are strays I picked up. I brought them all in except a beagle pup which I bought. The strays gotta live too."

Joe's shop, which is adjacent to his house, is about ten feet wide by thirty feet long, and has a rustic appearance about it. In the shop are his tools, some of the rifles he's built, and others he's in the process of building. The floor is wood with a strip of carpet covering the center. There's an old wood

PLATE 325   Inside the shop, a wood heater dominates one wall. Hanging behind it are several guns in various stages of completion. Just beyond the heater, Missy lies asleep in her favorite chair.

stove for heating, and on the back wall is a stereo tucked away so he can listen to bluegrass while he works. One long workbench runs almost the length of the room, and the bench is filled with rifle parts, barrels, planes, rasps, screwdrivers, nails, and screws, and all the other things he needs for his work. Above the counter are shelves filled with more tools and parts. The one comfortable chair he has was long ago claimed by one of the dogs, who sits and watches as Joe puts his rifles together.

When we asked Joe to tell us how he got started in rifle making, he said, "I first started building rifles in 1959. That's when I found out I had multiple sclerosis. This makes up about half my living. I've got a caretaker's job that I work part-time on. I've always been interested in rifles and in shooting them, so I just decided to build one. I acquire my tools over the long run, collecting slowly as I go. I build the guns almost from scratch. Never have used a kit. They take me about three weeks apiece, and I guess I've built about two hundred by now. When I first started building them, I sold the fancy ones for $150. Now, if someone wants me to make one, I just have to sit down with them and work out the price according to what they want. I never advertise about selling rifles. I just go by word of mouth. And then I go to the shooting matches, and people see the guns I make and like them and ask me to build them one. But I don't go to many matches now. I'm not able."

Joe told us a little about the rifles he makes:

"I use G. R. Douglas barrels. I use .32, .40, .45, and a few .50 caliber. Most are .45 caliber. Those are on my match guns. I make a lot of match guns. I've made only two or three flintlocks since I've been building rifles. I like caplocks because I think they're more reliable. I can make flintlocks on request, though. The barrels I use are already rifled. I have a rifling machine, but I don't use it. I started rifling the barrel once but the bench it was set on got loose so I quit. You have to have time and a good back to rifle barrels."

For the Tennessee-style rifles he makes, which are his favorites, he often uses Siler locks intact, but sometimes he uses only the works from the locks and makes the hammer-and-lock sideplate himself to his own specifications. He also makes the double-set triggers, triggerguard, toe plate, buttplate, end cap, sideplate, and ramrod thimbles for each gun. Since most of the guns of this Tennessee-style were iron-mounted, he continues the tradition, making these parts of iron. He also makes the sights himself, fashioning the rear one of iron and the front one out of either silver or brass. He has made his own ramrods before, but usually buys them now. When he was making his own, he would cut a straight hickory tree three to four inches in diameter, season the portion of the trunk he was going to use, and then split it up into

PLATE 326   Three
finished guns on a wall of
Joe's shop. Note the hooded
rear sight on the match
gun at top.

PLATE 327 A powder horn
and pouch Joe made hang
ready for use.

ramrod sizes. Then each ramrod would be scraped and sanded to round it, and then saturated with raw linseed oil to harden it.

Joe uses curly maple stocks almost exclusively and finishes them with chromic acid rubbed down with linseed oil. For the ramrod, he uses linseed oil alone. The barrel is drawfiled and then coated with browning solution made from a recipe he found in an old book. Not knowing what the old chemical names meant, he took the recipe to a chemist in Hazelwood who mixed it up for his use.

PLATE 328   Joe shows Stanley Masters and Mark Palpal-lotic one of the guns he made inspired by a Baxter Bean original.

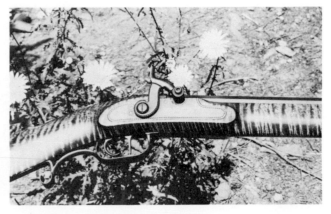

PLATE   329   The   lock plate of the gun is one he made himself.

PLATE 330   Joe also made
its silver front sights.

On the match guns he sometimes makes, he adds a shade over the sights, and he told us. "The design for the shade you see over the sights is my idea. It's for when you're at a shooting match and the sun's on your sight one time, and then the next time you shoot, a cloud is over the sun and your sight gets a different shade of light. With this metal shade, your light stays the same always.

"I do some repair work on guns, too, but it's not as big as it used to be. I used to repair a lot, but now it's mostly building rifles. The most popular rifle I sell is a Pennsylvania style I build. *My* favorite rifle, though, is the Tennessee. I got my patterns off an original Baxter Bean gun. Bean was a noted Tennessee man. He built rifles for a while, and every one of his sons followed him. I guess the reason I prefer the North Carolina and Tennessee types over the Kentucky and Pennsylvania is that I'm from here. My mother's a McCracken and she's Scottish. My grandfather has been along Camp Branch here for sixty years, and I was born just across the ridge here and then moved to Camp Branch when I was two years old and have been here ever since. I can just picture the man who made those Tennessee rifles. He didn't have the fancy shop or the fancy tools that northern makers had. Maybe just had a bench under a tree somewhere and made just very simple guns. But they were good guns. They're still my favorites."

Article and photographs by Jeff Lane, Stanley Masters, and Mark Palpal-lotic.

PLATE 331   W. A. Huscusson in his shop.

W. A. Huscusson

W. A. Huscusson was born in Macon County, North Carolina, in 1899. He lived there until 1920, when he moved to Lawrenceville, Georgia, to work in the sawmills there along with several other people from our area, including Lake Stiles (see the previous *Foxfire* books). He worked in sawmills there for forty years.

His first wife died in 1961, and a year later he moved back home to be near his mother, his stepfather, and his son Gene—one of three children. Five years after he returned to Macon County, he married again, and he and his wife live a relatively quiet, peaceful life outside Franklin, North Carolina. He spends part of his time doing odd jobs around their home and keeping the garden in good shape. On our second visit, he had just been to town to get some window curtains and had helped his wife hang them. When we arrived, he was looking over some of the coins he has collected over the years and lamenting the fact that he is becoming forgetful. Not long ago, for example, he lost eighty-one silver dollars and found them a month later behind the boot of his car. On the day we visited, he had just found two more in the glove compartment. He was getting ready to give them to his son.

Though he doesn't travel now, he once went to see a sister in Lyman, Washington, and wants to go out West again. He's afraid he's going to have to pass that trip up, however. Laughing, he told us that his wife even got

PLATE 332   One wall of his shop is filled with guns he has made, or is in the process of repairing.

nervous when he hiked up neighboring Mt. LeConte with Rufus Morgan (see *Foxfire 4*) and fourteen others in April of 1976. He was determined to go, though, and did.

Though he claims, "I don't get nothing done much no more," he does stay busy. For example, he still makes knives with deer antler handles, and hunting pouches from leather or groundhog skin. And he makes guns.

The little shop that he works in is behind his trailer. On our first visit, we had noticed with amusement a mother cat and five very young kittens in one corner of the shop near the pot belly stove. Several adventurous, pure white ones refused to stay in their box, and we had to constantly watch to keep from stepping on them. By the second visit, he had given up the stuggle to keep them put and had let them out in the yard for the first time. They were clustered happily around the door of the shop as we walked in.

We talked for a long time that day, especially about how he got interested in guns. He told us how, when he was little, he wasn't allowed to handle guns at all; but one day when he was about fifteen, he and his first cousin took one of his uncle's muzzle loaders into the woods. His cousin knew how to use it, and when they treed a squirrel in a big hickory, he shot at it nine times. Finally the squirrel began to come down the tree, and it dropped off dead. One of the bullets had hit home, and W.A. has been crazy about muzzle loaders ever since.

The first gun he owned was a Stevens Crack Shot .22 that cost $3.50. At that time flintlocks were really going out of style—a phenomenon that W.A. never completely understood: "Some people thought that flint was all there ever was, and they didn't change. They *still* buy flintlocks. But lots of them changed right away, just like they do everything else. Just like an old car that runs good, doesn't use oil, and they'll trade it in right away anyhow."

PLATE 333 Standing with two of his rifles: a flintlock and a percussion.

As he grew up, he continued to shoot flintlocks when he had the chance, and he kept the memory of them when he moved to Lawrenceville. He got the chance to make his first one when he found an old hand-forged barrel in Lawrenceville and bought it for fifty cents. He took the barrel to a man who re-rifled it and reworked the breechplug for him, and then, from the memory of guns he had seen, he made the rest of the gun and gave the finished piece to his daughter who still owns it. Later, he got a pattern from a gun he especially liked that was in a neighbor's gun collection in Lawrenceville. It was a half-stock, however, and since he prefers a Kentucky-style, full-stock flintlock over others, he rarely uses that first pattern.

He began his first serious gun work after he moved back to Macon County. Though most of his business comes from people who bring him guns they want repaired (or bring him a barrel and some pieces from one

PLATE 334 Two guns he made from kits, along with a knife, pouch, and powder horn he also made. The gun at the top is a blunderbuss.

PLATE 335 Marty Henderson firing the blunderbuss.

they want rebuilt), he has managed to build forty rifles, six shotguns, eighteen pistols, three derringers, and one blunderbuss from a Dixie Gun Works kit.

A typical Huscusson gun would be made mostly from parts (buttplate, triggerguard, trigger, barrel, lock, brass-tipped ramrod, etc.) purchased from companies like Log Cabin Sports Shop and Dixie Gun Works. He uses Siler locks almost exclusively, saying, "They're well-known, they look good, and they work good. I like them." It would be a Kentucky-style, full-stock flintlock with a curly maple stock (though he has also used cherry and walnut). It would have a toe plate and a patch box, unlike the rifle Hershel made for us, and the cheekpiece would be quite pronounced—an idea he got from a picture he once saw. The one hundred twenty-five hours of assembly—including chiseling out the barrel groove and the ramrod groove and shaping all the wood—would be done by hand. He also makes his own sights. He makes the front one using brass for the base and German silver for the blade, and the rear one from angle iron. And he makes his own thimbles out of brass or steel. He sometimes makes the patch boxes, but he can buy them cheaper than he can make them.

PLATE 336 Mr. Huscusson also showed a hunting horn he made from a steer's horn.

He avoids engraving, saying that he started too late in life to learn how to do such fancy works, and customers seem to prefer the plainer, simpler flintlocks. If they want engraved metal decorations, however, he buys them and insets them by hand. Then the barrel is browned (if it's a more modern gun, he blues it). With an electric engraver, he engraves his name on the bottom side of the barrel.

The finished rifle sells for about $300. "I've sold some nice guns, but you can't make them if you don't sell them. My guns have gone to people from Florida, North Carolina, South Carolina, Ohio, New York, and Oregon."

He gets the word around about his guns and knives by taking them to shooting matches, county fairs, craft shows, and school classes. He enjoys the matches most, saying, "I can't shoot when I go. I can't see as good as I used to. But I go to see the guns. I like to watch them shoot, meet the people and see the guns. I really enjoy that."

Article and photographs by Jeff Lane, Stanley Masters, Marty Henderson, and Jeff Reeves.

Frank Cochran

A friend of ours named Winfred Cagle, who lives in Bryson City, North Carolina, told us about Frank Cochran. A blacksmith first and later a machinist, Frank was noted for the fact that he designed and machined his own percussion locks rather than relying on kits.

PLATE 337   Frank Cochran.

PLATE 338   Frank molds a lead ball for us and then . . .

PLATE 339   . . . watches, with his grandchildren, as Tinker McCoy tries her hand at it for the first time.

PLATE 340 Doug Cochran fires the gun Frank made for him at a target set up in the back yard of Frank's home.

Jeff Lane wrote to him asking permission to visit, received a gracious reply, and during the summer, as he requested, three of us visited him. When we arrived, we found to our surprise that he had gone to a tremendous amount of trouble to get ready for us. For example, he had spent days borrowing back a number of rifles he had made, so that we could see and photograph them. Two of his grandchildren had come over and helped him set up his bullet-molding equipment, and they had already made a number of lead balls by the time we arrived and were ready to teach us how. And his grandson, Doug Cochran, had set up a loading stand that Frank had designed and was ready to demonstrate target shooting with the gun Frank had made for him.

Except for the barrels, Frank fashioned nearly every piece for the thirty or so guns he has made. The trigger and lock assemblies, for example, were nearly all made from scratch in his machine shop, and it takes only slight familiarity with guns to be able to spot numerous innovations that he worked into their designs.

Two methods characterize the finishes he used on the stocks. For the gun he made for himself, he first fine-sanded the stock. Then he took undiluted nitric acid and dipped a ball of steel wool into it for a moment, lifted it out whereupon it rusted instantly, and then dipped it back into the acid for a moment to allow the rust to fall off and color the acid. Then he swabbed one coat of acid on the stock, left it on for a half hour, and then washed it off to keep it from turning the stock black.

On other stocks, he used three tablespoonfuls of Griffin liquid brown shoe dye mixed in one quart of linseed oil. Each stock received at least three coats of this mixture, rubbed after each coat with fine steel wool.

He browned all of his barrels except two, which he blued, using the same solution Joe Farmer uses. It is mixed for them by a local druggist. He

browned them in a warm, damp basement, used three or four coats on each
barrel, and then oiled each one well.

We examined each of the guns he had assembled for us to look at and
photographed several for this section, while learning how to mold lead balls
and watching Doug shoot. It was a full, fine afternoon punctuated regularly
by Kool-Aid breaks that Hattie Cochran, his wife, insisted we take. And as
we left, they filled several bags with apples for us from the trees in their
front yard.

Article and photographs by Linda Ledford and Tinker McCoy

My parents came from Swain County, North Carolina, and I was born
in the Macon County mountains on top of Winding Stair Mountain. My
mother died when I was two months and twenty days old, and my father
brought my mother back to the Alarka community in Swain County and
buried her and gave me to his mother and father. Their names were Mr.
and Mrs. Worth Cochran.

Times were hard in those days. We had a rough mountain farm and a
good apple orchard and a good peach orchard, and we made a little money
off our peaches and apples. And we kept a lot of bees and sold a lot of
honey.

When I grew up, I became a trapper and a hunter. I hunted a lot, and I
knew the mountains well in Swain County. I had a trap line in the winter
time, and I'd camp out every other night at the end of my trap line (it was
one day out and one day back) on the Fry knob. I caught lots of furs. It
was cheap then, but a little money was worth a whole lot. I was trapping
anything in the way of possums, polecats, coons, foxes—anything that was
of any value on the market. And then I did a good deal of hunting. Especially when I was camping. I had squirrels, rabbits, and sometimes pheas-
ants to eat. I'd choose my camping place in a laurel patch where there was
no timber in case a storm blowed in on me. A laurel patch was good protection from snow. We had some big snows. Lots of times I'd build me a fire
and melt the snow away and then move my fire and sleep where I had my
first fire.

I had one partner that I wish hadn't been around a lot of times. He was
a bad bobcat. He came around and did a great deal of hollering, but he
never did come around where I could see him. I finally caught him in a
double-spring wolf trap, but he broke my trap chain and got away. Some
men that had been coon hunting treed him on Conley's Creek, and they
dug in and killed him. They knew him by his foot being gone—his foot had
rotted off and he had lost the trap.

We had quite a few bobcats in them mountains. I lived up in the mountains where I was a good mile from anybody else, and lots of times in going home of a night, a bobcat would follow me home. When one hollers, you might as well depend on him going home with you. That was his intention. But he never would get out where you could see him. He'd stay off in the bushes out of your sight. They were pretty scarey. They scared lots of people.

Also we had lots of snakes on the mountain where I grew up. There wasn't too many rattlesnakes, but the copperheads was very plentiful. You had to watch out about snakes, especially in the daytime when it's hot. You didn't have to worry too much about them at night. [There were other things to worry about then.] If I was traveling at night in the dark timber and lost my trail, there's where I stayed until daylight. It won't never do to take a chance on traveling at night in the mountains because you might walk off over a rock cliff, and it would be a long time before you was found.

I one time had a dog that was good when I could have him with me. I couldn't take him with me on the traps because he'd get caught in a trap, but if I was just going somewhere at night, I'd take him because he would follow the trail and he wouldn't get away from you. He'd stay in the trail, and he'd stay the speed that you could keep up with him. I know one time I lost the trail coming home one night, and it was very dark. I thought, "Well, if my dog's anywhere around the house, he can hear me whistle." I was a pretty good ways from the house, but I thought he could hear me. I whistled good and loud a couple of times, and I heard him bark. In a short while, he was to me. I spoke to him, and started to move, and he went right to the trail and on to the house without any trouble.

He got bit three times by a copperhead snake when he was young. He didn't know how to kill snakes then, and he just went into a bunch of polk stalks and pulled this snake out. It bit him three times before he got it killed. He like to have died. But after that, no snake was able to bite him. He would run around one and bark till it struck at him and got out of its coil. Then he got it in the middle and busted it up over the ground right quick. Living in a place like that where we did live, a dog like that was worth a whole lot.

Another problem we had in the fall was with groundhogs eating our corn. They'd tear down and waste so much. If they'd just tore down what they wanted and hadn't wasted so much, it wouldn't have been so bad. But I learned to catch them in steel traps, and I thinned them down pretty soon till I wasn't bothered so bad by them.

Then I got the hankering to be a blacksmith when I was a boy, and money was pretty hard to get. There was a man that had a good small anvil. I asked him to buy it. He said, "I'll trade it to you for some honey."

I said, "How much?"

And he said, "Thirty-five pounds."

So I give him thirty-five pounds of good honey for the anvil.

Then there was an old man that somebody told me had a pair of bellows, and he had went blind. His name was Sam Cochran. He was my wife's grandfather. I asked him about selling me the bellows, and he said I could have them for six dollars. "Well," I said, "when I get six dollars, I'll come by."

He said, "Fine, I'll save them for you."

So I found out a blacksmith was moving from the Alarka Lumber Company to Smokemont, and he had a big cow he wanted drove up there, and he knew that I knew where Smokemont was. And he said, "I'll give you six dollars if you'll drive my cow to Smokemont."

Twenty-five miles I drove that cow, and took the six dollars and bought the pair of bellows.

Then I give a man fifty cents to make me my first pair of tongs. It wasn't long till I could make me as good a tong as anybody, and other good tools as well, so I soon had a good blacksmith shop.

I had to learn blacksmithing the hard way. I knew a blacksmith that taught me a good deal about how to temper. I learned how to temper steel starting with the information he give me. I had the bellows and built a rock furnace and it worked good. I would rather have it than any blower. In the blacksmith welding part, I learned it just by trying. Now the best thing to practice on blacksmithing with is something like a chain link that you've just got one piece to hold together. When you get it in shape to weld, you've only got one piece to hold. Now if you're welding two rods together, you've got to have somebody to help you. They lay one on the anvil and you lay the other on it and hammer it together. But when you get to where you know how to weld, it's not hard to do. Spring steel welds good when you learn the heat to use on it. If you get it too hot, though, it breaks. Just like an axe. It's easy hammered out if you won't get it too hot. But if you get a little place too hot, it'll break off. I've hammered out old axes and made them just like new.

I was up on Pigeon River one time at a blacksmith shop. It belonged to Tom Narr, and Preacher Allen was there, and there was some axes there, and I told Tom I wanted to upset [reshape and hammer out] some of them axes, and he said, "All right." And I hammered out both blades and put the handles on and retempered them. And him and Preacher Allen took one out to the woodyard and chopped a dead locust log up with it, and Preacher Allen came back and said, "Son, you're a good blacksmith." I was a young man then—probably twenty-two years old.

Then I left Swain County and come to Haywood County, North Carolina. I moved my blacksmith shop up on Dick's Creek, and shoed horses,

 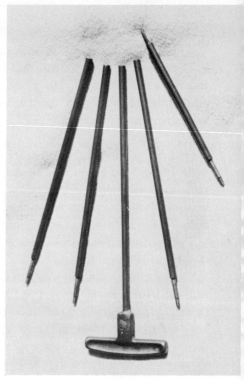

PLATE 341   The loading stand Frank invented. The stand won't turn over, can be raised or lowered according to the shooter's needs,. and collapses into an easily portable package.

PLATE 342   A ball-pulling kit Frank machined. Each piece screws tightly into the other to make a long rod that fits down into the gun barrel for removal of a jammed bullet, or a bullet that was accidentally loaded without a charge.

made trail grabs, J-grabs, spreads, whatever people wanted done. Lived with my uncle, Dan Cochran. I stayed there as long as there was pretty much logging work and acid wood work. I was mostly servicing the loggers then.

Then I finally sold the shop and went back to Swain County and married. Me and my wife came straight to Haywood where I got a job in a machine shop. This machine shop had a good blacksmith's shop and no blacksmith, and so I got a job there in 1938 and worked in the blacksmith shop. The Blythe brothers was putting in a sewer line from Hazelwood, North Carolina, to Pigeon River, and I done a lot of work for them that winter. There was quite a bit of blacksmithing for a few years till tractors took the place of horses and trucks took the place of wagons. Then the blacksmithing business got bad.

I took up welding then, and machine work, and I worked with that man at that machine shop for twenty-six years. When he died, I leased a shop from Paul Bryson at Hazelwood called the Skyline Machine Shop, and I worked there near about nine years till I got sick and had to retire. And I think I've done as good a machine work as most any machinist has ever done.

Now about the gunmaking business, there was a forge in Tennessee where blacksmiths got their materials. There's a place in the Smoky Mountains Park called Cades Cove, and there's a creek there called Forge Creek where they had a forge that smelted iron. Those gunsmiths made their gun barrels from a flat bar of iron, and they hammered them around a rod and welded them and rifled them with a hand rifle machine. Then they made their locks and everything. Tennessee had several gunmakers, and North Carolina had quite a few of them. The old Gillespie gun was made over about Brevard, North Carolina. They had a forge up there. The last Gillespie man that had that shop and made guns had to go to the Civil War, and he was said to be the last. Philip Gillespie. He had a pot of gold that he had sold guns for, and a barrel of brandy. He took an ox and a sled and hauled his gold and brandy back up in the mountains somewhere and buried it and told his folks that nobody wouldn't get any of his gold and brandy, and that it would be there when he come back. He dug a vault and lined it with rock, put his gold and brandy in it, covered it up with rock, and covered that with dirt, and it's never been found. He never come back. He left and took one of his own guns that he had made and went to the Civil War and never returned. He was killed in action and that was the last of the Gillespie Iron Works.

Now I know a man that owned a Gillespie rifle, and he died seven or eight years ago, and his wife sold that Gillespie rifle for five hundred dollars. I guess it's won more prizes at the shooting matches than any gun in western North Carolina. It was a big, heavy gun.

But all that early gunsmithing had ended by the time I got started. I got interested in guns by the first shotgun I ever worked on. It was for a neighbor boy when I had my shop over in Swain County. He had an old single-barreled shotgun, and something got wrong with it, and he brought it and wanted me to fix it. His name was Caney Barker. And I said, "Caney, I don't guess I could fix a gun."

He said, "You're the only hopes for me."

So I laid around there a few days and fixed Caney's gun. I said, "Well, if I can do that one, I can do some more." From then on, I got to working on guns. And then got into making gunstocks. I got into repairing more than anything.

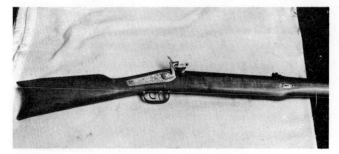

PLATE 343 Frank made this gun for Doug Cochran, his grandson. Doug's father made the maple stock for the gun, and Frank made the stainless-steel lock and hammer.

PLATE 344 One of the keys in the stock in Doug's gun. On all of Frank's full-stocked rifles, the owner has simply to push three keys out (one in the half-stocks) to remove the barrel.

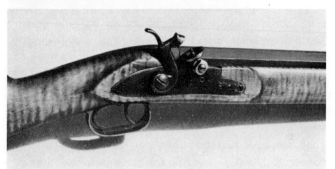

PLATE 345 Frank made this full-stocked (of curly maple) .44-caliber rifle for himself, and made every part of the gun except the 1⅛-inch barrel. The iron-mounted rifle intentionally has no grip rail, and the cup under the nipple was added to keep the stock from becoming scorched.

The first gun I made was a flintlock, and Earl Lanning helped me get started on it. I got an old barrel, and got Vee Jones to rerifle it for me. Then I made the flintlock by Earl giving me a few ideas on it. Well, it shot good. And later on I sold it to Earl for a hundred dollars and a .32-caliber barrel that's on my wife's gun. I would say that has probably been twenty-five years ago.

PLATE 346 The gun Frank made for himself is fitted with an old military sight which he salvaged and re-worked.

PLATE 347 Frank made this .45-caliber understriker for his nephew, Charles Cochran. The maple stock has a cheekpiece on both sides and is engraved very simply. Frank made everything for the gun except for the Douglas barrel and the sights. He got the understriking design from Mr. Ritter, a gunsmith in Virginia, but he made his own alterations in the design so that it would cock more easily. The advantage of the understriker is that the cap is not in the shooter's face.

Since then, I've been to the shooting match at Hiawassee, Georgia. That's a good place to shoot. I have won several times over there. I've found in the muzzle-loading rifle shoots that they're all good sports. I've not found anybody going and fussing and drinking. Everybody just goes for a good time. Nice, decent fun. They're all in a good humor and good fellowship. And then we have one here at Waynesville every July that's good fun.

But I don't make guns now. I'm not able to do it. I've got asthma and emphysema, and I've just got breath enough to do this stuff around the house. But the Lord's been awful good to me. And I give the Lord credit for everything I've ever done. Myself, I couldn't have done it without Him.

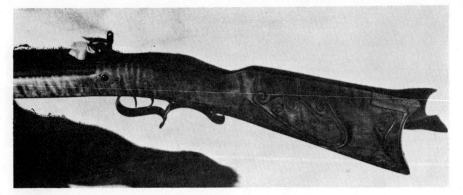

PLATE 348 Frank made this gun for Jay and Tommy
Masters of Asheville, North Carolina. The half-stock is
made of red maple, and the simple carving in the cheekpiece and the butt is of Frank's own design. He made every piece for this gun, including the steel hammer, the
brass triggerguard, and the brass patch box, except for the
one-inch .45-caliber barrel and the sights. The side screw
can be removed to allow cleaning through the drum into
the breechplug. The nipple can also be easily removed for
cleaning.

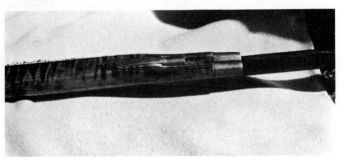

PLATE 349 Frank machined the ramrod entry pipe for
the Masters' gun in his shop, and then set it off with two
simple lines he carved into the stock.

My guns, I don't know where they all are now. I've made lots of them.
But I never signed them. I never got in the habit of it. A man said to me
one time, "Why in the world don't you sign your guns?"

"Well," I said, "I've never done it, and I ain't starting now because I've
sold so many without that."

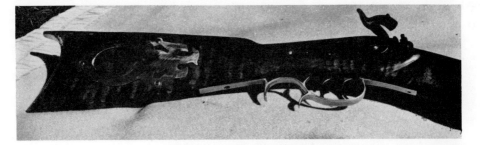

PLATE 350   Frank made this gun for Hattie, his wife. It fires through the breechplug unlike his other guns, which fire directly into the barrel. When the barrel is removed, the breechplug remains. Frank made the breechplug, the doubleset triggers, the triggerguard, the buttplate, and the stainless-steel patch box himself.

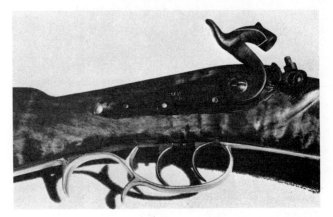

PLATE 351   Hattie Cochran's gun is fitted with a vintage 1830–40 Leman Lancaster lock.

But I've gotten lots of satisfaction out of it. One time I was at Hiawassee, and there was nine guns there that I made, and they was all shooting good. I was going in, and I met a man going out. He had already shot his round. He said, "Y'doing any good?"

I said, "No."

He said, "You should get you one of them Cochran guns. I hear they really do good."

I said, "I think I'll buy me one." I don't know if the man knew who he was talking to, but if he did, he could keep a secret good by not letting anybody know!

PLATE 352 Robert Watts with his wife, Sherrill, and his mother—all with guns that Robert made, which they use in shooting matches.

Robert Watts

Roberts Watts was born on October 30, 1936, in Marion County, Mississippi. He grew up on his grandfather's farm, and remembers long days spent hoeing corn, chopping cotton, plowing with the mule—as well as leisure time that included the swimming hole, fishing in the summer, and hunting game the balance of the year. Squirrels, rabbits, quail, and ducks were the primary small game; and raccoon, bobcat, turkey, geese, deer, and wild hogs made up the larger quarry. Marksmanship was stressed, and anyone who could adjust the sights of a new store-bought .22 so that it would shoot true had plenty of friends. On Sundays, when they weren't hunting, time was often spent shooting at Prince Albert tobacco cans and sharpening their skills.

PLATE 353   Robert Watts
with his assistant, Tom
Hayes.

*Robert was a skilled shot early in his life, and says the local people con-
sidered him a champion squirrel hunter since he nearly always head shot his
game unless he was hunting for his grandfather, who liked the heads. But
the stories he heard about the old muzzle loaders whetted his appetite for
something more than the .22s he and his friends were used to.*

*That interest blossomed to the point where he now runs a full-time busi-
ness in Atlanta making muzzle-loading rifles, is an officer in the National
Muzzle Loading Rifle Association, and is still a crack shot. In 1976, for example, at the spring shoot at Friendship, Indiana, he won the NMLRA's
Bicentennial All-American Aggregate with a score of 252 out of a possible
275. We found out about him at the 1977 NMLRA spring shoot in*

*Friendship. George Shumway took us to his booth to meet him, but he was
gone at the time. So we got his address from his assistant, Tom Hayes, and
visited him later in Atlanta. When we asked him to re-create for us how he
had become so deeply involved in muzzle loaders, he started with his
childhood:*

My father had his grandfather's old muzzle-loading shotgun, which he
was proud to be the possessor of, but he never used it *per se*. He had
acquired it from his grandfather when he was a young lad. There were several old shotguns in the family.

I have my great grandfather's old muzzle-loading rifle now. It's been
busted up a couple of times. It's one he acquired just before the Civil War
as a squirrel rifle, and he loaned it to a friend who elected to go join the
Federal forces in New Orleans. His father had been a northern preacher
who had taken a church down in that part of the country, so this fellow
elected to join the Federal forces. He got a few miles away from home,
and the local national guard—or buttermilk cavalry as they were called—
heard of his intentions and overtook him. They couldn't get him to give up
his intentions peacefully, so it ended up in a scrape and they shot him and
left him for dead. The rifle got busted all to pieces. The man's horse came
back, and my grandfather trailed him down and found him and put him up
in an old cotton house and nursed him back to where he could travel. Eventually my great-grandfather's son married this fellow's daughter, but that
was years later and a whole different story. Anyway, I grew up around that
kind of story.

So my great-grandfather restocked the old rifle, and then a couple of
years later when my great-grandmother was in town getting supplies for the
farm, the Federal forces decided they had to requisition her horses, and the
rifle happened to be on the buckboard there so they busted it up again. So
he restocked it all over again, so now probably the only thing that's original
is the barrel and the buttplate. Maybe the triggerguard, too, but it shows a
lot of twisting and straightening. The trigger and the lock are neither one
original, I'm sure.

Then when I was about twelve or thirteen years old, I found an old muzzle-loading barrel in an abandoned log cabin. I talked with the owner, and
he gave it to me in exchange for some work. It was in reasonably good
shape, and I visualized putting it back into firing order and condition. But
starting with just a barrel and not much else in terms of knowledge or anything, it was a slow process. I did rough a stock out of pine, and I acquired
an old Bluegrass lock from a local antiques person, but I decided that the
lock was not quality enough to make a decent rifle out of.

I sort of gave up accumulating any parts after a while because I just didn't know enough about what I needed. Someone, for example, gave me a brass door handle and said I could make a buttplate out of that. I probably could *now,* but it would have been hard then since I didn't really visualize how a buttplate should look not having any pattern or good references. Nowadays it would be hard to imagine someone having as hard a time with it considering the wide range of mail-order houses available, and the number of people that have castings and locks and triggers—anything you would need along those lines—available. But at that time those things just weren't generally available.

So I never did finish the gun at that time. I think it was ten or twelve years later before I did. I had spent four years in the Marine Corps—the last year coaching on the rifle range at Camp LeJune and shooting with the Second Division Rifle Team. Then I enrolled in the pre-engineering curriculum at Mississippi Southern, got married to my chemistry teacher, Sherrill Glenn, and finally moved to Atlanta where Sherrill continued graduate work at Emory University and I was studying architecture at Georgia Tech. Shortly after arriving here, I related the story of the old muzzle-loading rifle barrel to a friend one night, and the next night the friend introduced me to Schley Howard, a lawyer in Decatur who had a shop in his attic and was one of the few people in the country that was engaged in the repair, rebuilding, and rerifling of old muzzle loaders. He was also a particularly good shot, and we soon became good friends. I would get over and work with him when time permitted. He liked to tell his friends, when he would introduce us, that he was filling me in on everything that they didn't teach at Georgia Tech! Eventually we had the old barrel in a brand new stock, and had it rerifled and fitted up with the proper furniture, and I won my first muzzle-loading shooting match with it—and quite a few thereafter.

I was real enthusiastic about it, and I started demonstrating it all to my folks; and they were enthusiastic about it too having the background that they did—being raised in the country where rifles and guns were a necessary part of life. When my dad died seven years ago, I was building my mother a muzzle loader, and would have built him one too, if he had lived. Then I built rifles for the other members of the family, and we all shoot now.

I didn't go right into gunmaking out of school, though. I worked for a while for an architect who worked for Union Oil designing gas stations and special projects. It had been Pure Oil, but it was taken over by Union, and it became apparent that my boss, who was a registered architect, was not going to be allowed to have the architectural freedom he had enjoyed in the past. That meant I would never be able to get registered working with him. Anyway, jobs were kind of scarce in architecture at that time, and I took a job in construction, and then later I took on a job as trouble shooter for a metal manufacturing company. I worked for them for about three and a half years. During this period I had been making rifles and had a number of personal orders outstanding, but with that trouble-shooting job, I was on the road about 80 per cent of the time, and I hadn't made much headway on the guns. When we had a cutback in the company, I had enough business stacked up so I just stayed busy. I really didn't intend to go into business. I really just intended to get some of those orders off my back and then go back to work, but several other folks heard that I was making rifles, and they came along with orders, so I never have gone back to work. I "play" about eighty hours a week now, and I have an eighteen- to twenty-month backlog of orders.

I've had a shop here in my home ever since I've had the house—about ten years. And I have a production and machine shop out at Stone Mountain where I do a good bit with machinery turning out a powder measure we designed that helps a lot toward keeping the business going. The type of rifles we make are by and large strictly individualized and made for a specific person of a specific physical build. Each one has differences in drop and length of pull and barrel weight and caliber and stock length. These are all various aspects that suit a rifle to the individual so he can do his best with it. That's the beauty of custom-making rifles: You can take advantage of the chance to scale each one to the size of the person. Very few people really fit the universal standard rifle unless they're contortionists, or happen to be the right size physically just by luck. That's why virtually all of the matches are won by people shooting custom or homemade rifles.

Whether the rifle is plain, or has a brass patch box and raised carving and inlays and a swamped, flared barrel just depends on what the person wants. I've made a lot of rifles that are relatively plain because the people who order them seem to consider them more honest in some way than the heavily decorated ones. Other people feel that if you leave off the patch box and the carving and so forth, you're just building an incomplete rifle. I enjoy building highly decorated rifles, but the plainer look can be, I think, very appealing provided the architecture and the general shape and workmanship are well done. That would be true whether the item is a rifle or an automobile or a saddle for a horse. If the workmanship and design are good overall, then perhaps it doesn't need a lot of decoration. It can stand on its own as a fine piece of craftsmanship.

We do some restoration work, but often it's impossible [to tell what the original gun looked like because so many different gunsmiths have altered it over the years]. I've run across rifles where you could tell by the lugs on the bottom side that the barrel had been in at least three or four different

PLATE 354   One corner of Robert's shop.

stocks. The lugs might have been moved, and then it might have had a rib on it at some time to convert it to a half-stock, and then this might have been removed and the rifle reconverted into a full stock, and so forth. And you never know if the buttplate is original or not. You usually can't tell if it had a high, thin buttplate at first, which would have caused the buttstock to be high and thin; or whether it had a wide, broad buttplate, which would have given the stock an altogether heavier shape.

We are called upon to make quite a variety of rifles. These range from period pieces to shooters. Typically, they are brass- or iron-mounted, curly maple, full-stocked rifles intended for combination duty on the range and in the woods. These are both squirrel rifle sizes—.29 to .40 caliber—and deer and target rifles sizes—.40 to .50 caliber. Fifty caliber and above can be used very effectively on the range, but we don't recommend them for anyone but a veteran target shooter. We use Siler locks, and we use a good number of G. R. Douglas barrel blanks, which we have found to be of a consistently high quality. For special calibers and contours—tapered and flared, for example—we use handcrafted barrels as made by some of the custom barrelmakers. They'll plane them most any way you want them, which allows you complete control of the weight and balance of the rifle. For a heavy hunting rifle, for example, you'd want it plenty strong for heavy loads with enough weight that you don't get the tar kicked out of you every time you drop the hammer. So you might order a barrel that would be one and one eighth inches at the breech tapering down to seven eighths of an inch and back up to one inch at the muzzle. And you could get it.

I make virtually everything except the barrel and the lock. It's more economical to buy them. I make all the inlays, saw out all my own patchboxes. On the iron-mounted guns, I start with sheet iron to make the buttplate, the triggerguards, and other furniture. I think I could make the barrels, too, but I don't know that I would want a job making a three-thousand-dollar rifle where I had to weld up the barrel and forge out the lock and all that. The first reason is that I don't know how economical it would be. The other reason is that I just couldn't spare the time from my other commitments. I have orders on hand now for people that are friends and so forth, people that I like and care about, and I'm overextended already. I have done a little forge welding, but I have not forge welded a barrel. I think I could, though, if it came to that. I have made a barrel out of solid stock, and out of tubing. I have a rifling machine, and I rifle and bore out old barrels on guns that I restore or rerifle for other people. There's not too much demand for that kind of work anymore, but I do a little of it occasionally. In fact, there are about three or four barrels out there now that I need to do.

PLATE 355 Watts rifles
in various stages of completion.

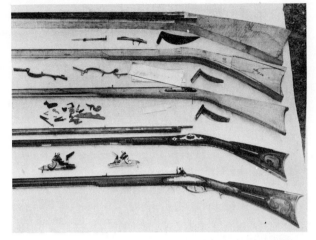

I haven't made a great number of real nice rifles—maybe twenty-five or
something like that. We also sell a semi-finished rifle, made to fit the customer, but lacking the finish—no sanding, no browning, no staining, no
linseed oil. It's got the sights on it, the triggers are working, and the locks
functioning properly. You can take it and shoot it just like it is. In fact, I
have used semi-finished rifles frequently at local matches. I'd get one at a
semi-finished stage and for promotional advertisement and so on, take it out
and maybe win the match with it. That sorta helps sell them. Of course,
usually the rifle would already be sold. I'd just ask the person that bought it
if I could shoot it at the match. He'd usually be delighted, just to see how
it would do. Almost invariably on those days, I'd get lucky and shoot better
than I would do shooting mine.

I enjoy variety, and I enjoy doing interpretive things. I've made many
different types of rifles from the mountain type to the Hawken, and I guess
my work is characterized by more variety than almost anybody else I know.
The typical rifle maker today more or less sticks with one style and interprets
within that style. A lot of makers make nothing but Hawkens, and a lot
make nothing but Bedford County, Pennsylvania-style rifles, and a lot of
them make nothing but their own style of rifles.

I guess, though, that if there's any one rifle that a number of people
would associate with me, it's the mountain rifle that I build, which is not a
copy of any original. There's some similarity to the typical mountain rifle,
but the architecture is slightly exaggerated in the direction of an earlier period which a lot of people kind of revolve back to. They appear to be very

simple, but the effect comes from any carving or decoration being very so-phisticated and subtle. Most of them are iron mounted with a combination of hand forging and riveting.

The price varies due to the extreme variation in the amount of work and time required. I have more or less a bottom line starting price to give the customer an idea of what he's looking at. But a customer can easily double this by specifying time-consuming work such as carving, inlays, and engrav-ing. The parts have gone up, and the quality of workmanship in this coun-try has increased, too. I guess some of the nicest rifles that ever have been built in the United States are being built right now. There are a lot of peo-ple capable of doing really good work. Many of them are people who only make one or two rifles a year—maybe for themselves or their wives or their best friends. Of course, this requires more and more of the builder who fan-cies himself staying on the top of the pile—abreast of the quality that's being turned out. I won't say that I've ever made a rifle that I'm ashamed of because I haven't—but the evolution of the continuation in style of the longrifle, as opposed to "reproduction," which none of us like very much—as far as the interpretation and authenticity of my design has come along considerably in the last ten years. This is partly due to the wide range of books that has become available in recent years. Also people are now inter-ested in getting a rifle of a particular period, people who wouldn't have known what you were talking about ten or fifteen years ago because there were so few references. And it's now possible to buy swamped barrels and parts of that sort which make possible a variety that wasn't feasible earlier. And that all makes a difference in price, too.

But our business stays steady. More and more people have become inter-ested in the longrifle from the historical aspects as books have become more available. Muzzle loading has a lot of appeal from the standpoint of, I guess, common nostalgia.

But it also has an appeal from the relationship it has with our nation's history. From the American Revolution on up through the Civil War, these guns played an integral part in our history and our way of life. There was that whole thing with the fight for freedom, and the pioneer spirit—that's part of the attraction. There are a lot of people who are seeking some con-nection with this spirit now, and if they can capture a little of it on one weekend a month, they're willing to go to the sacrifice monetarily to do it. And from a historic standpoint, there's now such a wide range of areas that a person can get into and branch off from that a lot more people are being attracted to the field. They can go from the guns on into things like birch-bark canoes and log cabins of the period they're interested in—into a lot of the things that you hit on with the *Foxfire* books. The reason there's this new

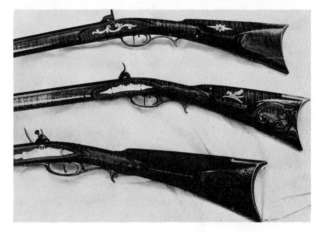

PLATE 356 Three finished Watts rifles.

interest in muzzle loaders, I guess, is part of the same reason why the books have been successful. I expect a lot of those books sold at Friendship, for example, and in the muzzle-loading community. There's more and more emphasis among many shooters on authenticity of dress and to some extent, even mannerisms. In the primitive group, for example, you are expected to be very aware of tepee etiquette on the primitive range at Friendship. They probably wouldn't want to embarrass you by correcting you, but they'd know you were a "flatlander" or so-called "pork eater." But you don't enter a tepee without invitation, for example. And you don't walk between someone and the fire. Every well-equipped tepee has a willow frame seat— kind of an A-frame affair—that sits on the ground and you can lean back against it and stretch your legs out while everyone else has to sit cross-legged. This is, of course, the owner's seat and his wife's. However, if he insists that you sit against it, that implies that you are the guest of honor at that time, which is not important except when there's a group of a dozen people there, and any other guest is not supposed to insult the guest of honor in any way. And so on. There's a lot in there I don't know, but I think one of the other sort of traditional things is that if you invite someone to come into your tepee, then the proper etiquette is to share whatever you have.

Of course, with all these different interest groups, you've got some infighting, which I think is sad. I've always kind of tried to push the idea of the whole entity. I figure we all kind of need each other, so to speak. Everybody likes to be a member of some sub-group, which I feel adds interest and variety to the overall group. I think a lot of the charm of any group is lost when you start trying to make everybody come out of the same-shaped mold. A lot of the charm in the mountains of North Carolina and north

Georgia has been lost in the last twenty years because people seem ashamed to wholeheartedly exhibit their ethnicity. However, I think that there's a real need in mankind to be a part of an exclusive sub-group that has some characteristics that they can be proud of. Whether it's the group of top shooters, or a group of the top tepee pitchers, or the group that rides their horses to the matches, or runs the furtherest downhill, or whatever—they need a special club to belong to. That's not to say, however, that they should be only interested in the welfare of that particular group. Just because there are shooters who aren't interested in wearing buckskins, for example, doesn't mean that they should be looked down on, or excluded. Some people are in muzzle loading purely because they like the idea of competitive shooting. They like the idea of competing against their fellow man in a sport that is not going to make or break them if they win or lose. They get some enjoyment out of coming out on top occasionally, but they're not necessarily interested in wearing moccasins to shoot in or buckskins to sweat in. There should be room for all of them in the larger fraternity of shooters without condemnation. Some people are interested in muzzle-loading rifles purely from the artistic standpoint. To me, building muzzle-loading rifles is one of the earliest and most encompassing forms of folk art. One has to be a good wood craftsman, a good metalsmith, a mechanical expert as far as the lock and trigger mechanism is concerned, and have talent in design and the ability to put things on paper. Some gunmakers don't even shoot. They're in it purely as a sort of artistic craft and personal expression. There's room for them too.

One of the best things about the whole revival of interest in muzzle loaders is the number of friends of common interest you make. I know people in virtually every state through muzzle loading. In fact, when I had the trouble-shooting job I was talking about earlier, no matter where I was I knew somebody local that was interested in muzzle loading, and I found myself going to funerals and weddings and everything else just on the spur of the moment. I'd be in town and call some person that I knew or had met at a match, and their daughter would be getting married and I'd be included. That gave me the opportunity to visit around a lot of what were mostly small, attic non-profit shops and get a few ideas and see how other people did things. It was a great opportunity, and almost without exception I was warmly received and usually had dinner with those people and so forth. A lot of times I would have been entertained for two or three more days if I could have afforded to stay around. And we've had the opportunity to return the hospitality a lot of times, too. A lot of people come through Atlanta. I've had people through here from California, Arkansas, Mississippi, Pennsylvania, Ohio, Indiana, Illinois, Texas, Florida, North

PLATE 357 Two types of buttplates Robert makes. The ones on the left are sand-cast brass; the ones on the right show two stages of iron buttplates for iron-mounted rifles.

Carolina, Virginia—and all this year. I think muzzle loading is a great game in that respect, and it's a good family sport, too. Most of the newcomers tend to be thirty to thirty-five years old, so there are plenty of new ones coming along that will be in it all their lives. And my mother is a good indication of the fact that there's plenty of room for older people too. She's won or placed in state championships in Arkansas, Mississippi, Louisiana, Georgia, Tennessee—and she didn't even get into it until she was fifty-five years old.

There are a lot of teens making rifles, too, but between the ages of eighteen and twenty-eight they tend to be pretty badly distracted and not able to give it the attention they can later.

But it's amazing to see how it has grown. When I finally got the old gun that I mentioned restocked, I started going to matches. But at that time, the opportunity to go to matches was pretty limited. The local club would have maybe one or two a year, and the next closest place was in Franklin, Tennessee. Then the only other place in this region was in Pensacola. Now there are eight or ten clubs in Florida—maybe twelve. You could go to a match virtually every weekend in this region if you could spare the time.

I'm first vice-president of the National Muzzle Loading Rifle Association. It's been growing steadily ever since I joined it in 1963. At that time, there were something in the neighborhood of five or six thousand members. There were about twenty-five members in Georgia. Now we have in excess of twenty-two thousand members in the NMLRA—up from about fourteen thousand three years ago—and about two hundred and fifty living in Georgia. So it's growing, and growing exponentially.

Our official position as a group is that a citizen's right to keep and bear arms shall not be infringed upon—the Second Amendment. We haven't had an active lobbying organization because our size couldn't support it. However, we are fortunate in having Colonel Vaughn Goodwin in the Washington, D.C. area, and he has been able to stay abreast of developments in Congress and maintain a close liaison with the National Rifle Association. We're not part of the NRA. We probably would be closer except for a couple of incidents. At one time, it was presumed that one of the officers of the NMLRA wanted to consolidate with the NRA. I don't know exactly what the details were, but there was a lot of opposition. Of course, at that time the NMLRA was pretty much a provincial Ohio-Indiana club, and I guess the officers were afraid that it would have just been absorbed by the NRA, which was and is a huge organization. So there's no formal affiliation whatsoever, even though the NRA has made some steps toward establishing closer relationships in the last three years. Maxine Moss and Doc Johnston —both prominent NMLRA members and officers—are on the muzzle-loading committee of the NRA. And Doc Johnston is also a director of the NRA. Al Hill, who is president of the NMLRA, is also on the board of directors of the NRA. At the NRA shooting preserve out in New Mexico, the primary use that the area has been put to so far has been muzzle-loading activities—rendezvous, that sort of thing. I think better relationships are desirable myself. I'm a life member of both groups, and a good many other people are. There must be a lot of mutual memberships. I'm concerned about both groups, but it's a lot easier to be concerned about the welfare of the smaller, more human-sized organization which you might have a little input into the destiny of than the sort of corporate organization that the NRA represents. Of course, their size, financial backing, and all is necessary in order for them to have any muscle with Congress. Both groups have their own work to do—their own styles. It's important, though, that we all remember that we're both in the same business. We're both concerned about the Second Amendment.

Jim Chambers

Earl Lanning urged us to see Jim Chambers, so we drove up to Canton, North Carolina, to see if we could find him. At first we couldn't find his house, but one of the local policemen offered to lead us there, and we followed him right to Jim's door.

After we had explained who we were and what we were looking for, Jim took us inside and downstairs to his basement shop. The low-ceilinged room was tiny—it was barely possible for all of us to squeeze in—but out of that room come some of the finest guns we saw during the course of researching this chapter.

Article by Jeff Lane, Stanley Masters, Mark Palpal-lotic. Photographs by Linda Ledford and Tinker McCoy.

I made my first rifle when I was fifteen. I'm thirty-one now. I'd been shooting in some of the shooting matches around here. They used to have one at the Cataloochee Ranch every summer, and at the age of thirteen, I started shooting in that. I borrowed a fellow's rifle, shot, and won third place in that first match. They really got me hooked. So I bought an old gun—a Hawken-type rifle—and shot it the next year. The barrel was pretty well worn—a lot of pits, rust, and so forth—so I didn't do quite so well. I won third place again. I was never satisfied to be third, or second; I have to be number one in everything I do. So the only thing to do was to make a new rifle. I started searching for parts, looking through catalogues and buying the parts I thought I needed. Then I happened to run across Earl Lanning. Earl lived not far from my home and was [and still is] one of the most knowledgeable men in the country on the subject of Kentucky rifles, and he was considered by many to be one of the finest makers of Kentucky rifles around anywhere. He kind of took me under his wing when he saw I was really interested in the old guns, and showed me what to do and what not to do. I was more or less an apprentice to Earl. This gun [see Plates 358–367] is one that he designed and I made. It resembles very much the York County guns with a little bit of Lancaster County in it also. This was more or less Earl's adaptation of a 1770–80 Revolutionary period gun.

I was really making this gun for Earl. He had started the gun but didn't have time to finish it, so really the architecture and design was already set by him, and I just went ahead and did all the actual work. I ended up keeping the gun as my own personal rifle. It's a good one to keep around as kind of a pattern. It has almost perfect architecture for a Revolutionary period gun. If you have something you can look at, touch, and feel, it's a lot easier to make other guns from it.

Earl helped me complete that first rifle. He did about as much work on it as I did. I shot for several years in the matches and did rather well with it.

In 1965, I started college at Western Carolina University [in Cullowhee]. I went a year and a half and then dropped out and went into the Army. I spent a year in Vietnam; came back and went back to school and got a BS degree in biology from WCU. I had intended to work for the National Park Service, but they said their first assignment for me would be in an office in either New York City, Philadelphia, or Washington, D.C., and my third or fourth assignment might be in one of the parks. I just couldn't go that route; never did care for city life. After checking around and trying to get jobs with wildlife people and so forth, I ran across an announcement that said there was a great shortage of medical technologists. I went back to WCU in that program, graduated in 1974, and have been working ever since as a medical technologist with the Veterans Administration.

While I was going to college, I became more interested in making these guns than in shooting them. At that time, Earl was doing a lot of restoration work, so I got involved in some of that, too. In 1970, I guess it was, I was at Earl's shop one night. We were restoring a real fine relief-carved gun —one that had been made by J. P. Beck. I was restoring the fore end of it. I'd made a couple of Beck-style rifles and knew his work very well. I completed the fore end of the gun—added some wood using his style and his technique. Earl asked me, "How would you like to work at Old Salem in Winston-Salem, North Carolina? I heard John Bivens is looking for someone to work in the gun shop." I said, "Yeah, I'd love to." [Old Salem is the historic restoration of the town of Salem which was founded by Moravian people from Pennsylvania in the mid 1700s. Salem was a highly respected craft center of the eighteenth century. Today many of the original businesses and homes have been restored and are open to the public.]

We called John, and I went down and had an interview with him. I got the job and started work there in 1970 during the summers when I wasn't going to school. It was really quite an experience. I worked there in the gun shop just like the old-timers had worked in their shops—carried on business just like they would. I made the guns and sold them to customers who came in. The only difference was that I had many more people coming through the shop than old gunsmiths would have and had to do a lot of talking, answer a lot of questions. But that was good because when you have people asking questions, then invariably they're going to ask questions that you don't know the answers to. I took it as a personal challenge not to let any question go unanswered. If I didn't know the answer, I kept a bunch of books behind my forge there in the shop and I'd tell the people I simply didn't know the answer but that I would find it and tell them the answer before they left the restoration. So I would go through my books until I found it. By looking up all those answers, I gained a lot of knowledge. I can say with a great deal of pride that the questions there *were* answers for did not go unanswered. In the process I learned a lot about gunsmithing in general.

To an eighteenth-century man a rifle was just as important and just as big an investment as an automobile is to us today. Gunsmiths back then made various items other than guns. They made tomahawks, knives, traps, and so forth. Most of the women in town would bring their knives in to get the gunsmith to sharpen them. They really had to have a mastery of many different kinds of materials. The gunsmith did work as fine as any cabinetmaker, and did as fine work in metal as any blacksmith; he even had to be a little bit of a silversmith and engraver. Many were prominent citizens in their communities, too. Some of them even went into politics. Most of them

PLATE 358   Jim Chambers as an apprentice to John Bivins in the gun shop at Old Salem in Winston-Salem, North Carolina. (Photo by David Herbert Hauser.)

were rather cantankerous fellows; they didn't put up with a whole lot. Gunsmithing was a very involved craft, and they were rightly proud of it.

Many of the characteristics the gunsmiths used were the same from one rifle to the other. There was one eighteenth-century gunmaker by the name of Leonard Reedy. He came up with a carved design that he apparently liked very well because he repeated it over and over again. All of his guns have the same design. Most frequently, however, the designs were changed from one gun to the next—changed just a little bit. But there were still certain distinctive things about the work that would tell you that, even though the design itself was different, it was done by the same gunsmith. You can tell each maker's work whether the gun is signed or not. You can look at the details on the signed gun, compare it to the details on an unsigned gun, and if the similarity is there, you can say with certainty that J. P. Beck, or whoever, made it. So really a gun doesn't have to be signed to be attributed to a particular maker.

Some gunsmiths would sign their name on the top flat of the barrel, and this adds a bit of value to the guns now. But many of the early guns were not signed—those made before the Revolution especially. Joe Kindig stated in his book, *Thoughts on the Kentucky Rifle,* that he feels that the reason many of the early guns were not signed was that people were very religious back then; and the gunsmith felt that if he signed the gun, it would have been boastful and bragging. They felt that this was their God-given talent, and to put their name on it was taking away from His work. I kind of agree with Kindig there. I'm not certain that this was the reason for them not signing, but it is for me. I feel that God has given me this talent, and I should give Him the credit. I do not put my name on the top of the barrel, but I *do* put it underneath the sideplate. I carve it down in there, along with the date, and the number of the rifle. I number the rifles in sequence and sign and date them to keep someone from passing them off as originals. If someone buys one from a dealer and pays the price of an original for it, and then happens to take the sideplate off and sees the date that it actually was made, then, hopefully, he can go to that dealer and get his money back or else beat the crook severely!

As far as parts for my guns go, I get my barrels from one of two places. Some I get from Bill Large in Ironton, Ohio. He makes very good barrels; many people say he's the best barrelmaker in the world. Then there's another fellow in Gettysburg, Pennsylvania, named Robert Parris. He makes very fine barrels also. The rifling is already cut in the barrels. Someday I hope to do my own rifling. I have a rifling machine that was made by a fine gentleman and gunsmith named Frank Cochran [see page 354], in Waynesville, North Carolina, but I don't have enough room in my shop to set it up.

The sights I make myself. The gunsmiths had their own little design that they used on their sights, and I've developed my own. I use that same design over and over. The sights are dovetailed on and adjusted. You don't have any trouble hitting what you're aiming at—at least up to a hundred yards.

The triggerguard and the buttplate are sand castings. They come out very rough. I have to file those—smooth them down and polish them. So, the barrel, triggerguard, and buttplate are the only parts other than the locks that I buy. The locks are made by my good friend Bud Siler. I usually get the kits and put those together. Bud's locks are the finest locks around.

Everything else on the gun is handmade. The sideplate is cut out of a flat sheet, filed, polished, engraved, and so forth, as are all the other inlays. The ramrod thimbles or pipes are made from a flat sheet of brass. I just cut out a small strip of brass the width that I want the pipes to be. Then I anneal the brass—heat it and dunk it in water to soften it—until it can almost be bent with your fingers. I get a good start on it with my fingers bending it around a mandril and then clamp it in the vise and tighten the vise. That bends the brass tightly around the mandril. I remove the mandril and add a little

PLATE 359 One of the rifles Jim made. Its front sight, a man's face, also incorporates carving in the barrel.

PLATE 360 Jim uses Siler locks and sand-cast brass triggerguards. He makes his own triggers.

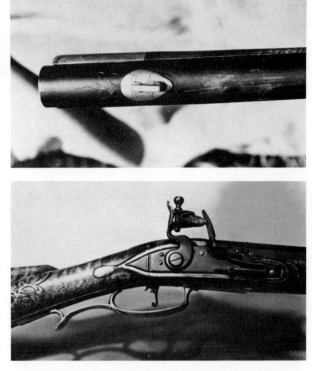

bit of solder to the seam to make sure the pipe stays closed. Then I file whatever design I want on it. Most of them are octagonal. Some, however, are diamond faceted. This is a detail that was used quite often by John Phillip Beck who was a Lebanon County, Pennsylvania, gunsmith. He worked back around the Revolutionary period and a little after that. He used the diamond-faceted ramrod pipes on some of his finer pieces, and I imagine he'd charge a little bit more for those. But normally just the regular octagon-shaped pipes are used. I start with a perfectly round pipe and then file whatever design I want on it.

The rear ramrod pipe can be made in different ways. Some of them are made out of two pieces, but I generally make them out of one piece. It's easier for me to go ahead and make one piece and be done with it rather than making it out of two pieces and trying to solder them together and taking the risk of it maybe coming apart later. It's made from a flat piece of brass, part of which is cut, rolled, and filed, and part of which is left almost flat and inletted into the stock.

The ramrods can be split out of a hickory log. They have to be split out lengthwise with the grain running straight from one end to the other to

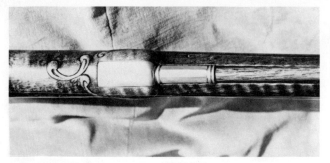

PLATE 361 Jim makes the rear ramrod pipes out of single pieces of sheet brass.

make it limber. They're also slightly tapered so they will fit easily under the barrel in the wrist portion of the rifle. The ramrods can be purchased as straight rods from several sources. I still taper them myself.

I make most of my screws. I start out with a chunk of steel, heat it a little bit, and hammer one end flat for the head of the screw. Then using a hand drill, I can turn the screws and hold the file up to one edge and shape them to whatever shape I want. I put the threads on with a tap-and-die set. Back then they had what they called a screw plate, which accomplished the same thing.

For the stock, I usually purchase a board, although I have been known to go out and cut down the tree and saw it into boards. I like the boards to air dry for several years before I use them for a stock. I don't like to use anything less than 2½″ wide for the early guns. They were wider, and the architecture was different from the later period ones that were made from, say from 1820 on. So the board has to be at least 2½″ to get the width you need out of it and to get the cheekpiece standing out.

I make my own triggers—cut those out of a solid piece of metal with a hacksaw and files.

The fore end or nose cap I make out of sheet brass. There are two different ways you can go at it. Earl makes a cap, puts this piece on first while the gun is still in block form, and then shapes the gun to the shape of the fore end cap. I go ahead and finish the forestock the way I want it shaped and then make the cap to fit the wood. Both ways work equally well. Again, I anneal the brass and bend it around the fore end. It's made in two pieces—the end is soldered onto the other piece. Some of them were made out of one piece.

There are two different types of patch boxes. One is a sliding wood patch box and the other a hinged brass box. The sliding wood type is a carryover from the European guns—the Jäegers—which were made in Germany. They were brought to the Colonies by settlers, and most of them had sliding

PLATE 362   He also makes the nose caps out of brass.

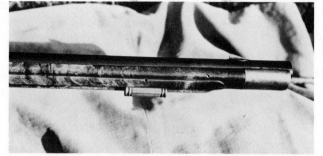

PLATE 363 The catch at the butt releases the sliding wood lid of the patch box —all handmade.

PLATE 364 The patch-box lid removed and turned upside down to show the catch.

PLATE 365 The cleaning jag and cloth found in each patch box.

wood patch boxes. Everyone pretty well agrees, the hinged brass patch box is totally an American innovation. It originated right here with the American gunsmiths. They started off rather simple. Most of the early patch boxes were just a hinge, the head portion, and a lid. Later on, they added side pieces to it and cut out areas in the brass and left wood showing up through the brass, and so forth. They really got fancy with them and did some engraving as fine as anything you find on the old silverware.

The lids of my sliding wood patch boxes are dovetailed into the stock. I cut out the hole in the stock, dovetail the edges of it. Then I cut out the lid and dovetail the lid to fit. I put a little spring-type catch on the lid to keep it closed.

The early gunsmiths usually made a worm to go with the guns. It's really a cleaning jag [see Plate 365] that screws onto the end of the ramrod. It was used for cleaning the gun and occasionally pulling a ball out. If you happened to put the ball down the barrel before you put the powder down, you were in trouble. Sometimes you can catch the ball with the worm and pull it back out. But primarily it was used for cleaning. They used toe for cleaning—the leftover stuff that is thrown away when you make flax into linen. It was kind of rough and abrasive, and fit well around the cleaning jag or worm. They carried those things in the patch box, as well as some extra flints.

To assemble the gun I start with the stock—lay the pattern on the board and trace around it and cut out the rough stock blank. I usually use curly maple. That's what the early gunsmiths used. They also used some walnut, and some of the fruit woods—apple and so forth—occasionally. Cherry is an excellent wood for gunstocks, but primarily they used curly maple.

Now on the early guns, the wood is not nearly as curly as on the later guns. Before the Revolution just a few gunsmiths were making guns. During the Revolution many people turned to making guns for the war. So after the Revolution you had this tremendous number of gunsmiths. There wasn't a need for that many, so the competition increased. Better gunsmiths made better guns—more decorative and so forth. The ones that couldn't measure up went back to being blacksmiths or whatever they were doing before. But these gunsmiths, primarily because of the competition, started using much better wood so that the grain and the stripes in the wood used was much more pronounced after the Revolution.

The next thing I do is inlet the barrel, get that set down in the block of wood, and try to fit it up just as tight as I can. The tighter the fit, the better it looks when it is finished.

After that I put the buttplate on. The buttplate determines the whole shape of the buttstock. You have to have that on before you can do any shaping of the stock. So I put the buttplate on the block of wood, and then using the rasps, files, and chisels, I can go ahead and shape the stock. If I'm making a gun of a particular style where the triggerguard and buttplate are not commercially available, I make them myself. Just take a flat piece of brass and hammer them out into whatever shapes are necessary, and then braze them together. In the near future I plan to sand-cast these parts just as the eighteenth-century gunsmiths did.

PLATE 366 The wrist portion of Jim's gun is beautifully tapered and finished.

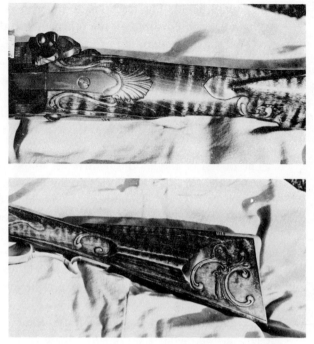

PLATE 367 The relief carving, wire inlay, and cheekpiece are all smoothly, gracefully integrated.

After the butt portion is shaped and the wrist partially shaped I inlet the lock. The lock plate is first inlet in the correct place and then each individual internal part of the lock is inlet. The trigger can be positioned and inlet any time after the wrist and the area around the lock has been shaped. I install the triggerguard after the stock has been completed. The sights, any inlays, ramrod pipes, relief or incised carving, and patch box are added after the stock has been fully shaped.

The hardest part of the gun, I've found—and Earl and most other people agree—is the wrist portion. That's especially true on the early guns where the architecture is so important. On the early guns, the architecture is really beautiful. You don't see that so much on the later guns. When you get into the percussion era, they went in more for inlays than they did the fine detailed carving and fine architecture. The later guns were narrower and flatter all over, and they just weren't nearly as appealing to the eye, in my opinion, as the early rifles were. On the early ones every line has to flow smoothly into every other line. Everything flows. There is really no straight line anywhere in the gun. Some were flat on top of the comb, but they are really more appealing if you have just a very slight curvature to that area. The same goes for the bottom of the buttstock. When you get up into the part of the stock that holds the barrel, the stock follows the barrel, which is tapered and flared. The stock has to taper to go along with the barrel. All the lines have to flow into all the other lines so there is nothing to snag the eye. That's really important in the early guns.

I have to plan for the relief carving and leave a little excess wood where I want the carving to be. The carving doesn't have to be very high, a sixteenth to an eighth of an inch is fine. It should be fairly low but still high enough so that you can tell it is raised. I draw the design on the stock and remove wood from it using mostly a pocketknife and one or two small wood chisels.

The design of the carving can be as simple or as elaborate as the customer wants. I try to add a little carving to every rifle I make. On the more expensive guns I add elaborate designs behind the cheekpiece, in front of the cheekpiece, in front of the patch box, around the barrel tang, and around the rear ramrod pipe tang. The designs I use follow the traditional eighteenth-century rococo style with C-scrolls, S-scrolls, etc. I usually incorporate silver-wire inlay into the design which, together with the carving and engraving, really makes the gun an art piece rather than just a sporting arm.

I've got some engraving tools I use, some small chisels, for engraving designs in the metal. I use a small hammer and peck along the lines I've drawn. The chisels are called die-sinker's chisels.

I inlet the sterling-silver wire into the stock with a pocketknife. I just draw whatever design I want on the stock, then take a pocketknife and carve a groove in the wood. Then I take a small hammer, hammer the silver wire into the grooves, then smooth it off with a file, and sand it.

For finishing the wood, there are different finishes that can be used. Some gunsmiths use chromic acid or nitric acid. I used that for a while and found that the wood looks good when you first put it on, but after the gun is a year or two old, it will get a greenish tint in it which is not found in the old guns. They have reddish tints and yellowish tints and browns in them, but you don't see much green in the old guns. I like mine to look like the old guns—that is, to be as authentic as possible—so I quit using the acids on them.

Instead, I mix up my own stain. I get a stain from one of the gunsmith suppliers which is too red for my taste, but it is the proper base to start with. Then I get some brown and black shoe dye and mix in various portions of all three of these and try it on different pieces of wood until I come up with the color I like—kind of a reddish stain with a little bit of yellow, red, brown, and so forth. It looks very much like the finish on the old guns.

That's just the beginning. I put that on until the stock is really dark.

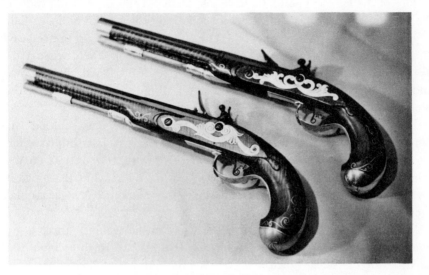

PLATE 368   Jim also makes pistols for special customers. Of his pistols he says, "They were made primarily for the more well-to-do citizens in Colonial America. Your average Joe couldn't afford one. So, as a general rule, they were decorated a little bit more than the rifles, but they are made about the same. You basically have the same jobs to do in terms of construction."

Then I use very fine steel wool—the finest I can get—and take the color down to the darkness I want. Then I start rubbing the stock with linseed oil. I put on linseed oil until the stock won't soak up any more of it. When I get all of that on, then I start with what is called the hand-rubbed finish. Just take your hands and rub them back and forth over the stock. This will give it a real glossy finish. It takes several weeks to do that. Or if the customer is impatient for the gun, I sometimes take some linseed oil and mix a little bit of varnish with it and apply that. The combination of the linseed oil, the varnish, and some rubbing will give a pretty shiny finish.

Today the modern gun barrels are blued. Way back, the barrels were browned. What is involved is really a rusting process. I mix up a bunch of chemicals according to an old recipe—various acids, and so forth. Then I clean the barrel thoroughly to make sure all the grease is off. I scrub it good with soap and water and then use acetone, or something like that, to remove all the grease from it. Lighter fluid works just about as well. Then I put the browning solution on the barrel, let it sit, and it gradually rusts the

surface of the barrel. You really have just plain old rust on it. I put more of
the solution on every day until I get a good even brown finish on it—usually
anywhere from four days to a week. The rust will get built up pretty heavy
on the barrel, so I keep it smoothed off with steel wool. Then, when I feel
like I've got a real smooth, even finish on it, I wash it good, dry it down,
and rub linseed oil or some other heavy oil all over it to stop the rusting
process.

There were many different formulas for the browning solution that
ranged all the way from those I make up with acids to just simply urinat-
ing on the barrel and setting it outside. That will work. If you don't do anything to the barrel, it will gradually turn brown by itself, but there will be
areas that are browner than others. By using the solution, I can get a quick,
even, and smooth brown finish on it.

My guns start at about $600. I usually work in the evenings, three to five
hours an evening, five or six days a week. It takes two to three months to
make a rifle or pistol. When you consider the number of hours that I put
into one, I'm not making very much. I estimate somewhere around two to
two-and-a-half dollars an hour, maybe. The parts are getting quite expensive. I got in some barrels the other day, and one barrel was $93—just for
one barrel, and they go up every year. The lock kits cost about $36, and if
you buy them assembled, that runs it up to about $60. Wood has gone out
of sight, $50 to $100 per stock. So you can get an idea from that how much
is involved just in parts alone.

I try to price my work in such a way that anyone who really wants one of
my guns can afford one. I often take items as a trade for part of the price,
and I will sometimes allow the customer to pay for the gun in several small
payments as well.

I love to correspond with or talk to anyone interested in my work,
whether they're wanting to purchase a gun or just wanting a little free advice. If anyone has any questions, just drop me a line at Box 32, Clyde,
N.C. 28721.

THE NEW AGE

There are many clues to the size of the muzzle-loading movement. One is
the number of thriving manufacturers turning out both finished rifles and
the parts with which to make them. Another is the number of successful
trade publications, like *Muzzle Blasts, The Buckskin Report,* and *Black
Powder Times.* Another is the size of the membership rolls in organizations
like the National Muzzle Loading Rifle Association (NMLRA) that serve
the movement. At last count this organization, founded on the almost pre-
posterous belief that an antique weapon could acquire a vocal and devoted

following, had over 23,000 members. But nothing brings it all home in quite the way that a visit to one of the annual NMLRA shooting matches does. It is, to put it simply, unbelievable. Three of us went to the annual spring shoot in 1977 to see for ourselves, and from a hill overlooking the narrow valley outside Friendship, Indiana, where it is held each year, we became convinced from the almost unbroken roar of guns that one of the larger battles of the Civil War must have sounded almost exactly the same.

Shooting matches are a tradition that goes back into time as far as the guns themselves. Their variety would fill a book nearly this size. Thousands of them are he'd each year around this country, and so it is appropriate that in the new age of muzzle loading, we devote this section to these tests of skill.

A Local Turkey Shoot

Bonnie Mize and Donna Griggs attended a shoot sponsored by *Foxfire* and Lawton Brooks, and they put together the following as a result. Though muzzle loaders are not used today in this particular shoot, they were once, and the match itself still survives.

One important pastime for mountain people was shooting matches, and one of the most popular types was the turkey shoot. It was popular not only as entertainment, but also as a way for the sponsor to make a little money.

In the earliest shoots, the participants would actually shoot with flintlock or caplock rifles, in turn, at a live turkey, and the one that killed it first won the match and the turkey. Later, people began shooting at targets with shotguns and the prizes were live turkeys. More recently, with fewer and fewer turkeys being raised and the almost universal shift to shotguns instead of rifles, turkey shoots have been used more as fund-raising events with the prizes ranging from hams to bags of groceries to cases of beer and soft drinks. If any turkeys are involved, they are usually frozen, the winner often receiving a coupon which he can redeem for the prize at a local participating grocery store. The targets the contestants shoot at are usually three-by-five index cards (one card per man per shot), and the winner is determined either by counting the number of shot each gun put through its card, or by measuring to see which man's gun put a shot closest to an X drawn from corner to corner on the card. Matches can go all day. The sponsor announces at the beginning of each match what the prize is going to be ("We're going to shoot off a ham now.") and how much it will cost to enter (usually one to two dollars per chance). The men who want to shoot pay the entry fee, and when enough have entered to pay for the cost of the prize and earn the sponsor a few dollars profit, the contestants step up to a rail and shoot—in turn—at the numbered card they have been assigned, each man getting one shot. Then a runner goes and collects the cards and brings them in for the judging and the awarding of the prize.

When *Foxfire* decided to sponsor a turkey shoot to raise money for a scholarship fund, we decided to have Lawton Brooks run it for us, and the experience was so interesting that we asked him to come to our class and talk to us about it. He remembered not only the earlier shoots (where each man would pay fifty cents for a chance at a live turkey, and the men would takes turns shooting until someone killed it) up to the present to shoots he still participates in regularly. He explained part of the motivation behind the shoots this way: "You can make some money if you run one right. You put up a ten-pound bag of sugar and everybody'll take a chance on it at a dollar a shot. They don't look at how many's shooting. All they think is, 'If I can win that for a dollar, it will be better than going to the store and buying it.'

"And then they have side pots going on now at the same time, too. That's just gambling. And sometimes people get into arguments over that, but I never heard of anyone actually getting hurt at a shoot. Some drunk or someone might come around and get into an argument. He'd think he ought to win when he knowed he couldn't see the target, let alone try to win anything. Somebody'd tell him to take his old gun and go home, and he'd leave."

The stories Lawton told were really interesting, and I hope you enjoy them as much as we did.

BONNIE MIZE AND DONNA GRIGGS

I can remember going [to turkey shoots] with my daddy when I couldn't hold up a rifle. Them old hog rifles is heavy. They ain't like our guns nowadays. They weigh as much as two of our guns weigh.

And I can remember going with him, and he'd take that old rifle and he'd just whack [the turkey's] head off nearly everytime. But I couldn't shoot it.

He finally bought me one of them guns—the first one I ever owned. It wasn't so awful heavy. Awful long barrel, but it wasn't so heavy. And it shot good, but I wouldn't put too much powder in it at a time, so it wouldn't kick me so bad. But I'd shoot me a little old bird sitting around the cornfield, and one thing or another. Get out there and shoot him.

[It was hard to get used to shooting with a gun like that, though, because] sometimes it would make what they called a long fire. The cap will bust and then it's just a second before the powder gets caught, you know, and then it goes off. Them old son-of-a-guns will do that sometimes. I'd done be fixing to move when it'd go off! Just takes them a second to get connected up, I reckon, to where the powder burns.

They didn't use targets in the beginning. They used real turkeys. Nearly everybody raised turkeys back in them days. Everybody had farms, you know, and they had stuff sowed for the turkeys to eat, and they raised them. We always had a bunch of turkeys at home running around all the time. They were easier raised back in them days than now. Now you can't hardly raise them out loose. Something will happen to them, and they'll just go to dying out on you. I tried it when I lived up here at Dillard. I raised around a hundred up there one time, but it was rough. Used to be we always had rye and wheat and everything sowed around the house for them to eat on, and the old turkey hen would take a bunch of little ones out in the rye field and you wouldn't see them for two or three days. 'Course they'd come back to the house, and by the time they came back, they'd be great big turkeys growing right on up. You'd just catch 'em up and go right on to the shooting match. They'd put one in a box and put his head up out of the box and everybody shot at that. Shoot right for his head—that old red head up there. Shoot right for his eyeballs. The man who shot the turkey and killed him, that was it. It was all over with. The other man didn't get to shoot. Had to put up another turkey and start again.

But that turkey'd stand there with his old head up and just turn his old head around. Never would hardly keep it still. But about every time you shot his head, it would fly off or flop down on top of the box. They'd really knock him in the head. They didn't hardly ever miss with them old hog rifles. They're just as true as they can be. They don't wobble off or nothing. That old bullet goes exactly where you aim it, and them old fellers were trying to aim right because that's the only chance they had. Like when they was hunting—see, that's what they hunted with all the time. If they found them a deer or wild hog or something they wanted to kill, they shot at it, and if they missed it—good God. By the time you got reloaded he'd a'been from here to Franklin. They waited till they knew what they was a'doing before they pulled the trigger.

But at these shoots, they'd be about fifty yards away—that turkey in a box just big enough for him to stand in. He'd keep his head up. I've also knowed of them hunting up a big log to put the turkey behind. I heard my daddy talk about that. They'd put him where his head would come up just above the log [when he raised up]. That was harder 'cause the turkey could get down behind that. Sometimes a turkey would go through two or three shoots. Every man shoot one and miss, and have to go again with the same turkey.

But about ten years ago [they stopped shooting *at* the turkeys and started shooting *for* live turkeys by shooting at targets]. People would bring them to wherever they had their old shooting match. They'd have their old turkeys tied up to bushes and everything around there, you know. Everybody would have a turkey they wanted to shoot off. They'd bring him and tie him up. And the man that brought the turkey would get the money. See how many he could get [shooting] on it. If he could get enough [shooting] on it to pay for his turkey, he'd let them shoot it off.

The last live turkey shoot I went to was down at what they call Joe's Creek on Cartoogachaye up there at a church. They had'em alive, just tied up around there. And there was one of the biggest gobblers there—oh, man he was a whopper. Weighed thirty-five pounds, and I wanted him. So I had some awful fine shot, but I thought they might have a rule, you know, about what to shoot and what not to. I wanted to be fair about it, and I didn't know none of them there—I had just heard of the shoot being there, and I thought I'd go down there. So I waited and watched them shoot a time or two. Then I asked a man, "Now what are you shooting here? Are you furnishing the shells?"

"No," says he. "A fellow has to furnish his own shells."

I said, "Well, what do we shoot? Do we have a certain number size shot that we have to shoot?"

"Na. Just anthing. Just as long as you don't shoot buckshot."

I just thought to myself, "Good. When that big turkey comes up, I'm gonna take a chance," 'cause I had some number twelves. They didn't have nothing finer than an eight.

So they had their signs out on a big poplar tree. They went and got that ticket [target] every time you'd shoot. They'd go get the ticket and put up another one. Just had a tree there to put them on. So that turkey come up, and I give'em a dollar and cut down on that thing, and it just filled it full. They kept a looking at that ticket and looking at that ticket and counting and looking and looking. So when they all got done shooting, the boy come up and said, "Well, boys, I'll tell ya, they ain't a bit of need nobody else counting. We've already counted over two hundred and we ain't got nothing like all of'em counted." It had it just filled. Looked just like a sifter. So they said there wasn't no argument about that. Said I was the man that won the big turkey.

So they begin to move around there and I decided then that I didn't want that old turkey; I'd shoot him off. But I couldn't get but eight men to shoot, and they had got ten on him the first time around. So I said, "Boys, I'll be a'losing two dollars if I shoot him off at eight."

"Well," some of the boys said, "just take a chance yourself." Said, "You take a chance."

Well, I knowed if I did, I'd win him again, but they wanted me to do that. Said it was all right with them for me to take a chance. Said, "You can't do that every time."

"Well," I said, "all right. Put him up." So when I come up, I done it
again. Then they begin to scatter off then. So I brought the old turkey on
and I sold him to an old conductor on this Tallulah Falls train right here.
He give me eleven dollars the next day for that old turkey. He said he had
two grandsons, and he said that they was always aggravating something
and he wanted that old turkey. Said he bet that old turkey would fight, and
boys, he would fight. He said he wanted it to learn them grandsons something. So I sold it to that old conductor that worked on that train, and I
made that old turkey pay off.

I've won a lot of stuff. I went up to the Rabun Gap School one time, me
and this other boy. Me and him went up there one time when Mr. Burden
[the vocational agriculture teacher at that time—now the Superintendent
of Schools for Rabun County] was having one shooting off live turkeys.
And they had eight down there, and me and him won all eight of them,
and I bought his four from him. We was using that old single-barrel gun of
mine, and it was just filling them cards full. Every time they'd count, we'd
win. So we got the eight turkeys, and I bought his four and took them over
on Jones Creek to my wife's first cousin and put them up and had me a
shooting match with them. I made some good money off of my turkeys. I'd
get about ten or eleven shots on a turkey.

[You have to watch when you're running a match. Some people will
cheat.]

One way you can cheat is if you're supposed to shoot with an eight and
you shoot a nine [instead]. You'll have a better shot.

And then you can reload a shell. You don't put too much powder and
you leave out some of the waddings and put in a good many more shot. See,
the more high-powered a shell is, the more it will scatter [the shot]. They
got so much force when they come out of there they go to scattering. They
got too much powder. If you just got enough powder to kinda throw the
shot out there, they'll just slap out there in one place and don't scatter and
maybe come up in a wad. Now that's the difference in that. That's where
your reload comes in. And you needn't to shoot much against a reload
'cause they got an advantage over you if you ain't shooting reloads too.

I can tell when he shoots if he's using reloads. I can tell by the noise.
When he shoots a reload, they don't sound like any other shells. And if
you'll look at it good, you can tell a difference. You look at the shell that's
supposed to be like it [and compare] and look at the difference in the
primer. There will be a difference in the color of the primer most of the
time. Most of them have got a lighter color than the others.

But you can hear one. I can be at a shooting match and I can tell when
one goes off just like that. A lot of people are doing that nowadays, and

they'll slip them in on you. Any way to win. They want to win, and they'll do anything to win. That's the reason. I say a man [that's running a shooting match] just has to give them the shells [he wants them to shoot] and see that every man shoots the same thing, and then if he wins, you can't grunt at that man, 'cause he's got a better gun or is a better shot than you. You have to watch them, though [if you're running a match]. It's easy to have where they come up and get their shell from you and then switch anyway. That'd be easy done for me to have me some shells in my pocket and then I come up and there and get one off of you, and while the other fellers is shooting, I drop that one in my pocket and use one of mine. I've got a good chance of winning then. Where you shoot with so many at a time, you can't hardly keep them from slipping in on you. Somebody's going to do something wrong. They've got different ways that they can really beat you.

Them number nines are supposed to be a regular target-loaded shell. That's what everybody generally shoots is number nine. And so if that's the way it is, that's what people should shoot. They ought to shoot number nine, and then there wouldn't be no growling about it. I think we ought to have someone stand right there and hand them their shell and see that their gun isn't loaded, and watch them [put the shell you gave them] in their gun. Then nobody could have no complaints. Nowadays people don't like two or three to carry off everything there is [in prizes] and them have just as much money in it and never win nothing and go back home empty-handed and their pocketbooks flat. That's the way I always done it. I'd always shoot till I got out of money! [They do too.]

Now there's some variation in the factory-loaded shells too. I've tried it. I've got out there and shot a big old pasteboard and counted the shot, and some had a lot and some didn't hardly have any. [Even the factories] don't get them loaded *exactly* the same. [But at least you don't have reloads, and everyone takes the same chance with the same kind of shell. They're all working under exactly the same kind of handicap.] But it's fun. I don't mind losin' as long as I'm losin' fair. I could lose all day. I'm just as satisfied, just so it's fair. I've always been crazy about going turkey shooting. I don't win all the time. I've lost money. I've lost a lot of money shooting, and then I've won some. A man ain't gonna win all the time. He's just gonna have to trust his luck. But it is luck shooting at these crosses [on a card] sure enough. It's all in luck because half the time a man will take an old scatter gun and he won't hit [the target] with but four or five shot, but one of them might be right in there right next to that cross. And maybe you'll put fifty or sixty shot in there and you won't have nary one within a quarter of an inch of the cross. That's luck now.

Really the best way, and the fairest to everybody, would be to count the shot, and that would be shooting for the skill of a man's gun. He'd know then if his gun would stand up or not.

The Cataloochee Shoot

Another type of shooting match was called an "across the log, 'X' center" match. Earl Lanning, who lives in Waynesville, North Carolina, teaches a college class in muzzle-loading rifle building, and he got involved in the field through one of the Cataloochee shoots. Held each year near Waynesville in the Cataloochee section of the mountains, the shoots were patterned after some of the oldest traditional types where participants won quarters of beef.

Here, Earl tells about his experiences and about the shoot itself.

I got into [muzzle loading] about '53 or '54 when I went to a match at Cataloochee. That was the first time I ever had one of those guns in my hand. Back then you could buy a pretty decent old gun for about fifty or sixty dollars, and I went through several of those and tried to get them to where they'd shoot, and that was kind of tough. In the meantime, I heard about men like Lester Smith that were building rifles, and so I had Lester Smith build a rifle for me using an old barrel; and then I had Hacker Martin build me one. That was after Hacker moved to Virginia. And by that time I had been around it enough to learn a little. Went up to the shoots at Friendship several years, for example. Vee Jones was building some guns at the time; and there used to be an old fellow named Ed Browning that lived above Joe Farmer—he's related to Joe—and I used to go up there and watch him sometimes. Then I got to studying the old guns a lot, and I could see that some of these guns these old fellows were making weren't up hardly with the old ones, so I said, "What the heck. I'll try it myself." So I got into it—I built fifteen rifles. Then I heard about still other folks around the country, and back at this time, you didn't have all these books, and there weren't many parts available. You just had to bow up on a work bench and file the parts out working with photographs. Bud Siler and I became friends, and we were trying to learn together.

Well, we got along, but it was slow. And I've always been willing to drive halfway across the country to see something. I never was one to just sit around home. I heard of Carl Pippert, and just drove up there. When I went up to Carl's the first time, he did more for me in the first hour than all the years before had taught me. He completely enlightened me on a multitude of things I had done wrong. So for years I'd build guns and take them up there, and Carl would go over them and correct them and show me.

Then along about that time I met Joe Kindig, Jr. (author of *Thoughts on the Kentucky Rifle in Its Golden Age*) with that tremendous collection of fine-carved rifles he had, and Joe was a real nice collector and perfectly willing for me to go in there and look at anything I wanted to. I learned a whole lot of things there.

So I progressed right along and I got up to a point where I thought I could build a gun just about as good as anyone else's. My favorite period was the Lancaster County, Pennsylvania rifle of the 1770s. So that was the niche I put myself into, and everything I made was pretty much as though I had lived right in that area. It was all pretty much in character with that time. But eventually I got worn out with it, and I started showing other people instead, and that's what I've been doing ever since. In my class at Haywood Tech, I've had as many as thirty-nine students in one quarter, so I guess we're going to keep the class a while. There's been some fine gunsmiths come out of it. I've had a few guys that were just as good as I was, and that's all you could ask for [as a teacher].

Tom Alexander started the Cataloochee match back in the early 1940s and one of the distinctive things about it was the location—it was isolated way up there on top of that mountain. Even though it was in August, it was always pretty cool—nice atmosphere. And another thing that was distinctive about it—and one of the reasons it caused a lot of interest—was that it was like the matches were back in the old days. It was started by old-time local match shooters, and they conducted it pretty much like it had always been done. They weren't the gun-collector types or anything like that running it. It was strictly old-time. Each shooter used any kind of target he wanted to—any shape. He could shoot at a *Life* magazine if he wanted to. The only stipulation was that he had to put his own X on the target; then he'd fire three shots and come as close as he could to that X.

In the very earliest shoots I can remember, they would have a stack of oak boards up there and a fire built, and they'd throw those boards over there in the fire and scorch them black. Then the shooters would cut out all kinds of little cardboard targets for themselves, and put one on each oak board. One of the most popular was a square with a V cut right in the top of it, and they'd aim right at that V—right at the point of it. But they could choose their own type of target, which was important because during the first matches, they used all old guns—I didn't see any new guns at all the first year—and with those old-time hunting sights, maybe one type of target didn't work so well. You had to have a target that would relate to those sights, and everybody had his own version of what he could see and shoot

PLATE 369 Left to right, Harvey "Cap" Price, Bill Large, Earl Lanning, and Vee Jones at the 1959 Cataloochee shoot. Vee Jones holds the record for the best target ever shot at a Cataloochee match. He put three .45-caliber bullets into one hole in the dead center of the "X." He had one of Bill Large's barrels on his rifle. (Photo courtesy Earl Lanning.)

PLATE 370 Shooting in the 1955 Cataloochee match. The man on the far left is the famous photographer and gun enthusiast, J. T. Holley. He is shooting a gun, dated 1804 on the breech, that was used in the Battle of New Orleans. He called the gun "Old Kellem." (Photo courtesy Earl Lanning.)

PLATE 371 Left to right, Judy Lanning, Earl Lanning, Bud Siler, and Joe Farmer at the 1963 shoot. (Photo courtesy of Earl Lanning.)

the best. But they didn't have these modern sights like they've got now. Those old Kentuckies had the old-time hunting sights on them: sort of a semi-buckhorn-type affair on the back, and then they had a little silver or barleycorn sight in front, and they were tough to see out in the sunshine. That's the reason some of these guys used copper hoods to shade them.

Anyway, they'd choose their own targets, and put their own X on them, and shoot at those. Three shots. And they shot across a log. It was a laying down deal, and it was at sixty yards, which is pretty far. It's a little too far, actually. Most matches around the country have been fifty yards for a long time. Then another thing that made the match tough was the fact that you had to stand in line to shoot. You would shoot one shot, and then they would take your target down and put up the next man's, and you'd go to the back of the line. Then when your turn came again, they would set your target back up, and it might not be set up exactly the same way. It was a crazy, hard way to shoot, but it was an old-time match, and you just had to put up with that. Of course, everybody kind of liked it that way, and it kept up the interest.

When they got ready to score, they'd have a lead bullet that they had cut in half through the middle, and there'd be an X marked on the inside of it. They'd set that bullet down in each of the three holes in the target, and take a set of dividers and measure from the center of the X on the bullet to the center of the X on the target. Say maybe one was a quarter inch from center to center, and the second shot was a half inch, and the third shot was a quarter inch. Well, that man's score would be the total of those measurements, or one inch.

Another good thing about Cataloochee was that they always had a live steer, and at the end of the match, the two hindquarters and the two front quarters were given away to the four highest scorers. The shooters were divided into age groups: up to twenty, then twenty to forty, then forty to sixty, and then sixty and over. But they didn't go by age groups for the winners. The four best boards of the day got the beef, no matter what age group they came out of. The very best boards always got the hindquarters, and the next two best got the front.

There were a lot of things about the match that were hard—and made it maybe not quite as democratic as some of the more modern shoots today— but I don't know. You lose something when you gain something. Some of the old-time heritage goes when you modernize the darn thing, and you lose when you try to make it better. The old shoot is phased out now, and there's a new shoot over here at Waynesville [to take its place]. They don't have a live steer. They just buy beef and give the beef away. Then there's a nice big trophy that goes with it, too. It's a good match, but it's not quite the same as the old one.

A Shooting Club:
The Blue Ridge Mountain Men

All across the country, local clubs are being formed, most of which sponsor local shoots for trophies and cash prizes. We found, to our surprise, that our own area has one, and Mike Drake and Bobby Rholetter visited one of their shooting matches and talked to their president, John Harkins.

Most of the members in our club are deer hunters, and they like to shoot muzzle loaders. It's just something different than shooting a cartridge gun. It's educational, and you might say it's a challenge to see if you are as good as your forefathers were. In those days they shot to live and to protect themselves, and it's fun to test your skill against theirs. Today there are probably more people in it than there were in those days. Today mostly it's just target shooting, but generally in the hunting season a lot of them go hunting deer with muzzle loaders.

These guns are surprisingly accurate. I saw in one of our *Black Powder Times* that they put up a bunch of police department people shooting cartridge pistols against a muzzle-loading club, and the muzzle loaders came out far ahead over the pistol shooters. They're just that much more accurate.

PLATE 372 Left to right, John Harkins talking to Mike Drake and Bobby Rholetter at a recent shooting match sponsored by the Blue Ridge Mountain Men.

We've been a chartered NMLRA club since we formed four years ago. It wasn't too hard to get up because for some reason or another, there were a lot of men who were getting interested in it. And one good thing is that the NMLRA doesn't tell us what to do. If we need to know anything, we can write them in regard to the national rules or something we don't understand, and they'll help us. But members don't even have to have a gun. They can just be a member, and that's it if they want. Our treasurer doesn't shoot targets with a muzzle loader, but he has shot deer before. He doesn't participate in these matches, though.

We try to have meetings once a month. Sometimes we give the club members notice on a short order because something has turned up that we wish them to know about. Generally we try to have a meeting a week before we're going to have a shooting match so that members who have been assigned to a detail can get together and understand what they've got to do, or they can pass on their duty to someone else if they aren't going to be able to make it.

The dues that come into the club go for operating expenses, and generally most of the money goes to pay for the trophies. What money is left goes to buying targets, stuff for a little food concession set up at each match, and general operating expenses. The club's not a profit-making deal. We try to make just enough money so we can stay solvent and not lose.

Most of the members of the club are from right around here. Right now we don't have any women shooters in the club as members, but we have women shooters come to the matches, and they tote those trophies off!

There are lots of different kinds of targets used at these matches. Each shooter picks up the kind he wants to shoot at, and then the highest score on

PLATE 373

PLATE 374 Even young-
sters participate in shooting
matches.

PLATE 375   Scoring targets.

that particular target for the day wins a trophy. We change targets that we buy from match to match, so there's plenty of variety for people to pick from.

It's not a big, nationally important shoot or anything. We just get out and try to have a good time with these muzzle loaders, and some of the best people in the world are in muzzle loading. And more are coming in each day. Like today, someone came to this shoot that's not a member of the club. He'd never been to a shoot before, and he walked off with a first-place target score—won a trophy. So muzzle loading is a coming thing, and I expect it will be here a lot longer. More and more people realize it's an easy thing to get into. It can be expensive, but you can make your own lead balls at a much cheaper price, and your own percussion caps and your own patches and knives and ramrods and cleaning jags and things of this sort. Some members even make their own guns. In the near future I want to build a Bedford County percussion rifle with brass furniture. I already have some of the parts to build it with, but I haven't got the wood yet, which is very costly.

It's a most relaxing, enjoyable thing to shoot a muzzle loader after you understand the principal workings of these guns.

The NMLRA Shoots

The biggest shoots of all are those sponsored in the spring and fall by the National Muzzle Loading Rifle Association in Friendship. Though growing pains are obvious, the shoots are still spectacular occasions. Divided in half by a small river, the site breaks perfectly into two separate shooting areas. One is devoted to those individuals who wish to compete by shooting at targets from a formal range. There, there are matches especially for those who shoot flint, percussion, pistol, trap, skeet, bench, or slug guns. Participants camp in tents, vans, trailers, their cars, or rent rooms in local motels.

The second area is devoted to the primitive range where participants dress in buckskin clothing, camp in tepees or lean-tos, and engage in matches that can bewilder the novice observer.

Jeff Reeves and Kirk Patterson spent an afternoon with two men on the primitive range and talked with several people.

Dale Black is a warehouseman at Scott Air Force Base and has also worked in grain mills, aircraft factories, and automobile assembly plants. He has been involved in the primitive side of muzzle loading for twenty-five years.

Hawk Boughton received basic infantry training in World War II at Camp Forrest, Tennessee, and subsequently served in the U. S. Army in the South Pacific. At various times he has worked for the U. S. Forest Service, has done technical writing in the missile business and for the Allis-Chalmers Company, and has spent two years as a cook on river boats. More recently, in an attempt to find employment closer to his home and to a mother who was getting up in years, he took a job as a parts inspector at an Emerson Electric Company plant in Paris, Tennessee. Aside from the spare time he spends going to muzzle-loading events, he also co-operates with the TVA, running "Wilderness Weekends" where he teaches participants such survival skills as how to make a fire without matches, find and prepare wild goods, cook without utensils, snare small game and use fish traps, sleep in cold weather, build shelters, use a canoe, and find directions without a compass.

Hawk is the only man who has won the Mountain Man Aggregate match at the NMLRA three times, and Dale has won it twice. This match requires that participants wear period clothing of the type that was common from 1750–1840, and that they use a flintlock rifle equipped with open, non-adjustable sights. Each participant must build a fire with flint and steel

within a specified time period, make three difficult shots with a flintlock rifle, throw a knife three times, and throw a tomahawk three times. The targets and their locations are changed from year to year to keep it competitive. This year, for the three rifle events, a participant had to shoot at the edge of a playing card and split it completely in half, shoot at a barely visible target in the woods, and shoot at an axe blade mounted in a stump. The latter shot, if done properly, would cause the lead ball to split in half on the blade and break two clay pigeons simultaneously—one mounted on either side of the blade. Hawk did it while we watched. Dale split the playing card, but Hawk missed.

When they had finished shooting for the day, we talked to them:

DALE: I've been interested in early history all my life, ever since I was in grade school. When they'd give me a history book, I'd read it the first day. That was all I'd do. I mean, I liked it. Hawk and I, I guess, go back about ten years. We kind of started in muzzle loading, and then we went off on a little different path. We wanted to follow the historic way of doing things,

PLATE 377 Hawk splitting a lead ball on an axe blade and breaking two clay pigeons.

PLATE 378 Dale Black split a playing card in the Mountain Man Aggregate and tucked half of it in the horsehair band of his hat.

and dress like it, instead of just saying, "Well, I'm going to shoot a muzzle loader." There's really more to it than just having a rifle and a pouch and shooting a few targets. You get to reading history and you get interested in it, and the more you get into it, the more history you assimilate. Right now I've joined a Civil War outfit, and that's an entirely different part of muzzle loading. We re-enact certain battles, for example. It just all depends on how far the individual wants to go. Maybe at some point in time a man reaches a plateau where he's satisfied with himself and what he's doing. But we're usually working on a part of our gear, like authentic type moccasions or authentic type belts or some ironware for our cooking. It's a continual thing for us. We're all the time trying to better our gear and be more authentic with it. I might say, "My cooking utensils are not quite right," and I'd spend a lot of time going to museums until I found a part I was really interested in that suited me. Or I might spot a knife and say, "Well, gee, there's just the knife I want. That man carried that knife to skin beaver and stuff." And I'd go down there and try and make a sketch of it. And if you're lucky, the people might let you draw a line around it and get a pattern, and then you go home and do your best to re-create it.

HAWK: Dale here's a blacksmith, and he's hand-forged a lot of his stuff.

DALE: We're not trying to go and fake it in any way. We don't try to fake anything. The idea is, if we make something, we want to make it of a type that was used during the time we're interested in, the time we're depicting. It's just like a hobby. You're constantly bettering yourself.

Some people think we're stupid, I guess, and they have different viewpoints and one thing or another; but I believe if I want to have a tepee or live in a lean-to or dress in buckskins, I shouldn't be frowned upon. There are a few people who don't think too highly of it, but I feel they're welcome to their viewpoint just like I'm welcome to mine.

In fact, I think the fastest growing part of muzzle loading is the primitive part of it, and if our National Association [NMLRA] decides not to go along with it, then they'll be making a big mistake. It'll break off as a splinter group and go its own way. The National Rifle Association many years ago pooh-poohed muzzle loading. Said, "If you want to go out and shoot stinky black powder and get your hands dirty, then it's your business, but we don't have to be interested in it." So it broke away, and now you have the NMLRA. The NRA could have had all of it, but they didn't want it.

But there are all different levels of interest. If you'll notice around here at Friendship, there's some people that wear a hat with a feather in it, and they could have on a blue serge suit, but they feel content. They say, "Well, boy, I'm game. I'm authentic." And then you meet another man and he's in full skins that he's tanned and sewed himself, and he says, "I'm portraying what I want to be." So it's just how far the individual wants to go. But

PLATE 379   Dale Black.

PLATE 380   Hawk Boughton.

you never seem to reach the end of the rainbow if you're really into it. It's like the process of learning in school. When you're at the end of the freshman year, you think you know everything there is to know in the world. And at the end of the sophomore year, you find out how dumb you were in the freshman year. That's the way life is.

HAWK: I think one thing we all have in common is that we enjoy reading the old books—the original manuscripts if possible—written by people who helped settle this country and went through the blood, sweat, and tears of the frontier period. I get a big kick out of finding something in one of those books that tells me how they did some small thing. To them it may have been a simple and everyday way of doing something, but it's often been lost and is unknown to the modern generation. To me and to many others like me, it becomes very important. One book I was reading, for example, was *Seed Time on the Cumberland* by Harriette Simpson Arnow. She tells about a frontiersman who was coming back from a deer hunt, and he had stopped to cook his supper. He wanted to make some bread, but because he traveled light, he didn't have any pots or pans. So he dug a hole in the ground, scooped it out bowl-shaped, took the fresh hide of the deer he had killed, laid that hide down in the hole flesh side up, and he had a perfect bowl in which to mix flour.

And in another book I saw the other day, a man said, "You know how the old-timers made a hat sometimes?"

This other man said, "No, I have no idea."

He said, "they took a piece of rawhide, wet it, made a bowl-shaped hole in the ground, cut the hide round like a brim, and pressed it down into the hole and put something flat on it and let it dry. When it dried, he took it out and he had a hat made out of rawhide. And then he smoked it over the fire to make it waterproof."

Another old book I have was written by a minister who lived as a boy on the frontier of what is now West Virginia, and he tells how most boys learned to throw the tomahawk. He said they'd be going out in the woods, maybe to get the cows, and as they were walking along, they'd throw at a limb or a dead tree. That way they'd learn that a 'hawk had to turn one turn for a certain distance, and a turn and a half for another distance, and two turns for a longer distance. They learned that way, and they kept that knowledge with them. The tomahawk, like the knife and longrifle, could be an instrument of entertainment because they didn't have TV. A tomahawk, knife, and gun were three items that they had with them at weddings, funerals, and cabin raisings. When they'd get together, since they had no other real way of entertainment, it was just natural for the men to shoot or throw knives and 'hawks; and it was also a useful skill for them, of course, for these were skills on which they relied in their scrapes with Indians.

PLATE 381 Jeff Reeves and Kirk Patterson tape recording Hawk and Dale. When asked about their buckskins, Hawk said, "The story is that it helped water drain off in a downpour instead of soaking into the cloth, but I don't go along with that. I think it's just style—it was the style in those days. You even see people with a little fringe over their pockets where it would do no earthly good in a downpour. But I believe that one thing that it *did* do, whether they realize it or not: It helped break up their silhouette when they were in the woods. I mean, if you were dripping with fringes and things, you would blend in with the woods easier than if you were just a hard silhouette.

PLATE 382 Hawk, due to his nickname, was given a hawk's claw which he wears around his neck. Beside it is a hinged cow horn he uses as a powder measure.

DALE: They've got bales of volumes on the mountain men and trappers in historical societies in St. Louis because St. Louis was a jumping-off place. They just haven't gotten around to publishing the manuscripts yet, but when the interest of the public is great enough, I guess they'll be bringing them up. Something like this is fabulous because so much of this has been lost and few people really care about it.

PLATE 383   Hawk's fire-starting kit, worn
on his belt.

And we have our get-togethers at historic sites lots of times. There's an
annual shoot at Fort Chartres, Illinois, for example. Only part of the walls
are left there, but in the eighteenth century it was the most impressive for-
tress in what is now the United States. It was the seat of the French empire
here—the hub. French officers from Detroit would come down for four or
five days and meet with the people down at Fort Chartres to decide how to
get rid of the English.

HAWK: And canoe brigades made regular trips from Montreal clear
down to New Orleans taking goods down and getting supplies to bring up
to the fort.

DALE: There have been at least three forts on that same ground. Part of
the walls of the powder magazine is all that's left now. The walls were six
foot thick in the main fort, and they were used to build a bridge across the
river at St. Louis because the rock was there available and already quarried.
They just hauled it on flat boats down to St. Louis and built their bridge out
of it. It's an impressive thing, but many people don't understand the
significance of it: that that fort was there before George Washington was
born, and that they brought in a thousand stoneworkers from France and
built it on the banks of the Mississippi as their capitol. Quarried the rock by
hand and hauled it down there in wagons and built it.

HAWK: That's the same kind of thing that got me interested in all this,
too. In 1968, I organized a group of buckskinners to duplicate the march
that George Rogers Clark made across the Illinois Territory to Fort
Kaskaskia. It was a hundred-and-twenty-five-mile walk. Clark and his men
did it in five days, and we had to do it on the same days he did it. And it
worked out fine.

PLATE 384 Dale with a white oak split basket and a meat-cooking fork he made.

We think that by learning to be self-reliant and passing skills on and reminding people of their tradition and heritage, we're doing some good in the world. It's not all for our own enjoyment. We do think that sometime it might help because you can't guarantee we're not going to have another war. Our country might even be invaded. And if this should happen, the people who know how to survive on the land as far as finding food and shelter, snaring animals, fish trapping, making fires without matches, cooking without utensils, and getting along without all the modern things—they may help save our civilization.

DALE: I don't think these things should be forgot. There should be as much as possible put down with the written word. 'Course, the written word leaves a lot to be desired.

HAWK: That's right. You can talk all day about wild foods you can find, but if you don't actually find some and go to the trouble of cooking it and trying it, chances are the knowledge won't stay with you. It's a college from which you never graduate.

DALE: It's the same with the muzzle loading. Once you get hung with the muzzle-loading bug, you never graduate from it. If a man says he knows everything there is to know, he's an idiot because you never get to know it all.

More and more people have gotten interested in it. It's really something to watch. When I first came to Friendship twelve years ago, there was just a small area being used, and there was plenty of space to spare for camp grounds. Nobody had any tepees or anything like that.

HAWK: I have friends who say they'll no longer come here to Friendship because they don't like so many people, but I still find that here's the place to come to see your friends from all over the country, to shoot and talk and have a good palaver, and that's the main reason I still like it here.

DALE: And also there's a lot of people that come down here and they're interested: "How do I get into this; how would I get a tepee; where would I get a lean-to; how do I get my buckskins together; where would I buy an authentic-looking rifle?" and all of this and that. And if some of us older people sit around and ignore them and don't pay any attention to them, we're defeating our own purpose. If a man's interested, I'll go the other halfway and tell him what I think he should know and what might be the pitfalls that I have fallen into over the years. Then if he ain't got sense enough to at least listen to what I've got to say, that's tough. That's all you can do for him.

HAWK: You might be able to keep him from blowing his head off with one of those cheap imported guns and get him started right so he doesn't get disgusted and drop the whole thing.

DALE: The biggest thing that's come up now is a lot of Japanese-made and foreign-made rifles. They may be safe with light loads, but whoever's getting into this should at least do enough research to find someone that's already preceeded him and learn what might be the best kind to have, rather than just going and buying something that's off the shelf where all the salesman is interested in is the 20 per cent commission he can make.

Also we come in here to Friendship to outfit ourselves for the following summer until we can get back again.

HAWK: It's a big rendezvous in one way of speaking.

And over the last eight years, the "primitives" have become more numerous. They like to practice as near as they can, in the spare time that they have, living the ways of their forefathers. Their number has grown tremendously, and they have a good primitive program here for those people who want to live in lean-to's and tepees, make their fire with flint and steel, and eat just the foods of the old days—not the canned stuff.

Now the American Mountain Men is a separate organization that has taken the cream of the crop of the primitives. It started about six years ago. It's formed along the lines of the old fur-trapping parties. Although we know that the common idea of the mountain man is the beaver trapper of the West, we had our own mountain men here too. In fact, many of the ones who went West came from here originally—all of them practically.

PLATE 385 The primitive camping area at the 1977 Friendship spring shoot.

PLATE 386 The primitive area features numerous areas where handmade goods can be purchased or traded for in the old tradition. The area also has booths like this blacksmith shop in full operation.

Jim Bridger, Kit Carson, Joe Meek, and Jedediah Smith are good examples. So we kind of lean toward our eastern forefathers.

The American Mountain Men is a national, non-profit association. We have about five hundred members now, and we're growing. The headquarters is in California, and Walt "Grizz" Hayward is the director, or *Capitaine*. When we have a rendezvous, nothing is allowed in the camp area that wouldn't have been found there from 1760 to 1845 or 1850. These are patterned after the original rendezvous on Henry's Fork of the Green River in Wyoming.

That original rendezvous began a system that the fur traders set up to outfit their trapping brigades—to make it possible for the trappers in the West to get all of the things that they needed to sustain themselves for the next year out there in Indian territory. These included powder and lead, cloth shirts, fish hooks, knives, beads, salt, pepper, right down the line. And they could trade their hides that they'd got for the year and get their necessities for the following year. That saved them from going clear to St. Louis or Independence, Missouri, to pack this stuff in.

So we've formed along those lines. Today, the men bring their handmade items—their skins, knives, horns, tomahawks, and things like this—and take them to rendezvous to swap and sell. It's a gathering where the accent is not on shooting. It's an affair—a frolic—where they can talk, swap, lie, exchange items, goods, and stuff for things they need; and if somebody bets another man that he can hit something at a distance, the two of them might get up and shoot. Or they might throw the tomahawk in a contest. But it's not a gathering for shooting *per se* like you have at the other shoots.

We've got men from all occupations in the group. In fact, last night I met Leighton Baker, a former state senator from Florida, and he's the "booshway" of our Florida brigade. "Booshway" is from a French word, *bourgeois,* meaning "middle class," and in the fur trade, he was the leader of a fur party. Leighton is a descendent of Jim Baker, one of the old trappers.

I'm what they call a "Segundo" in the organization. It's Spanish for "Second." I'm over the Eastern Territory. We have a Western Segundo also. But we don't have membership drives. Men have to ask to get in. I have to sign every application from the East, and if I sign it, he's in under certain provisions. There are a number of requirements he has to fulfill before he can become a member, and they're the kinds of requirements that the average man who puts on a pair of blue jeans and carries a Spanish-made rifle wouldn't care anything about fulfilling. It's just not his sort of thing. He doesn't want us, and we don't want him.

A new man is called a "Pilgrim" and he has that first year to get all his gear together. We prefer that he handmakes it, all except his rifle. We don't require that. But he should try to make as many of the other things as he can. He can get his clothing and everything together, and then he should take time to attend a couple of shoots or rendezvous and see how he likes us —and give us a chance to see how we like him. And if either side is not satisfied, he can join another club that's more suited to what he wants.

So he has a grace period of a year. And if he's still acceptable after a year, he is promoted to what they call a "Bossloper," and after one more year, he may qualify for the third and highest degree of "Hiverano"— which means, roughly, "a person who lives or has lived in the area." A Hiverano to the mountain man was someone who had been in the mountains at least a year and wintered in the wilds either with the Indians, or at least at one of the fur posts. That man was experienced; he could take care of himself in a hostile land. He could survive. Any of our members who holds the Hiverano degree can do the same.

DALE: The average life was only two years in the mountains. Often less than two years. Something would usually happen to them. They'd be killed, or die of natural causes, or—

HAWK: Give it up and get out.

DALE: A broken leg or anything could just put you away. So the average life span was about two years.

HAWK: The primitive life, even for a few days at a time, is definitely not for everyone. But lots of people, once they try it, find it answers a deeply felt need. I don't know. I may be all wet. But we're all descended from primitive people. The campfire and the lure of the wilderness is in us all. Now I feel some of us have these feelings stronger than others. They may be handed down in the genes of people, I don't know.

DALE: Some of the things you do it seems like you've done before in another life or something. I want to tell you, I don't believe particularly in reincarnation and stuff like that, but you'll find a man that's never seen a flintlock before, and in five minutes he'll be shooting like a pro. Then another man, poor devil, he can work at it for years and never shoot one right. The same with a boy. I've seen boys in high school that never had a saw in their hand, and they'll be doing great carpenter work quickly because they seem to know naturally how to do it. I've seen it happen too many times— there's just something there. It's just one of those things.

But the thing that bothers me, like I said before, is how much of this old information is getting lost. I was at a sale one day where they sold out a blacksmith shop that had been in business since 1855, and I bought a box of junk because I wanted some buckles in there, and there was a little notebook in there written in old ink that gives all the measurements for making a single buggy harness, double buggy harness, work horse harness, and a soda harness. I never heard of that—he could have meant something else—but he had it s-o-d-a. I'd like to know what that was. But I was fortunate to get that book, and I'll save it as long as I'm around and pass it on to somebody. But a lot of people are just throwing information like that in the trash can. They'll carry it home, and they won't give it to nobody—it'll just go "whop" in the can, and it's gone forever.

You all at *Foxfire* are doing a lot of people a lot of favors by saving some of that, because it's preserving a part of history that should be preserved. The younger generation like these boys here [Jeff and Kirk], I'm so glad they could be here and soak up any information they can get because these people want to put it out; and when you put an old person away in the ground, just think, all that information went to thunder right then. And so many of them will just do their darndest to help you if you ask. When I was about nine years old, my old uncle who had been a railroad blacksmith in the yards, had a bad stroke. But if I was interested, he'd totter out there, and as I remember it now, it probably was a supreme effort for him to get out to the shop 'cause he'd sit on a chair for a half an hour after he got there. But he tried his best to show me how to blacksmith, weld, and stuff with his cane, "You do this," and I was small, but boy, I tell you, when I started really getting into it a few years ago, it all came back to me just like he was there. At the time, I didn't comprehend everything he said, but somewhere back in there it was stored. When it's in your head, it comes out, if you give it time, when you need it.

Those old people really want to teach you, but the school system is so messed up nowadays that they won't let them do it unless they've got ten years of college, and that to me is nothing. If somebody has made shingles for fifty years, he probably knows more about certain skills than a college professor ever got by reading books.

We talked to both Earl Lanning and Garnett Powell about the Friendship shoot and its evolution. Earl Lanning said:

I went to Friendship in 1955 the first time, and the whole shoot was contained in just a little compound. Then they bought the area across the river. I can remember when there wasn't but one tepee, and it belonged to John Barsotti, the famous artist, who's one heck of a nice guy. He had this tremendous big tepee, and any time of the night you pulled in, nobody worried about a place to sleep. You just went and crawled in John's tepee. Of course, you might be sleeping with eighteen or twenty people. You'd have to move the paintings and guns and all that stuff out of your way and make a bed and go to sleep. But it was a great period right in there. I'd just as soon not go back, now. I remember the way it used to be [before it got so popular and so large], and I'd rather keep it that way. Everybody knew me back in those days, you know. I guess they've all forgotten by now. Back then, they'd find out where I was camping and shoot a cannon over my tent wherever I was at—three or four o'clock in the morning they'd drive a cannon up and shoot it over the top of you—blow you out of bed. There wasn't anybody supposed to rest up there. You didn't go there to rest. You stayed up for days at a time. It was a crazy place. Used to be a guy up there who would haul all the gunpowder in an old Chevrolet van, and he smoked a big black cigar. He had the gunpowder in big twenty-five-pound kegs, and it was plumb to the ceiling in that van. And he'd come in there smoking that cigar, and we'd buy those kegs of powder for fifteen dollars.

And back in those days, there weren't any sale sheds. It was a bunch of cars, like a flea market. I remember when Dixie Gun Works was in the back of a station wagon. They'd build up these little old tents and lean-tos, and they'd have their whole deal in those. Now they've got the commercial row and the sheep shed and all those booths.

Back then there wasn't hardly any water, and there weren't many bathroom facilities. Pretty primitive, but everybody just went along with it. We didn't care. Everybody just had a good time.

Garnett Powell, who is active in a number of gun-related organizations and is highly respected in the field, talked to us for several hours about Friendship—its roots and its evolution:

I started going in 1950. They had around 470 registered shooters that year and several hundred spectators, who were mostly area people. The shooters, of course, would come from all over the country since these were national matches. And for muzzle loading, at that time, these were the *only* national matches. There were muzzle-loading clubs still holding regional and local shoots all over the country, but the National Championship was always at Friendship, Indiana. In those days, the big one was the fall shoot, five days through Labor Day. Over the years they kept extending it until now it's nine days. Then in addition there was the spring shoot and a turkey shoot, which was in November, a beef shoot, which was held between Christmas and New Year's. The first beef shoot I ever attended was held at WLW "Everybody's Farm"—then the world's most powerful radio station —in Mason, Ohio. This was a farm owned by the Crosley family, and we shot there. I went in December between Christmas and the first of January, and there was snow on the ground about a foot deep. They had several big oil drum barrels all fired up for heat. The temperature was probably fifteen or twenty degrees, and there was a group of fifty or sixty people out there with their rifles. I remember "Bull" Ramsey let me shoot his famous big rifle "Ole Seiberts." It was so typical of early day matches held two hundred years ago.

PLATE 387 Walter Cline during the 1930s when he was an early president of the NMLRA. (Photo courtesy of C. Frederick Beck and Garnett Powell.)

The most heavily attended shoot, of course, was the National Shoot over Labor Day. In the early days, Bill Large and John Barsotti would have been there, along with Merril Deer, Carl Fuller, "Boss" Johnson, John Amber, Charlie Ruark, Neil Wesley, Walt Muething, Bull Ramsey, Judge Resley, and Dr. Duncan from Texas. I remember also a Mr. Cline; he was a jeweler who made some gorgeous silver mounted and engraved rifles. And A. O. Neidner, the great gunsmith from Michigan, who was in his eighties; and, oh, numerous other gunsmiths from all over the country. Walter Grote from Canton, Ohio, was a famous slug-gun man who was still shooting records in 1976. He was always there for the matches. In other words, if you go back through *Muzzle Blasts*, the who's who of muzzle-loading rifles, at one time or another most of these people were in attendance at the early shoots. Every night there was a campfire and everybody gathered around in a huge circle, and the talk would range all the way from the battles of the Civil War to the Western Wars and Custer's defeat. In fact, I probably learned more about history around those campfires than I could ever learn out of a library of books.

PLATE 388 Walter Grote (left) and Pete Menefee (right), both ˎearly NMLRA members. (Photo courtesy of C. Frederick Beck and Garnett Powell.)

Many of those people had lived great personal experiences, and tales of fighting Apaches and Little Annie Oakley's shooting feats, great forest fires in Idaho, logging days and buffalo hunting on the Great Plains would be related in much detail. We had a gentleman named Hampton Swain from Canada who was in the employ of the Hudson's Bay Company and worked with many of the trading posts up there. I talked with him one day because I had always been interested in fire steels. He told me there were Indians up in Canada who were still using flint and steel for making fires, and he drew some sketches which I still have in my files of some of the fire steels that were traded to the Indians by the Hudson's Bay Company. And then, of course, we talked about the trade guns, the Fusil Indian muskets, they traded to the Indians. A very rare and colorful person. He knew all about tomahawks and axes and sleds and ivory of the Eskimos—just a tremendous knowledge of the Great Northland.

The NMLRA started in Portsmouth, Ohio, February 22, 1931. Many of those people who started the whole thing are gone now. Red Farris was one of the founders—first secretary—and, I think Oscar Seth was the first president. Red Farris and Bill Large are the two remaining people that signed up and paid their fifty cents at the first shoot that was held by the railroad YMCA in 1931. There was another group near the same time that

PLATE 389 Oscar Seth, one of the founders of the NMLRA. (Photo courtesy of C. Frederick Beck and Garnett Powell.)

PLATE 390 Boss Johnson, without whom no shoot was complete. (Photo courtesy of C. Frederick Beck and Garnett Powell.)

had been doing some shooting out near Rising Sun, Indiana. This was the WLW muzzle club under the direction of Boss Johnson who worked for the Cincinatti radio station. And Bull Ramsey went out to one of the shoots they were holding out near Rising Sun, Indiana in 1934. Bull visited with Boss Johnson and they talked and they merged the two groups into a single group that met in Rising Sun, Indiana, which is not too far from Friendship, and held probably the first combined national NMLRA shoot in 1935. That was the beginning of it. How different it is now. Elizabeth and I, right after we married, went to the spring shoot in 1956. We got in on a Friday night. Turner Kirkland was there camping in a tent, and we didn't even pitch one. We slept in the club house. And the two of us and Turner were the only three people on that entire range the night before the shoot. That's just how different it was. Today you can't even get a spot to camp there. We used to go in there and pitch our tent just about anywhere we wanted to. We all had regular places to camp and we kind of staked them out, but nothing permanent. Today you have to reserve camping a year ahead to get within miles of the range, I understand. But in the early 1950s it was just like a big family reunion.

I have a letter in my files from Merril Deer who has been president two or three times. He's still on the board of directors. And [what he said] is a

PLATE 391 An NMLRA award ceremony in Dillsboro in 1938. Here, Boss Johnson in ceremonial Indian costume presents the Crosley Trophy to Andy Whitehurst (who had scored 48 out of a possible 50 at sixty yards with a hundred-year-old muzzle loader) as Walter Cline looks on. (Photo courtesy of C. Frederick Beck and Garnett Powell.)

PLATE 392 Gilbert Angel, the champion of Tennessee, at an early shoot. (Photo courtesy of C. Frederick Beck and Garnett Powell.)

PLATE 393 Henry Pancake, a regular at the early shoots. (Photo courtesy of C. Frederick Beck and Garnett Powell.)

good illustration of the closeness of the thing. He wrote me after one of the shoots and said that he suddenly looked around and I was gone and two or three other people were gone, and the thought hit him, "It's all over for another year and I didn't even get to say good-bye. I just felt like sitting down and crying." It was an emotional thing. We were all so close and all so keyed up for four or five days, and this went on day and night: gun talk, history talk, shooting, visiting, and taking notes and photographs of rare guns and people, and it was an incredible environment to be a part of. Then, suddenly, in a matter of minutes to an hour—zam—everybody was gone in every conceivable direction to California, Texas, Virginia, West Virginia, Canada, New York, Ohio—all these places. And you look around the range and here, suddenly, all this came to an end and everybody's gone home. And I don't think the old days could ever be recaptured. I talk with [John] Barsotti occasionally about it, and he doesn't enjoy it like he used to. I think he went last year, and he said it was just too big. The old spirit is gone and it's just not the same. We talk about the old times and the old acquaintances—like Bull, whom both of us knew—and find that most of the old-timers we knew have passed on. John was fortunate in getting there in the early 1940s. He was on the board of directors in the early days and was technical advisor of pistols and revolvers in 1941.

It has just grown too big—crowds in the thousands—too many people. But even if the present directors wanted to scale it down, I don't think they could now. I'm watching the same thing happen to the Ohio Gun Collec-

PLATE 394 Bill Large in buckskins at an NMLRA shoot. (Photo courtesy of C. Frederick Beck and Garnett Powell.)

tors. Here's an organization that every time we have a meeting—which is about six times a year—there's probably a couple hundred new applicants joining. It's outgrown every facility around the state to where they have to have it in Columbus almost totally now because of the size of it. The first time I went, there were probably a hundred tables in a hotel in Cincinatti; and now you have over a thousand tables full of guns at one of these meetings, and probably five to ten thousand people converging in the basement of the exhibition center. It's a mad scramble to where you have to fight your way through crowds to even get to a table to look at something. It's almost getting to a point where I hate going—as much as I love going. And each year they're adding, probably, another five hundred or a thousand people to the membership. And where is it all going to end?

I know Bill Large is concerned about what's happening to Friendship because I noticed in a recent ad of his, he pointed out that he had a range up there on his farm where he makes his barrels, and he said something to the effect of, "We need another place since Friendship is such a mess that it can no longer serve our needs." Now he's one of the founders, and I am sure he never thought that it would someday come to this. It's bad, you know—one of our two remaining founders to have taken this attitude.

But I believe the success of the whole muzzle-loading thing is beyond the wildest dreams that Farris could ever have. I was quite close friends with Red. We corresponded for years and watched the NMLRA grow. I was at the twenty-fifth anniversary shoot, for example, in August 1957. And even then, he was still forecasting for the future. He had no idea where this was all going to lead, but he was always the optimist. Always forecasting a bigger, better range, more members, and better things. Suddenly in a period of about fifteen years, all of this really happened. It just suddenly burst upon the scene, and I don't think anyone, even including the people who administer it, know what to do about it. They must have problems galore. I remember when we were going back in the '50s, we had one john there and we had sewer and water problems then. How in the world do you cope with ten thousand people? You know, this is like another Woodstock. Serving food to this many people, keeping law and order, the traffic problems. How many automobiles can you crowd into that little narrow valley there? I can't imagine ten thousand people. I remember when our little hoard of a few hundred went into the village of Friendship, it was like State Fair day. I just can't imagine it all now.

My start in the muzzle-gun shooting is an interesting little story. I was teaching school at the time at a vocational high school in West Virginia, and I had gotten acquainted with a teacher on our faculty from Charleston who was a good friend of G. R. Douglas, the barrelmaker. Douglas had bought a barrel machine out of the old ordnance works in Charleston, and he was rifling barrels. The teacher friend had some of Doug's barrels made up in custom calibers and he was the machine shop teacher. So we had a sort of common interest in guns as I had taken over the Junior Rifle Club. I was the faculty instructor for our NRA club. This teacher got me interested in bench-rest shooting, and I acquired one of the Douglas barrels. I had a gunsmith in Charleston make me up a fine .22–.250 varmiter-bench gun. I was hand-loading my ammunition, and I was learning all the technical side of bench-rest shooting. So I decided at this point that since I was also doing small-bore target shooting, I would go to the NRA matches at Camp Perry, Ohio, and shoot in the .22-caliber championship matches. I made a trip up there, and I ran into the most snobbish bunch of shooters I have ever met. A rather distant, inhospitable group of people. You'd go up and try to talk or make friends, and nobody would talk to you. It was void of everything. So you sat around by yourself on the line and waited for your target to be scored; you shot and you went your own way. It was a terribly impersonal thing.

Well, my grandparents were living in Ohio at the time, and as I traveled by to visit them I was looking for primers and powder for my varmit rifle. On my way home, going through Portsmouth, Ohio, I saw this little store on the street called "Farris Muzzle Guns." I stopped the car and went in to see if I could find some powder and primers, and as I walked in this store building I noticed glass show cases along the side. And down the middle of the store was a rack, and there must have been fifty to seventy-five long mountain rifles stacked in the rack. I went over and looked in the glass show case, and here were all these Colt 1860s Army revolvers and Navy revolvers and cap-and-ball pistols on display. I engaged the little proprietor—who was almost bald except for a fringe of red hair, and had a big nose and glasses—in conversation. And I said, "Do you sell this stuff? Who would buy this old junk?" Here I was going after these beautiful custom rifles with the fancy checkering and polished blued barrels. His guns were like something he would have to pay me to haul off.

And he said, "Oh, yes. We've got quite an enthusiastic group who collect. In fact," he said, "we have a shoot where we shoot these."

I said, "You *shoot* guns like these?"

"Oh, yes. We've got national matches, and," he said, "we've got just a ball of enthusiasm." He seemed to jump up and down as he was so enthused. You couldn't believe Red's great drive unless you knew him. He was really something. And I related my experiences at Camp Perry and I kind of started out shaking my head. So he gave me a couple of copies of *Muzzle Blasts* that he had on the counter. "Now, I'll tell you what," he said. "Where are you going to be during the last week of August?"

I said, "Well, I finish up summer school in August and I'm going down to Virginia to my home."

He said, "Well, you're not going to be back in school." He said, "Why don't you take a day or two and come out to Friendship, Indiana? I promise you an unforgettable time."

I'd never heard of the place. I said, "Well, I'll think about it, and if it's convenient, I might do that."

He said, "I'll guarantee you that if you do, you won't believe what you see. It's the greatest bunch of people that you've ever met."

Well, I came home and sat around three or four days and got bored with everything and I decided, "Well, I'd like to go somewhere before school starts." So I got the car and I went back to West Virginia, and I ran into one of the students from the school rifle club and we got to talking and I said, "Why don't we go somewhere before school starts?" So, to make a long story short, we loaded up the car and took off to Friendship, Indiana. Had no idea, in fact, exactly where it was located. We slept in the car. We hadn't taken anything to camp with or cook out. I didn't know what to expect. So, anyway, we got there and here was this atmosphere that was just amazing. The evening we arrived some guy under a great big umbrella he put on a tractor had a shooting bench set up on the range. It was almost dusk and he had this big monstrous bench gun he had built with a barrel he had won the year before. His name was Ralph Dunn. He was a farmer from Indiana. I had never seen a gun like that before. This gun must have weighed fifty pounds. He had been sighting it in, so we were watching him shoot and he began to talk to us and we began to ask questions. And he said, "Sit down and shoot her."

"Oh, no," I said, "I wouldn't dare touch your gun."

"Oh," he said, "you can't hurt the damn thing. Sit down and shoot it." That's just the way the people were, you know. At Camp Perry you couldn't get within six feet of some of these guys and their guns. He said, "Here, let me show you how to load it." So we put a target up and that was the first bench gun I ever shot. He said, "Keep shooting it."

Well, I got so excited and so involved in asking questions and talking and trying to load and shoot that I rammed a bullet down without the powder. So we had to tear the whole blessed thing down, unscrew the breech plug and run that ball out. Embarrassed the life out of me. Well, it was a big joke to him. "Now," he laughed, "you've graduated. You're one of us." I was fond of Ralph because he was such a genuine person. He passed away five or six years ago, I guess. I read of his death in *Muzzle Blasts*.

PLATE 395   One of the booths in commercial row at the Friendship shoot.

Then the next day they had what they called "commercial row" which was then just a bunch of cars backed up with the trunks opened. And here was all sorts of gun parts, guns, and scopes; there was bullets, there was lead, there was antiques, pictures, cow horns—a gunbugs' fleamarket. I looked around, and we began to examine old and new guns and went up and down the firing line. Spent the day. There was a little restaurant built onto the range house and the ladies from the Lutheran Church were doing the cooking. The food was superb—great home-cooked country food. Everyone ate there. And everybody was friendly. Just the nicest kind of people. They'd come up and introduce themselves: "Where are you from? I'm so-and-so."

Well, a fellow came up the second day I was there in a A-Model car. Real old fellow with two or three boys. Looked like a farmer. And he had this real nice half-stock rifle that had a .59-caliber bore that he had made. He had put it all together from old parts. His name was Schoonover. I'll never forget it, because he was carrying this rifle around trying to sell it. It was kind of a heavy stock. So finally he came up to me and showed me. I said, "How much do you want for it?"

He said, "I want twenty-five dollars for it." Had a maple stock on it, buttplate, set trigger—not the finest workmanship, but a pretty good shooter. Such a big bore, though. Well, to make a long story short, I bought it. It was my first muzzle loader.

I took it back down to the school and we took it to our club range, and I had written to Farris and he had sent me a mold for this big .59-caliber ball and we had molded some bullets in the plumbing shop. Farris had sent me a pound of black powder. Anyway, we got to shooting it, and the rifle club had more fun than you could shake a stick at. Found out it didn't explode, it didn't tear my shoulder off. In fact, it was called a "stinking" time by one of the kids as he smelled the aroma of black powder for the first time.

PLATE 396 A small portion of the firing line at the 1977 Spring Friendship shoot.

PLATE 397 Shooters at Friendship retrieving their targets . . .

PLATE 398 . . . and stapling up new ones for the next round.

Well, the next spring I took a couple more of the kids and we went back up to the Friendship range to the spring shoot, and I met a few more people that shoot. By that time a couple or three of the kids had gotten real enthused about the muzzle shooting and were trying to buy a rifle. Then, that fall, I went to the fall shoot again. And I registered for the shoot that time, and I took my rifle to shoot. Of course, I didn't do any good. I never was a good shot. But I had a lot of fun. A friend, Jack Kalasky, and I got in there for that shoot about two days before it started. Took the tent and everything to camp. So Jack and I pitched our tent, and right over from us was this great big old canvas fly and tent, and here was this great big old fellow over there. We were the only people on the range, and he was really surprised to know that somebody else had seen fit to come that early. So we were pegging down the tent and he came wallering across there and said, "I'm Bull Ramsey. Who the hell are you?" I introduced myself and Jack and he said, "Come on over." He said, "Have you all had anything to eat?" And we said no. And he said, "Well, we got an iron pot of beans over here, cooking out over a fire." His wife, Pearl, had cooked up a big pot of beans, fat back, and corn bread, so we spent the evening with Bull. And that was the beginning of a friendship that lasted until he died. Well, from that moment on, as everybody arrived, Bull was there to greet them, and I got to meet everybody. I think Bull knew everybody in the shooting fraternity. The second day, John Barsotti came. Well, I had heard of Barsotti. I had been reading some of his things in *American Rifleman* magazine. He was quite a celebrity himself. This past year we celebrated twenty-five years of friendship. I didn't realize we had been friends that long. But that was also the beginning of my friendship with John.

After that shoot, I went back and traded off all the modern stuff I had and began to get totally into the old guns, and I cared nothing about modern guns from then on.

At that very first shoot I went to, Red Farris had a little gun supply stand set up and I went over to see him. He was quite pleased, you know, that I had showed up. In the past twenty-seven years I've often thought about what I could have missed if I had decided not to stop in the little shop in Portsmouth, Ohio, that day. I still might be a frustrated small-bore rifle shooter. Perish the thought.

I think it's an interesting time in the muzzle-loading game because each succeeding generation that comes up seems to come up with a little bit more of a degree of enthusiasm toward these old guns. It's a growing thing. This has been helped along, again, by the Civil War Centennial and the Bicentennial. These two things, I think, have spurred the growth of this more than any other factor.

PLATE 399   Overlooking part of the Friendship scene today, including the primitive camping area.

[When we expressed some doubt that even those two events could be solely responsible for the tremendous surge of interest, he elaborated]: I've got [another] theory on it for what it's worth. Most of the Americans, I think, have a void in their lives [caused by the fact that] they can't attach themselves directly to the long lines of family that Europeans, for example, can. I think that they want to identify themselves in some way with yesterday—with their past. The movies, and I guess history in general, has dealt with the romantic side of America's past. But there's a violent sort of spirit that makes up the American culture. Firearms were an important part of the founding of the nation. Had it not been for the ability of the Colonies to arm themselves, we'd still be under the English crown. This sort of identification with our freedom—if you go the roots of the thing—is part of it. I think every American, by in large, is looking for a certain identification with the past. And I think within the last twenty years that the social conditions in America have wrought upon this nation an evil situation to where, with the politics and the other things that have gone on, people have just sort of been disillusioned with the present, and a little bit disillusioned with the future. There's uncertainty. So people are beginning to go back. And this is not only true with guns. It's true in everything old. It's true in primitive furniture. It's true in antiques. It's true in literature. There's a tremendous revival in classical music. And I think it's the fact that people are turning away from the future and today to try to identify and grab something which they feel is secure and something they can hold onto.

Well, the firearm is a part of this past. There's the romantic side of the firearm, plus the fact that with a firearm in your possession, you have a feeling of security. As the psychologists say, it's the womb concept. You want to crawl back in and wrap it around you in order to protect you. So the firearm is part of the psychological hangup that Americans have. The younger generation—I see more and more young people today that are gun crazy. The first possession they want, outside of a car, is a gun. And not really because they *need* it for protection, but for the assurance. "If I need it, I've got it." I think we're all a little paranoid that way.

And then, again, you know, we go back to that Second Amendment. You really can't forget that, because if they ever abolish this, God help us. Because it's not the principal that we could take up arms and go overthrow the Government. This isn't possible. But it's the simple fact that we have the right to defend ourselves and our property. It goes back to this spirit we were talking about that's in the mountains—this independent thing that makes up America. It's the one ingredient that makes us different from the rest of the world. And it's associated so closely to our freedom that whenever these anti-gun people begin to try to nibble away at the Second Amendment, they just stir up this group of gun collectors and Second Amendment believers, and so far they have successfully fought the worst of it down.

I abhor violence, and I try to look at both sides. And I'm frightened with these "Saturday night specials" and the fact that every would-be assassin has got an arsenal that he could fight a good army with. This scares me because I know that sometimes these things can be turned against our civilization. And yet, you can't really cut it off. You can't say, "You can have muzzle loaders but you can't have the other guns." If they are going to confiscate guns, they're going to have to take them all. I mean, where are you going to draw the line? You can't discriminate against one group. There are people, for example, who collect pistols and love them and cherish them as much as people like ourselves who collect and shoot the old longrifles. And their rights are just as important, and I can't say you should confiscate hand guns and leave the rifles alone because that isn't right. It's a paradox. And I don't really think we'll ever see the solution to it. Even if they pass legislation in this country that would confiscate guns, they would never get them all. First of all, the criminal element is not going to come in and turn his guns in. So confiscation, to my way of thinking, is a fallacy because it won't work. All you'd do is disarm the honest citizen and leave the criminal element with his gun because there's no way you can get those guns away. They'll manufacture them if they can't get anything else. You can make a gun out of a piece of pipe, and you can shoot nails, and you can make explosives out of fertilizer, so where are you going to draw the line?

But it's something America has to deal with. Somewhere along the line, this thing will come to a vicious solution thrust on the people. When that happens, for whatever it's worth, at that point, I feel America will die. I don't think it can survive because that freedom is so much a part of us that in that spirit of it, I think you would destroy what little bit of human rights a person has left.

PLATE 400

BIBLIOGRAPHY

Selected books available in reprint editions from
George Shumway,
RD 7, York, Pennsylvania 17402:

THE KENTUCKY RIFLE. John Dillin. National Rifle Association, 1924. ($20)

LONG RIFLES OF NORTH CAROLINA. John Bivins. (Will be back in print from Shumway in 1980).

MUZZLE BLASTS: EARLIEST YEARS PLUS VOLUMES 1 AND 2 1939–41. Shumway, 1974 ($15).

THE MUZZLE LOADING CAP LOCK RIFLE. Ned Roberts. The Stackpole Company, 1940 (no price listed).

RECREATING THE AMERICAN LONGRIFLE. William Bruchele and George Shumway ($7.50).

THOUGHTS ON THE KENTUCKY RIFLE IN ITS GOLDEN AGE. *Joe Kindig, Jr.* George Hyatt Publishers ($35).

Other Books

THE AGE OF FIREARMS, A PICTORIAL HISTORY. New York: Harper, 1957.

ARMS AND ARMOR IN COLONIAL AMERICA, 1526–1783. Harrisburg, Pennsylvania: Stackpole Press, 1956.

DECORATED FIREARMS 1540–1870. Wallace B. Gusler and James D. Lavin. Williamsburg, Virginia: Colonial Williamsburg Foundation, 1977.

EUROPEAN AND AMERICAN ARMS, C. 1100–1850. New York: Crown, 1962.

THE LURE OF THE GREAT SMOKIES. Robert Lindsay Mason. New York: Houghton Mifflin, 1927.

THE MUZZLE LOADING RIFLE THEN AND NOW. Walter M. Cline. Huntington, West Virginia: Standard Printing and Publishing, 1942.

MUZZLE LOADING SHOOTING AND WINNING WITH THE CHAMPIONS. Max
Vickery, Webb Terry, Bob Butcher, Don Davis, Walter Grote, Bill Car-
michael, Peter Allan, Warren L. Boughton. Friendship, Indiana:
Powder, Patch and Ball Publications, 1973.

THE PENNSYLVANIA KENTUCKY RIFLE. Harrisburg, Pennsylvania: Stackpole
Press, 1960.

Film and Film Strip

"Gunsmith of Williamsburg." Film Distribution Section, Colonial Williamsburg, Box C, Williamsburg, Virginia 23185. (This fine film and
film strip shows Wallace Gusler making a rifle from beginning to end.)

Trade Publications Mentioned

BLACK POWDER TIMES $6.00/year
P.O. Box 842
Mount Vernon, Washington, 98273
THE BUCKSKIN REPORT $12.00/year
220 McLeod Street
Big Timber, Montana 59011
MUZZLE BLASTS $8.00/year
P.O. Box 67
Friendship, Indiana 47021 (The publication of the NMLRA.)

Organizations Mentioned

American Mountain Men
P.O. Box 259
Lakeside, California 92040
National Muzzle Loading Rifle Association
P.O. Box 67
Friendship, Indiana 47021

BEAR HUNTING

THE HUNTERS

When Mike Clark, the director of the Highlander Center in New Market, Tennessee, and one of the members of the *Foxfire* Advisory Board, found out that some of us were interested in meeting some bear hunters, he offered to meet me, Danny Brown, and Eddie Brown at his home in the Cruso Valley outside Waynesville, North Carolina, and introduce us to some. His ancestors had been bear hunters [see photo], and so he had met many men in the area who hunted for sport and for the meat.

We contacted Mike and decided on a convenient weekend for all of us to visit the hunters he was going to line up for us. When we arrived at Mike's place one morning, he took us to meet Bob Burress, Glenn Griffin, and Lenoir [Bear Hunter] Pless, three men who turned out to be our best contacts.

After Mike's mother had served us coffee, we jumped in the Blazer and headed down the valley. The first thing I saw when we pulled in Bob Burress' rocky driveway was a big red barn with a white star on it, and a white, suburban-looking house. Mike led us to the front door and introduced us.

As we walked into the house out of the cold, windy mountain air, the warmth of a blazing fire hit us. We sat down on the large sofa and began to talk. Bob told us that he was born near Cruso, and that he has always lived here. He said that his father hunted: "He was about as big a hunter as Rex Pless, Mike's great-uncle. In fact, back then I don't know if people hunted for sport or not. They hunted for meat. But he got me started. He learned me all he knows. And that's the way I did that boy of mine." Bob worked for a while at the Dayco Rubber plant in Waynesville. After that he was in the Army for three years. He works at the Champion Paper Company in Waynesville now on the night shift, and he has worked there for thirty years.

Next we went back to Mike's mother's house where she had cooked us a big country dinner with chicken, vegetables, salad, and corn bread, and then we headed down the curvy mountain road toward the other end of the

PLATE 401 Mrs. Clyde Clark, Mike Clark's grandmother, supplied us with this photograph of her father, T. R. Pless, Mike's great-grandfather. T. R. Pless came from Germany, settled near Canton, North Carolina, and became the local sheriff. He raised his family largely on wild meat and garden produce. A legendary hunter and fisherman, he would often hunt on Cold Mountain until late at night long after his children had gone to bed. When he came in, he'd place whatever he had killed on the fireplace hearth. Mrs. Clark remembers that in the mornings, she'd come down out of the loft of their log house and look at the hearth to see what her father had brought in the night before—and he nearly always brought in something.

Sometimes, during the day, he would send her downstream, and she'd wade out in the stream and pull out wild ducks that her father had shot upstream as they came floating by.

When the photo was taken, Mrs. Clark was a girl of about twenty. Mr. Pless was coming from Crawford's Creek with his dog, Ring, his gun, and the bear and coon he had just killed. He was stopped at Laurel Creek by a traveling photographer who took this picture. It is one of Mrs. Clark's most prized possessions.

valley. Mike said we were going to see Glenn Griffin. We turned off the main road and headed up a steep, gravel road and drove all the way to the end to a small, worn-looking house where we met Glenn, who was very friendly and showed us the way to his living room. The room was large and warm. The walls were filled with pictures of the family and hunts. The tables had plants sitting on them. Glenn obviously came from a hunting family: "My daddy's killed a hundred and three bears by himself. Got an old shotgun down there that's flat laid the bear out. Old Wirebarrel River-

PLATE 402 Jeff Fears, Bob Burress, and Eddie Brown in the midst of an interview in Bob's living room.

PLATE 403 Coon hides stretched on boards in Bob Burress' barn.

side—single-shot 12 gauge. At a hundred yards, you can put all nine double-ought bucks through one with that thing. I mean it'll flat work on one. He'll be eighty the eighth of next month. Momma died about two months ago. Well, the twentieth of January. Daddy can't even remember now half the time where he's at. [Elbert Glenn, his father, died on November 11, 1976.]

"Me and Lenoir Pless started hunting with them [Daddy and Rex and Wes] when I was just twelve or thirteen. First time I ever went, I went with Guy and Rex and Wes and Daddy. Me and Lenoir did. We killed one of them just below where me and Tommy killed that one. He weighed 500 pounds. Daddy told me, said, 'Don't you run in there.' Said, 'Them there boys'll shoot you.' Said, 'They're a flat a'workin' on that bear.' They shot him all to pieces. He looked like a sifter bottom. Wes had that .35-Remington automatic. He's had it as long as I can remember. It's an old one. I'd a'loved to get ahold of that gun. I don't know who got it.

PLATE 404 Glenn Griffin and part of his family with Mike Clark (the tallest one) outside his mountain-side home.

PLATE 405 Glenn Griffin and Jeff Fears.

"When we were boys, instead of running down the road or anything, we had work to do when we came in from school. We were glad to get to go hunting to get away from the house. We used to skin possums and sell them hides. And we used to walk miles to get to go fish or go in swimming. That's how come one of my hand's off. I fell down on my shotgun, and it went off and blew off my hand. That was back when I was fourteen going to school. Someone tore a rail fence down and I was climbing over them rails and had the gun with the stock behind me. The rails flew out from under me and I threw up the gun and it shot through my hand.

"Later, after I was finished with school and started working, I kept on hunting. I'd walk about two and a half miles to catch a bus to go work at Enca [a nearby manufacturing plant]. That winter I trapped muskrats up Coffee Branch and made more catching muskrats than working that winter. I'd get $3.50 to $4.00 for a good hide.

"And I've killed about nineteen bears myself. I killed one old she bear with my pistol. They treed her three times. I'd get nearly to her and she'd jump out."

When Mike Clark remembered a story about his Uncle Guy chasing a bear that passed over into the refuge, Glenn picked up the story right away: "Yeah. He went after it with his pistol and got so excited that he shot all his bullets before he got to the tree. He beat that'uns brains out with a pine knot. Little old .22 pistol was all he had. That was on the head of Sorrel's Creek. Guy wasn't too old then. He wasn't no more than about fourteen or fifteen then. Me and him was close to the same age. He was a little older than I was.

"There's a lot of fun in it. I don't care nothing about shooting a bear. If I can get where I can hear that fight I'll let somebody *else* shoot him without [unless] it just runs over the top of me or goes to hurting the dogs. If I can beat the rest of them there to hear that fight, I'll be there."

Slowly the discussion with Glenn ceased after he had talked to us for several hours. It was hard to get away, but we were soon on our way again. We stopped by Mike's house again briefly, and then we headed out a third time that day only to go about a mile or so in the darkness, park at an old wood-rail gate, climb a fence, and then walk several hundred yards up a rocky road to a small log cabin. The cabin was old and was about twenty-four feet square. Lenoir's dogs let him know we had arrived, and so we were met at the back door by Lenoir Pless who is known as "Bear Hunter" to most people. He brought us into the cabin through the small kitchen that had a woodstove and into the living room that had a large gas heater to warm the small room. The walls and floor were quite aged and worn. The windows had plastic over them. It was barely big enough for the six of us, but we crowded around and Mike helped us get one of the best interviews of the day. Bear Hunter is a distant cousin of Mike, and Uncle Rex, whose name you'll hear mentioned many times, is Bear Hunter's father. "I've hunted ever since I was big enough to follow my daddy through the woods." Bear started out coon hunting. He'd work all day, and when the chance came, he'd go hunting all night. He has killed three bears himself, but says he has helped carry out more than he can count. "You've got to be in pretty good shape to bear hunt like that. I'm telling you, there's a lot of sport in it, and there's a lot of hard work in it, too." Bear Hunter has worked most of his adult life as a mechanic, but recently he was visiting a friend in the hospital, and as he was leaving, he had a serious stroke right in the hospital parking lot. Had it not been for the fact that he was at the hospital at the time, he might not have lived. He is now recovering, but will probably not be able to hunt again for a long time.

That night, after a long day, we headed back to Rabun Gap and I worked on the tapes and photographs for nine months. When I found out this year that Wig had to give a talk at Haywood Tech near Waynesville on a Friday, I talked with him and we decided to make an all-weekend thing out of the talk. I needed to take the information we had gotten before around to all the contacts and have them read through it and check it all for accuracy, so it worked out great. Wig gave the talk, the audience found out I was working on a bear-hunting article, and all of a sudden James

PLATE 406 Bear Hunter, his daughter, and his new dog.

PLATE 407 Bear Hunter's log house.

Moody, the Director of Occupational Education there, was leading us off to meet a bear hunter he knew named Jerald Cogdill. He wasn't home at the time [he happened to be out at that moment with some friends hunting for bear signs], but his wife invited us to come back later, which we did. We checked all our information with the first three hunters we had interviewed, and then returned to Jerald's nice red house. It sits on the side of a mountain with his own sawmill in the back yard. Jerald and his friends hadn't had any luck finding signs. He said, "There ain't enough game around here anymore to pay to feed my dogs. We've been hunting several years, though, and we've killed several bear. We used to have a club, but it didn't work out too good so some of us just come along and say, 'Let's go hunting' and we go hunting. We kill the biggest part of our bears in Michigan anymore. We've been going up there four years. We generally average somewhere's in the neighborhood of three or four a year.

"But I really like it. To get out a week, camp out, and have good luck is my favorite time. And I go with the dogs. I can't hear what's going on if

I'm in a stand. I go to hear my dogs. If it wasn't for a bear running over the top of me, I wouldn't even take a gun any more. I've killed all I want to kill."

Jerald has done logging and sawmilling all his life with the exception of working five years at Dayco. For the past three years, he's been working at Haywood Tech at their sawmill [Haywood Tech is one of the only schools in the United States that has a sawmill and trains sawyers].

Several weeks later, Wig and I were on the road again, this time to check out some bear-hunting information that had been gathered by another student several years ago from Taylor Crockett who lives near Franklin, North Carolina. After a short drive, we arrived at his beautiful two-story log home, the front yard of which has just been paved over by the new four-lane highway that pushes through the mountains toward Murphy and west. It was chilly inside the house, so we built a blazing fire in the large fireplace. The walls of the living room where we sat were covered with pictures of people and bear hunts. Also on the wall was a large trophy deer rack and an enormous trophy boar head with long tushes. Taylor Crockett, a well-educated, intelligent man started telling us of his long, well-traced ancestry. He said, "My father was a minister. He didn't hunt much except birds— quail, pheasant. They came from Scotland, my ancestors did. There's an old story about one of my ancestors who was knighted, given a coat of arms, because he killed a great boar that was committing depredations around over the countryside. Of course, that's a legend, you know, about the fierce boar that was committing all these depredations, and he killed it with a spear. So he got a coat of arms for that.

"And, of course, I'm descended collaterally from Davy Crockett. Same family he was from. Not descended right from him. I'm descended from his grandfather. In other words, my great-great grandfather was a first cousin to Davy's father, or something like that. Davy traveled all over Tennessee on horseback when he was electioneering, you know, and he'd bear hunt with these different people. And he even came over here in North Carolina around Asheville and Maggie Valley and hunted there. Some of those people to this day bear his name. One fellow I know was named Crockett Campbell, and another was Crockett Evans, and they said that Davy come and hunted with their families years ago, and they named some of the kids after him is how they happened to have that name.

"Like I said, their outlets in those days for recreation was limited as compared to ours now, and that was one of their means of sport. I guess that activity to them kind of compared to what football is to us now, don't you think? Possibly. It's a more aggressive outlet."

We then went over the stories we had from him that had been passed down by the student who had interviewed him previously, and made a

PLATE 408 Jake and Bertha Waldroop in their back yard. Jake is holding a 12-gauge Texas Ranger shotgun he has had for fifty-five years.

number of changes. We also noticed the dogs in his back yard and asked him about taking some pictures. He agreed, and we put on our coats and headed out the door. He leashed up two of his Plott hounds, we got the photographs, finished up, and headed back to Rabun Gap again with yet another pile of material.

Several days later, I was going through some more old, unpublished material in our offices, and I came across several transcriptions concerning bear pens and traps. It had been gathered several years ago from two favorite *Foxfire* contacts, Lawton Brooks and Jake Waldroop.

And so, after a year's work, here's what I've got. The contacts were great. All of them were really friendly and helpful and went out of their way for us. I have been given the names of even more contacts, of course, as I've put this together, and so I'll be following up on this. For example, I'm going to talk to some of the descendents of the Plott family to get the background on the Plott hounds that were bred in this part of the mountains.

JEFF FEARS

Article researched, photographed, written, and diagramed, by Jeff Fears. Students who helped with interviews along the way include: Randall Hardy, Danny Brown, Eddie Brown, and Mark Burdette.

BEAR HABITS AND HABITAT

The bears that live in the Southern Appalachians are all black bears, and most of them range in size from two to three hundred pounds. Jerald Cogdill told us, "The average weight of the bears we kill is two hundred to two hundred and fifty pounds. A lot of people see one, you know, and their eyes get big and then the bear gets big, too [laughing]."

Their main source of food is the mast of the forest—hickory nuts, acorns, and so on. They also eat worms, berries, grapes, and insects in season; and, if hungry, they will sometimes venture into communities to visit apple orchards or garbage cans and dumps. They will rarely kill stock like sheep and cattle. Jerald said, "There's one that killed a cow on I-40 the other day because this year there ain't nothing much in the woods for them to eat. If they can get things to eat, they won't generally bother animals."

In the fall of the year, they do their main feeding for the long winter months, raking back the leaves to find mast, or even climbing up into the oak and hickory trees to break off nut-bearing limbs. Jerald said, "Before the apples start falling, if there isn't a lot of mast in the woods, a lot of times you can check an apple tree and find where he's climbed it by the claw marks. But usually they stay in the woods and hunt. They rake the leaves up in there. Just looks like a bunch of hogs have been in there rooting around."

The female will go to den in November or December if she has enough fat stored up to last her through the winter. If not, she'll generally keep hunting, sometimes being forced to eat bark in the worst part of the winter. The male does not go to den, but keeps prowling. "In bad weather," Bear Hunter said, "he'll crawl under something or 'nother—under a tree or a limb or something. Or if they ain't nothing for him to get under, he'll break laurel and ivy like a hog and make him a bed. I've found several of them in the summer time. Be a huckleberry picking or something and find them in them laurel thickets where they've just broke them and made them a pile as big as—well, I bet you can't get what they break and pile it in this room right here. And they just crawl right in the middle of it and lay down there just quiled up. Maybe lay two or three days and get up and go on. Maybe another bad spell come and they do the same thing again. Never go to den.

"But the female always goes to den when she's fat enough. Her cubs are born there in February and March. Sometimes the mother will have two cubs and occasionally three, but when the mother has just one, it is generally larger. The mother will go out during these first spring months to get water and food, but she usually doesn't bring the cubs out until up in April when it's warm enough for them to follow." By hunting season, the cub will usually be ready to take care of itself, and will weigh about fifty pounds by then.

In the spring and summer while the cub is still following its mother, the mother will be very protective. Bear said, "You better *watch* when they've got cubs or little ones. They're like a dog or a wildcat or anything else. They fight for their little ones. If you ever find a cub, don't never try to catch him without you *know* it has got away from the mother. If he ever makes a squall [and she's around], she'll be there in a minute."

A bear will range for miles hunting mast, but will generally stay in the same area where he was raised. Jerald said, "They sometimes range as far as twenty miles in one night. A lot of people won't believe it, but they will. Bears will move until they find food. They have to." The bears are not territorial in the sense that they fight to keep other bears out of their area. Sometimes there will be six or eight or ten bears all feeding in one area. But they will occasionally fight one another—though not over territory.

Most hunters claim that the bear population has declined drastically over the last few years. In fact, many of the hunters we talked to now hunt in Michigan instead of around their homes. Jerald Cogdill, for example, goes to Michigan every year with a hunting party; he puts a freezer on the back of his pickup, plugs the freezer in at the campsite, fills it full of bear meat, unplugs it, and drives straight through to get home. The meat stays frozen on the trip, and as soon as he pulls into his back yard, he plugs the freezer back up at the porch outlet.

There seem to be many reasons for the decline in the bear population in this area. The scarcity of mast since the death of the chestnuts and the beginning of extensive hardwood logging are certainly factors. Another is the increasing encroachment of civilization on bear habitat. Still another, of course, is the increase in hunting activity that has taken a real toll, combined with the opening up of some forest areas to hikers and jeep traffic. As Glenn Griffin noted, "Now the Forest Service has dug a road all the way from the Ranger Station and trimmed a trail two can walk side by side in plumb to Shining Rock for them hikers. I told them that if they had thought they was helping us bear hunters, they probably wouldn't have trimmed a foot of that! Then they made one from Shining Creek Gap going up Slashy Springs and out over old Bald through Spanish Oak Gap and up Bear Pen out over Dog Loser to Shining Rock to the grade; and set in there and come from the end of the grade down over Winding Stairs and Balsam Springs to the Narrows and into Deep Gap, and went plumb to the high top of Coal Mountain with it. Trimmed a ten-foot trail all the way up there. That just makes it better for us! You can flat scoot one of them ridges when you're running one of them trails trying to head a dog off, and ain't got to worry about them bushes slapping you in the face. You can flat put her down getting on one of *them* [trails]."

PLATE 409 Kim Griffin, Glenn's granddaughter, with Trim, a half pit bull and half black and tan.

PLATE 410 Glenn Griffin with Bo, Drive, and Smoky. Bo is half pit bull and half black and tan. The other two are half treeing walker and half mixed.

THE BEAR DOGS

All the men we talked to had strong feelings about the kinds of dogs they felt made the best bear dogs, and they were all fiercely loyal to those dogs they owned that had done a good job over the years. However, they were also quick to get rid of those dogs that began to fail them. As Jerald Cogdill said, "We use mostly mixed-breed dogs: Plott, blue tick, black and tan. Well, we've got some full Plotts, and they're just as good as any that we've got. That's a black Plott right down there [pointing to a dog in his front yard]. They say he's full, but it looks like he has a little blue tick in him to me. I trained that dog. Raised him from a pup. We groundhog hunted him a little and then got him running rabbits, and then we just packed him in right behind the rest of them [on a bear hunt]. He's eight and a half

PLATE 411   Queenie, Glenn's blue tick bitch.

PLATE 412   Glenn, Checkers, and Dexter, one of Glenn's grandsons. Checkers is half blue tick and half treeing walker. At right are Eddie Brown, Jeff Fears, and Mike Clark.

months old, and he runs them rabbits all day and half the night, but he won't quit a bear for a rabbit. Once you put a dog like that on a bear's track, they'll stay on it and won't hardly pull if you have a hot track.

"I had one dog, though, I got rid of. He was four years old. He fought bears last year, and the year before last. He got torn into by a bear, and this year, why he picked him up a deer. We couldn't get him on a bear. I sold him for twenty dollars."

Glenn Griffin said, "I used to keep mixed Plotts. I don't like full Plotts. Most thoroughbreds are selfish—a one-man dog. I had one of those dogs. Only one I had in my life. Every time she was turned loose, if there was a screen on them windows and them windows raised, she'd jump through that screen. I'd whup her till I felt sorry for her, and then I'd quit whupping her and she'd be right back in the house again. I sold her to Roy for

PLATE 413 Blackie, a full black and tan that runs only bear and boar.

PLATE 414 Taylor Crockett in his back yard with two of his Plotts.

twenty dollars. I had her sitting in the back of the truck one morning vaccinating her. Giving her rabies shots. He asked me what I'd take for her. I said, 'I'll take a twenty-dollar bill for her.'

"He said, 'Go ahead and give her that shot and I'll give you an [extra] dollar for that.'

"Only dog I ever sold in my life. I turned down five hundred dollars for one, and it got killed in the next bear fight. I couldn't have replaced him— not as good as he was. I had a dollar in him besides what food I had in him. Lord have mercy! He killed bear after bear, that old Ranger dog I had. I give a dollar bill for him. I brought him here with a baling wire

PLATE 415 Training four-month-old Plott puppies by using a lead coon (coon on a collar and chain). This teaches them to run a track. Taylor Crockett was training these puppies, and he loaned us this old photo.

wrapped around his neck for a lead on him. He was just about a year old when a man that lived down in Florida—one of them big shots—offered me five hundred dollars for him.

"But I mean I *really* love to hear a good fight. That's the reason I feed these dogs the year round [even though I can only use them for a few weeks each fall]. Got all kinds. Mixed up stuff. Them old cross-breeds is the toughest things you can find. I've got a dog that's half walker and half blue tick. John sold his mammy and daddy for eleven hundred and fifty dollars. Priced them, and the old man just wrote him a check for them. Old John just cried. Told Sally Ann, he said, 'Go down there and get that check.' He said, 'I opened my big mouth and that old man wrote a check right then.'

"He give me the pup.

"And we've got a black and tan like the stock Guy used to have. Now them last two dogs Guy had was out of that old Ranger dog I had and a black and tan bitch he had. We bred her, and then just stood the pups up amongst us. Kept the pups. We've fooled around and just about got out of our old stock of dogs.

"My son, he had a short-haired black and tan here, and we bred him to a pit bull bitch that old Sheridan had. That little old black bitch—you may have seen her. She barked at you when you come up. Tied up up yonder. She's a half black and tan, but she's like her mammy. She's black sparkled. And her brother down here in the lot looks like an old brindled Jersey cow! Roy named him Bodyguard. They took him to Michigan when he was seven months old, and he just wanted to stay right in under Roy's feet. He said, 'I don't need no bodyguard,' and he said right then, 'I know what I'll name him. I'll just name him Bodyguard.' We call him Bo all the time. And you ought to hear that bulldog fight one.

"We're out of Airedale. We did have some that's had some Plott in them, but they're gone. We mostly got walkers, Roy and them has. Sheridan's got a black and tan down there that won't run a thing but a bear or hog. He'll stand and watch deer just flash by, and when he gets after a bear, he'll take it right through all them deer and never mess with them. He wouldn't run a coon to save your life. We bought him off my first cousin out there at Cherokee."

Taylor Crockett prefers full Plotts. He bears out completely Glenn's statement that they are one-man dogs, but he prefers them just the same. "I've had dogs that way. Be camping out in the mountains, and nobody'd come anywhere around. They wouldn't let you. Had one in the car, and I sent a boy one day to get a coat out of my car. He come back. I knew what had happened. Kind of long-faced. Said, 'If you want that so-and-so coat, you go get it yourself!' The dog wouldn't let him have it, you know.

"My brother's eighteen years younger than me, and when he was just a toddler, I had an old Plott female. We lived over here on this farm and had big old turkey gobblers running around, geese, and the big old sow might be out, and a young bull. You had to *watch* kids, you know. He'd get out of sight, but I didn't have to worry because that old female stayed right with him; and if a chicken or anything got anywhere near him, she'd put it in high gear!

"Another example was John Siler. He was one of the earliest settlers in Macon County, and he was a big landowner and had many cattle and horses. This place I live on now belonged to one of his brothers. And he would have his cattle driven to the Siler Bald in the Smokies for summer pasture.

"One of his herdsmen that lived on Hazel Creek was going one day to see about the cattle and didn't come back when he was supposed to. So they sent out a search party and found him sitting against a tree with his gun across his lap, dead. Apparently a heart attack.

"And this fellow had two big brindle Plott dogs that had gone with him, and they were standing guard and would not let the rescue party come near. And they had to go back and get the man's wife to come and quiet the dogs before they could carry the man in."

Training his dogs is naturally an important part of just about every serious bear-hunter's life. What he's after are a group of dogs that are aggressive enough to make a bear tree, but smart and quick enough to stay out of its way as it fights back. Often the most highly prized dog in the group is the strike dog that is talented enough to follow even a cold track, and smart enough to stay quiet until the bear has been located and the other dogs brought up into place for the chase. Bob Burress told us about one of the best dogs he ever hunted with: "Some dogs can smell a colder track than others. Now I remember one time we were hunting over on the West Fork, and we had a two-day hunt. We went on the day before our hunt and found some signs, and we went back the next morning and the bear hadn't been back there. Well, we hunted the territory out and couldn't find the bear. We just decided to go back to that sign that we had found which was then two days old. We got this dog on that bear's track and we tracked the bear up, and she jumped him out of the bed. After we jumped it out of the bed, why it was no problem then. But this was an exceptionally good dog. Now when we train that strike dog—the leader—she'll track it right on till you get to the bed and will never bark. Now when you turn her loose, she'll bark every breath.

"Now we use a mixed breed of black and tan and Plott. Also we like to cross in a little pit bulldog with hounds. We start training them when they're young. If they'll fight, they'll fight, and if they won't, they won't. You just don't make them fight.

"We start them on mean stuff like coons when they're about five months old. Nothing big that will hurt them, though. When they get older, we put them on a bigger challenge. I have turned pups six or seven months old on a bear. They can't keep up, but that's the time to start them. If the young dog tries to keep up and don't come back, that's a good sign—if he'll keep going on. If he just runs out there and back, that don't look good.

"[You also don't want them running anything *but* bear]. About the best way to keep a dog from running a deer is to catch him when he runs over the top of one and get you a brush and beat him half to death. That's the only way you can break them. And a lot of them you *can't* break. There are more of them you can't break than there are that you can. But mostly nine out of ten dogs won't run a deer because them dogs like that bear better than they do a deer."

Glenn Griffin often yokes a young dog and a more experienced dog together when he's training one. "We take us a yoke then till we get him learned to lead, and put him with one of the old dogs. That old dog'll take him whether he wants to go or not. He'll give up sliding directly, and he'll go to trotting along with him."

Bob summed it all up when he said, "It's just an enjoyment to start a pup and train it right on up and watch it through the years as it improves fall by fall. We get to where we can tell the different dogs apart. We can tell about every one of our ten to fifteen dogs apart by the bark. There are

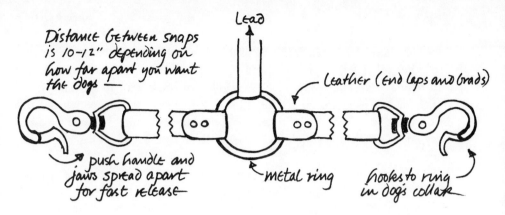

Distance between snaps is 10-12" depending on how far apart you want the dogs —

Lead

Leather (End laps and brads)

push handle and jaws spread apart for fast release

metal ring

hooks to ring in dog's collar

PLATE 416

hardly any two dogs that bark exactly alike. There will be a little difference somewhere. A lot of times we get into discussions over whose dog that bark is!"

After the bear is killed, one of the problems is to keep the dogs, who are highly keyed and excited, from fighting among each other. Bob deals with that problem this way: "We let them dogs wool the bear for about five minutes. Then we get the dogs off. You can easily get your dogs in a fight right there where you've killed the bear. It has happened. Them dogs is mad. I mean they're *mad* when they're fighting a bear. When you pull the dogs loose, you have to watch out or they'll snap at you. So after about five or ten minutes, we start pulling the dogs back out and tying them up. Some of them you have to separate and put single because they'll fight right there."

Glenn agrees completely: "We had two dogs that always fought. When we'd go to take them out, they'd go for a fight. And when they got ahold, they stayed no matter where they was at—neck or throat—whatever they got. Once they got ahold and we couldn't get them loose. We had a pond out there that we'd swim in, and we were going to throw them in that and drown them to get them loose. But it was dark and we couldn't see, and the water had been turned out of it. There wasn't no water there. We just reeled them right off in there, and they held on. Right across the other side, we had another pond made to fish in. Daddy said we'd put them in there. We just hauled them right across to there and there wasn't no water in there either. That one was dry. I said, 'Just get out of the way.' I said, 'I'll get them loose.'

"He said, 'You'll never get them loose.'

"I said, 'Just wait a minute.' I looked, and there was a big old beech tree standing there. I just reached and grabbed a limb out—jerked it down and broke her off. I fell in on them and it wasn't a minute till they come loose, I'm telling you. They may have been give out some with us carrying them out there and us trying to get them loose, but they turned loose when I fell in on them with that limb. It was a great big limb, too. It wasn't a little bitty one. I said I'd get them loose or kill them one. I said, 'They're coming *loose.*'

"The third lick I hit, they come apart. When they come apart, he grabbed one of them and I grabbed the other. Took them back and tied them up. You could turn them loose in the woods and they'd run just like any other dog would. But whenever the bear was killed, if you didn't tie them right then, they'd fight.

"You've got to keep them tied up 'cause with real bear dogs, that is what will happen. They'll fight."

The dogs' main responsibility of course, is to hold the bear, after they've tracked it down, until the hunters can get there and shoot it. They try to kill it, and in the process many get hurt. There is almost no way to train dogs against this—they just have to have instinct enough to stay out of the way as the bear swings. As Jerald said, "For a hog dog, you want one that will catch and hold on because if he turns loose, that hog'll cut him to pieces. But for a bear dog, you want one that will go in, snap, turn loose, and come back. If he holds on, he gets killed because that old bear can reach around and get him.

"My brother had a dog that got his heart and liver knocked an inch and a quarter out of place. It took a three-hundred-dollar doctor bill, and it still ain't no count. And I've seen dogs get slapped so hard they were addled for days; and another dog I saw got cut up like you were making shoe strings out of him. Of course, the only dogs you get killed are your best dogs. The sorry dogs hang back.

"We've had several dogs killed. Never had a man get hurt, but we've had a bear to bite his gun strap. We'll shoot one, and maybe the dogs'll have it down, and it'll get one of the dogs and start to bite it or something and we have to run in there and kick it loose and stick the gun right down against its head and shoot it so it won't kill the dogs. I've seen them get a dog up and start to lay the teeth to them. Just pick the whole dog up and pull him right on in and pop the teeth to him. If they get ahold of one, they'll tear one apart. That bear hunting's rough. I like it, though."

Taylor Crockett said, "A good fighting bear dog is supposed to use judgment—catch a bear and turn him loose and get out of the way. But lots of times they'll miscalculate, and the bear'll catch him and kill him. As a rule, you try to kill the bear as quick as you can for fear that it might get away or might hurt a dog. And you want to kill it dead because a wounded bear is more dangerous to your dogs. Your dogs get more courage when you shoot one. They'll just lose their caution and pile in and the wounded bear forgets about trying to get away. He just tries to kill a dog."

Glenn Griffin said, "If you've got a bunch of dogs that'll really fight one, then they's some dogs get hurt 'cause when that gun fires, every one of them'll freeze him—grab him—and then just hang on, and that's when you get your dogs hurt. They're fighting him just the minute that gun fires. Or if he's in a tree and you shoot him and he hits the ground, it's just like you'd shook a possum out. They *cover* him right then—just all over the top of him. And that's when he does the biting and the hurting. They'll flat work on one. Old bear'll get up on his hind feet and walk around and slap one just like a boxer. He can use them front feet just like a man a'slapping at anything.

"We killed one on North Fork at 3:30 in the evening, and at 4:30 the next morning we loaded him on the truck. We had ten dogs, and they was three of them that could walk. We carried the rest of them out in our hunting coats. We'd take our dogs a piece, and then go back and get the old bear."

Bob agrees: "We've carried a lot of dogs out of the woods. A bear'll stand on his hind legs and slap them dogs for a loop. We've had seven dogs killed, and lots of times we have a dog to get hurt bad. We've had them sewed up in just about every way. In fact, there's a boy named Billy Fingers that I hunted with two years ago this fall. Bear bit his dog's jawbone plumb in two, and he took it to the University of Georgia to have a man fix its jaw. That man completely made the dog a lower jaw—made him some teeth, too—and he's back in action now."

Dogs are lost in other ways, too. Bob suspects that some of the dogs that fail to return get caught in traps. Some simply get lost, or stolen. If the hunters lose sight of the dogs and give up the hunt and head for home without the dogs, Bear said they will "fight till they give out and then they come in. And that's all your time lost for nothing then. Or you lose the dogs completely. Lots of times they run off. Might be gone two or three days before they come in. May be so weak they can't walk hardly by the time they get in. But if you've got *good* dogs, they won't quit. They just keep going. They go plumb through into Davison's River and everywhere through there. That's where you lose them, see, when they cross these mountains. They just make a swipe or circle and right on through yonder they go and they're *gone*.

"But if somebody don't bother them or nothing, they come back eventually, most of them will. They backtrack theirselves and come right on back after one gets a little age on him to where he can get around. And most of them come back to where you turned them loose at—where you turned them out at, that's where they'll be. That's where a lot of people finds their own dogs. They just give out, or they get tired and quit. Just like people, you know. Some people's long-winded and they just hold right on and on. And then they's others that can't do it. That's kinda the way it goes. And maybe a dog's sick, or maybe he don't feel good, and he can fall out. Just like fox hunting. You take fox dogs and run them, and maybe one be sick or something or'nother and not feel good, and he'll fall out and come back. He won't go no more. And the others just keep a'running. That's the same way with bear dogs or anything like that. And then a lot of times [they get killed]. If they catch a bear and he kills one, why that's the end. He's just piled up right there. Or one cripples him and maybe he'll starve to death before he gets in.

"Some of them after they've hunted enough—after they learn it—if they're able they'll take the near cut and don't have to backtrack theirselves all the way back. But anymore there's so much traffic on the road and so many people [that will] steal them that you've *just* got a chance to get one back. You go coon hunting, and nine times out of ten somebody'll steal them before you get them back."

Though there are many dangers involved, and a very real chance that dogs that have been worked with and trained for years will never hunt again, the excitement of the chase and the fight still makes it worthwhile for those men that have it in their blood. They get a good scare once in a while, but that's all part of it. The danger is part of the excitement. Bear Hunter almost got killed once, but he kept right on hunting: "When I saw that big one I was telling you about earlier [see the section on stories] coming through that laurel and ivy looking like a cow coming out on me—I'll tell you, it's frightful. If you've ever been around one, you know what they are, and when one gets mad, why what they can do. If one gets ahold of you, it's just too wet to plow! There's no way of getting him off of you."

Taylor Crockett just laughs at the times he's seen men scared:

"Of course, if you come in and the bear and the dogs are fighting, it's more exciting because maybe you're crawling through the ivy and you can't see over ten feet ahead, but you can hear the bear growling and popping his teeth, and the dogs hollering; and maybe you'll see one get slapped and fly over the laurel—bear'll hit one and it'll just throw it.

"I've gotten a pretty good lick now and then out of people I have taken hunting. One time I took some young men who were inexperienced but enthusiastic, and I said, 'Well, now, boys you all are young and stout. You can outrun me. So if we get after a bear, I want you to take after him just as hard as you can and catch up and kill him!'

"And so we turned on a bear, and they lit out in good style, and oh, they left me behind pretty quick. But I soon noticed that I was gaining on the boys. The closer we got to the bear, the slower they got. Just before we got to the bear, I had caught up with them. I could hear the dogs and it sounded like one hell of a fight. You could hear the dogs barking and the bear growling and the brush popping. And I came around a little turn in the trail, and there stood the boys. I said, 'Boys, why don't you get gone in there and kill that bear?'

" 'Well,' they said, 'we believe you better kill it for us!' What happened was they got there and it kindly got their nerve [laughing]!

"And another old boy, I took him. He says, 'Crockett,' he says, 'I just thought all my life about killing a bear.' Says, 'That's my greatest ambition.' Said, 'If you'll see that I get to kill a bear, I'll pay you extra.'

" 'Well,' I says, 'we'll see what we can do.'

"And so that day we got after a big bear, and we had a good race, and the dogs stopped him in a little narrow ravine—just real steep-sided. Just ran up a little holler, and then he couldn't climb out. He just run up against a rock cliff like, and the brush and ivy and rhododendron was real thick in there.

"And this boy that was helping me with the dogs, we caught up and we could hear the bear down in there and the dogs fighting and the bear popping his teeth, and I said, 'Get that old boy, and we'll let him kill this bear!'

"He ran back and got him and brought him up there. It was kinda open out in front of the ravine, but you couldn't see back in there very well. That fellow ran up and down the bank a little bit, and he *looked* in here; and he ran up and he *looked* in there, and he listened a little and he says, 'Crockett, I guess you better kill this bear.' He just didn't quite have the nerve to crawl in there!

"So that's kinda the way you feel when you get there. Your hair seems like it just sorta rises up on the back of your neck a little bit, you know, and you get goose pimples. Of course, that's the charge you get out of hunting. The excitement. If they wasn't some excitement to it, why there wouldn't be any point in going.

"Couple of years ago, a young man went with me boar hunting. Hunting one that had been committing depredations to a corn field. He could really get through the woods, and I told him to go ahead and try to get the boar, and he did. I heard him shoot, 'Bang, bang, bang!' I was pretty close. I went on. He owled [made a sound like an owl as a signal to let Taylor know where he was. A man would owl once if he wanted to know where you were, or three times if he wanted you to come]. I answered him. When you kill a boar, you shoot two shots about five seconds apart a few minutes after you've killed it so they'll know you've killed it. He didn't shoot any shots in the air. I got to him and the first thing he said to me was, 'I guess I did something you won't like.'

"I said, 'What? Kill an old sow?' We had not planned to kill any sows that trip.

"Says, 'No.' What he'd done was kill a bear. He was up there crawling around looking for a boar on the ground, and this bear jumped out right by him—lit right by him—out of a tree. And he shot all his shells up and killed him, and that's the reason he thought he'd done something I wouldn't like because it was out of season for bear.

"And I said, 'Well, did it scare you a little bit?'

"And he rared back and says, 'No-o-o-o-o! Not a bit!'

"And I just thought, 'Well, now, that's a lie.'

"And then after a while, he said, 'Well,' he said, 'it did sorta excite me a little bit.'

"I can imagine. It would have excited me—one jump in on me like that!"

LAWS AND REGULATIONS

In the earlier days of hunting there were no restrictions on families as to how much game they could kill, or the time of year in which it could be killed. Later, however, such restrictions became necessary. Even now, they are constantly being revised, and areas that were not once sanctuaries are now.

At the present time, however, bears may only be hunted in season, and on areas set aside for such hunting. The season opens on the fifteenth of October, and stays open until the first of the new year with the exception of a two-week period in November when bear season is closed and deer season is open. There is no limitation on the age or sex of hunters now, and a person can hunt every day except Sunday during season.

Each hunter must have a license, which costs twenty-five dollars and includes the hunting license and the big game stamp. Each hunter may kill only one bear per season, and neither cubs nor she bears with cubs weighing under fifty pounds may be killed. Some hunters object to this as it is often hard to tell how much a small bear weighs until it has been killed, but that's the law. No hunting is allowed in the sanctuaries.

Bears that are killed are supposed to be taken to a ranger checking station to be weighed and recorded so that officials will have some idea how many are taken every year and may keep track of the bear population.

Although there are a number of rules governing hunting now, some of the restrictions that used to be placed on hunters have been lifted which has meant more and more hunters in the woods than ever before. Many of the older hunters grumble about this, seeing it as a way the Government has devised to bring in more money through the sale of extra licenses, and seeing it as the main reason for the decline in the bear population.

Those rules that are in force, however, are enforced more strictly than in the past. This makes for complications when a bear is jumped out of its bed on open land, and then chased by the dogs onto a bear sanctuary. Whose bear is it then? Glenn Griffin told us just such a story: "The dogs treed a she bear in Greasy Cove just at dark. Crossed [Route] 276 four times with them back and forth up the river. When they got to where they could hear the dogs at Greasy Cove overlook, there was the game wardens and park wardens all there waiting on them. Well, they just come on back. Come to the house. And at nine o'clock the next morning, them old dogs was still sitting there counting it off [but it was sanctuary land]. They've closed all the bear sanctuaries now to hunters. No guns or dogs on it, period. Them coon hunters done that themselves. They can't blame us bear hunters for it for we didn't have nothing to do with it. They caught two coon hunters one time and another bunch the third time. One of them the first time had a little 128-pound bear. The second bunch had an eighty-six pound bear. And the last bunch had one that weighed twenty-eight pounds. That's just waste."

Men that go onto closed land despite the laws can face stiff penalties if they're caught. Glenn said, "My first cousin's bad to get on the Park, and he got his last warning [from the wardens]. They flat been a'making it hard on them old boys out there. Five hundred dollars first offense. There's four dogs in jail in Gatlinburg now. Some of them said to that old boy [who owned them], 'Why don't you get somebody to go down there and get your dogs?'

"And he said, 'The man that goes after *them* dogs is going to the penitentiary.' He said, 'Nobody *better* not go down there and get them.' He said, 'I'd a'done been after my dogs if it'd just cost me a thousand dollars, but,' he said, 'there's a penitentiary sentence buying *them*.' They got his truck. Brand new four-wheel-drive Chevrolet. Got his dogs. His dogs have been in jail down there three months.

"And they made it hard on these old boys from around here down in Georgia this year, too, now I'll tell you. Let's see now. They had thirteen [from] in this section here in jail down there at one time. They was just infractions that they wasn't a'paying any attention to. One old boy had went down there and falsified his statements on his license."

PLATE 417 The Cables were legendary bear hunters who lived at the lower end of Swain County until they were moved out by the Government when the Great Smoky Mountain National Park was formed. This seventy-five-year-old photo shows them at their stock camp on Siler Bald.

HUNTING CLUBS

Before the hunting laws were so drastically revised, men would group themselves into bear-hunting clubs. During the season, the clubs would compete through drawings for the right to be on a certain open piece of territory for a two-day period. The club that won the drawing would be allowed to be in that section, alone, for that two-day period. Each club would pay fifty dollars [it was later raised to seventy-five] and put in an application to be eligible for the drawing, and the money was refunded to those clubs that lost. The losing clubs could then compete for the right to hunt during the next two-day period. At least ten men had to sign each application.

Most hunters we talked to really liked this system because it assured them of two full days in an area without competition from other hunters. The two-day periods would run on Mondays and Tuesdays and Thursdays and Fridays. That way, if the group happened to get rained out on one of these days, they would have either a Wednesday or a Saturday built in to fill out the two-day period.

Some clubs still function, but they have to compete with each other in the open areas. Glenn Griffin belongs to the Griffin Bear Hunting Club. One man keeps the books and the bank account. Each person in the club pays ten dollars a year, and that gives them some money ahead that can be used for flowers if someone dies or is sick, or for veterinary bills for dogs that get cut up on a hunt.

Glenn has belonged to two or three different clubs. He quit one because he and two other members had to furnish the dogs for every hunt, but the club at large wouldn't help them with the feed bill. Now he's more satisfied, for the members of his club all have their own dogs—enough for two good packs—and they all chip in to help with the feeding.

No drinking is allowed on a hunt. Glenn explained, "He may go with us one time, but if it's smelled on him, or we see him take a drink somewhere a'hunting, he's done. That's his last trip. It's dangerous. He may kill your dogs shooting at a bear or something and him half-loaded. Or he may shoot *somebody*—like somebody coming through the woods or moving around, and him just haul off and go to shooting. That's for the birds. We just won't fool with that."

Bob says, "We take anywhere from five to twenty-five men on a hunt. Every man is allowed to kill one bear apiece. We've never had ten men and killed ten bears. We usually take four to five hunts a season. Now back when they drawed hunts, there was nobody in there. When we would draw a hunt on the East Fork, there was nobody hunting in there while we were hunting. We had it to ourselves. That's the reason it cost pretty high, but I'd rather do it that way. It was worth it to have two days in there just to your party."

HUNTING AND TRAPPING

Every hunter that we talked to agreed that the first step in any hunt was the location of fresh signs that would show where the bears had been feeding. Some hunters would go into the woods around October first and locate signs in order to be ready to take their parties in when the season opened on October 15. The oldest hunters, however, would just go to the woods and camp, find signs, and do their hunting all at the same time.

On the morning of the hunt, "standers" would be put out on ridges overlooking gaps that the bear would be likely to pass through once the dogs started chasing it. Once they were in place, the dogs would be put on the trail, and the bear would be located, and then either killed by one of the standers as it fled by, or treed by the dogs and held in one place until the hunters could get there and kill it.

The signs the hunters would look for would be such things as places where the bears had raked back leaves looking for mast—acorns and hickory nuts. It the nuts hadn't started falling yet, you might be able to find places where they had climbed up into oak trees and broken limbs trying to get to them. Bob Burress said, "We call it 'lapping.' I reckon what give it that name is a bear'll just reach out and lap 'em in." Glenn Griffin added an interesting note when he said that if you find a place where a bear has stooled in its mast, then that's a sure sign that the bear has moved on because they never foul their feeding grounds.

Once the feeding area is located, the hunters are ready to begin. Taylor Crockett described the oldest style of hunting as follows:

"The younger men, they did the hard work. They got in the woods and made camp; and the older men, they furnished the brains for the hunt. [After camp was made] the younger men, or the men that were able, would go out and hunt signs the first day and come back and report. Then the older members of the party would plan the strategy of the hunt—that is decide which way to drive with the dogs and where to place the standers. [The bear might] be laying up in a woolly head up a ridge. Well, he'd say, 'Well, we'll jump it there in the morning; and if we come in from above, why, he'll run west. If we come in from below, he'll run north. And so we'll put standers in such-and-such a gap that he's likely to go through.' And before they took the dogs out, they would send the standers on ahead to be there waiting.

"Now they might send the standers out five miles, and maybe the dogs would go the other way. [That stander] might never hear a dog all day. But he was supposed to stay there till up in the evening so if the bear happened to come that way, he'd be there. And if he left his stand or did something he wasn't supposed to, why, they wouldn't take him hunting again. He had to go according to the rules.

"And then the drivers—the men that led the dogs through the woods to pick up the track. Generally they'd have one dog that was bolder, better trained, and more experienced. They'd turn him loose first and let him get it straightened out, and then they'd turn the younger dogs loose one or two at a time on the track so they wouldn't fight. They were so high-keyed that they just wanted to jump on anything they might run across. They'd jump on each other they were so excited and wanting to go so bad.

"But the older, more experienced dog is your strike dog. He generally has a little better nose and can smell a colder track. He's maybe a little smarter. Won't get excited and get off the track and lose it. And they use him to start the other dogs. And sometimes they'll have a dog or two that just barks big mostly and doesn't fight much. He just chases the bear, but they can hear him a long ways. Then maybe they'll be another dog—sometimes they'll use a mixed-up [breed of] dog—that doesn't bark much, but he fights hard and tends to stop the bear. You need both kinds. A dog that won't stop the bear is not much good, and one that'll stop him but you don't know where he is, is not too good. So you use a combination—a team—gathered in a pack of six to twelve to fifteen. Seven or eight is enough, but sometimes you get men with you, and they all want to bring their own dogs, and you just keep adding on till you get, really, more than you need. Sometimes they get split up and confused. I used to do better with just five or six old dogs that knew exactly what they were doing. I'd hardly ever lose a bear.

"Some hunters will use their dogs such a long time that they won't run anything *but* bear. You want them to lead the young dogs because the young dogs want to run deer or coon or just pretty near anything they can get after.

"Then the drivers, of course, fall in behind the dogs in case they stop the bear long enough for them to catch up—tree him. And the standers, they could tell by listening at the dogs coming if they were going to come close. If they were, they'd try to run in and cut him off—try to kill the bear.

"And it would generally take them a week for a hunt. Now, why, they just jump in a jeep and run out here, you know, ten or fifteen miles to hunt, and come back that same day. Not the same as it used to be. That's the reason that the game is getting scarce. Too accessible."

Jerald Cogdill is one of a number of bear hunters that represents a bridge between old and new hunting techniques. He and his partners begin scouting for signs two weeks before the season opens in the fall, but return home in the evenings since most of them have to be at work the next morning. When the season opens, they head for the most likely spot they have found [it is common for a man to set up his job at a local plant so that his vacations fall at the beginning of bear season], put out their standers, and bring in their dogs: "We use a strike dog—a trail dog that we call a strike dog. You have him on a lead. He trails the bear on to where he has bedded down, and then the track's ready to run. We just trail the dogs out about fifty feet apart, one right behind the other. When the man with the strike dog knows the dogs can run it [they can either jump it out of its bed, or it has left its bed so recently that they will be able to catch up with it], he stops and hollers back at us and we bring them on up and unsnap them [one at a time]. Just unsnap one, and then unsnap another one, and just trail them up to where they look like a bunch of ducks going through. If you just turned them loose at once, why they'd just run every which way. That lead dog will lead them on this way, but turn them all loose at once and that's when they scatter. They wouldn't know what they were running, you know. Sometimes they might run a half a mile behind and never get caught back up. But if you turn that lead dog loose, then they'll follow that dog. They know what they're doing.

"And we use radios. With a radio, you can tell a man which way the bear's going; and the man that's like the stander up here, why, if it's going through yonder, he'll be listening on his radio and he might come back down here to where we turned loose at and get a vehicle and go around and cut that bear off.

"We use eleven dogs in all, and they know what they're doing. You need six good dogs to get ahold of the bear—not ones to run along behind it and bark at it. You'll never tree a bear that way. They've got to get ahold of it [and aggravate it until it stops running and trees]."

Like Jerald, Bob Burress begins looking for signs about the first of October. "You've got to go way back. The rougher the country, the better the bear likes it." Glenn agreed, saying, "A bear can run within twenty feet of you in that ivy [laurel and rhododendron] and you can't see him. You can hear him a'slashing it down, but you can't see him. He likes that kind of country. He'll run through it just like a horse."

When the season opens, Bob and the hunting party he's with go to the spot they've found, send out the standers, and then head out with the dogs. He, like most of the people we talked to, would rather run with the dogs than stay in a stand, even though keeping up with the dogs is the hardest part of hunting. "Some men prefer that job over all others. They like running with the dogs. The men that follows them dogs is the ones that's really got it tough on these bear hunts. The way it works is that you have one strike dog out front that leads the other dogs. The strike dog trails the bear from the feeding grounds to the roughs where he's laid down. Then the dogs jump him out of his bed, and the men following the dogs try to make sure all the dogs get after the bear. The men in the stands wait for the bear to come through or to be treed near them."

In many cases, however, the men who are following the dogs, if they can keep up with them, have a better chance at getting the bear. They are really the ones who are in the middle of everything, and often they look down on those who prefer to be standers. As Bear Hunter said, "If you *really* bear hunt, you'll run with the dogs unless you do like a lot of them does—get out [in a stand] and pile up and lay there while everybody else does the work. They'll go to a stand and then they'll stay a little bit and they'll leave it, and maybe if you jump one, right through there he goes and gets away. When I could get about, I stayed with the dogs."

Glenn agreed: "I used to run with the dogs. Sheridan and Roy and them still does now. They know all the ridges. They'll stand and listen at the dogs the way they're going, and they'll cut him off over yonder somewhere. They'll be on the next ridge waiting for him when he comes through. I had the yellow jaundice twice, and I can't anymore. I can go as long as I go uphill and take my time. I can go good around the hill, but when I turn down, I have to watch it. My knees gives way on me. That's the reason I stay skinned up all the time. Falling."

Taylor Crockett, who also always runs with the dogs, said, "Bear hunting is the most rugged sport we have in the hunting line. To do it right, you have to be in good physical condition. You find the bear generally in the very roughest place that *he* can find. Calls for a lot of endurance and determination and perseverance. Just *everybody*'s not a bear hunter. Now there are a good many would-be bear hunters, but they just go out somewhere and park their jeeps on the road and listen to the dogs is about all they do. A real bear hunter likes to get in there with the dogs and find the track and turn loose on him. That separates the men from the boys is the old saying."

Once the dogs actually begin chasing a bear, the bear will run until it is shot by one of the standers or is cornered or treed by the dogs. They usually head for the roughest country they can find. As Bear said, "That's where a bear goes—them thickets. A bear can get through them and a dog can't."

And they may run for hours before they're caught, if they are caught at all. Glenn said, "Lord have mercy, the way they wind around and swarp around through them roughs and maybe make three or four trips around one knob, why, you may travel a long way. Sheridan and Rogers ran one, I guess, twenty miles."

There are several general rules of bear behavior that most of the men we talked to agreed on. Bear told us that most bears would tree fairly quickly after the dogs began to aggravate them unless they were old and experienced. "When a dog goes to chasing him, he'll usually go down the hill or around. Doesn't usually take up the grade. They don't *pick* fights. And then when it gets rough, he'll either go up a tree or whip them. Most bears, when a dog goes to fighting them, they'll climb if there's anything around they *can* climb.

"But these old big ones, it'll *take* something to make them climb. They've really got to fight him. Has to be a bunch of dogs that work together in order to put him up a tree. And it takes a pretty good-sized tree for one of them to climb. Old bears are a whole lot worse to fight because they've been hunted with dogs until they've learned how to get away or how to whip a dog.

"And, if you're hunting at night, the dogs can tree a bear a lot easier. The bear hates the dogs to catch him, and he's afraid at night, so they'll tree fast at night."

Glenn agreed: "You can hunt them of a night and it don't take too much to put'em up, period. They're afraid. See, they can't stand for a dog to catch'em. If a dog catches'em, or if he pinches'em, they'll go up something if there's anything there for them to get up. *But* if you've ever shot at one of a night up a tree like that, he'll not tree anywheres in the neighborhood. He may leave the country and *then* tree somewheres when he gets a way back, but you'll never get to him in a tree. The dogs will eat him up, but he'll come out of there if they *do* eat him up."

Jerald added, "A fat bear will tree where a poor bear won't start to tree. They're easier worried and slower getting around, and the dogs can bite them a whole lot quicker. That worrying a bear is what puts him up a tree. They don't go up a tree 'cause they're whipped. That worrying is what puts them up there."

Bob said, "The more you run a bear, the meaner they get. And some just get away. Since I've been hunting, we've had bears just outrun us—just outrun the dogs and leave. We have a lot of bears like that. Your smaller bear, if he's not fat, is the one to cause you that trouble and run off and leave them. Your big bear is not as bad. I'd rather turn on a big bear as a small one.

"Now, when the dogs catch up with them, the smaller bear can't put up as big a fight. But sometimes them little ones—especially an old she bear—will put up a rough fight if they've got a cub with them. If she's got a cub when you turn on her, she may take a big circle off five or six miles away from that cub. She'll get the dogs away from that cub if she can. And sometimes you never kill the bear right away. You just never know."

Once the bear is in a position where it can be shot, it is up to the men rather than the dogs. Almost every man we talked to preferred a different gun ranging from straight .44-magnum automatics to .32 Winchesters to .30-30 carbines to .22s, but all agreed that one bear is just as easy to kill as another if you hit him in the right place, and if you watch his behavior carefully. Glenn said, for example, "If he's whipped good, and he's away up in a tree, and he looks down at you and then turns his head away, just don't worry about him coming out. You've got time. But now if he goes to slinging that head and a'looking, you better do some shooting and shoot him fast 'cause he's coming out of there. He'll leave there when he goes to slinging that head and a'looking trying to see you. He's going to go somewhere, and he'll jump just as far as he *can* jump when he comes out of there. He'll come right out of there, and then it's all to do over again then. And it may be five miles from there when you *do* do it again, too. He'll leave there.

"But if you shoot it in the right place, you can kill it with just about any gun. I killed one that weighed 485 pounds with a .22. Little old single-shot Winchester I've got hanging on the wall in there. They tell you a .22 won't crack one's head, but I can flat bust one's brains out with that. I got him right in under the chin. Just shot him one time and he rolled. A bear's not any harder than anything else to kill. Just place your shot. Make that first one count. That's the biggest thing. Don't just cripple him. If you cripple him, then you're in trouble."

Bob said, "When you've treed the bear, it's best to shoot the bear between the eyes. If you get too high, or if you hit too low, you may not kill him. But if you hit him right, you can kill him first shot."

Bear told us what happened once when a man used the wrong gun: "Once a man jumped a mother and two cubs. He hit the mother in the rump with a .410 shotgun. She scooted around that hillside on her rump just about like a bunch of yellowjackets had hit her is what it was like. That'll kill a squirrel, but you don't want to use it for nothing bigger. But you can take a twelve-gauge and use buckshot or a pumpkin ball, and now they's some damage done when you fire one of them."

Of course, there's no guarantee that the bear will be killed at all. Often, it just disappears leaving several wounded dogs behind. Or sometimes both the bear and the dogs get out of hearing, and that ends the hunt for that day. As Taylor said, "If dogs have one treed and you don't come, the dogs'll eventually get tired and quit, and the bear'll get away. Fact is, more get away thataway than you kill, actually. 'Cause he goes through the very roughest terrain that he can find—rock cliffs and thick ivy thickets, you know, that slow you down and don't slow him as much; and he gets out of hearing and you don't know where he's gone, and he gets so far that you never catch up sometimes."

Or Jerald: "These boys trailed one the other day over yonder twenty miles, I'll bet. Close to it. It had fed, and they found where it had fed under this tree, and then they'd go on and find another tree that had acorns on it that it had fed at, and gone on. They trailed it from seven to four-thirty that evening with the dogs running loose and never did get to where it laid down. It never had laid down and was still going. No telling how much further it went before it ever laid down."

When the bear was killed, the old method of getting the other hunters to the location so they could help out was a system of signal shots. As Glenn said, "We'd shoot a rifle and one of them would hear, and he'd answer you with one shot. We'd shoot twice and then count to ten and shoot again. Say I was shooting and you heard me, why, you'd pinpoint them shots and then you'd answer me with one shot, and then keep a'coming and keep a'shooting. I've shot a box of shells like that trying to get Carroll and Daddy and them to us.

"One problem was that [as years went on and radios began to come in] sometimes they wouldn't pay any attention to them. Maybe have to climb back out on the highest top they was and hoot and holler till you got somebody to you. I have had to come out and come back to where we was supposed to meet at and then get them and go back. It got to where nobody never did pay any attention to them signal shots. That's the reason I said them young fellers didn't know nothing about them. If *Roy'd* a'heard them, he'd a'knowed what was what. He'd a'knowed they's somebody a'wanting some help somewheres.

"But now they've got the radio and we use them. But sometimes we can't get ahold of you with the radio, and we'll have to come back high somewhere to where he can get ahold of you and talk to you. Sometimes you get down in one of them deep coves and them little radios won't reach out."

Eventually, however, help is reached, and the bear is field dressed, divided, and carried out of the woods.

TRAPS AND PENS

We asked all the men we talked to how they felt about traps, and every one of them disagreed with their use. Glenn Griffin reacted very strongly against them: "A man I know set him a trap and caught one that climbed way up in a maple tree [dragging the trap behind him]. See, they got an old pointed grab on them. A blacksmith, or any man that welds, can build one for you. Put the trap on this big chain and then just set the trap. [When the bear gets caught] he drags that trap along and after awhile he eventually gets wound up; and he will be worn down most of the time by the time he gets wound up, you know, and he can't get loose. That grab will hook onto anything. It will turn in bushes and stuff and get caught.

"But this man I'm talking about went back and got the dogs to come back, and they were going to have a fight out of him and then shoot him. That old bear just lunged out of that tree and the grabs was still hung in the tree, and his whole weight went against that trap and he jerked them toes right off. Just stripped his toes off and then whipped the pups and got away from them.

"But I never did like a trap for a bear. I know an old boy that used to trap in the Park all the time. He's dead, but his wife still has two sixty-pound traps, and if somebody was to get caught in one of them things, your leg's ruined. If you ever step in one, you're done. The way they're made, see the teeth on them jaws come together and they counterlock. You can drive her plumb through the bone sometimes.

"A boy told me on Cooper's Creek up here three or four years ago, said he was up there coon hunting. He said he just started to step and he didn't know why he didn't make that step, but he stopped and shined the light down and saw he would have stepped right on the pedal of a trap. He was by himself, and he would have been hung up right there. He'd of had to carry that thing out of there—hopped or crawled or someway—because you can't open one by yourself. You have to use clamps on them to mash the springs together to open one.

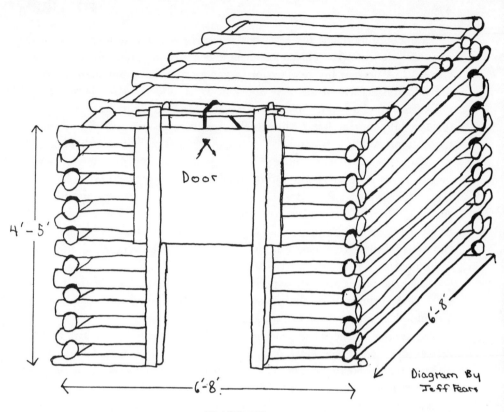

4'-5'

Door

6'-8'

6'-8'

Diagram By
Jeff Fears

PLATE 418

"I ain't got no use for one of them. If I have to set one of those things, friend, to get a bear, I just won't get one. I have more fun hearing my dogs running him and fighting him than I do shooting him. That's just like shooting a hog in a pen. Ain't a bit of sport to it."

Both Lawton Brooks and Jake Waldroop remember another way men used to catch bears: by the use of pens rather than traps. As Lawton remembers the ones he saw, they were made of logs like a little log house with a flat roof. The pens usually measured about six to eight feet square, and four or five feet high, using logs about six to eight inches in diameter. Any kind of wood was suitable, and the logs were simply notched to fit together at the corners, and then spiked together. They had to be spiked as the pens weren't very tall, and didn't have enough weight to keep the bear from lifting the logs up. The roof was also made of logs, spiked down, and there was no floor put down, as bears "won't try t'dig out." Spaces of three or four inches were left between all the logs, with no kind of mortar used.

An opening large enough for a bear to get in was made on one side of the pen, and wedges were placed between the logs and spiked in, to keep the logs level. A door of heavy planking, a good six inches larger than the opening all around, was suspended above it. The door was set between four poles [in sort of a frame] to act as "runners" for it. The poles were eight to ten feet tall, four or five inches thick, and were driven into the ground at the bottom. At the top another short pole was nailed between them so they wouldn't spread apart, or squeeze the door so it couldn't drop easily. A rope or chain was fastened to the top of the door, ran over the short pole on the top of the frame, down between two logs of the roof, to the ground inside the pen. There it was tied to some bait, and staked just firmly enough into the ground above the opening. For bait almost anything could be used as bears have sensitive noses, and will eat almost anything—hog meat was often used.

When the bear entered the pen and moved or began to eat the bait, the stake tied to the rope or chain would pull out of the ground, and the door would fall, covering the opening, and trapping the bear.

People used to check the pens every day when bear was plentiful, and less often otherwise. When they found one in their pens, they would shoot it.

Jake Waldroop remembers the pens being essentially the same as Lawton's description, except that many of the pens he heard of when he was young were covered over with branches and leaves and moss to "disfigure them so bears wouldn't booger at them." He also thinks that they were floored with logs about six inches in diameter so that the bears couldn't tunnel out. And he has heard of pens where the doors were triggered with large triggers like those described it the deadfall traps section of Foxfire 4 (pages 198–99). He says the door rested on the deadfall trigger to provide the weight necessary to hold the trigger assembly together.

Jake also told us that a local gap named Bear Pen Gap got its name when Barak Norton, Priest Norton, Jim Hopper and Fate Hopper set a bear pen there. It still carries that name today.

AFTER THE KILL

Today, as in the past, when the bear is killed, the dogs are tied up and then it is field dressed. Then a decision must be made as to whether it is to be skinned and cut into quarters or divided up to be brought out, or brought out whole. Most of the men we talked to tried, whenever possible, to bring out the whole carcass in one piece, but sometimes the size of the bear and its distance from a road demanded that it be brought out in pieces since it was so much easier to handle that way. Most of the men agreed that

PLATE 419 Henry "Chick" Farmer, Billy Farmer, Ronnie Hendrick, Daryl Frizzell, Tommy Frizzell (the Frizzell boys are Glenn's grandsons) Pat Frizzell (Glenn's daughter), Glenn, and Terry Wilson. The bear was killed by Tommy.

if the weather was warm, and if it was going to be some length of time before the bear was going to be brought out, then the meat should be cooled by whatever means available—putting it in a creek, for example. One man, however, as you will see, felt that putting the meat in water while it was hot would harm it, not help preserve it.

Jerald Cogdill said, "We gut it when we kill it. We short gut it down its back parts just you field dress a deer. That makes it lighter, and every pound helps—especially in places where you have to start uphill with it.

"If you're around a creek, it's good to wash it out. That gets that body heat out of it quicker. If you cut it up with that body heat in it, it'll ruin every time. Hang it up if no creek's around. If the weather's hot, you need to cut it up pretty quick, but if it's cold, you can let it hang there two or three days."

PLATE 420   Part of Bob Burress' bear-hunting club after a successful hunt about ten years ago. The men got one bear one day, and one the next. In the front row, the men are, left to right, Jimmy Burress (Bob's son), Billy Finger, E. B. Rickman, Professor Hutchinson (in hat), Bob Burress, and Jim Mehaffey kneeling at far right. Standing, left to right, Dude Howard, John Kinsland, unidentified, Stokey Caldwell, Albert Rich and Edward Messner between the bears, Roy Smith, and Billy McCracken.

PLATE 421   Fawns Cable (on the left) had the record for beating everyone to the dogs. This photograph was taken about 1920 in the Smokies.

PLATE 422   A group of bear hunters returning successful, 1885–90. The location is what is now the corner by the Episcopal church in Highlands, North Carolina. Note that the bear has been divided up, and the man on the far left has the head and the hide, while the other men carry the meat on poles. Note also the muzzle-loading rifles.

Glenn Griffin said, "We [always] just split the bear's belly till we can get his guts out; and when we get down here next to his rump gut, if we can't get it all, why we pull it up there to where we can tie it off with a string and then cut it off and then sew him back up. We whipstitch him back up to keep him from getting full of leaves and stuff. And we don't never put no water in him if we can keep from it, 'cause that cold water'll make him spoil quicker.

"Now ordinarily a dead bear'll run over you, you know, downhill in the leaves or anything. You just get him on a steep place and turn him loose and he'll flat scoot. [But one we killed on North Fork] wouldn't scoot. We'd drag him across a dead chestnut pole and his old hair would just screech like it was trying to hug onto it. There was just four of us, and we [were determined] to bring head, hide, and all out [in one piece]. We gutted him—took everything out plumb to his goozle—heart, lights, liver, entrails and all—but he was still almost more than we could handle."

Bear Hunter said, "If you're by yourself and you kill one, you better get him gutted just as quick as you can get to it. Get his insides out to keep him from ruining. They'll ruin in three hours if it's warm weather. You better believe it. If you can skin it, and if there's water around, put it in the water. It'll hold. You can cut out all you can carry, and then come in and then go back and take some help with you to get [the rest]. But I'd take me a big chunk of it!"

If there are a number of men on the hunt, then at some point a decision has to be made as to how the bear is going to be divided up. Bob Burress told us of several methods:

"First we skin it out. We usually lay it out on a piece of paper and skin him out on the ground—just split him down the legs and start skinning him out. Sometimes we hang him to skin him. We start at his heels and skin plumb on out down to his head. Most of the time we don't skin his feet. We just put a ring right around his back legs and split it right on out. Skin right up his legs to his chin and then just peel that off.

"Then however many men we got on the hunt—say there's ten men—we cut that bear's hams up into ten pieces and put them in ten piles. [Then we cut the rest of the bear up the same way and distribute it among the ten piles.] It's divided just as equal as we can divide it, and then put into bags. Each man just goes and gets him a bag of meat.

"But now we used to just face a man against a wall there, and another man would put his hand on a pile and say, 'Whose is this?'

"And [the man facing the wall would say], 'That's Stewart's.' He'd have a list in front of him and just call out the names [as the other·man went from pile to pile].

"They said that seventy-five years ago, they put the meat in piles. Then they'd take a man, blindfold him, and spin him around a couple of times; and he would point with that stick and say, 'This is Joe's,' or somebody's, so no one would be cheated. We've done that."

Taylor Crockett does it essentially the same way: "You cut the bear up and try to make an equal portion for each member of the party. If there's ten men, you take the ham and cut it in ten pieces; and you'll take the back and cut it in ten pieces, so everybody'll get an equal amount as near as possible. And then a man'll turn his back on the meat, and another fellow'll take a stick and just touch a pile of meat and say, 'Whose is this?' And the man that's not looking will call one of the party's names. He doesn't know what pile of meat the other man pointed to. And that man steps up and gets his pile of meat. That was one way of making it fair. We did that just the other day. We still go by that."

Jerald said, "When we kill a bear, we just cut it up in chunks and mix it all together—hams, shoulders, and all. If there's six [hunters], put six bags out there and start throwing chunks, putting them into each bag till we run out of chunks. Then we pick them up and bring them in. Everyone just grabs one bag. Each bag's got some ham, some shoulder, and different parts of the bear in it. The man that shoots the bear gets the hide and the head. If he don't want it, we give it away, and [if the person we give it to] wants to donate [some money to the club], we take it. You ain't supposed to sell that. We say, 'Here it is. If you want to donate us something for dog food, why you can have the hide.' Most people give us fifty dollars."

Bob said, "A lot of the boys has tanned them bear hides and made them a rug. And we've sold a lot of hides. And we could sell them teeth, them tushes, for fifty cents apiece. And we'd take them claws and sell everyone of them for thirty-five cents apiece. You'd be surprised at the amount of money that adds up to. We put it back in the treasury in the club and kept a little money ahead that way. But now it's illegal to sell the hide. A lot of these tourists out around Maggie Valley coming in, they was the ones buying them. They really wanted them."

If someone killed another man's bear, a different set of rules for dividing it came into play. Taylor Crockett said, "One of the unwritten rules of the old-time bear hunter which was strictly abided by was that if you were in the woods and killed a bear [being chased by] *another* party's dogs, you shot the signal shots so he would know there had been a kill. And if he came on, why you were entitled to a share of the meat. It was divided according to the number in the party. And if he *didn't* come, and you and your party had to take the bear out and skin it and butcher it, why then you took him the hide and half the bear, and you got half the bear. That was an old custom that seems to have pretty well gone out of style, or been forsaken, in late years."

"I'd rather have bear meat than beef."

Every man that we talked to said that one of the biggest reasons for bear hunting, besides the excitement of the hunt, was the taste of the meat itself. And each had his own way of cooking it.

Bob Burress said, "It takes special preparation to cook it right. I like to smell it while it's cooking. You can make steaks out of it, but I like it better in a stew. That's the way my wife fixes it all the time. There's several that fix steaks out of it, though. When my wife cooks it, she uses all kinds of pepper. You've got to kind of spike it up a little bit. Also, it's better to cook the meat slow. You know, to just put it on the stove and let it simmer for a while instead of rushing it. It's tender meat if it's cooked right."

Jerald Cogdill said, "We cut the bear meat up into chunks, put it in the pot, and parboil it. Chop up all parts of the bear and mix it up and parboil it until it starts getting pretty good and tender. Then just add potatoes and peas and all that good stuff in there. By the time your potatoes get cooked, your meat's good and tender. It takes about five hours to make a big pot of stew. It takes a pretty good while unless you've got a pressure cooker to cook it in. I like it that way. I don't like roast too good myself."

Bear Hunter said, "It's worth every penny it costs me to get one. I really like the meat. I can eat it three times a day and then between meals. Now if you want something good, take a piece of it and cook it of a night. Say

PLATE 423 Bob Burress with the frying pans he uses for cooking both fish and bear liver. Bob is flanked by the three students who did the interviews for this article: (left to right) Jeff Fears, Danny Brown, and Eddie Brown.

you're going tomorrow: put it in a biscuit, wrap it up in a piece of paper, and stick it in your coat. Along about one o'clock, I'm telling you it goes mighty good. Most people don't know how to cook it right, and it just don't taste good unless it's cooked right. But if it's cooked right, you can eat if for dessert. I just cook it like chicken. I parboil it till it's tender, and then I salt and pepper it up. Bear grease is good too. It's good for anything. Makes the best fish that you ever put in your mouth. Just fluffy and light. You can eat them, too. They still got the flavor to them.

"Now that grease: One time a bunch of them was a'hunting and they killed a big one and gutted it to keep it from spoiling, and they cut out a bunch of it and fried it and eat it. And when they got it fried and they all got done eating, they had a big pan full of grease left. And some of them was cleaning up the things—putting things up—said, 'What we gonna do with this grease?'

"He said, 'Don't you waste that grease.'

"'Well,' they said, 'we got to do something with it. Got to empty the pan.'

"And he said, 'Let me have it.' He just reached and got that pan and turned that pan of grease up and drunk the last drop of it. And they said time he got the last of it drunk, it was done running out of his britches!

"I'll tell you what you can do. You can take a gun barrel and put a plug in one end of it and pour it full—rifle or shotgun—and not spill nary a drop and pour that gun barrel full. Stand it up out there in the corner, and in the morning you can take your hand and rub the oil off of it. It goes through it. Sure does. It'll go through the gun barrel, and it'll be on the outsides. It will sure do it. You may not believe that, but it's a fact."

When Glenn Griffin cooks it, he leaves about a half-inch of fat on the meat, and cuts off the extra. He said, "I like it any way I can get it. Steaks, stew, or roast. Don't make no difference to me. It's good any way you go at it. I'd rather have it any day than deer meat. I *like* bear meat."

"I'm telling you, they's a lot of sport in it, and they's a lot of hard work in it too."

Most of the bear hunters we interviewed had a few stories that were their favorites. The following section is made up of those favorite stories of interesting bear hunts the men have been on.

PLATE 424

Bob Burress

Right here is as big a bear as I've ever killed. Five hundred and ten pounds. But that's an exceptionally big bear. We killed that bear right down here below the house. They was five of us when we killed that big bear. We were lucky on that one. We had to pull it straight down the mountain to get it to the trucks. That bear killed one of the dogs.

That bear had come down to a trash can to eat. That was one of them years that there wasn't much for them to eat. That's the reason that they come down. If there is not enough mast, then they come down into the settlement. Now that bear there is a bear that come down from Newfound Gap in the Smokies. It was a mean bear that was doing damage around the campgrounds. Well, them wardens tracked him, and I think they used some barrel-type traps, and they caught it, and hauled him and turned him loose in the Pisgah Forest. Now what that bear was a'doing was making his way back to the Smoky Park. They was a boy called me and said, "Do you want to kill a bear?"

And I said, "Yeah." So I took my dogs over there and went over there and looked at his track. I said, "Just wait till I get some help." I called them boys from Maggie Valley, and it wasn't but about thirty minutes till they got there. There was twelve dogs that we turned on that bear, and that fight lasted something over six hours before we got the bear killed. We turned them loose down on Hungry Creek over here, and we went all the way across Old Man Dave's Mountain and all back in there.

My favorite hunt? They were all good. You know where the Looking Glass Rock's at? That's the first one that entered my mind when you said that. We run a bear up on that rock one time. See, that big rock cliff starts back out here gradually going up, and it just keeps getting higher and higher. On out here at the highest end, it's probably four or five hundred feet high. We turned on this bear one time out there at the highest end and run it all the way back to where the bear could get up over the rocks but the dogs couldn't. There was two boys about ten minutes behind the dogs that helped the dogs on up, and they came back to the highest part and treed that bear in a hole. And this boy on the ground, he walked around here to the dogs listening to them, and saw the bear come out of the hole up a tree. Well, he shot it from the ground, and it lodged up in that tree. That right there is all that saved our pack of dogs. It would have rolled off that cliff if it had come out of that tree, and them dogs would have been holding on. They would have come down with the bear.

When you shoot a bear, that's where your dogs get hurt mostly. Especially when you shoot one out and just cripple him. If you kill him dead, you've got no problem, but when that bear hits the ground, every dog you've got will grab him [even] if it is alive.

Glenn Griffin

I've seen that bear named Honest John. He was as big as a mule. I don't know what happened to him. He must have died by the lake. Never did hear of anybody that killed him. The old Sherwood area in here is where he ranged. There used to be a little old shack around where the bear was just when you cross Turnpike Branch up Crawford's Creek. We called it the Champ Butler shack. Old Champ Butler used to live there. Champ's old lady was named Melviney. And right out next to the bank she was washing there, and there was that bear. And they run that bear right straight off

PLATE 425

that steep bluff. That bear was right over Melviney when she was a'washing. Old Champ said that she was scared for a week.

He was a big old bear. He had three toes off of his right forefoot. You could see his tracks in the dirt where somebody caught him in a trap and pulled them toes right off. On his right foot you can see this toe and this old claw on the side right here. They say that Bennie Moody caught him on the Little East Fork. They say all he had was three toes in his trap.

I don't know why they called him Honest John. That was back when I was a boy. We ran him in there for fifteen years. Nobody ever could get him. You never could get a shot at him. There was a lot of people who shot at him, but he was just too far away. He flat could run away.

I had something funny happen to me this year that I never had happen. My wife was sick that morning, and I was late. I fooled around here till about nine o'clock. Got up there and old Chick said, "You better be getting that gun on that back and get in the woods! Old Roy, they're taking the dogs to him now!"

That was the old she and two cubs that Sheridan had tracked. [The woods] was green. You couldn't see nothing. I said, "Well, I'll get in the woods."

Them boys was plumb in on Turnpike in yonder. I thought, "Maybe I can get up there and hear the race anyhow."

When I go in the woods myself, I always put a shell in the barrel of my gun, but old Chick a'aggravating me and a'talking to me, I loaded my magazine and just hung it on my shoulder and went up a little old branch to where the woods opened up, and then I crossed over and got in the old trail and went up. Just crossed the branch again—maybe like from here to the outhouse up there from where you cross the branch—and I got up on that little old steep place. I just stopped and turned my radio on, and old Chick just blasted me out of the woods. I had to turn it down. Roy was a'talking and Chick answering him, and Chick was just below me with that mobile unit. I had to turn it down just to listen at Chick. I couldn't hear Roy. Chick said, "And you say you've turned the dogs loose, Roy?" I know Roy said, "Yes," and Chick said, "That's a 10-4. Which way are they going, Roy? I don't hear them."

Just in a minute Chick said, "Well, if they're going right up that gorge," said, "they'll pop out in a minute till I can hear them," and I knew right where they was at then. I was standing there talking on the radio and had my gun a'hanging on my back. Decided I'd relieve my kidneys. I heered a brush pop behind me and I just cut my eye back over my shoulder right back down the hill the way I'd come up. I said, "Well, I wonder whose black dog that is [that] didn't go when Roy turned loose," and I said, "Just wait a minute, Glenn." I cut my eye back, and I said, "*Yeah.* You ain't no dog. You didn't look like one to *start* with." Little old cub bear standing in twenty feet of me. He was about that high and about that long.

I put the antenna of my radio down on the ground and then just dropped it so it wouldn't whiplash the antenna off of it. That radio a'laying there just a'talking. Old Chick just a'yowyowing on. I never ever cracked my gun to see if there was a shell in it 'cause if they's somebody with me, I won't carry one in the barrel, but if I'm by myself, I'll always slip one in the barrel. I just kept pivoting around and got my gun off my shoulder and I laid her right between his eyes. He was a'looking right straight at me, and when I started to turn around, he said [snuffing]—just a'*smelling.* [I said], "I think I'll shoot the end of your nose off." I laid me a dead bead right on the end of that nose and that gun snapped. His tail end's all I seen. Just one jump. I never did see him no more. I heered him tear the side of that hill down!

I went on up the end of the grade to Chick and I said, "Well, I'll tell you about this one later. There was just one walked up and smelled of my back end a minute ago."

"Well, what are you a'doing a'standing up there blind in the woods like that? Ought to be paying attention!"

Directly the dogs come off and run right over old Chick in the road. He was trying to turn his Bronco around, and the bear run within five feet of the back of that Bronco and crossed the road. Got nearly to the top and the dogs just about caught it, and old Hershel killed it right in the road there. I got'em to come back up there, and they brought them dogs back up there and we run that little old bear from ten o'clock that morning till dark that night and they was five dogs *still* running it. Hadn't never caught it. It just a'whipping them little old rough knobs just like a fox. Running through

them roughs. I heered it twice, but I never could *see* it no more. I'd hear
him just like a rabbit in the leaves go by, you know. He wouldn't a'weighed
thirty pounds, and I'd a'had to hid him to brought him out. And I'm glad I
didn't kill him. Anything under fifty pound and you've flat got a hundred
dollar ticket. I got to thinking after that, though, if I could have killed him,
I'd a'slipped him down there and put him in Chick's dog box while old
Chick was talking to somebody on that radio, and not said a word about it!
Old Chick'd a'raised cain, I'm telling you!

I guess an old she bear me and Daddy and Riggin Wells got on was the
meanest I've seen. She was flat a mean one. Old Riggin—we called him
"cliff climber" after that. He kept on wanting to shoot one. It was on
Ripshin there. You know, them old rock's on Ripshin's rough. That
Ripshin, now, that's bear country anyhow. If you go through it, you crawl
most of the time. Sometimes you can get up, but it's growed up in laurel
and ivy and rocks and little old pines till you have to crawl. Doug told old
Riggin, said, "Well, why don't you get in there and shoot it?"
  They had an old bear bayed right in at the foot of one of them cliffs.
  And old Riggin was going to go down that rock and get right above the
old bear and shoot her. We'd fought her all day. Old Riggin got right
down next to the old bear and his feet flew from under him and he went
right in *on* the bear and the dogs, and here he come, coming back up that
rock hollering "Shoot her! Eb, shoot her!"
  Old bear slobbered on the seat of his britches. They'll get you when
they're mad like that if you get in on one too close. Old Riggin tore his
fingernails off and the hide off his fingers. Now he flat clumb that cliff coming back! Now he was a'getting back out of there!
  You get scratched up, bit a time or two. Better not tell you that one,
though!

We've had some rough ones. Had a whole lot of dogs get killed. That one
that Sheridan killed that was so mean up here this year would a'killed that
blue tick bitch. She had her hugged up and was gonna bite her, and
Sheridan said, "I knowed I wouldn't kill [that bear], but he shot her right
there. Made her turn the dog loose anyhow. Then she come on off Tater
Hill.
  I fell in the creek trying to get up there. Lost my gun. Creek was up. It'd
been a'raining all day and all night for about two days and nights. Come
that storm and washed that kid away up there at Harold's. Washed Cove
Creek away up there. Ain't no logging road [anymore]. You know the logging road used to go plumb to the forks of the creek, and then a good one
went up the left-hand prong. It ain't there no more. It just washed it out. I

was going around through there and I hopped for a rock and I never did hit the rock. I hit right in that creek flat on my back. It was cold. You could a'heered me holler for a quarter [mile]. Then I had to go back down the creek and get my gun. Old Charles Clark had caught up with me, and he said, "Boy, they're flat eating him up."

Well, when we got up there, they told me and him to stay in the road on Crawford's Creek so we could go around, and I heered Terry Wilson come on the radio—him and Billy Fingers—and Bill said, "They're going right down on that little sharp piney knob on Cove Creek."

"Well," I said, "they're going to the Tater Hill, then. You'll hear from me directly. I'll be gone for a while." Me and old Charles lit out and come around there and Lester Heatherly and his mammy was a'standing out in the yard and I run up and stopped. She said, "Glenn, is that your'un's dogs?"

I said, "Yeah."

"Boy, now," she said, "I slap been hearing a bear fight I want you to know." She was standing out in the yard a'listening at us!

I got right up at the falls on the left-hand prong of Cove Creek, and I told old Charley Clark, I says, "Stay right here. I'll go above the falls and come around the hill and maybe we can get it between us to keep it from going to Little Creek." If they get in on Little Creek, you've flat had it in there. You have to crawl if you get to'em. And I just got nearly to the falls when I heared old Sheridan set into shootin' right above me. And here come him and bear, dogs and all right off that knob. He wore the seat of his dungarees out a'coming down through there!

It cost us forty-eight dollars to get our dogs sewed up. We flat had a six-hour fight out of her. We fought her all over Sorrel's Creek, Dick's Creek, Lenoir Creek, Anderson's Creek, and killed her on Cove Creek. Old Sheridan and Harold Rogers after her all the time through them roughs follering the dogs. I was nearly to her when Sheridan shot her.

My grandson, Tommy, got his first bear this fall. That hunt really showed how dogs can get mixed up sometimes.

Sometimes you run onto several bears and the dogs switch back and forth. On that big one that Tom killed, the dogs swapped bears three times. Roy said he knew that that big one was in there. We found where he'd been —crossed the trail twice before the season opened. There was plenty of acorns in there, and we knew he was in there. It was just a matter of finding him.

So we went back in there, and old Roy found where he was feeding, and he took the dogs in the next day. But there was also an old she bear and two cubs and then two or three year old yearling bears loafing around too.

PLATE 426 Glenn's grandson, Tommy, with the head of the first bear he killed. It hangs on the living room wall of his home.

Finally two dogs—Old Sailor and Queenie—got up with him, but the other dogs [had taken off after the other bears] and they was at Maple Ford on Crawford's Creek, and it took them about an hour and forty minutes to get to them. Those two dogs interested him enough till the other dogs could catch up, and then it was *on*. But there was *still* two bears there —that big one and another. And so then the dogs split again. That's how come Roy's strike dog, Sailor, was the only dog after the big one, and the whole rest of the pack was after the other one.

Anyway, we heard Sailor coming lower down on the ridge than the rest of the pack, and coming straight to us in our stand. When we saw the bear, he was headed right for us, and Tommy started shooting at him. He shot three times and killed him on the third shot. And that was the big bear.

There was a hippie there. He'd been right there with us the whole time watching everything—just curious. And that big bear came right at that hippie in the middle of the trail and just fell dead. That hippie froze with his eyes bugged out and his thumbs hooked in his overalls.

Tommy tried to holler and just went, "Whe-e-e-e." Couldn't talk.

I said, "Son, why don't you rare back and holler till your mother can hear you three mile down yonder." His mother hunts with us—my daughter.

He said, "Paw-paw, she won't come out from right in here [throat]."
Said, "That's the best I can do."

And I knew he was going to take the buck fever 'cause that's the first one
he'd ever shot at or seen a'running in the woods.

I heard a racket and I looked around and that *hippie* had it! He done
had the Saint Vitus Dance. Them packs was just a'rattling!

And I told Tommy, I said, "Son, lay your gun down over there because
you're going to start in a minute." He laid the gun down and boy, it set in
on him—buck fever. I've took it myself, and I know what it is. It's a nerve
reaction is what it is. You shake like a leaf in the wind.

"Boy," he said, "Paw-paw, I didn't shake when I was a'shooting him."

I said, "That's what you're supposed to do. Shoot him and *then* do your
shaking."

That old hippie turned around to Tommy and said, "Hey, boy, does
them things run wild in the woods like that?"

Tommy said, "Yeah." Said, "They'll slip around and *watch* you!"

The hippie had told us he was going to stay at Shining Rock that night
camping with his friends. Directly Tommy said, "Hey, Paw," he said, "that
hippie ain't going to stay at Shining Rock." Said, "Look going down that
trail yonder!"

It was about two hours before anybody got to us, and then the work set
in. Bringing that bird down Shining Creek about four and a half miles was
a job. At eight o'clock that night, we loaded him in Chick's Bronco.

Old Tom, he was tickled to death. We're having that head mounted for
him. His old tushes was about two and a quarter inches long. The boy who
mounted it said that it was the biggest bear head he'd seen. And he got
twenty-two bear heads this year. Said that was the biggest one he got. He
said now that was a corker. Weighed 375, and he wasn't fat. Had about a
half inch of fat on him.

Rex and Guy and Wes had one, one morning. Me and Dad and Johnny
Michael was going up from Rich Knob. That's the first time I ever
knowed that old feist and that bulldog and that old Plott of Wes' and Guy's
to get whupped. We topped out on Rich Knob and I told Daddy, I said,
"Old Wes and them's ahead of us." I said, "Listen in yonder on the side of
Old Bald." Now they was flat having a bear fight in there. We'd done
turned our dogs loose.

And that old Ranger dog that old Guy liked so well that I had—he was
about halfway around in toward the slipoff into the head of Little Creek. I
heared him set in around there, and Daddy said, "What about that?" Said,
"That's that bear old Wes and them's after up there." Said, "Old Ranger's
run right smack into her."

And we flat had it right in there for about three hours. Old Rex finally shot the bear, and then we had to get a long dead chestnut pole and punch her out of the tree. She just slid down the forks of it and set there, and her dead. Lodged in it.

PLATE 427

Bear Hunter

We decided we was a'going bear hunting, and we camped up here right below Camp Hope. About twenty of us went. We spent the night up there is what we done.

And the next morning, we got our dogs and started. Took right up that ridge up Ugly Creek to where they'd already found the sign where he'd been a'feeding. We got up there and led the old strike dog around to where he could smell it, and they led him just a little ways and got to where they couldn't hold him. They had to turn him loose.

They turned him loose, and then turned all the other dogs loose, and from that, the thing started. They run him just a little ways and jumped him. Took right up the ridge and went out the top, and they was fighting it then. And they went off into the splash dam at the head of Shining Creek. We run on up through there trying to get to the dogs, and when we got to the top where the standards was, we run right over the top of them. We passed them up and kept going. Some of them laying stretched out in the sun, some of them sitting up half-cocked, some of them asleep. We went over one boy that was asleep and he didn't even know we'd ever went through. The dogs was down in the holler and they couldn't hear them, and they was just laying around there.

We just kept going, and I guess we went three miles through them roughs in there when we come out right under where the dogs was baying. And just as we come out below where they was baying, why, Wes Pless set in to shooting. We jumped behind a tree—afraid he'd hit us. We didn't know what direction he was shooting in. And when he ceased, we just broke on out to him. And he said that was the biggest bear he'd ever looked at. But he said he'd went on. He shot three times, but he never stopped it.

See, what had happened, he was starving for water. He just stood his gun down and laid down in the creek to get him a drink, and when he laid down to get him a drink, this bear slid right off in the creek just above him. And there he was. And he grabbed his gun and he had the safe pushed on it and he couldn't find his safe, and the bear jumped the creek and hit on top of a log that was laid up against another tree. When he finally got his safe pushed off—he'd had to take his eye off the bear and look down to see where his safe was because he was so excited he couldn't even see to find his safe—he got three shots at it before it got out of his reach.

I went up that log he had been on trying to find if there was any blood, but I couldn't find any. I went to the tip of it and jumped off and took the grade of the hill and went back around to where Daddy was at. I wasn't looking for no sign. I was expecting the dogs to be a'baying it, you know. And when I got to him, he said, "Whatever you do, don't step on no stick or nothing to break it and make a racket—scare it." He says, "It'll be gone."

And I told him, "Well."

We was going right around the side of the hill, and before he hadn't much more than got it out of his mouth, me or him stepped on a stick and it just went like the whole side of that mountain blew up. I never heard such a racket since I've been born. It was one of the dogs made all the racket. He thought there was another bear coming in on him, I reckon.

Daddy said, "Too late now. He's gone."

I said, "Maybe not." I said, "I could track him." I just wheeled and went back up there where he went off that log [and looked a little closer this time], and there, where he'd jumped off, was a track so big your hat wouldn't cover it. You could see it just like a cow's track, you know, where he'd jumped off. And when he went to walking, why you could see his track right on around through there just the same as a cow track.

The dogs had quit, so I just took its sign and was tracking it just like tracking a dog or a cow. I just left Dad. I never paid no more attention to him. And first thing I knowed, I walked right in on it! And he was in laurel thick as your fingers. He was going right around the side of the hill from me. I pulled out my pistol and fired. That's all I had was a pistol. A .38 special is what it was. Held nine shots. Well, when I done that, he just throwed his head up, turned, and was coming up towards me! I fell down and emptied the gun. I didn't have time but to put two more back in the magazine. I had a pocket full of shells, but didn't have time to put them in! That thing was a'getting so close I didn't feel good waiting to put in any more! So I had two more shots, and the last shot that I fired, he jerked his head thataway and I hit him right in the lock of the jaw, and his mouth flew open, and you could have set a small dog in his mouth without a bit of trouble. And the blood just a'gushing. I didn't have sense enough to shoot over his head. He had his head down. If I'd gone over his head, I'd done good. But I didn't. You just as well spit out there in the yard for all the good that'll do to shoot one in the head. But when you're in a laurel patch and you're going in on him and he's coming out at you, you don't feel good! That's the way that one was. He was close as that chair there to me, and I'd done made the will to run when Daddy slipped up behind me and said, "Where's it at?"

And I said, "If you'd look right there, you'd see where it's at!" And that bear's mouth was open that big. You could have thrown a dog in his mouth.

Dad had a .30-.30. He jerked that .30-.30 in to his face, and when the gun fired, the bear just wheeled and right off the side of the hill he went and went over a cliff about forty foot high.

We went up to the top of that cliff where we could see him. Went up to the top of that cliff to look down. He was getting up on his four feet. Dad just turned the gun down thataway and finished him out.

We went around the cliff, went down to where it was at; and we got down there and we took two chains. He took one and I took one, and we tied around his feet till we could drag him. And we just took right down the holler with him. And we come to this log a'laying across the holler where a tree had fell, you know, and it was everything in the world we could do to get it over. We like to never got it over. Both of us pulling all we had just like two horses. They're hard to carry. They're limber. They're just like a dishrag. They'll just roll and waller every which way. You take a deer and kill it, and it gets stiff in a few minutes after you kill it. But a bear don't. He's just like an old dishrag or something, flopping around.

I said, "If there's ary another log," I says, "we'll go around somehow or another." I says, "Ain't gonna drag it *over* it."

He said, "All right," and it was open from there on in to Shining Creek. We drug it to Shining Creek, nothing else in the way, and we was both busted when we got there. I said, "This is as far as we're a'going!" Just about that time, the standards just poured off the hill right down in on us. They said they'd never heared such a war since they'd been born—me a'shooting that pistol. They set in, said they was going to bring it out whole. They yow-yowed around there a little bit, and I listened at'em. Finally I said, "Nope, not *this* chicken! I've done had all I want of it. You'uns can carry out every bit of it if you want, but," I says, "here's one that won't have none." I said, "I wouldn't tote a pound of it. Not nary pound. I won't touch it." I said, "That damn thing's fat." I said, "I'll lead the dogs, carry the guns, anything else you might want me to carry, but." I says, "I ain't carrying that no more."

And when I said that, everything fell. They commenced grabbing their knives and went to skinning. We skinned it, split it open, quartered it, and made four pieces out of it. Cut the head off and the hide. And about like as far as from here to the barn out there—about three hundred yards—is as far as one man could carry the hide and the head. You can figure what it was. We tied each quarter to a pole, and about the same distance is as far as a pair of men could carry a quarter of it to save your life. They'd have to change and two more take it. We got it out to the ranger checking station. Now you talk about a bunch being white-eyed, we was! What meat we had —just the meat—dressed out over six hundred pounds. You take a horse or a cow that'd weigh six hundred pound and start dragging it and drag it on the ground, and you'll know just what we had. I can pull a whole lot. My daddy can, too. But it was everything in the world we could do to drag it.

That was the biggest bear I've ever seen in the woods. And it was about as frightful a thing as I've ever seen, too. They let some of the rest of them have the head and the hide. Might have had it mounted. I don't know. I never did know what ever went with it, but that was the biggest one that I've ever seen yet.

Old bears are worse to fight. They're a whole lot worse. See, they've been hunted with dogs and all till they learn how to get away or how to whip a dog.

One time we ran one with one eye. An old she bear. And she'd whip the dogs off every time they turned loose on her. She was laying on the Cove Creek side up here. We found its sign. We didn't know what it was, and we turned loose on it. And they was three of us standing at the Green Knob. And they jumped it right down in under the Green Knob there down in the Cove Creek side, and she took out up through there and she went out up over a cliff at Old Bald. And we had a bunch of dogs, and one of them went in. You could see it run in and grab it by the hindquarters, and she'd just wheel before you could bat your eye, and you could see that dog come changing ends coming out there over top of that laurel and ivy. That's the way she whupped them.

My daddy was right under the gap there, and he says, "I can't stand that." And he just broke right through and just when he got down under the top a little, it was open timber through there. And he broke right on through, and the bear went on through the gap. And they just went from top to top. He set in hissin' the dogs, and they went back in on it again.

Well, they turned off and down on Roy's Creek side they went, and they got it down at about the creek, and she whipped [the dogs] out again. And Daddy was just a'pulling everything he could do trying to get to it. And it just went up on the face of another side, and the dogs quit and come back to him. And he hissed them and they just wheeled and back they went. And he was just pulling trying to get to it. And they just went up on top of the ridge and they was a laurel thicket on top. And was coming back.

And he set in to hissing them, and they wouldn't go back, but he said he set into looking everywhere, and just in a minute, why they was one dog in the bunch belongs to Harrison Henson down here—just as black as a bear and it had brown on its nose and looked just exactly like a bear. And it come in below and was coming back up to them when every dog they had set in a'baying. I reckon they thought that's what it was [a bear]. And Daddy was right close on'em and he just wheeled and pulled the trigger on'em and fired. And the dog's heel went up, and he said as soon as the dog's heel went up, he seen what he'd done.

He said he wheeled around and looked, and there, standing right above him—there it stood on its hind feet with its head stuck out of the laurel. And he just wheeled and fired and down it went the same way.

And I was up on top of Cold Mountain, and I got to him before anybody else did. They just had a short cut across there to get to him, and I run three miles! I came in a little of breaking my neck too. I had an old shotgun, and I stumped my toe on a root or something and started to fall. And I went as far as from here to that gate right down that ridge just a'hanging and a'jumping and grabbing trying to keep on my feet. And finally I got straightened up and on right down through there I went. If I'd a'fell, ain't no telling what'd a'happened to me.

There was eight or ten of us hunting then, and we tied the bear's feet together and run a pole between his legs and got one man on one end and one on the other and down the mountain we'd go. Lay it down every once in a while and two more take it and keep a'going.

We got down to a logging camp that Wilburn Clark [Mike Clark's grandfather], Eldon Burnett, Guy Clark [Mike Clark's uncle], and Elbert Trull had in the woods. We just throwed it down to rest where they was at, and Elbert started calling me "Bear Hunter," and everybody in the country started calling me that afterwards. That's how I got that name. Sometimes I have to stop and think what my real name is anymore! If you ever get a nickname, it'll stay with you. You'll not get rid of it!

There was another one over at Cove Creek. They sent me to the stand on Green Knob. And when I got to Green Knob, why, I heard the dogs bark. I ran over trying to get to them, and I got up pretty close, and I couldn't see the dogs. They were in some laurel and ivy, and the bear was in a flat-top pine. The pine'd been broken off or something at the top, and there he was standing up looking at the dogs. He never seen me or heard me.

I slipped by the side of the tree and took aim at about the middle of where I should fire. And when the gun fired, out of it he went. And this other fellow was coming up trying to get to it too, and when it jumped out, it tore a rock loose as big as a stove; and it went right down through there and he had to run to get away from it. He downed the bear—I hit it but I never killed it—but he said when it come down and tore that rock loose, it like to have scared him to death. He didn't know what had happened. He was standing right there when that big rock came down the mountain a'changing ends, and he had to run for his life!

One night I came in from work. Harry [my brother, who was fourteen at the time] met me down there and he said that he wanted to go possum hunting. I said, "I'm give out." I said, "I can't."

I had to come to the house and go back to the store. I came to the house to find out what they had to have. I just went by and told them that I'd go to the store. I got down there and when I come out from the store and turned back thisaway, there was one dog a'barking back thisaway and one back through here and one out through there. I heard them, and the fever hit me, tired or no tired. I come by Daddy's house, and Harry had his shoes off fixing to go to bed. He knowed he wasn't going to get to go. I said, "Get your shoes on." I said, "I'll be back in a few minutes."

I just run to the house, told my wife, "I'm going possum hunting a while." I grabbed my gun and I had two dogs—a young dog that I'd never had out, and an old dog—she'd fight one pretty good. But we were just going possum hunting. I wasn't aiming to go—nothing only to take mine and maybe one of his dogs and go around out through Grandpa's and back.

When we started, Daddy said, "What kind of gun are you going to take?"

I said, "I ain't taking nothing but a .22."

He said, "You're drunk." He said, "You're going to take something else." Daddy had a .22 special. He said for me to take the special.

He said, "What dogs are you going to take?"

I said, "I'm going to take two or three old dogs of mine, maybe one of yours."

"No," he said. "That won't work either." He said, "You're going to take them all."

I said, "I can't lead all them old dogs." I said, "I ain't going to the big woods. I'm just going possum hunting."

He said, "I don't care what you are going to do." He said, "You're going to do what I tell you, or you won't go."

I said, "All right, then." I got the special. I throwed it on my back and got the old dog tied then and let the pup loose. And Daddy's old dog was loose. And they'd been all over everywhere and around about. Just as we got out, here they come. They just run up and started jumping thataway. One went off—my pup—on the Burnette Cove side, and Daddy's old dog come out on the Cold Creek side. They was gone just a minute and here they come back again. They both set out on the Burnette Cove side like they were leaving the sticks. I didn't know what to do, hardly. I just went right to'em with that dog I had. I thought it snorted—or something snorted. They were horses in there. I thought they were going down there and that it was the old pup baying a horse.

So just when it snorted again, that dog I had tied was about to eat me up. I couldn't hold her. She tried to grab me by my arm right there, just the same as she was going to tear my arm off. I sat there just a minute and told Harry, I said, "Pull the collars off of them." I said, "If we have to go to the highway after them, we'll go."

The moment we turned them loose, I'm telling you what's the truth, it went just like the whole side of the mountain coming off. Harry had a flashlight. I didn't have no flashlight. I had the gun.

In just a minute they went to barking at that old bear. When I started through, they were still on the ground. They hadn't treed yet. I just took right down through there meeting them. I grabbed the flashlight, but when I got down to the tree, I couldn't hold my gun and hold the light too. I looked around for Harry. I thought he was coming with me, but nobody was there. I was afraid to say anything or holler. I was afraid to use my light. The moon was shining just enough to just barely tell where you was going. I just reared right back up through there, and I went and run just hard as I could.

I got back to where I'd left him, and he was still standing there. I told him what I wanted him to do. I said, "I'm going to give you the light." I said, "Don't you turn it on till I tell you." I said, "You get right square behind me," and I said, "when I punch you, you throw the light on." I said, "Don't take it off, but keep it on." I'd done got my gun ready and everything.

When I punched him, he flashed the light on. When he did, I done had the gun pointed to it. I just dropped in the bead as best I could tell, and fired. When I fired, it went about six feet right straight up the tree, and as it hauled it, I fired again. When I fired again, it dropped back down just like it went up. I fired again. When I done that, it just turned a somerset thataway and hit the ground. Right down the mountain it went, and me right after him. But I hadn't hit it enough. It still had a little life about it. When I got to him, there the dogs were a'baying and a'fighting. Just as I run up to it, it reared up on its hind feet. I took aim right in under him and right there that old pup I had ran in and catched the bear in the stomach. Just as he went in under it, the bear came down on his four feet thataway to hit the dog. The dog dodged it, and run out, and when it hit the ground, I grabbed the gun again. I pulled the trigger and killed it.

Well, there we was. I didn't think I could carry it. Of course, you get excited, and you can do a whole lot. I sat there a few minutes until I kind of cooled off and caught my breath. I got around down below it and told Harry, I said, "Now you tie them dogs up and hold them. Don't you let them loose." When I shot it, Daddy's dog was still mad and was bound to fight and jumped on my pup and about killed him, and he ran off. He wouldn't never come back around. He reckoned the bear got him it happened so quick.

I got around and tried to get it up on my back, but I couldn't get it up on my back. I told Harry, I said, "Tie Dad's dog up and come help me." I said, "We've got to get it back." I knowed it was too big for him to try to carry and come out of there. I got her on my back, got it rolled up, and I like to never got up. I finally got up on my feet.

I took right around the side of the hill, and we got up there, and just before we got into the snaking road, this big tree had fell down there. It struck me right about here [waist high]. I says, "I don't know how I'll get over that." I says, "I ain't a'going to climb that hill with it, and I ain't a'going to go *down* the hill with it." I says, "The only thing I know to do is try to hold it on my back and cross over." And I just walked up by the side of the tree and got myself balanced and throwed my left leg over and just got up a'straddle—settin' a'straddle of it. I didn't have my other leg over. That dog of Dad's broke his chain and here he come, and I was settin' on the tree with that thing on my back, and when he went over top of me, he grabbed a mouthful of it and turned it down and crammed my head right in under that tree and that bear on top of me! I said, "My soul." I was going to *die*. But I finally got out.

And I sit there a little bit till I kindly got over it, and I give Harry a good jacking up 'cause he *turned* the dog loose. And he just about cried 'cause I jumped on him, you know, for turning the dog loose; but he said he *didn't* turn him loose. He said he broke the chain. And about that time the dog come and made a run to me and he had a piece of chain about that long, and I knowed right then that he *had* broke it. And I had a chain in my pocket, and I *knowed* it was a good one, and I took it and told him to put *that* one on him, I said, "So's he won't get loose no more."

I wouldn't go as far as from here to the barn down yonder—I couldn't go more than half that—hardly that far. I'd have to throw that bear down. I'd have to rest, and then both of us would get him on my back again and go a little farther. Once I tried to pick him up by myself, and said, "I can't do that. That'll kill me."

And we got him back on my back and I carried him up there where Wesley Pless, my cousin, used to live, and I throwed her down. I said, "That's as far as I'm a'going." I says, "You're gonna help me."

In the meantime, my dogs were right down in the edge of the cornfield right out here. They was down in that cornfield after something. I didn't know what, but I thought it was a rabbit or something. There was a pole laying down there, so I just set it right down beside that bear and tied its front feet together and tied its back feet together. I had my dog tied with one chain, and had to turn it loose to get that chain to tie with. When I got it tied then, we got it on our backs and started.

Them dogs were barking right over here in the holler above where Wesley's house used to be. So we let out and we carried him on out to the next ridge coming thisaway, and we laid her down. I said, "We'll go down and see what it is." I said, "It's an old possum, I guess." I set in to shining the flashlight trying to see what it was, and I couldn't see a thing in the world. I could see that old dog of Daddy's up the hill. There was a locust up there that had fell into the top of another, and that dog was up that locust and was right in the pinnacle of it. It was about as big as my arm. That locust was lodged in beside this other tree, and he was barking every breath. "Well," I said, "the only thing I can do to find it is to get which way he's a'barking and shine the light thataway."

I just throwed the light back on him, and about that far from where he was there he sat. I said, "Yep, I see him. I see his eyes." I said, "I don't know what it is, but I'm gonna find out just in a minute."

I just turned around and got my flashlight and shined it right in the middle of it and fired at it. That coon hit the ground, and when it hit the ground, my two dogs—I had them all tied but my two—both grabbed it, and when they grabbed it, I got one of them—the old dog—and she turned it loose. And this pup, it got it and around the side of the hill it went with it. I had to run him down and catch him. I got back, and the other one got ahold of it, and they were both on it again. I said, "I don't know how I'm gonna get'em loose." I just grabbed her by one ear, and the other one by its ear, and I blowed in her ear and she turned it loose. Then I blowed in the other one's ear, and it turned it loose. I just throwed them both thataway [to either side], and grabbed that coon and stuck it down my coat. That was the only thing I could do.

I finally went back there, and there that dog was up in the tree. I says, "We got to go up and get him out." I says, "No, he may jerk me out too, but," I says, "he's got to come."

I lit out, and I was up that locust. I went, and I got up to him, and there was a snag about eight inches long about as thick as a broomhandle sticking right out up on top of that locust. And that dog had his leg hung right around that, and right there he was a'holding. I said, "Well, there ain't but one way to get you out," and that's by the tail and turn him around. I got a'straddle of that log so I could hold, you know, and he wouldn't jerk me off it if he did fall. I just got ahold of him and held him and got him by the back of the neck and held him by the tail and scooted right down that pole right on down till I got him off on the ground. And I got that coon then and we come on out and got the bear, and down the hill we came.

We come in, and I'd done told Harry what to do. I says, "We'll lay him on the porch, and you can take the coon around the house and show it to Dad." He was in bed.

Dad was like Grandpa was. He'd take on and get excited. He took on about the coon, and just in a minute, he wanted to know where I was at. I was standing out there in the yard, and says, "Come out here a minute." He was lying in the bed, and to tell you what's the truth, he didn't make two jumps till he was out on the porch. I never seen a man come out of the house so quick in all of my life. And I never seen nobody take on so. He was as bad to take on as Grandpa whenever somebody killed something. He'd take on more than if he'd killed it hisself.

He said, "I told you." He says, "That's why I was wanting you to take the dogs."

I says, "I see it now, but," I says, "I didn't know it [then]." So we went down there and took its insides out and hung it up and left him till the next morning and skinned him. But now I tell you, that came as near a'getting me as anything I've ever done. We just carried him from right up yonder above the house, and it like to have killed Harry. He was so sore for a week he couldn't hardly walk. And I'd done worked all day, and then carried the thing two thirds of the way down the mountain. My knees nearly buckled, but it got a little easier when I put it on that pole.

CARRIE STEWART

*M*rs. Carrie Stewart recently celebrated her one-hundredth birthday (November 1978). She still sews and quilts, works in her garden, keeps house, and attends the dinners sponsored by the Macon County senior citizens' groups "without the aid of a walking cane."

Carrie was the first-born of ten children. Her mother's mother was a "bound girl" to a family in Franklin, and her father was born a slave and told her he remembered being sold on the slave block in the Franklin, North Carolina, market. Carrie grew up on a farm near Franklin and attended a school established by the St. Cyprians Episcopal Church from the time she was six years old until just before she married at the age of eighteen.

She and her husband, Joe Stewart, had ten children, four of whom are still living. When I asked her why she felt she had lived so long and was still so healthy and active, she said she supposed it was because she has always been interested in learning about and doing new things, and because as a young woman, she had never had to go outside her home to work as so many other black women had to do. "I never had to work hard. My husband looked after me and treated me well." But if having and rearing ten children and also being a midwife isn't "working hard," I wonder what is in her estimation.

These interviews with Carrie Stewart were part of an independent Foxfire project I undertook as a senior. The purpose of my study was to talk to the black people of our area of Southern Appalachia about how they or their ancestors came to be here and to learn something of their life-styles. I was very surprised to learn that many slaves were bought and sold here and that many white families owned at least one or two slaves. I was quite shy talking to the first people we went to see. I felt I was prying into a part of their lives they might not want to tell me, a white teen-ager, about. But so many of the people I visited were helpful and did tell me whatever they knew of their pasts, though for many it was quite sketchy—some had never asked their parents, and others just didn't remember much about what they had heard.

PLATE 428

During this time, I visited with Reverend Rufus Morgan in North Caro-
lina, who has been a source of material on many subjects in the Foxfire
books, and told him of my project. He had been active in the work at St.
Cyprians Episcopal Church when he returned to Franklin in the early
1940s and knew Mrs. Stewart. They are good friends and he asked at once
if I had talked to her. When my answer was "No," he gave me directions
to her home. She lives with her daughter, Gertrude Conley, just down the
way from another daughter and son-in-law and 'heir family. We called on

Mrs. Stewart and Mrs. Conley a few days later, and they treated us as though we'd known one another a long time. We went back time and time again, taking beautiful pictures of Mrs. Stewart and hearing warm, wonderful recollections about life from times almost a century ago to now.

Mrs. Stewart still reads a lot and likes to be informed about what is happening around her today. "I read [about the moon missions] and part of it I believed and some of it I didn't. It said a man visited the moon and brought back some rocks and I said, 'Well, I don't know whether it is true or not. I didn't see it, and I don't know.'

"They might have visited the moon and all like that, but I just couldn't believe it much. Of course science has done a whole lot of things. I don't dispute it. Man can do so many things. He's made man every way, but he can't put breath in the body. That's one thing he can't do."

We would sit on her living room couch with the windows and doors open to catch the afternoon breeze, and while she talked, all my fears about not feeling welcome evaporated. She told of flying "on a 747 from Atlanta to California to visit my daughter. I was in the air four hours and didn't seem to be scared. I could look down and see what was happening. I was surprised that those wings were so big. I said to myself, 'I don't see how this thing stays up in the air.'

"The funny part about it was that the two men flying the plane were talking and I said to the lady next to me, 'I hope they will keep their minds on keeping this thing up in the air instead of talking. They may forget.'"

My initial shyness just didn't seem to be important as I listened to this black woman who feels she has had a very good life, in spite of obstacles placed in her way because of the color of her skin. Everything I had worried about vanished when she laughed. Sometimes sad, often quiet, and then again happy, her laughter sparkled those interviews and I knew that part of her secret for a long life was her ability to be happy. It sounds so simple: a hundred years' worth of "not working too hard" and laughter.

LYNN BUTLER

I've just come back from the dinner [for senior citizens] at the [Franklin, North Carolina] Community Center. There was quite a crowd there this morning, too. I said, "Well, I have the privilege of being the oldest lady in this crowd." It was so funny. I just looked around—so many were there that had to have somebody to help them get up and they had to take a stick to walk with and somebody to look where they're goin'. I have a walking stick, but I don't usually think about taking it when I leave home. I'm lucky that way. I don't really need it much.

My mother's been dead ever since nineteen and twelve. That's been a long time. I was born and reared here in Franklin and so was my mother.

My father—I reckon he was, too. I really just don't know. He was born way back there when they sold children as slaves. Put them on the block. He said he remembered being sold.

He said they'd have these auction sales [in Franklin] and they'd take a block out there and the people would all crowd around and bid on whoever it was being sold. If a man was strong and seemed to be well made, they'd go to bidding on him. The highest bidder got him then. If a white man wanted to buy a woman for a slave, he'd check out first to see if she was fertile and how many children she'd had. If she'd had a lot of children, he'd buy her right off because he'd know she could have more children and get him more slaves for nothing. They'd take care of her like she was a queen just about.

The McDonalds bought him. There was two McDonald brothers—one bought my daddy and one bought my daddy's uncle. We are so mixed up, I don't know who my relatives is and who's not.

My grandmother wasn't a slave. She was a bound girl. Way back then, if a white man wanted a girl, they'd bind her to this man and call her a bound girl. My grandmother was bound to Reverend C. D. Smith, and that was the name she had till she married. They taught her to read and write nicely. She married a Carpenter, but they didn't live together but just a little bit. She said she didn't like his ways, so she wasn't married long. Then she went back to using the name Smith. She lived on with the white people and reared her daughter, my mother, there so she learned to read and write with these white people, too. I knew several older people that couldn't read, but both my parents had enough education to read and write intelligently.

I think they said my grandmother's daddy bought his freedom. I never could understand how that was, but he wasn't a slave anymore. He made his living as a farmer. He could take care of his own business after he bought his freedom. He didn't have to go and ask someone else questions. That gave him his own chance then. That's been years and years ago, because I think there are about five or six generations of my family. Just immediately I have children, grandchildren, and *three* great-grandchildren!

My parents owned their own home. They bought an acre and bought my grandmother a quarter acre from an old man who owned a lot of land. They lived just right next to each other.

My daddy farmed. He used to raise corn and stuff like that. We children pulled fodder, picked peas and beans. We'd go out early in the morning and spread a great big sheet. We'd pick clay peas and put them on there. The sun was hot—it was at the fall of the year—and they'd dry. When we'd get the sheet full (about the middle of the afternoon), we'd sit down and beat the peas out with sticks. Then we'd take the hulls all out and sack them up, and sack up the peas. Then we were ready to go home. I don't know why people don't raise more clay peas now. They're high. They're called cow peas, too. A lot of people don't like them, but I do. I like to cook them today and warm them tomorrow. I think they're better then.

[We'd also shell beans] before we went to bed. We'd be playing around, and they'd bring in a big bag of beans and put them down. All of us children would get on our aprons and we'd shell beans. They'd save the hulls and feed them to the cows. Then they'd save the beans in big bags. We didn't have to go to the store to buy beans like you do now. We had them at home. They say now it's cheaper to buy them, than to raise them. Maybe so —I don't know. I'd rather raise my own beans and onions and things [than buy them]. I raise mine every year. I've got great big onions now that I raised last year.

Used to be there were plenty of children because everybody had a big family. There's not many families with children here now. Some of them moved away, and others have died out. These younger folks, they got on to this new way where they didn't want no big family, so they didn't have them. This community used to be full of children.

My parents had ten children—I'm the oldest of the ten. My full name was Minnie Carrie Ann McDonald. My granddaddy's brother's wife had sixteen children. How about that? He was Oliver McDonald, and when he visited me when my children were little, he'd say, "Well, sis, you're good for as many as my wife had."

I said, "I hope not." Can you imagine having sixteen children? They were all healthy—they played out in the dirt and they ate what was grown in their garden, and they had homemade syrup. It didn't seem like there was many people not healthy then.

It was nothing to see a lot of children in the field with a hoe—men a'plowing and the children hoeing corn. Everyone would have hoes—heavy hoes and light hoes. Every man owned his own set of hoes. We'd go and dig in the summertime. It was hot and we was barefooted. Many a time we'd stand there and dig a hole—playing, you know—and jump in and stand in the hole and dig as far as we could. We used to do a lot of funny things [to pass the time].

In the fall of the year, we'd pull fodder—tie it up in big handfuls, and when it cured out, the men would go through there and get four of those handfuls together and tie them into a bundle of fodder. After they were all tied up, the bundles were stood up in a hole in the field. This was used as a cow feed in winter. They'd have a pole standing up in the hole and a man would start tying bundles to the pole. He'd first stand up a lot of the tops of the corn and tie them around the pole. Then he'd get up on that. We'd throw the fodder up to him and he'd just go round and round till he got a great big stack. It was interesting.

People won't work that way now—no, no. They farmed and growed their stuff—Irish potatoes and sweet potatoes and tender green beans. We'd take a great big long string and string the green beans and hang them up [to dry]. Those were leather britches to cook in the wintertime. I do that yet! It didn't matter how old they got. They were still tender. It was nothing to go by people's back porches and see great strings of beans hanging up. They're good, too—cooked with plenty of fat meat. I like them good and greasy. They're not fit to eat if they're not good and greasy. No, no!

People had cane patches and made homemade molasses. They'd cut that cane down, grind it, and get the juice. They had a great big boiler and would boil the juice down to make syrup. Then the ladies would take some apples, put them in the syrup boiler, put it on to cook, and make apple butter. Then they had little gallon jars and put that apple butter in there. They'd melt beeswax and put it on a cloth and tie it on the jars. That's the way they sealed it up. I remember when they didn't have no glass jars to can things in like they do now. They did pumpkin butter the same way. That was pretty good eating in the winter, too.

My daddy was very strict about things, and on Sunday afternoons we didn't go out in the woods and pick up brush to kindle our fire with. We had Saturday to get our brush to kindle a fire for Monday morning. We didn't gather any brush on Sunday.

We went to Sunday service at nine o'clock and stayed for church every Sunday morning. Then we'd go home, eat our dinner and come right back Sunday afternoon at three for Sunday school. Then after Sunday school we'd go home. At that time they didn't have this fence law, and you could turn your cows out and they could go anywhere they wanted to. So after Sunday school, we'd go out and hunt up our cows and bring them in.

So Sundays we were in church [most of the day] and had a crowd. 'Course there was a lot of children then. There's not so many children now. They had the Zion Methodist church downtown, the M. E. Methodist church around the hill there, and the Baptist church across the river down here. We had Sunday service every Sunday here. So you had no excuse for not going to church.

I joined the Episcopal church after I was grown and married and had had my children. I moved my membership from down there at the Methodist church to here at St. Cyprians, and quite a few of the other members did, too, because the old Methodist church got so run down. I guess my grandmother was just about one of the first members at the Zion Methodist church—she was one of the founders. But so many of the members had got so careless and flighty in the upkeep of the church down there, and I don't know what happened to their minister. So I raised my children in the Episcopal church.

St. Cyprians is what you call a mission. Big [Episcopal] churches in the north would furnish things for these little missions for Christmas and Easter. For Christmas they'd fix up a big box of clothes, shoes, underclothes, dresses, and hoods (they wore them then, you know, tied under their chins). At Christmas we'd have a Christmas tree and all those things would be under the tree—a bundle for each family. We were just tickled to death. Those parents that didn't have sufficient clothes for their children were helped out in clothing their children. They didn't have any excuse to not go to church or school.

Lots of folks wouldn't start coming to Sunday school till along in the fall. Then they'd go every Sunday till Christmas. The minister caught on to it, so one springtime he told them, "Now, I want to inform you all—all that waits till the fall—they needn't expect any presents. Now if you want to be remembered at Christmas time, you start Sunday school early in the spring and go all the time. Sunday school is better to be in on Sunday afternoon than to be out playing." So we had a big Sunday school, and we had a crowd at Christmas time. We'd get a great big holly tree and put it in the church, and hang things all around on it and then put bundles under it. They had dolls that they'd hang around on the tree.

We didn't have many toys except what the boys would make. They made little sleds and things like that, but I don't remember any other toys. We did have dolls—they had a china head and china hands and the rest was cloth, filled with excelsior, like ground up wood or chaff. The head would just sit there, and you'd sew the body on to that. Then you'd sew the arms on and there were china feet and legs. That's the way our dolls was. We'd dress them to suit ourselves. We didn't have great big dolls like they do now. I remember poor folks wasn't able to buy them. I remember the first doll I ever had. I thought I had something great!

My parents generally gave us books. They were cloth books—ABC's, stories, and pictures in them. One time we had them out in the yard and it rained on them. That just ruined them.

I think families used to be closer [than they are now]. Children didn't get out and just roam where they pleased and run all over everywhere. We couldn't just go up to people's houses anytime we wanted to. If we were invited to come and play, we could stay an hour. When that hour's out, we came back home. And we didn't just step out and go like children do now. No, every child, when he was away from home, his parents knew where he was, but now you can't keep up with the children. They were quite different. They didn't do like they do now.

Used to be children weren't together as much as they are now—only when they were at school. They'd play some then and maybe they wouldn't see each other anymore from Friday till Monday, because they stayed at home with their families.

Their parents had chores for them to do when they got out of school. They didn't have this water system in the house like now. They'd maybe have a spring down below the house, and the children would have to go and carry water to the house. Sometimes we had to bring up the night water—fill up two wooden buckets with hoops around them to use [for cooking and drinking water each evening]. We had tin dippers or sometimes a gourd dipper.

In one way I think the parents are to blame for the children getting in so much trouble and all now. They don't give them something to keep them busy and interested in. They just turn the children loose and don't know where they are half the time.

And I just think if a young person doesn't get an education or get into something worthwhile, then it's because he or she's just too lazy to try. Then another thing, now when children get sixteen, seventeen years old, they think, "I can sort of do as I please now." And then they step out, and they step in the wrong place. They don't think anything about it till it's too late.

I had a wonderful teacher—Reverend Kennedy at the school over at St. Cyprians Episcopal Church. You didn't pass anything halfway with him. You had to know it. I remember we wore out the page in the book learning the multiplication tables! That was the hardest thing to learn. He made us stay right there till we learned those tables. In the five's and the ten's, we could just rattle on, but we couldn't keep up with the others! He made us stay right with it till we learned all of them. We had to learn, and you know, I'm proud of it, too. If he had let us go on, I'd never have known my arithmetic.

I get aggravated [with myself] when I think about it. I wasn't real strict about making my children learn things like that. When my children were small, I had a baby this year, then in two more years another baby. I didn't have time to teach arithmetic [laughing]. I could've done better than I did.

Reverend Kennedy lived to see me married and he knew some of my children. He said, "Now you keep your children busy. Give your girls a needle and thread. They may not sew good, but give them two or three pieces of cloth and let them sew them together, and if they don't sew it straight, make them take it out and go over it again. You might baste a line there—long stiches—let them sew and see if they sew right by that. If they don't, pull it out and start again."

He boarded with my parents [when he first came to Franklin]. He wasn't married then.

PLATE 429

Way back then the children didn't go to the table with the old folks to eat. They played and [then ate their meal after the grown-ups got through]. So when we children sat down to eat, we'd reach across the table and [use very bad manners]. Reverend Kennedy would come in and say, "All right, sit down. Take your arms off the table. Lay your wrists up there. Put your knife on the back of your plate. Put that spoon down and eat with your fork."

I said to myself, "I wish Mama would tell him to go on about his business!"

"Put each arm close to the table," he said. He'd make us do that. You know that now if I sit down to a table crossways, I think of that and I get tickled! I think of Reverend Kennedy saying, "All right, Carrie, sit up to the table close and don't brush crumbs off on the floor. If you have any crumbs, let them come in your hand and put them on your plate. When you leave the table, put your knife and fork on there decent."

Oh, he was very strict. His oldest daughter lives in Asheville and once when I was over visiting her, I told her, "I got my table manners, and all my manners, I think, from your father."

She said, "I know. He used to make me so mad [fussing at me to eat and behave correctly]."

He lived to be about ninety-nine, I think.

He taught me as long as I went to school. I was six years old when I started to school. It was across the road here at the St. Cyprians Episcopal Church. They had a private school for all the colored children in the community. My family didn't live here though. We lived a little distance away.

The county had three months of school every year [for the colored children], but we lived too far away from that school and never did go to it. We were too small to walk so far and our parents had no way to get us there. So I never went to anything but the Episcopal school—nine months a year, till I was eighteen years old! I ought to be highly educated. We'd start in August and end up the last of May or the first of June. We ought to have had all kinds of education, but we played a lots of times when we should have been studying. We had readers—first, second, on up. I went through all those. And we had spelling books and primary, intermediate, and high school arithmetic. That's the way our books run then.

I remember we had these little half-gallon tin buckets and our parents would put our dinner in that bucket with a lid on it. All the children brought their lunches in those little tin buckets.

One little girl was an only child and her parents were what we called pretty "high up." She'd have biscuits and cake or teacakes, and those of us from big families, we'd usually have cornbread and peas or beans. We'd rush through our lunch and go to where she was and help her eat hers. I think of that, and it still tickles me.

I don't think there's any reason why most every Negro, even from my age on down, can't read if they've had schooling available. Me and my class— we had a chance, because we had this school free from the time I was six years old on up till I was grown and had children of my own. I mean right here in Franklin.

I married when I was eighteen. I quit school in the spring and married in June.

I had ten children, nine confinements—one set of twins. The little girl of the twins didn't live but just a little while, and Canara lived to be seventy-seven years old. He died just this year here. I had two more babies who died in infancy. My oldest son's dead now and my second daughter. I still have four living children—Ella, Gertrude [who now lives with Mrs. Stewart], Emma, and George.

[There was a twelve-year period between the first nine children] and my last baby. Now you talk about somebody being mad! My doctor told me back before then—because I used to suffer with sick headaches—"Carrie, you're going through the change and this headache will torment you right much, but it'll quit after awhile. It might take a year, it might take two. In the wind-up, you'll most likely have a little one." And sure enough in twelve years [from the time my ninth baby was born], I had another boy. He was spoiled to death. Boy, he just thought he was it! He's always teased me and said he was an unwelcome visitor. I said, "You sure was!"

I never did go out to work or anything like that. My husband took care of the family—bought the clothes and food and we raised a big garden. The man he worked for had a big wheat crop, and we had whatever the rest of them had.

At that time most people made their children's clothes in the fall of the year. They had what they called "Kentucky jeans." We used to buy so much of that cloth in the fall and I'd make my boys' pants from a pattern that a white lady gave me. I'd also make their shirts and buy outing to make the girls' petticoats.

Back then, we made our soap out of lye and hog grease. We didn't know nothing about going to town and buying soap. We kept the soap in a gourd [it was liquid, not hard or a powder]. We'd boil the clothes in a wash pot. I have mine yet. It's out there in the yard. Back then we'd buy wooden barrels that kerosene came in from the merchants for fifty cents. We'd saw them in half and have two wooden tubs. We'd wash the clothes by putting them in the iron wash pot, pour some soap in there, and punch the clothes around in that boiling water with a punching stick. Then we'd put them in the wooden tub and wash them and then rinse them in another wooden tub. Then we had another tub that had indigo blue in it. We'd tie the indigo blue up in a rag, fix the bluing water, and blue the clothes, then hang them out. We went through with all that.

We didn't know what a washer machine was, and I've never used one. I don't have one now! We had washboards, and I have my washboard yet. You know, when things get really dirty, you scrub them on that washboard.

I still wash my own clothes. Now, since my daughter's been back here with me, she takes things to the laundry at times, but I never did go to a laundry. Not for myself. I washed all my clothes myself—quilts and all. Everything of mine, I washed with my hands. In the fall of the year, I'd wash up the quilts I used in the summer and get them dry and put them away and get out my winter quilts. Then in spring, I'd wash those winter quilts, put them away, and use my summer quilts. I still do pretty well washing for myself.

After one of my daughters got to be six or seven years old, I thought to myself, "Well, looks like I could go out and work, too." But my husband said, "No, the children would waste more than both of us could bring in." He said that the children could throw more out the kitchen door, wasting, than both of us could put in the front door. He felt we'd have more by me staying at home and having a little garden and raising some chickens and taking care of the young'uns than working out. So he thought it was better for me to stay home. He was right that way.

I'll be one hundred on November 28 [1978]. And I have never worked [outside my home]. My husband didn't believe in the mother going out to work and leaving the oldest child to take care of the younger children.

I was a licensed midwife. I started when my children were almost grown. I went to the class to take instruction regularly, every spring. When we started, I think there was four colored and several white women. Several dropped out, but I just stayed right in there. We had to have three permits. When you got an "A" permit, you had the highest one, and I was determined to get my "A" permit. I stayed right in there till I got it. Then I could go on any calls I wanted to. I had my bag with my own equipment— scissors, a fingernail brush, towels, face mask, and a big apron with pockets all round. Oh, we had to have all that. I went [on calls] all times of the night. [A doctor had checked out my credentials and knew I was capable of delivering a baby and looking after the mother], so when a patient called me, I was ready to go. I just wanted to keep up, and I did, too. I did!

I did [the midwifing for] a lot of my friends, too. 'Course you see there weren't many doctors then. There was several white midwives and three colored at one time. The father of a white boy I took care of passed through Franklin last summer. He laughed and said somebody had told him I lived yet. He wanted to come by and see me and said, "I wanted to tell you about your boy. He's married now and he's got children."

My grandmother was a midwife and she delivered several of my children. After she died there was another old lady that delivered one of my babies, and Dr. Harry Jones, a white doctor, delivered my last baby. Dr. Jones is dead now.

I followed midwifing a long time, but after my husband died, I quit.

I think to a certain extent, women have a right to go [out and work] and they have a right to stay home and let the husband carry on. Somewhere I read the woman wasn't supposed to speak in the church service. She was supposed to speak to her husband and let him take care of it. It seems to me that women now have the lead in more things than they've ever had before.

When it comes to the home, the woman has the whole responsibility of raising the family and the man brings in the food. To bathe and dress the little children, nurse them and tend them, put them to bed all times of night, not just daytime (anything can happen to the little one at night)— the mother has to take care of that. I know it would nearly kill my husband for the baby to get to crying, and I had to get up and do something for it. It would nearly kill him to have to wake up, get up, and get something for *me*. He'd say, "Why don't you get your things right here by the bed so you won't have to get it?"

And I said, "I ain't going to keep medicine sitting here all the time. You ain't got a thing to do but get it."

He'd laugh about that. He'd laugh years after the children were all grown about how he hated to get out of the bed.

I had three boys, Grady, Canara and George. Grady died fairly young, but Canara's only been dead a short time. He was a farmer. He was the life of the family because he loved parties. He could really call a square dance.

I never did like to square dance, but my children did. I thought it was very, very pretty to watch, but there was too much swinging around for me. I liked to go when they had a cakewalk—have two and two and play music and march. I didn't mind that, but for a crowd to get out and dance, and have a man calling—uh, uh. I wasn't in that at all! Some of those girls could dance—my, my! And those fellers could pick and sing—ohhh! I had a brother-in-law who picked the banjo and his brother could play the fiddle. That was beautiful music! Two men would face one another and buckdance. They didn't just jump up and down on the floor. They could use their feet!

I had a good marriage. My husband was good to me. He enjoyed parties and dances and things like that, but you know, I never did care too much about it. One time though he said, "Will's got a party up at his house tonight and they're having a dance. I thought maybe you'd like to go up and see'em dance."

I said, "You going?"

And he said, "Yeah, I guess I will."

And I thought to myself, "Well, I knew you was going," 'cause I knew he enjoyed dancing.

And he said, "I thought you'd like to go."

So I said, "Yes, I think I'll go and see how they do." I didn't care much about it, but I thought I'd go. I said, "Listen, if you'll come back to the house with me when I get tired of seeing them, I'll go." And he said he would. We went on to the dance. They was swinging their partners and singing and dancing. It was very pretty and they were all having a good time, but I got tired of it. I'd been used to going to bed. He came around and said, "Are you enjoying it?"

I said. "Yeah, but I think I'm about ready to go to the house."

He said, "Well, anytime you're ready to go, tell me and I'll go." But he didn't tell me that he was going to take me to the house and go back. I had a baby at the time, and I'd carried the baby with me. When we got home, he said, "Why don't you put the baby to bed?"

I said I was tired and I'd put it to bed directly. I said, "Why don't you pull off your hat and go to bed?"

And he said, "Well, I thought I'd go back up yonder awhile."

So I said, "Well, I'll just sit here. If you go back up yonder, I believe I'll go back, too." And it hacked him, you know. He thought I didn't mean it, but I sat right there and he said, "Well, I guess I'll go to bed. It's getting so late." I was going to go back with him, and he knew that'd embarrass him to death if I went back after we had left.

The next day his friend passed and asked how come he didn't come back [to the dance] and he said, "I got sleepy."

I said, "No, he didn't. I told him if he went back, I was going back with him, and that would've embarrassed him."

I didn't care much about dances and all. I'd rather just go to bed. I didn't mind him going. I let him come back when he got ready, except for that time. I never really felt he left me out. No. He always took care of me and our children.

The last dance we was at was down to Bryson City. That was my husband's last time. There was two teams that danced against each other and there was two men; one played a banjo and one played the fiddle. They had a great big round platform [they danced on].

My husband knew every step they was a'cuttin'. There was some old gray-headed men and some old ladies. They could dance! It is alarming. I knew two old people who were dancing. The lady had on a beautiful gathered dress. She could swing around that dress—it'd just be in a circle. She could dance!

During court week there was a man who'd come to town, and the people loved to see him dance. They'd say, "I'll give you a half plug of tobacco to dance for us some." He'd get out there and he could cut the pigeon wing and all kinds of other dances. Folks had good times then. They wasn't so particular and choosy about one another.

I remember they used to have dances at corn shuckin's in the fall of the year. They'd gather corn and put it in a great big pile and send out word, "Corn shuckin' tonight." They'd have supper and lots of times a dance afterwards. White and colored would go together. There wasn't no segregation to it. I don't know, they enjoyed being together to have a big time. They didn't do like they do now.

They'd have a red ear of corn in the pile somewhere. I forget how they done that. There was some kind of prize for the one that got the red ear of corn.

They'd also [have a gathering] for a "cleaning up," like if a man had a new ground he wanted to clean up to put in corn, he'd set up a time for [folks to come and help, and then they'd have a party] that night for them.

I don't think they had much trouble with people drinking [at parties] like they do now. Seems like people didn't drink and what I call "act a

PLATE 430

fool" then. They went to enjoy themselves. I don't remember seeing them drinking and cutting up like they do now. Everybody seemed to be so sociable and nice.

Oh, and I remember when the first automobile came through here. An old lady and her husband was goin' to town in a wagon and somebody passed them in an automobile and she like to have had a fit. She said, "Lord, old man, there goes a wagon that ain't got no horses!"

I never would try to drive. They tried to teach me how, but I never did care to drive. I'd go places, and if my husband wasn't going, I had a friend that had a son that could drive and I'd get him to drive a car. I always felt like if anything happened to the car, I wouldn't know what to do, so if I had someone else driving, they'd know what to do or who to see. My boys— from the time they was big enough to sit up under the wheel—was trying to drive. They wasn't allowed to use the car until they could drive, though.

We asked Mrs. Stewart her views on the transition from segregation to integration since she had one hundred years to observe the changes and has been so candid with us in her feelings on different matters.

Times [for blacks] are better now to what they used to be, quite a bit different. They're better in the way people feel about each other. It's calmer most of the time. Some [white] people are just as nice and they respect the colored. If the colored is anybody intelligent, they'll respect them and go right on. Then there are some they'd kick out of the way if they could. Well, you couldn't really blame them in a way. Intelligence demands intelligence. Anybody that wants to be somebody, wants to stand for something, they don't have any time to take up with anyone that's slowing them down. If they can't help them, they just got to go on and leave them. That's the best way, I reckon. If there's somebody just acting all kinds of ways and using all kinds of language, and you try to help them and you can't do nothing with them, the thing to do is just to leave them. As my grandmother used to say, "Leave Ephraim join to his idols." I don't know where she got it from but it says it. If you can't help anybody, the best thing to do is go on because you're wasting time there with them when you could maybe help somebody else.

I can remember way back [before segregation was ended] when the white people would eat in the dining room, and when they got through, then all the food was taken to the kitchen and put on the table in there and the black hands would eat. They didn't eat in the dining room at all or even look in there. I didn't blame [the white people] much because with those white tablecloths on the table and [the black workers] in there with their dirty shirts, they'd have had to change the tablecloths. Even if they were clean, they was a Negro and the Negroes ate in the kitchen then. It was just a rule, no matter what or how. I don't know why they wanted to be that way, but they did, because I remember that very well.

My husband, Joe, worked on a farm for a man named Mr. Crawford. [There were several black men] working for him, and he asked one of them to fill in on a different job one day and this man said, "No, I ain't going to do it. I'll go home first."

Joe said, "I hate to see anybody be so contrary."

Mr. Crawford said, "Well, I was trying to favor him and give him a job, but he won't accept it. If he had lived way back yonder during slavery time, why from what they tell me, he'd got in there and worked or he'd a'got his back torn up. I'm glad that it isn't like that now."

Joe said, "Well, if it was like that now, these men that done that to people wouldn't have a place to lay their head, 'cause I'd burn up everything they had."

Mr. Crawford said, "I'd be ashamed."

And Joe said, "I would. Before I'd be drove around and knocked like they done then . . ."

We asked Mrs. Stewart what she regarded as her most important possession.

My religion is more important to me than all this house and buildings and things. My life and the way I live means more to me than anything around earthly because this life is here, but when this life ends, your soul has got to go somewhere and it's either going to go where there's happiness and peace, or it's going to go to hell. That's the way the Bible teaches me. If you knew when you was going to die, that would be another thing. But you don't know. Only God knows that. That's why the Psalm says to "prepare yourself and be also ready" because you don't know when death's coming. Some people think they've got to get sick and lay sick a long time and they'll have plenty of time, but they don't know that. You can be going along thinking you're all right and all of a sudden drop dead right there. You don't know anything about what shape your system's in. If you've lived all kind of a life, where's your soul going? It's nice to have a good time but always put God first in everything you do. Put Him first and if you do that, you will make it all right because He's always been and will always be, and there's nothing that He put in this Bible that's wrong— nothing! There's no need now for anybody to say they don't understand right from wrong and how to live because you don't have to go to church to learn it either. You can read the Bible and learn it. Some people think there's nothing in going to church. Some go, I guess, because they like to go to service, and some go to have somewhere to go, and some go to see who's there—all for different reasons.

A piece in a book said that you can tame everything but the tongue, but the tongue is an unruly member and has never been tamed—never will be. Christian words and prayer come out of the same mouth that all these wicked words come out of. That's true! But that's why there's a God—to teach man what to say and how to say it. It's a difference in the heart. The Bible teaches that man was placed in the garden of Eden and he had a chance to be happy, but he sinned. A lot of people say I ought not to talk about it because it was the woman that caused him to sin.

I've lived to be a hundred years old and there's been so many things that's happened that I've been able to see and hear. Some of them I believe and some of them I didn't. I can believe what I want to. But I know there's a God somewhere. I know that, because man couldn't do all this. It took a high power to do that, and I know there is a God or it wouldn't have been like that.

INDEX OF PEOPLE